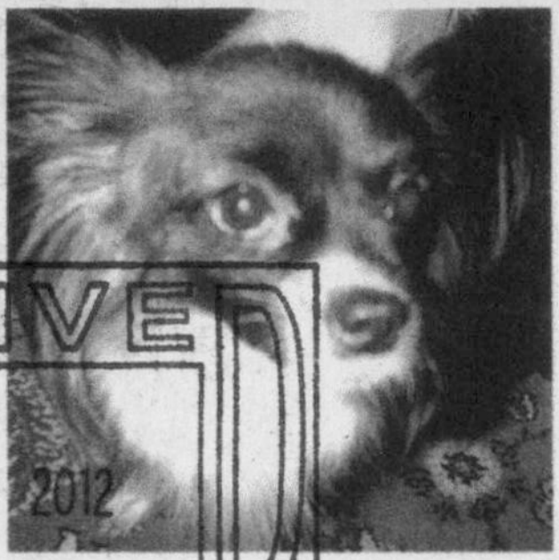

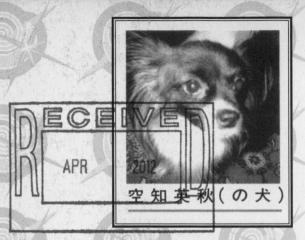

空知英秋(の犬)

Hideaki Sorachi('s Dog)

What? You're asking me what that jerk Sorachi is doing? I dunno. Isn't he doing his business? You're asking me if this manga is any good? I dunno. It's his business! What? You say this carpet is tacky? I'll whack you on the nose with a newspaper, you bad human!!

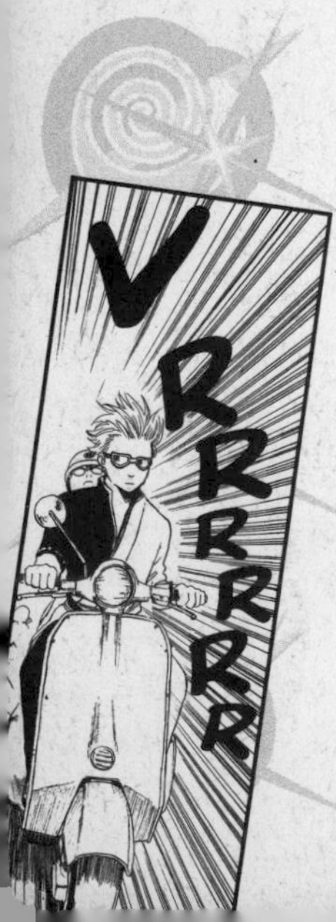
VRRRRRR

Hideaki Sorachi was born on May 25, 1979, and grew up in Hokkaido, Japan. His ongoing series, ***GIN TAMA***, became a huge hit when it began running in the pages of Japan's ***Weekly Shonen Jump*** in 2004. A ***GIN TAMA*** animated series followed soon after, premiering on Japanese TV in April 2006. Sorachi made his manga debut with the one-shot story *DANDELION*, which is included in this volume!

GIN TAMA VOL. 1
SHONEN JUMP ADVANCED Manga Edition

This graphic novel contains material that was originally
published in English in **SHONEN JUMP** #37, and #49~#53,
plus a bonus story not previously printed in English!

STORY & ART BY HIDEAKI SORACHI

Translation/Matthew Rosin, Honyaku Center Inc.
English Adaptation/Drew Williams
Touch-up Art & Lettering/Freeman Wong & Averil Averill
Cover & Interior Design/Sean Lee
Additional Touch-up/Josh Simpson
Editors/Yuki Takagaki & Annette Roman

Published by VIZ Media, LLC
P.O. Box 77010
San Francisco, CA 94107

10 9 8 7 6 5
First printing, July 2007
Fifth printing, November 2011

www.viz.com

THE WORLD'S MOST
CUTTING-EDGE MANGA
SHONEN JUMP
ADVANCED

Vol. 1

Nobody with Naturally Wavy Hair Can Be That Bad

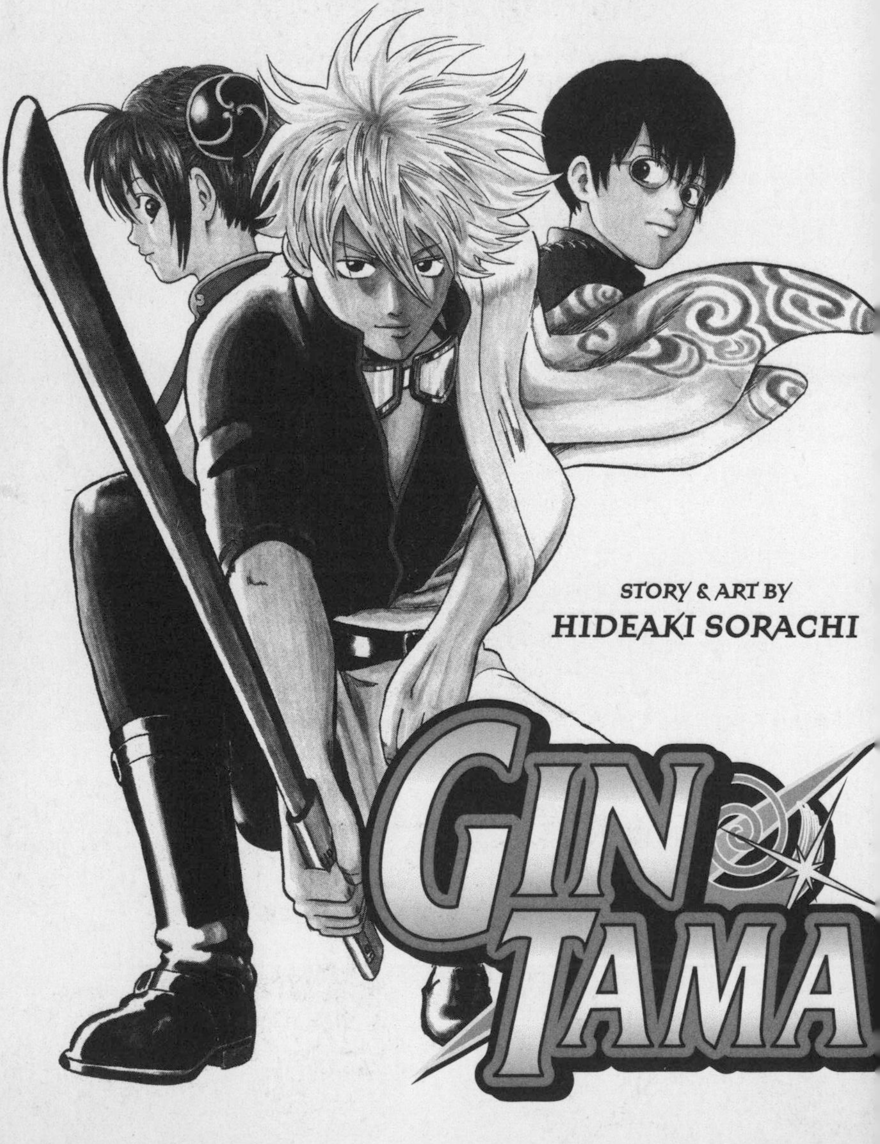
GIN TAMA

STORY & ART BY

HIDEAKI SORACHI

WHAT THIS MANGA'S FULL OF
vol. 1

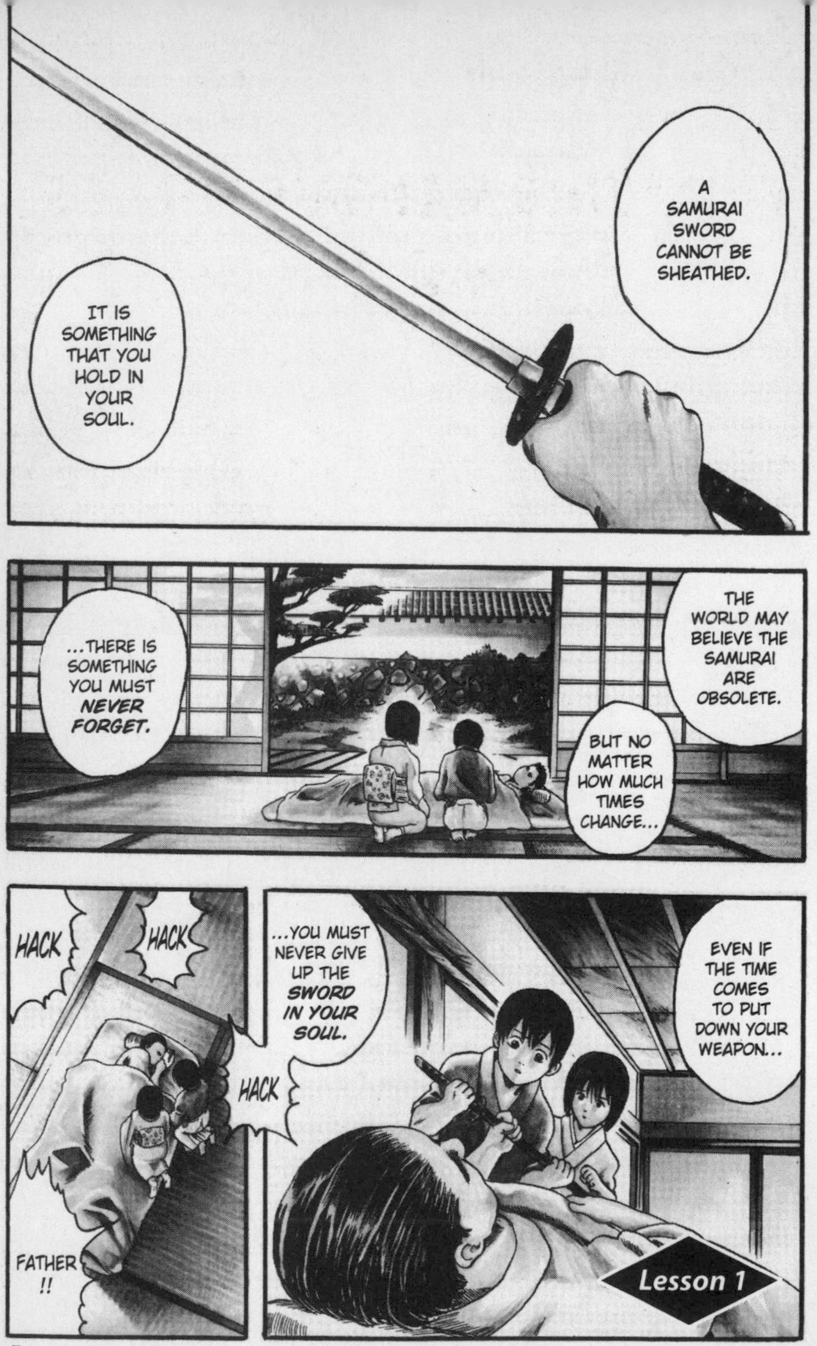
A SAMURAI SWORD CANNOT BE SHEATHED.
IT IS SOMETHING THAT YOU HOLD IN YOUR SOUL.
THE WORLD MAY BELIEVE THE SAMURAI ARE OBSOLETE.
BUT NO MATTER HOW MUCH TIMES CHANGE...
...THERE IS SOMETHING YOU MUST *NEVER FORGET.*
EVEN IF THE TIME COMES TO PUT DOWN YOUR WEAPON...
...YOU MUST NEVER GIVE UP THE *SWORD IN YOUR SOUL.*
Lesson 1
HACK
HACK
HACK
FATHER !!

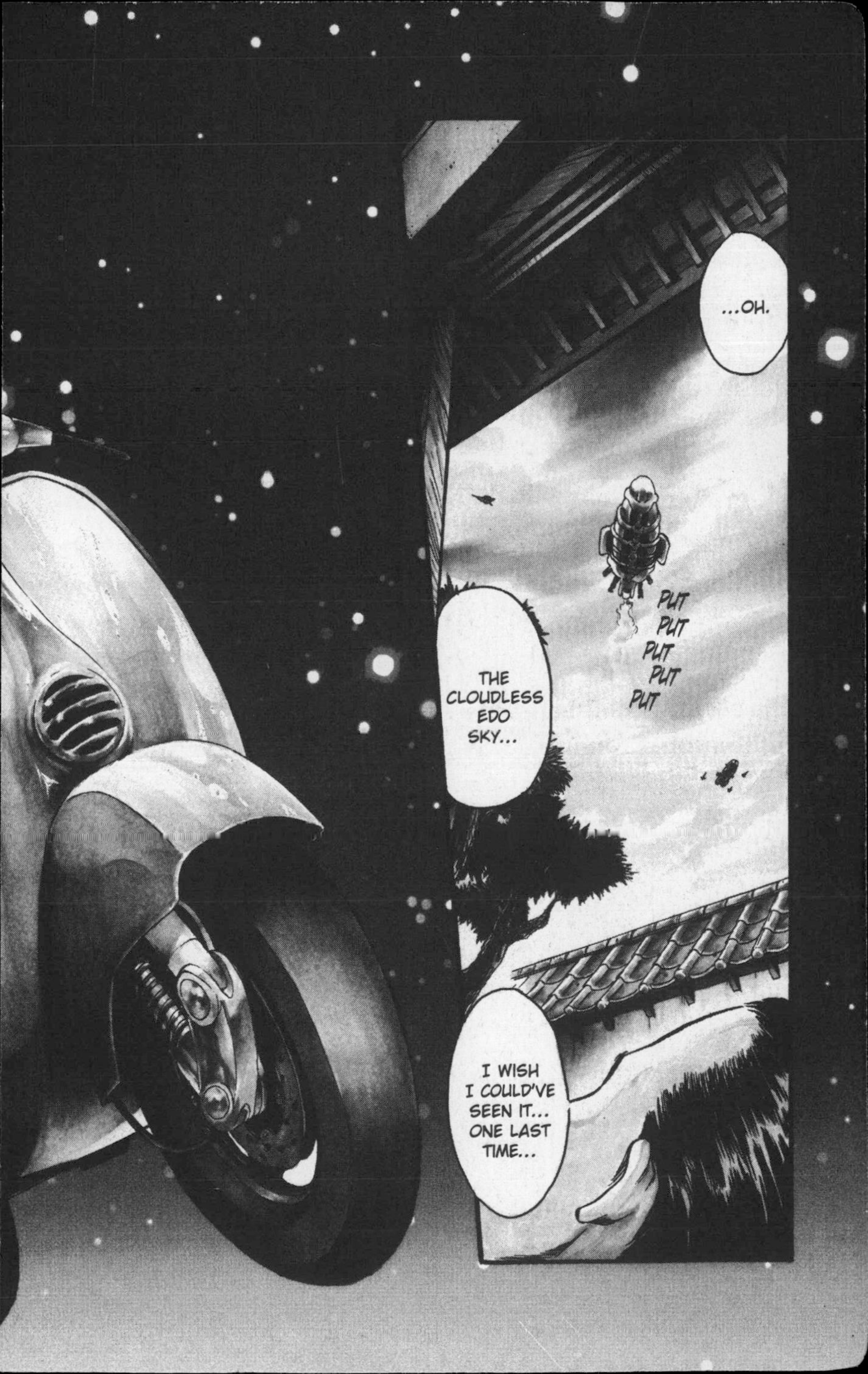
...OH.
PUT PUT PUT PUT PUT
THE CLOUDLESS EDO SKY...
I WISH I COULD'VE SEEN IT... ONE LAST TIME...

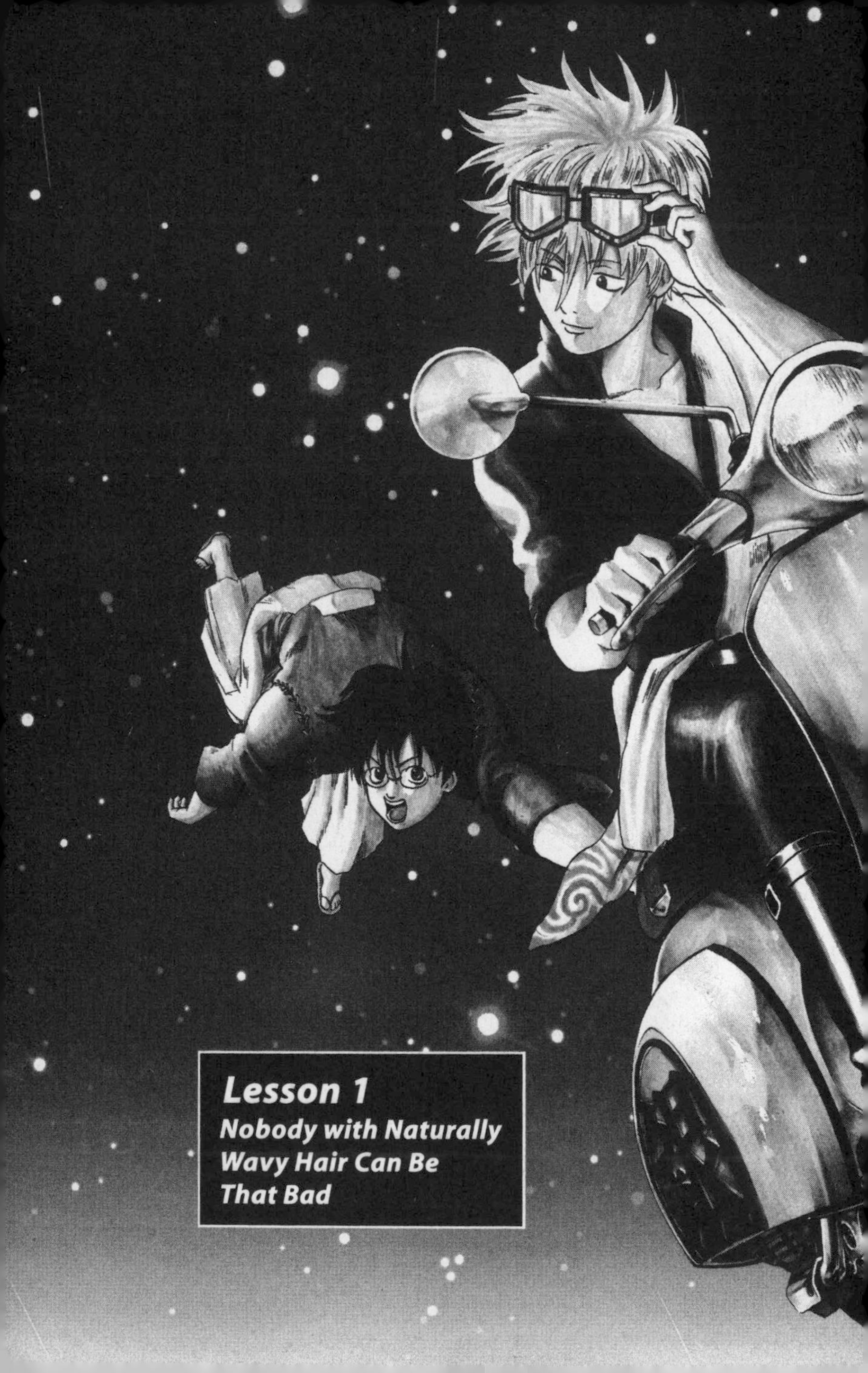
Lesson 1
Nobody with Naturally Wavy Hair Can Be That Bad

"SAMURAI COUNTRY" ...

THERE WAS A TIME, LONG AGO, WHEN OUR COUNTRY WAS CALLED BY THAT NAME.

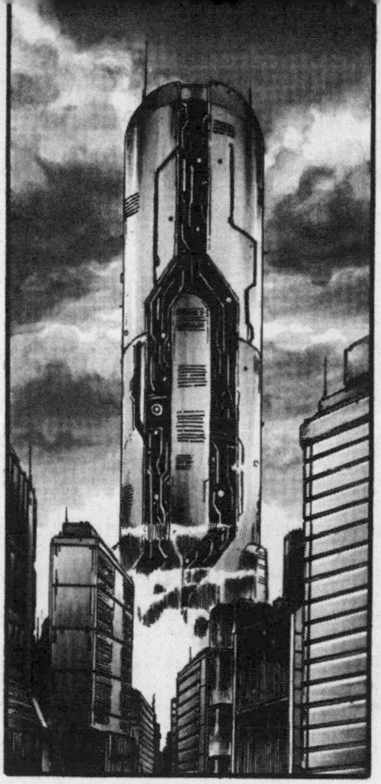

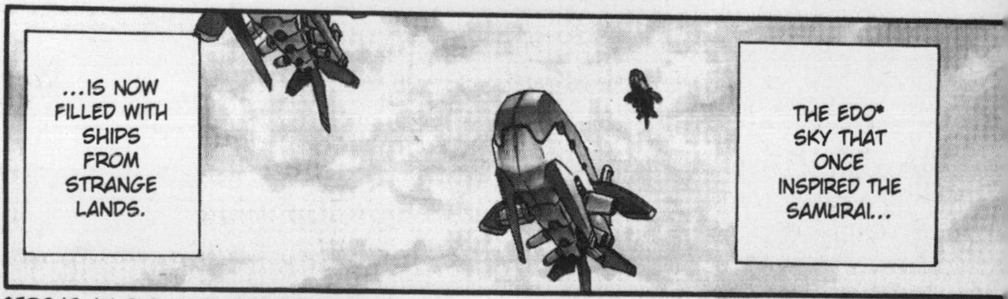
THE EDO* SKY THAT ONCE INSPIRED THE SAMURAI...
...IS NOW FILLED WITH SHIPS FROM STRANGE LANDS.

*EDO IS AN OLD NAME FOR TOKYO.

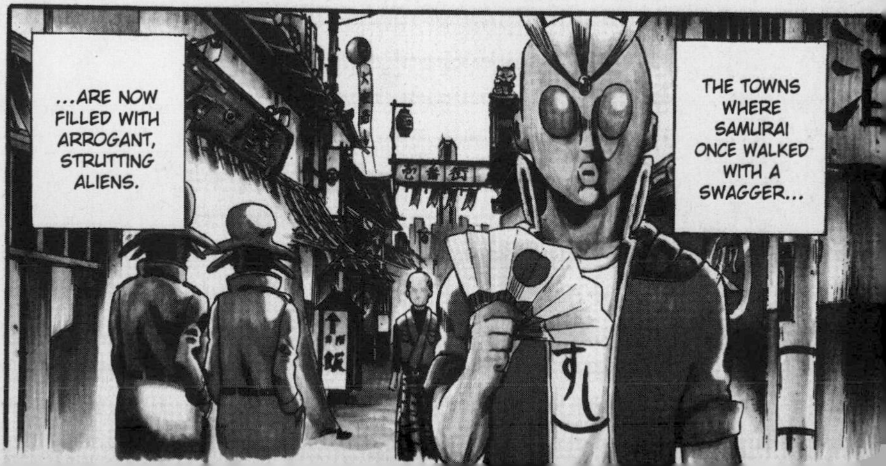
THE TOWNS WHERE SAMURAI ONCE WALKED WITH A SWAGGER...
...ARE NOW FILLED WITH ARROGANT, STRUTTING ALIENS.

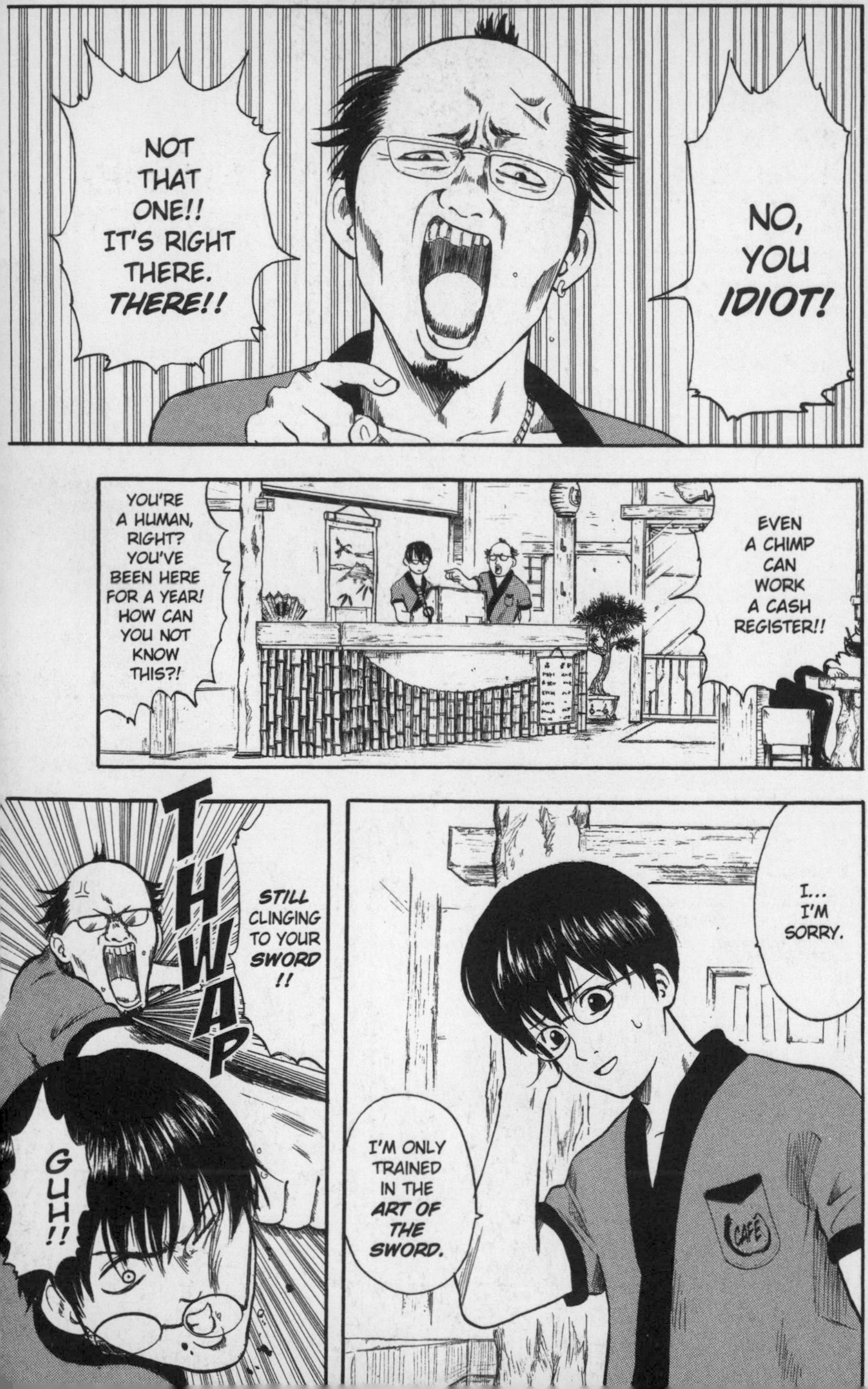
NO, YOU *IDIOT!*
NOT THAT ONE!! IT'S RIGHT THERE. *THERE!!*
EVEN A CHIMP CAN WORK A CASH REGISTER!!
YOU'RE A HUMAN, RIGHT? YOU'VE BEEN HERE FOR A YEAR! HOW CAN YOU NOT KNOW THIS?!
I... I'M SORRY.
I'M ONLY TRAINED IN THE *ART OF THE SWORD.*
STILL CLINGING TO YOUR *SWORD* !!
THWAP
GUH!!

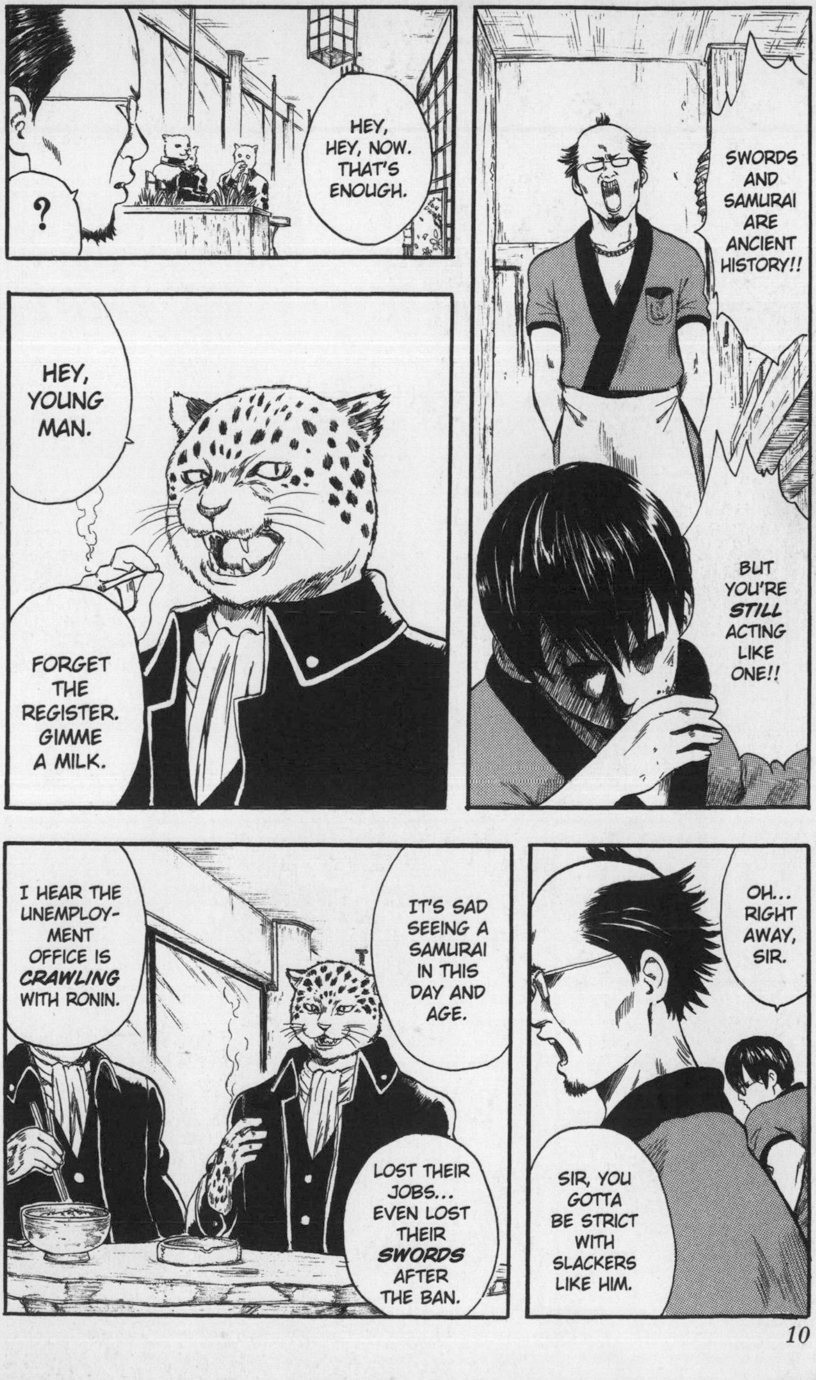
SWORDS AND SAMURAI ARE ANCIENT HISTORY!!
BUT YOU'RE STILL ACTING LIKE ONE!!
HEY, HEY, NOW. THAT'S ENOUGH.
?
HEY, YOUNG MAN.
FORGET THE REGISTER. GIMME A MILK.
OH... RIGHT AWAY, SIR.
SIR, YOU GOTTA BE STRICT WITH SLACKERS LIKE HIM.
IT'S SAD SEEING A SAMURAI IN THIS DAY AND AGE.
I HEAR THE UNEMPLOYMENT OFFICE IS CRAWLING WITH RONIN.
LOST THEIR JOBS... EVEN LOST THEIR SWORDS AFTER THE BAN.

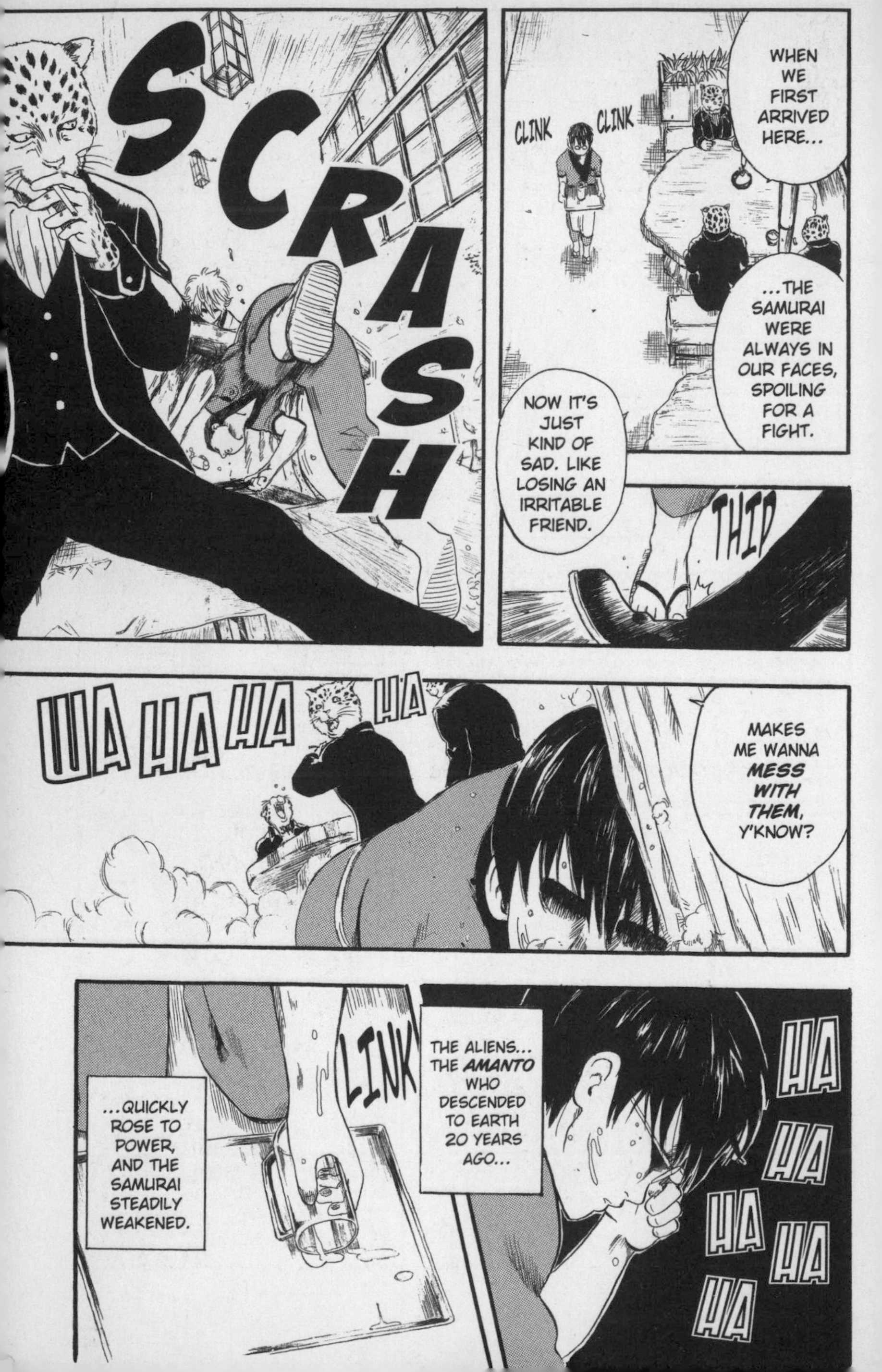

WHEN WE FIRST ARRIVED HERE...
CLINK CLINK
...THE SAMURAI WERE ALWAYS IN OUR FACES, SPOILING FOR A FIGHT.
NOW IT'S JUST KIND OF SAD. LIKE LOSING AN IRRITABLE FRIEND.
THIP
SCRASH
MAKES ME WANNA ***MESS WITH THEM***, Y'KNOW?
UA HA HA HA HA
HA HA HA HA HA HA
THE ALIENS... THE ***AMANTO*** WHO DESCENDED TO EARTH 20 YEARS AGO...
LINK
...QUICKLY ROSE TO POWER, AND THE SAMURAI STEADILY WEAKENED.

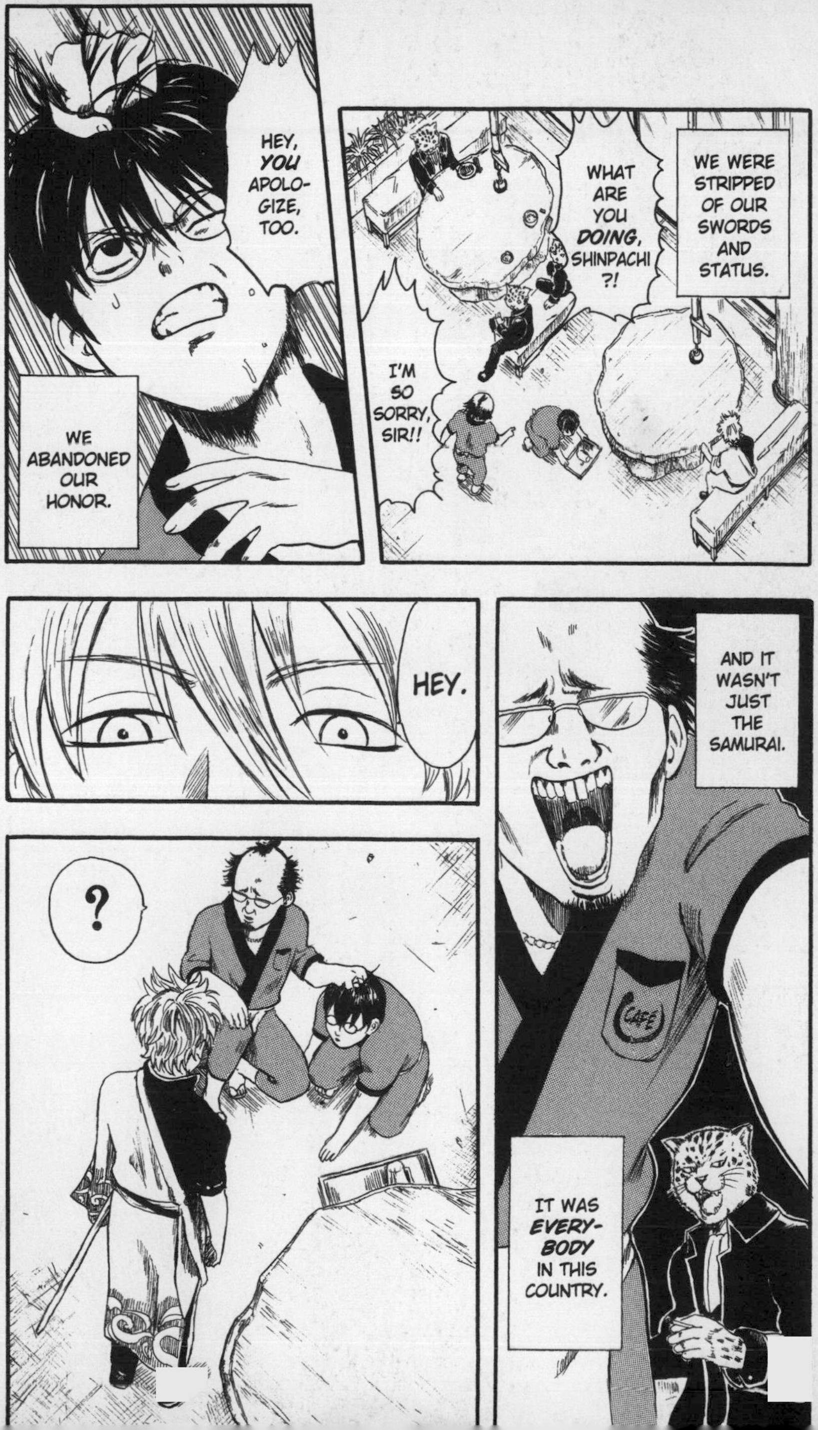
WE WERE STRIPPED OF OUR SWORDS AND STATUS.
WHAT ARE YOU *DOING*, SHINPACHI?!
I'M SO SORRY, SIR!!
HEY, *YOU* APOLOGIZE, TOO.
WE ABANDONED OUR HONOR.
AND IT WASN'T JUST THE SAMURAI.
IT WAS *EVERYBODY* IN THIS COUNTRY.
CAFE
HEY.
?

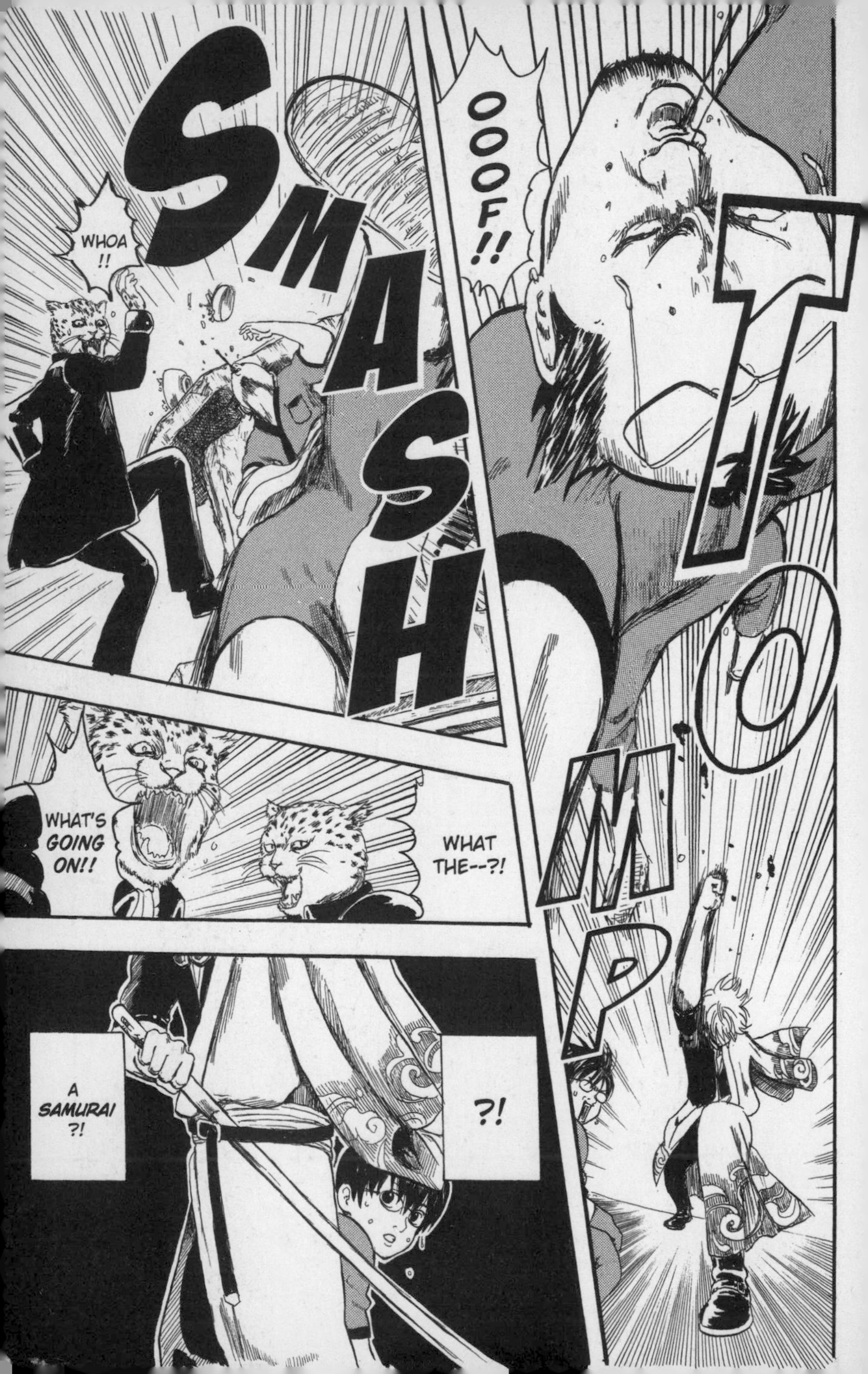
OOOF!!
TOMP
SMASH
WHOA!!
WHAT THE--?!
WHAT'S GOING ON!!
?!
A SAMURAI?!

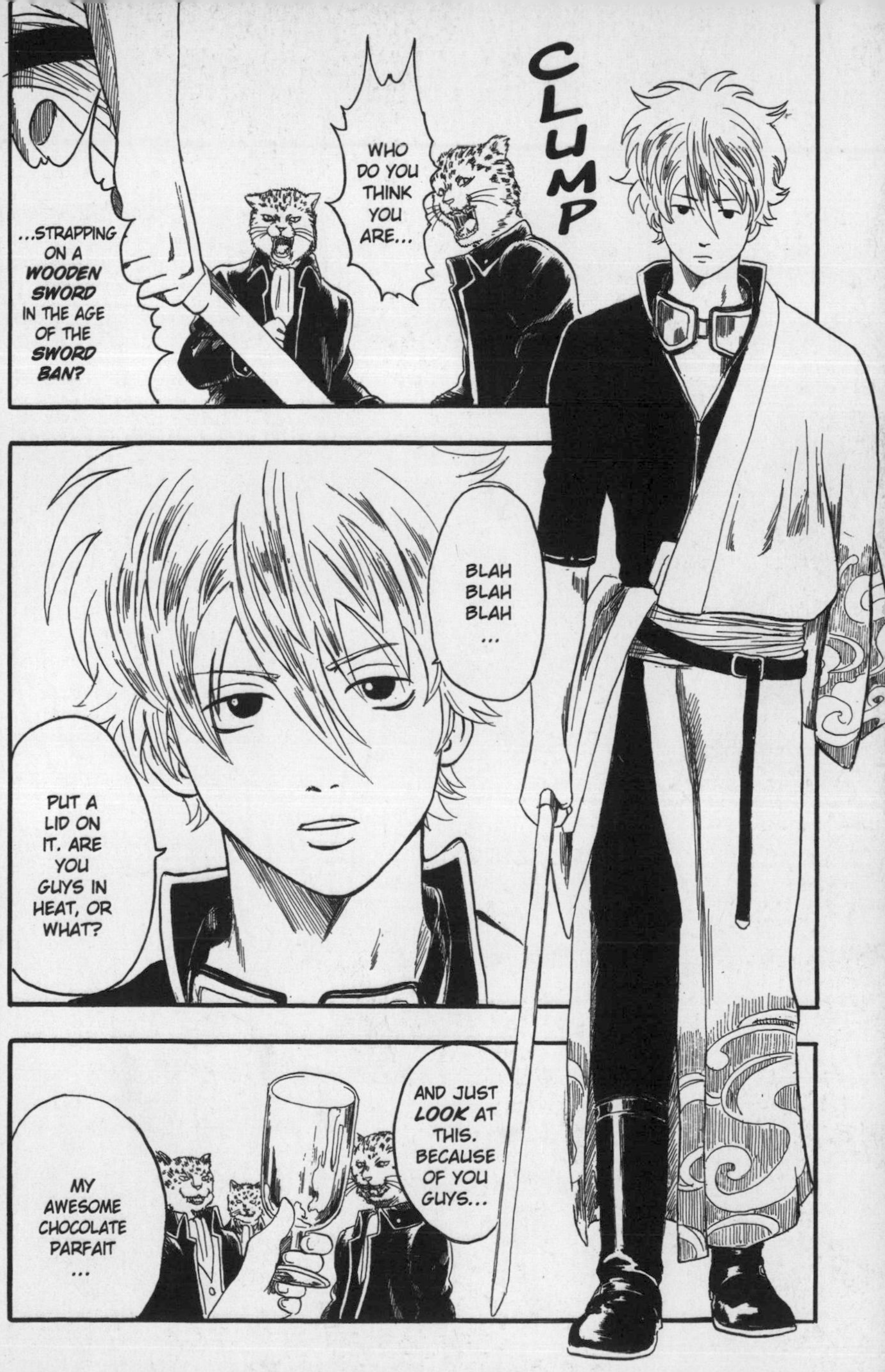
CLUMP
WHO DO YOU THINK YOU ARE...
...STRAPPING ON A WOODEN SWORD IN THE AGE OF THE SWORD BAN?
BLAH BLAH BLAH ...
PUT A LID ON IT. ARE YOU GUYS IN HEAT, OR WHAT?
AND JUST LOOK AT THIS. BECAUSE OF YOU GUYS...
MY AWESOME CHOCOLATE PARFAIT ...

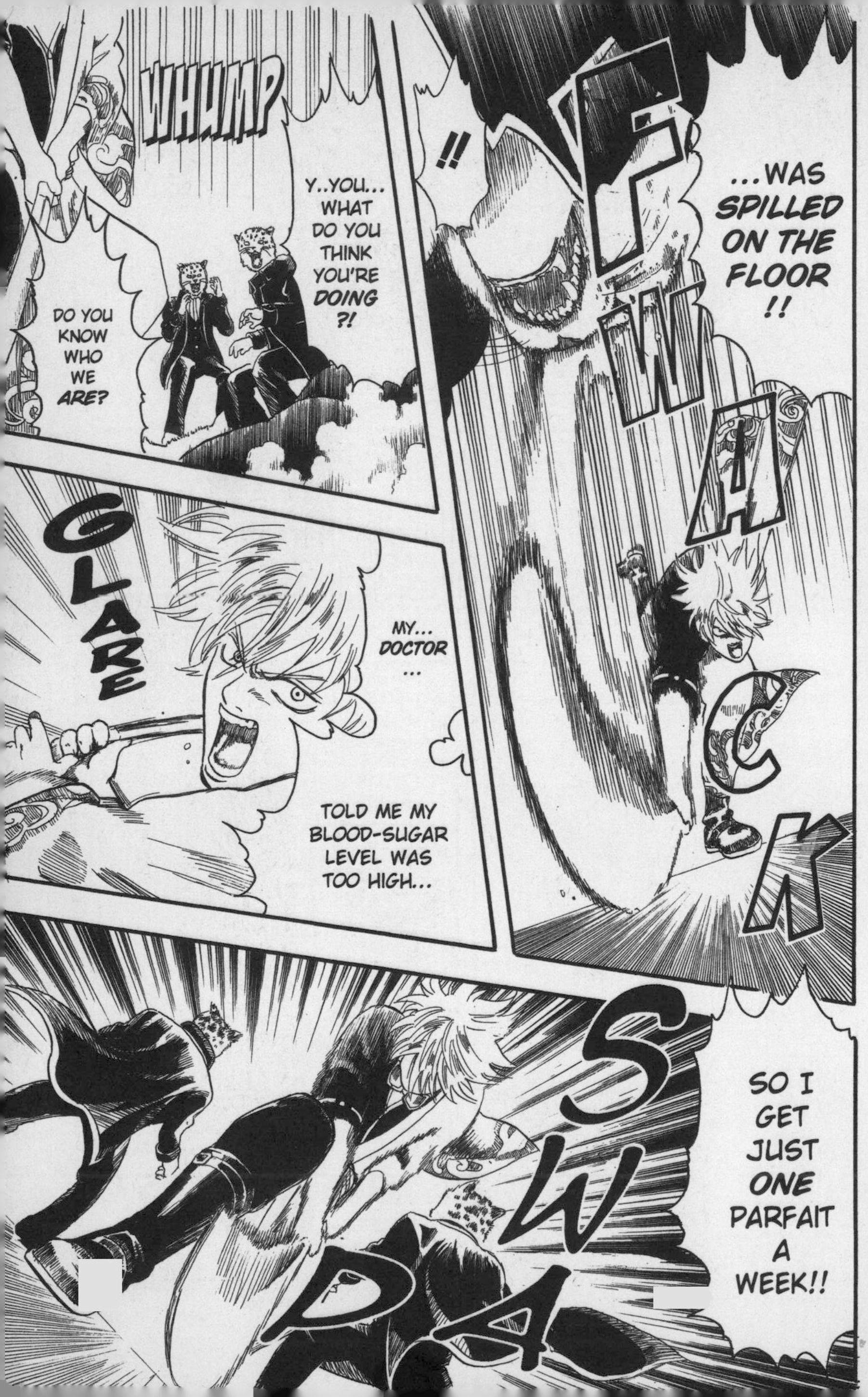
...WAS SPILLED ON THE FLOOR !!
!!
FWACK
WHUMP
Y..YOU... WHAT DO YOU THINK YOU'RE DOING ?!
DO YOU KNOW WHO WE ARE?
MY... DOCTOR ...
TOLD ME MY BLOOD-SUGAR LEVEL WAS TOO HIGH...
GLARE
SO I GET JUST ONE PARFAIT A WEEK!!
SWPA

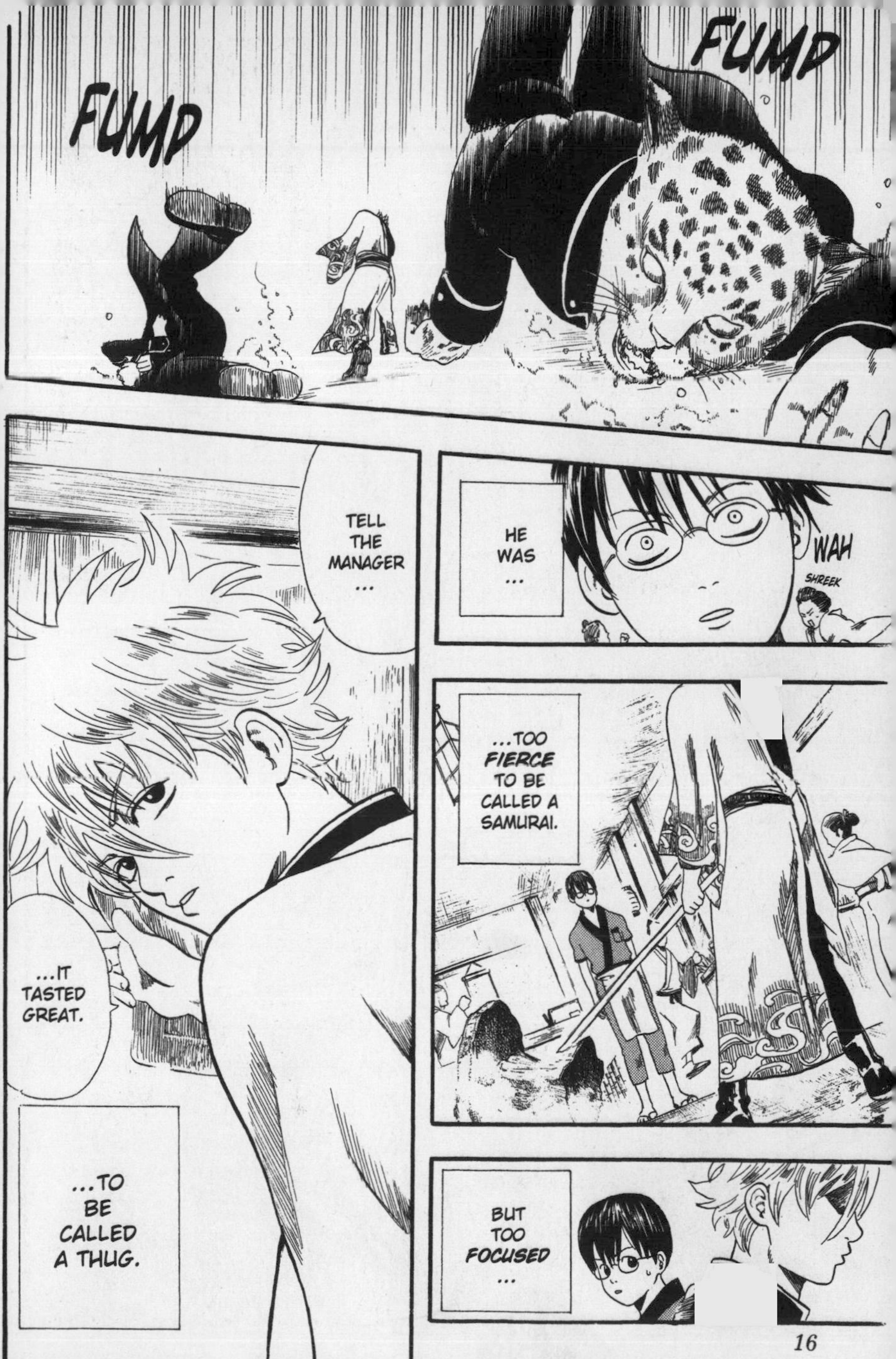
FUMP
FUMP
HE WAS ...
WAH
SHREEK
...TOO FIERCE TO BE CALLED A SAMURAI.
BUT TOO FOCUSED ...
TELL THE MANAGER ...
...IT TASTED GREAT.
...TO BE CALLED A THUG.

READ THIS WAY

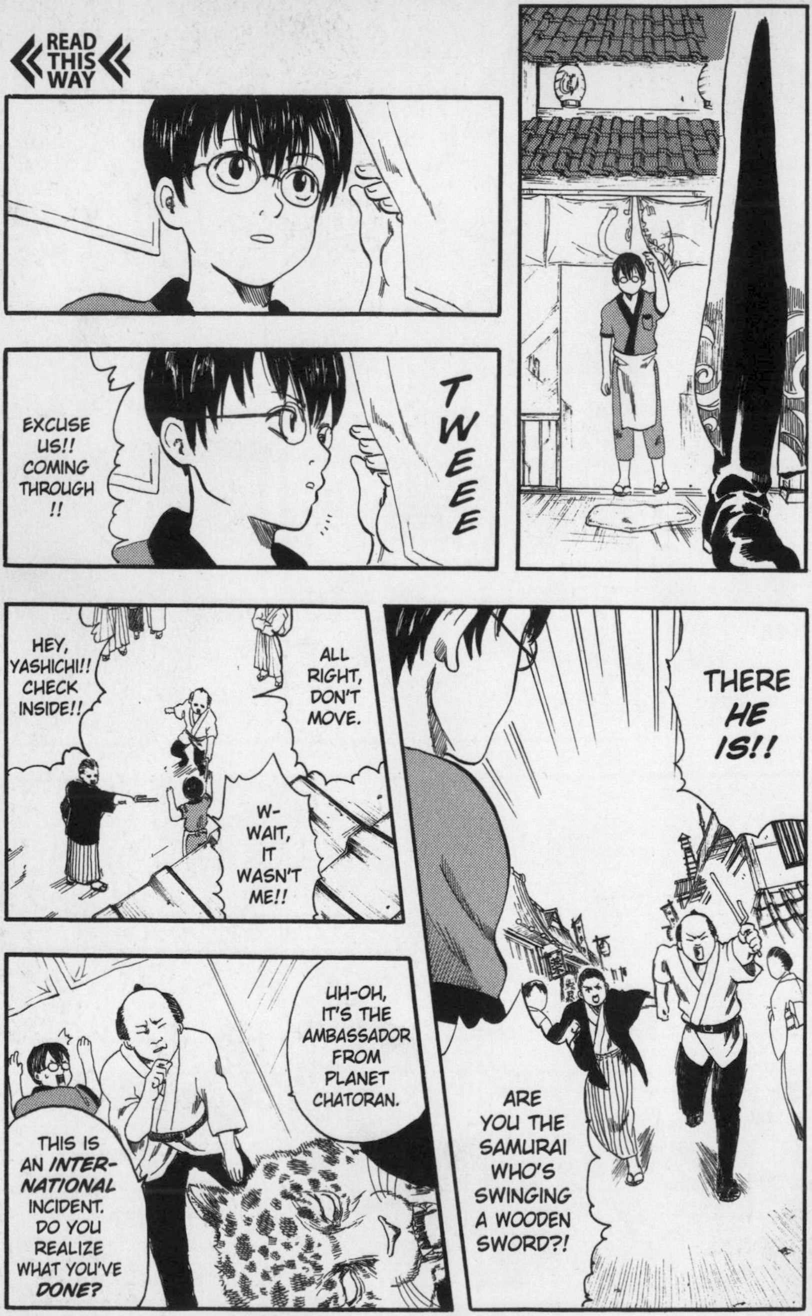
TWEEE
EXCUSE US!! COMING THROUGH!!
THERE HE IS!!
ARE YOU THE SAMURAI WHO'S SWINGING A WOODEN SWORD?!
ALL RIGHT, DON'T MOVE.
HEY, YASHICHI!! CHECK INSIDE!!
W-WAIT, IT WASN'T ME!!
UH-OH, IT'S THE AMBASSADOR FROM PLANET CHATORAN.
THIS IS AN INTERNATIONAL INCIDENT. DO YOU REALIZE WHAT YOU'VE DONE?

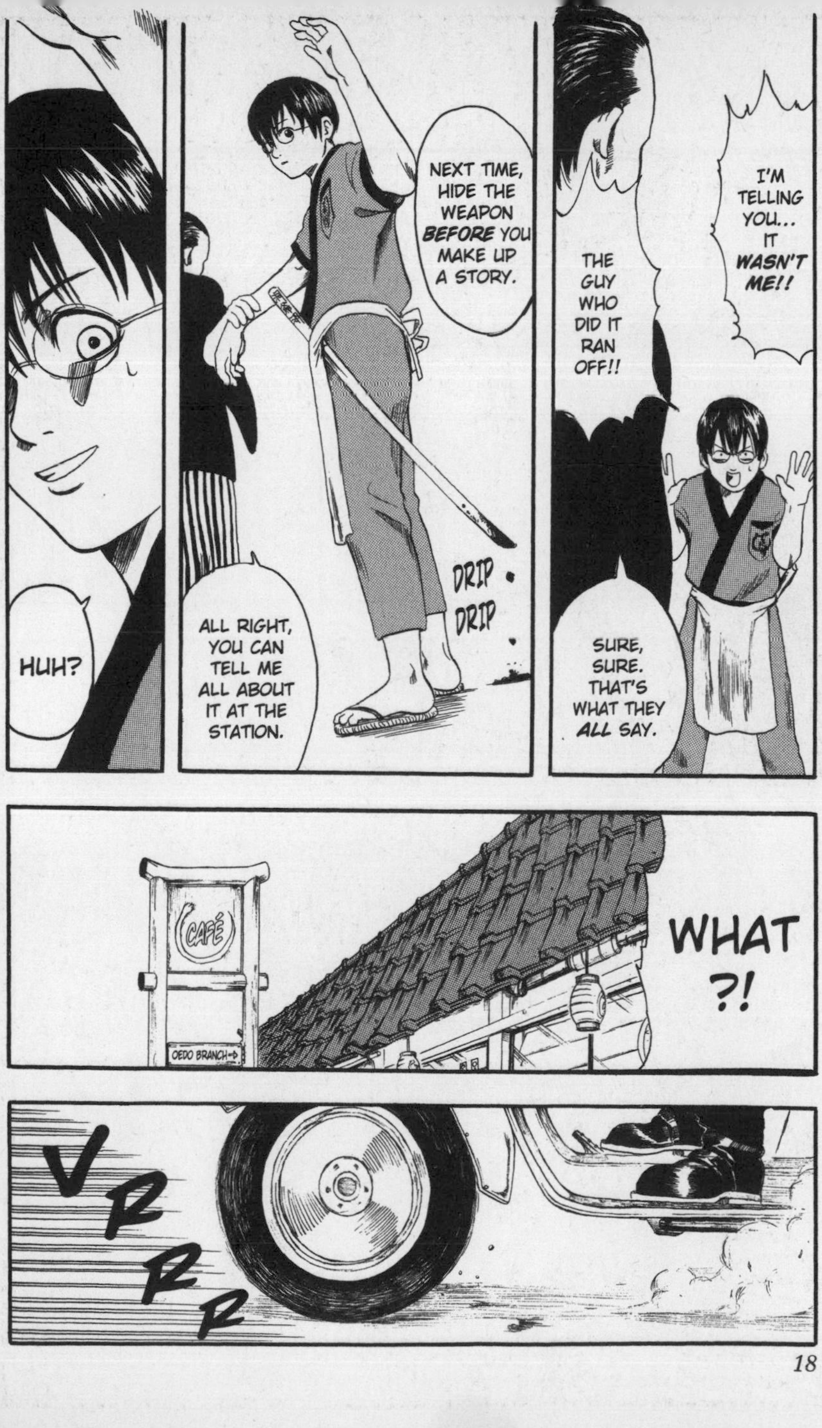
I'M TELLING YOU... IT WASN'T ME!!
THE GUY WHO DID IT RAN OFF!!
SURE, SURE. THAT'S WHAT THEY ALL SAY.
NEXT TIME, HIDE THE WEAPON BEFORE YOU MAKE UP A STORY.
DRIP DRIP
ALL RIGHT, YOU CAN TELL ME ALL ABOUT IT AT THE STATION.
HUH?
WHAT ?!
CAFÉ
OEDO BRANCH
VRRR

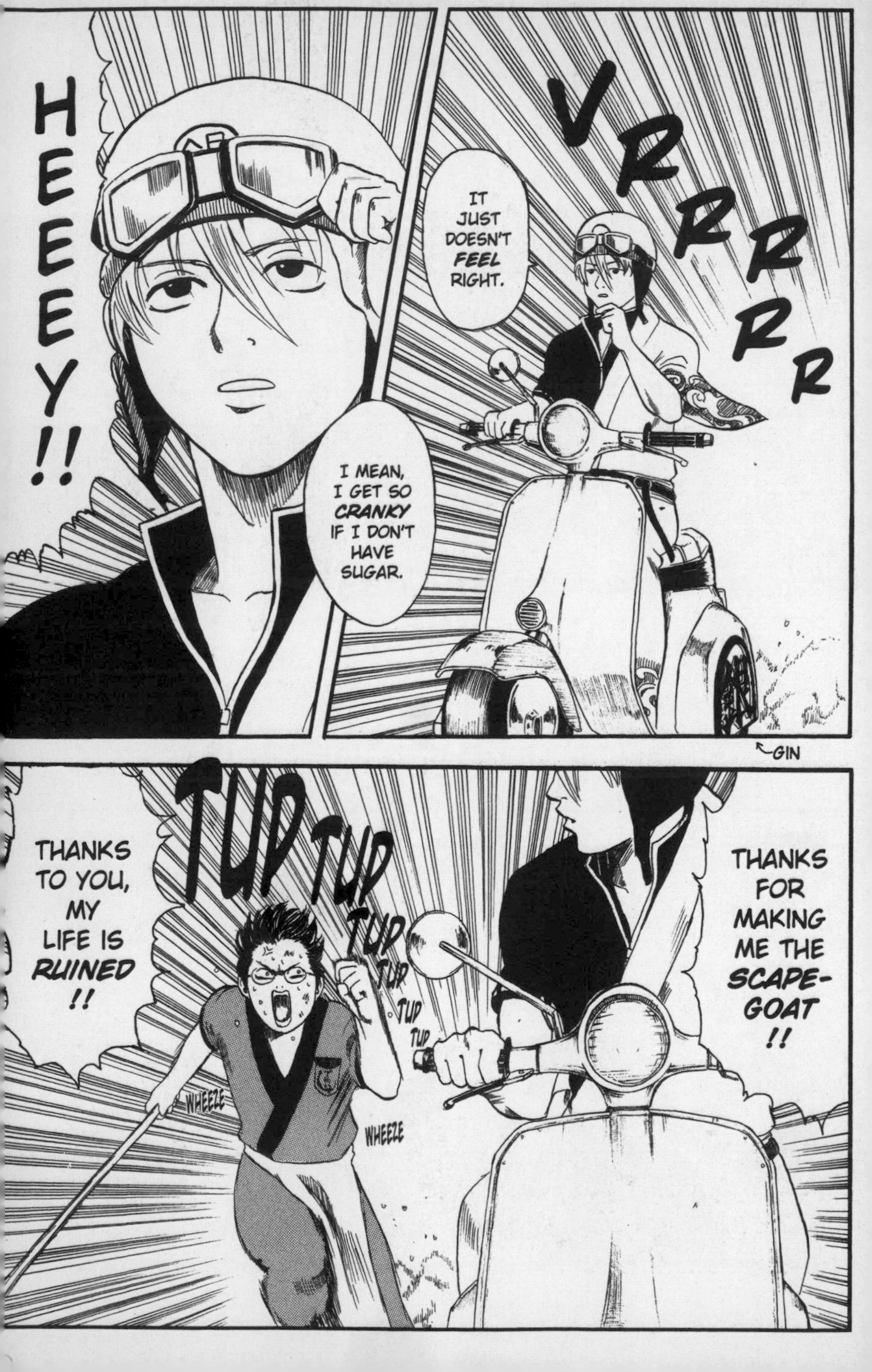
VRRRRRR
IT JUST DOESN'T FEEL RIGHT.
I MEAN, I GET SO CRANKY IF I DON'T HAVE SUGAR.
GIN
HEEEEY!!
THANKS FOR MAKING ME THE SCAPE-GOAT!!
TUP TUP TUP TUP TUP TUP
THANKS TO YOU, MY LIFE IS RUINED!!
WHEEZE
WHEEZE

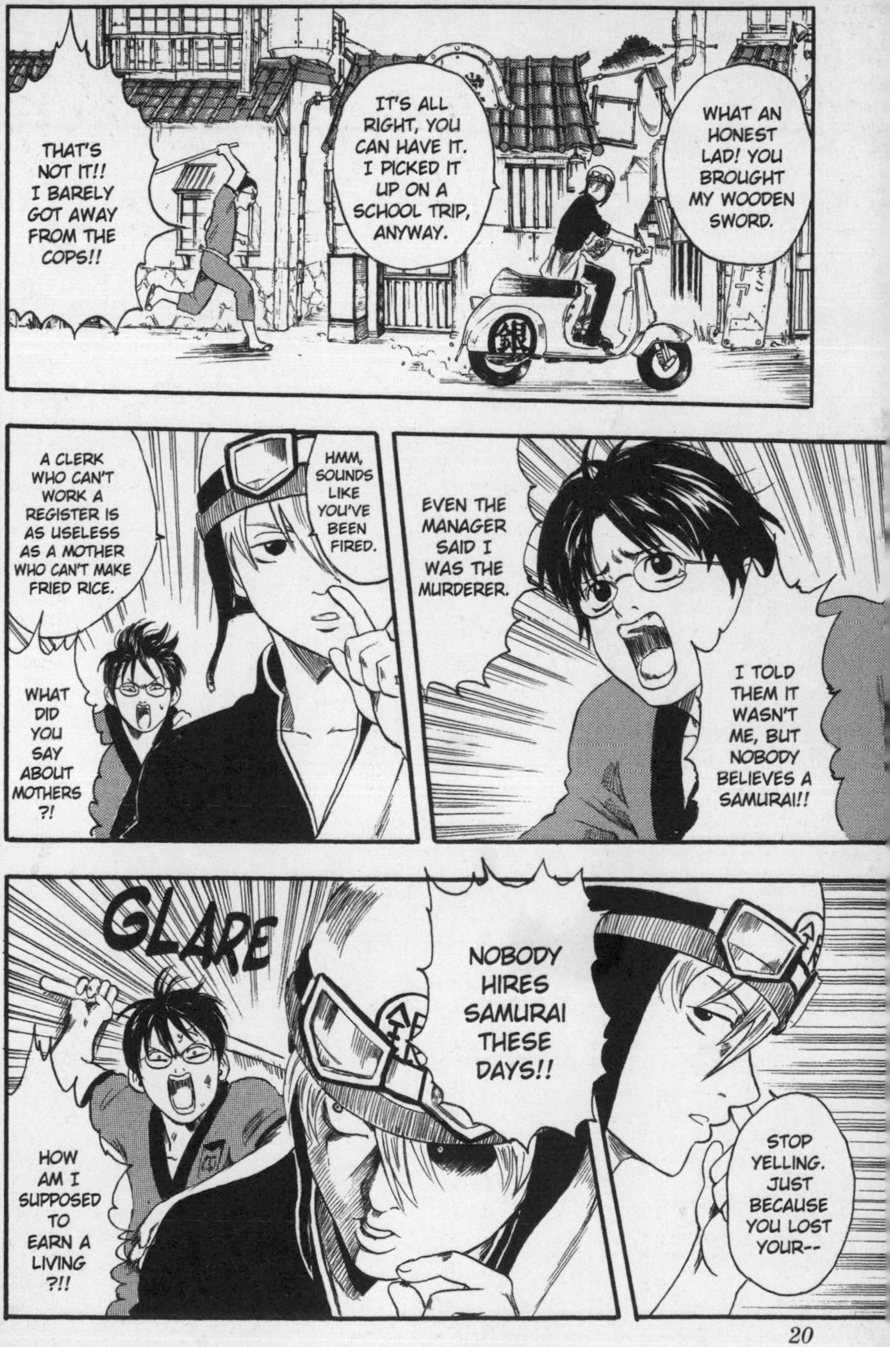
WHAT AN HONEST LAD! YOU BROUGHT MY WOODEN SWORD.
IT'S ALL RIGHT, YOU CAN HAVE IT. I PICKED IT UP ON A SCHOOL TRIP, ANYWAY.
THAT'S NOT IT!! I BARELY GOT AWAY FROM THE COPS!!
EVEN THE MANAGER SAID I WAS THE MURDERER.
I TOLD THEM IT WASN'T ME, BUT NOBODY BELIEVES A SAMURAI!!
HMM, SOUNDS LIKE YOU'VE BEEN FIRED.
A CLERK WHO CAN'T WORK A REGISTER IS AS USELESS AS A MOTHER WHO CAN'T MAKE FRIED RICE.
WHAT DID YOU SAY ABOUT MOTHERS ?!
STOP YELLING. JUST BECAUSE YOU LOST YOUR--
NOBODY HIRES SAMURAI THESE DAYS!!
GLARE
HOW AM I SUPPOSED TO EARN A LIVING ?!!

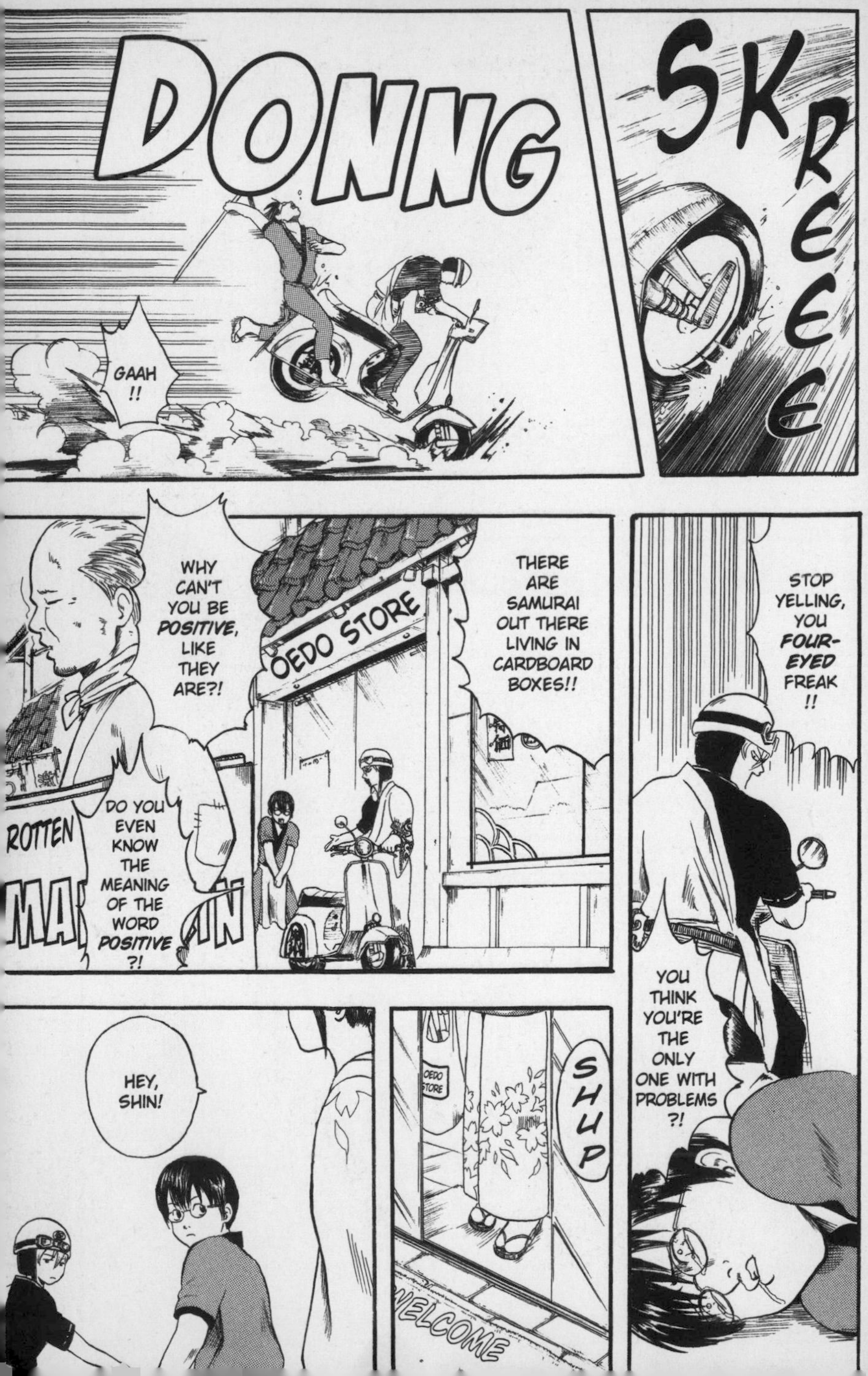
SKREEEE
DONNG
GAAH!!
STOP YELLING, YOU FOUR-EYED FREAK!!
YOU THINK YOU'RE THE ONLY ONE WITH PROBLEMS?!
THERE ARE SAMURAI OUT THERE LIVING IN CARDBOARD BOXES!!
OEDO STORE
WHY CAN'T YOU BE POSITIVE, LIKE THEY ARE?!
DO YOU EVEN KNOW THE MEANING OF THE WORD POSITIVE?!
ROTTEN
SHUP
OEDO STORE
WELCOME
HEY, SHIN!

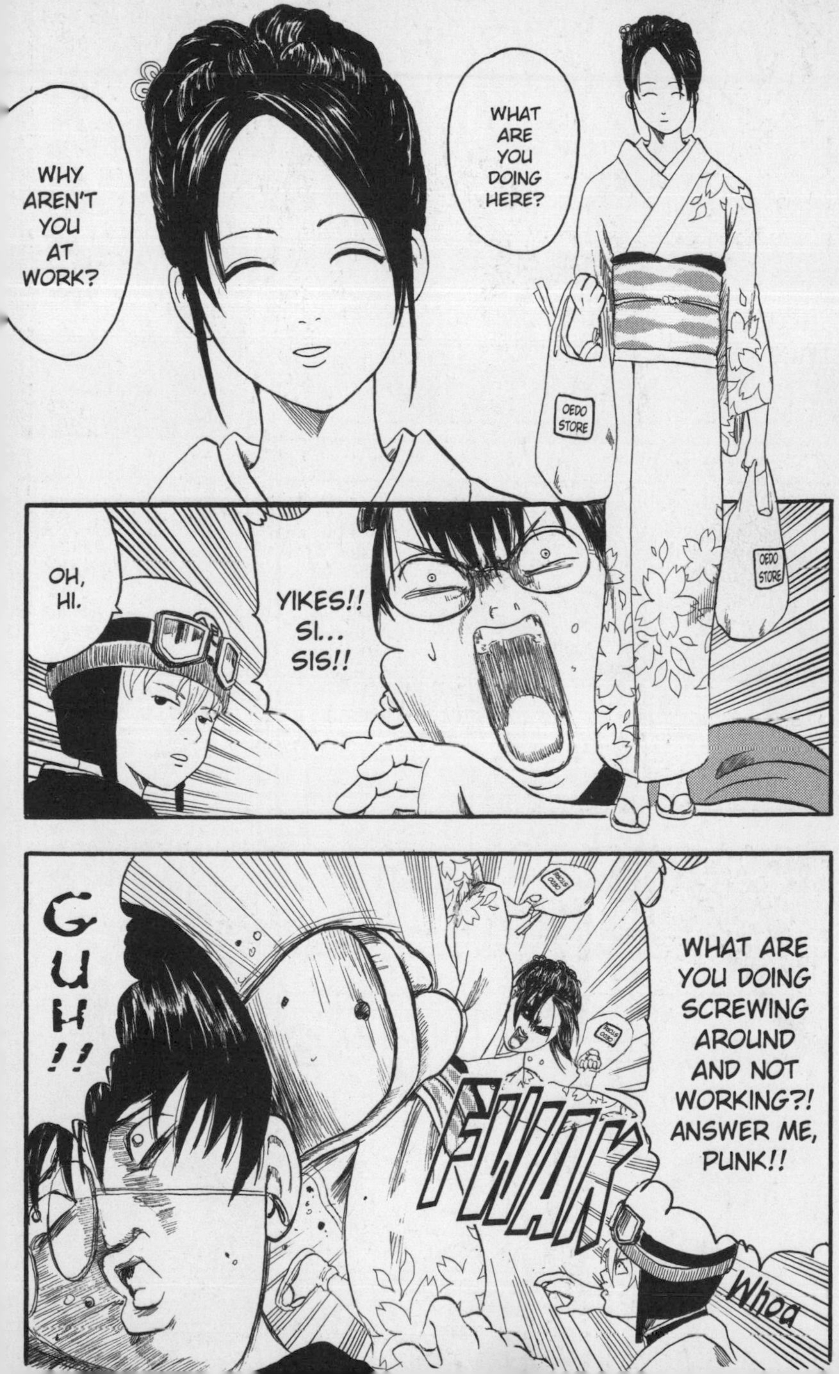
WHAT ARE YOU DOING HERE?
OEDO STORE
WHY AREN'T YOU AT WORK?
OEDO STORE
YIKES!! SI... SIS!!
OH, HI.
WHAT ARE YOU DOING SCREWING AROUND AND NOT WORKING?! ANSWER ME, PUNK!!
FWAK
Whoa
GUH!!

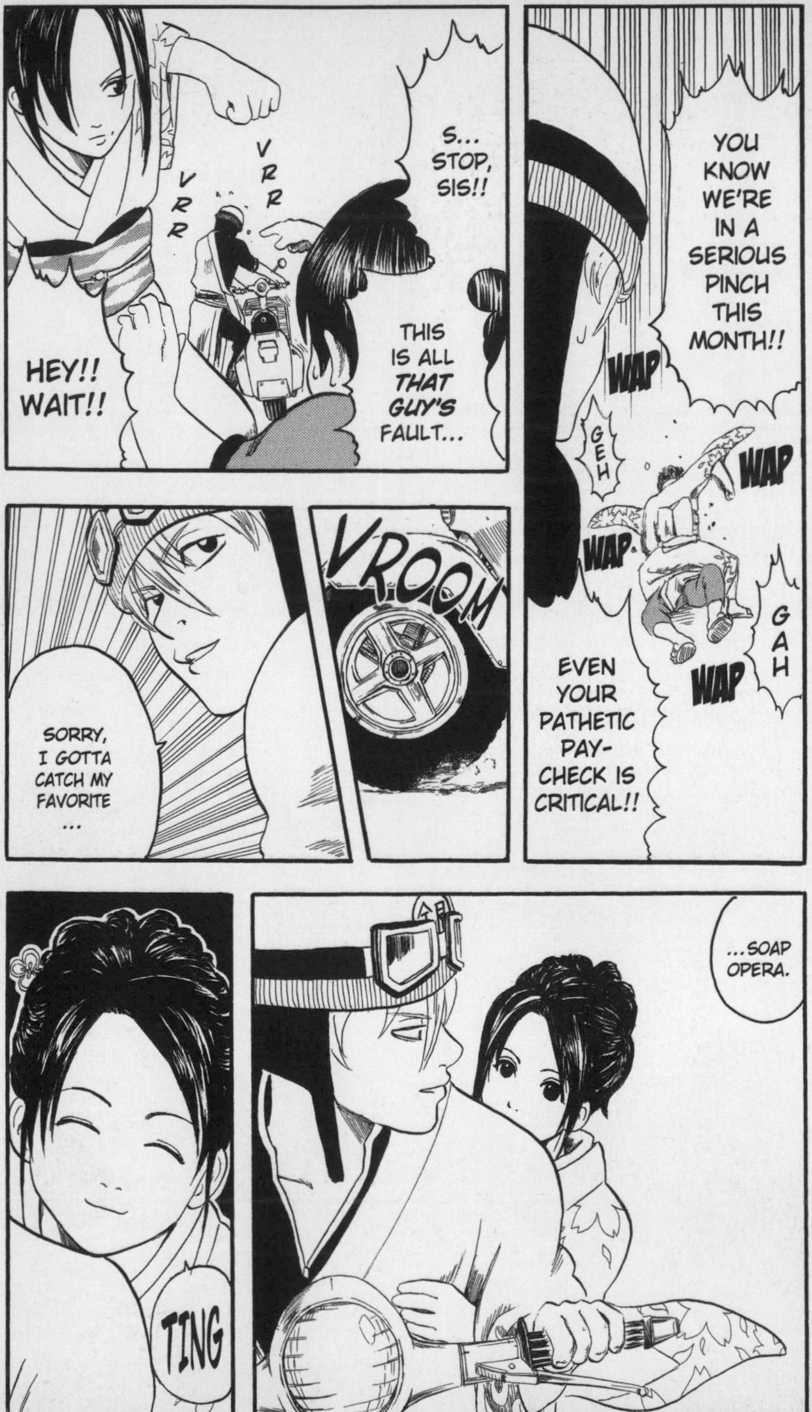
YOU KNOW WE'RE IN A SERIOUS PINCH THIS MONTH!!
WAP
WAP
GEH
WAP
GAH
WAP
EVEN YOUR PATHETIC PAY-CHECK IS CRITICAL!!
S... STOP, SIS!!
THIS IS ALL THAT GUY'S FAULT...
VRR
VRR
HEY!! WAIT!!
VROOM
SORRY, I GOTTA CATCH MY FAVORITE ...
...SOAP OPERA.
TING

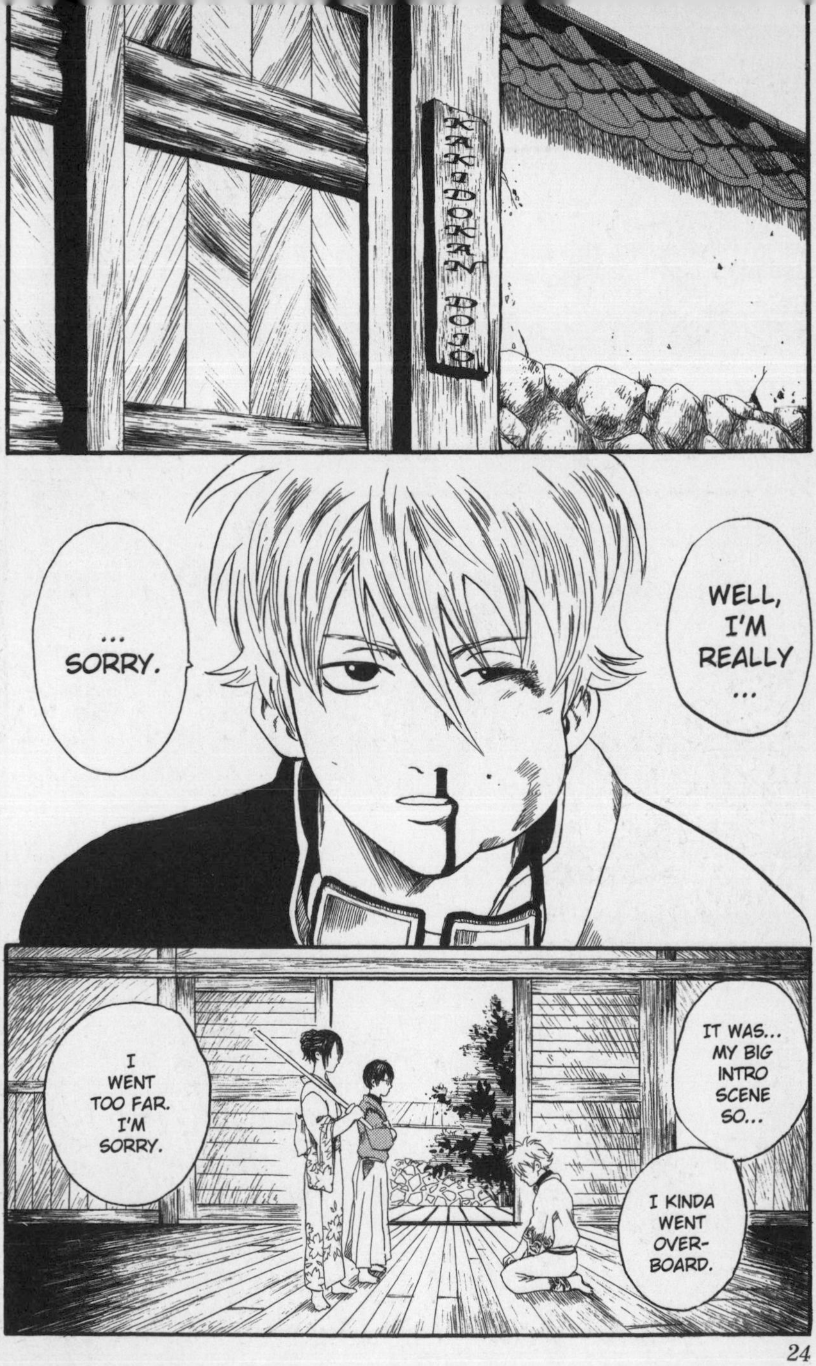
KAKIDOKAN DOJO
WELL, I'M REALLY ...
... SORRY.
IT WAS... MY BIG INTRO SCENE SO...
I KINDA WENT OVER-BOARD.
I WENT TOO FAR. I'M SORRY.

READ THIS WAY

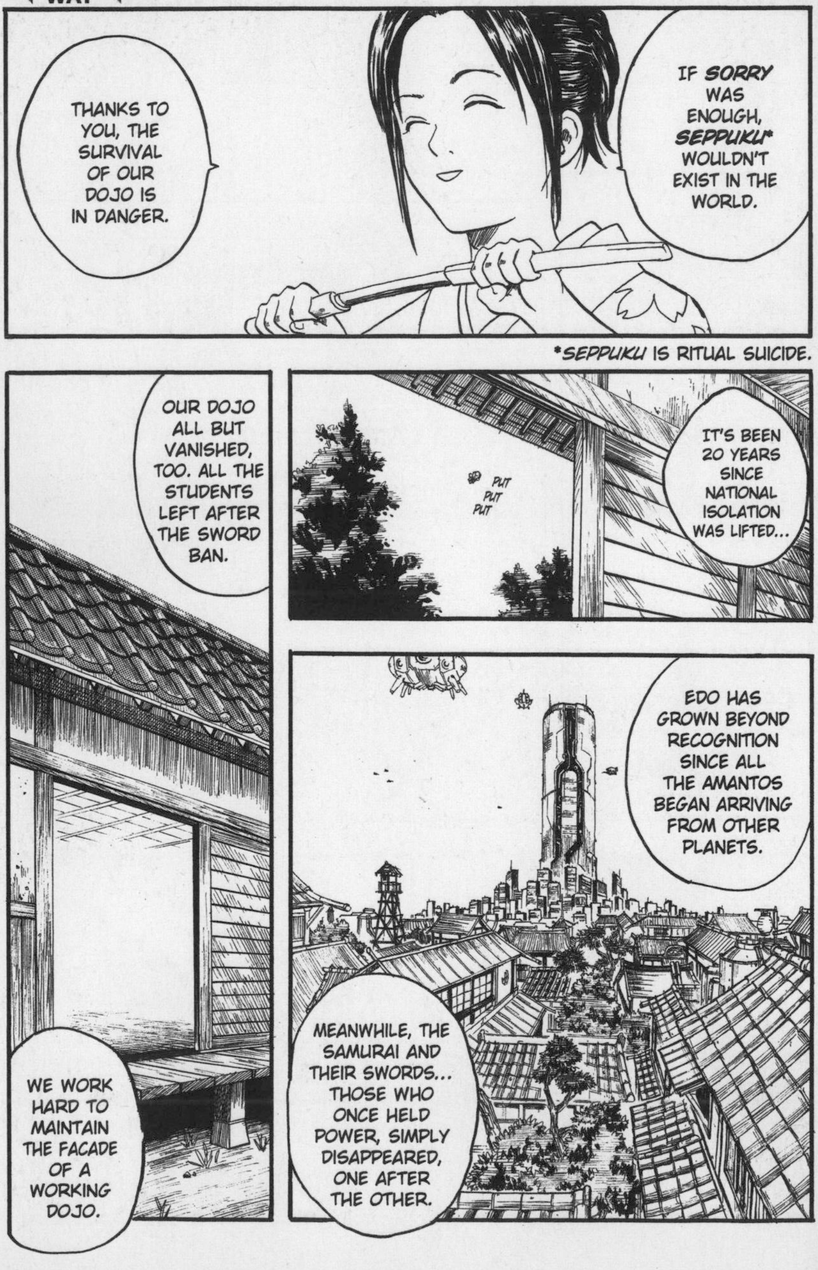
IF SORRY WAS ENOUGH, SEPPUKU* WOULDN'T EXIST IN THE WORLD.
THANKS TO YOU, THE SURVIVAL OF OUR DOJO IS IN DANGER.
*SEPPUKU IS RITUAL SUICIDE.
PUT PUT PUT
IT'S BEEN 20 YEARS SINCE NATIONAL ISOLATION WAS LIFTED...
EDO HAS GROWN BEYOND RECOGNITION SINCE ALL THE AMANTOS BEGAN ARRIVING FROM OTHER PLANETS.
MEANWHILE, THE SAMURAI AND THEIR SWORDS... THOSE WHO ONCE HELD POWER, SIMPLY DISAPPEARED, ONE AFTER THE OTHER.
OUR DOJO ALL BUT VANISHED, TOO. ALL THE STUDENTS LEFT AFTER THE SWORD BAN.
WE WORK HARD TO MAINTAIN THE FACADE OF A WORKING DOJO.

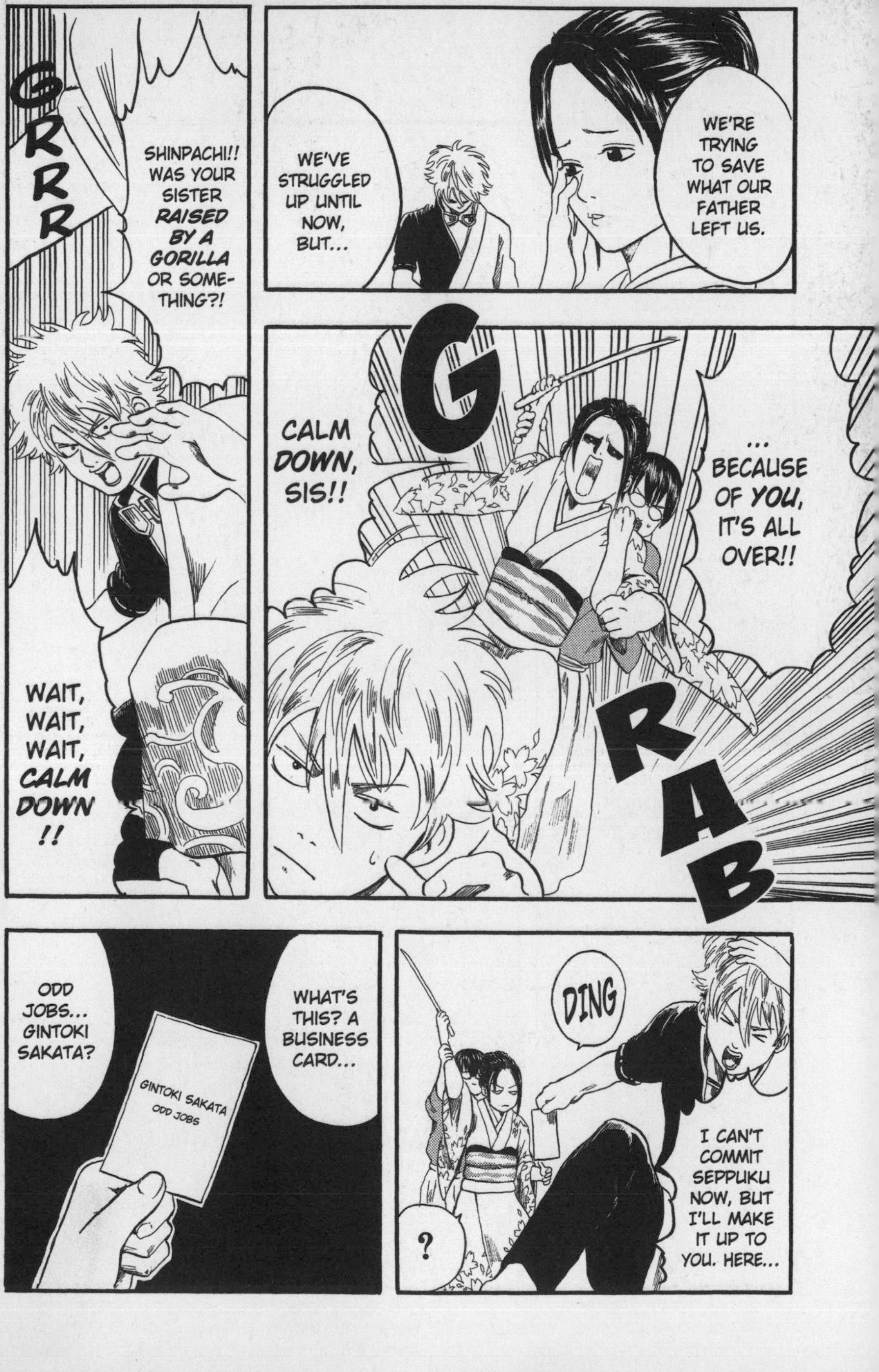
WE'RE TRYING TO SAVE WHAT OUR FATHER LEFT US.
WE'VE STRUGGLED UP UNTIL NOW, BUT...
... BECAUSE OF YOU, IT'S ALL OVER!!
GRAB
CALM DOWN, SIS!!
GRRR
SHINPACHI!! WAS YOUR SISTER RAISED BY A GORILLA OR SOMETHING?!
WAIT, WAIT, WAIT, CALM DOWN!!
DING
I CAN'T COMMIT SEPPUKU NOW, BUT I'LL MAKE IT UP TO YOU. HERE...
?
WHAT'S THIS? A BUSINESS CARD...
ODD JOBS... GINTOKI SAKATA?
GINTOKI SAKATA
ODD JOBS

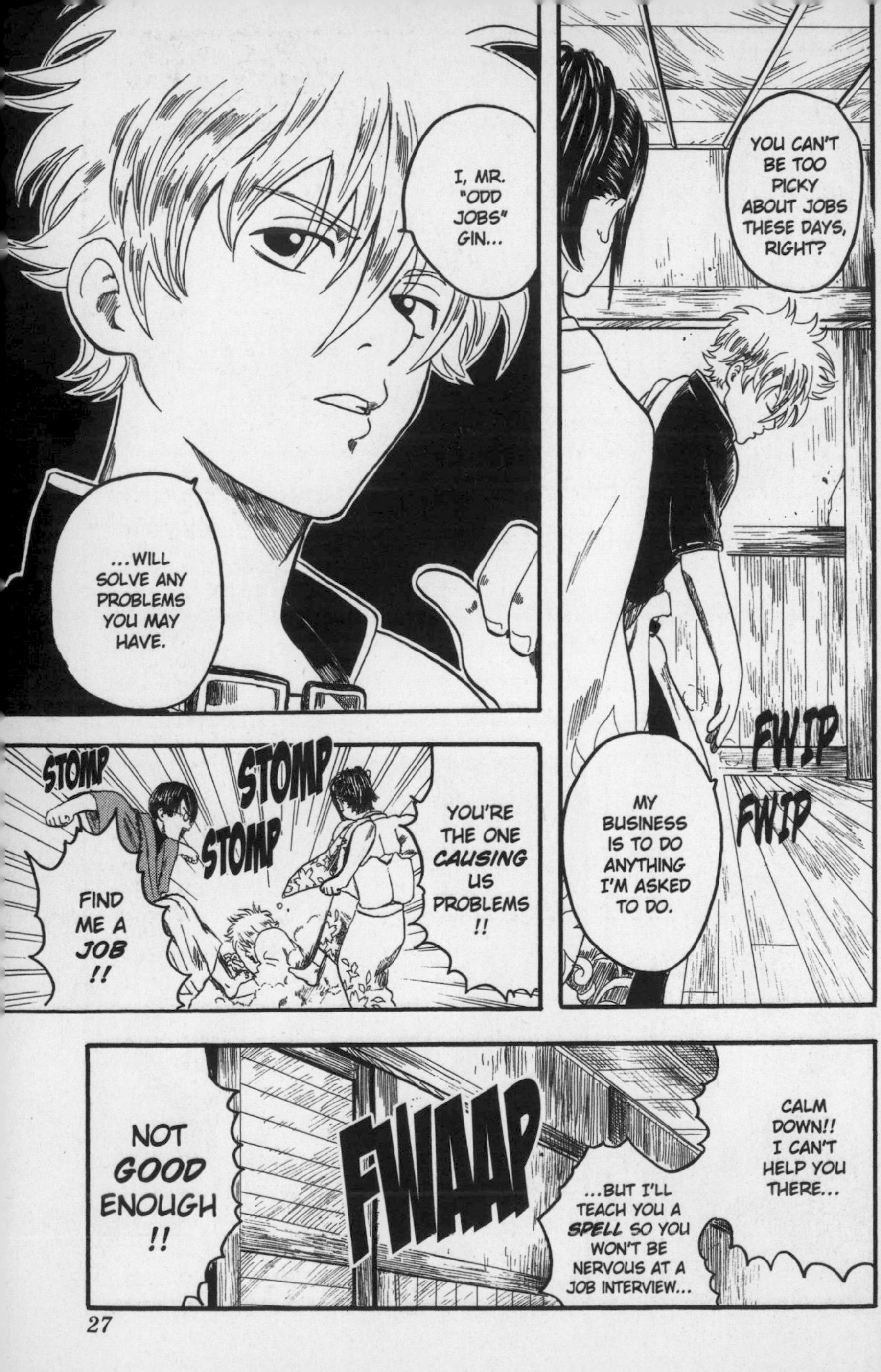
YOU CAN'T BE TOO PICKY ABOUT JOBS THESE DAYS, RIGHT?
FWIP
FWIP
MY BUSINESS IS TO DO ANYTHING I'M ASKED TO DO.
I, MR. "ODD JOBS" GIN...
...WILL SOLVE ANY PROBLEMS YOU MAY HAVE.
YOU'RE THE ONE CAUSING US PROBLEMS !!
STOMP
STOMP
STOMP
FIND ME A JOB !!
CALM DOWN!! I CAN'T HELP YOU THERE...
...BUT I'LL TEACH YOU A SPELL SO YOU WON'T BE NERVOUS AT A JOB INTERVIEW...
FWAAP
NOT GOOD ENOUGH !!

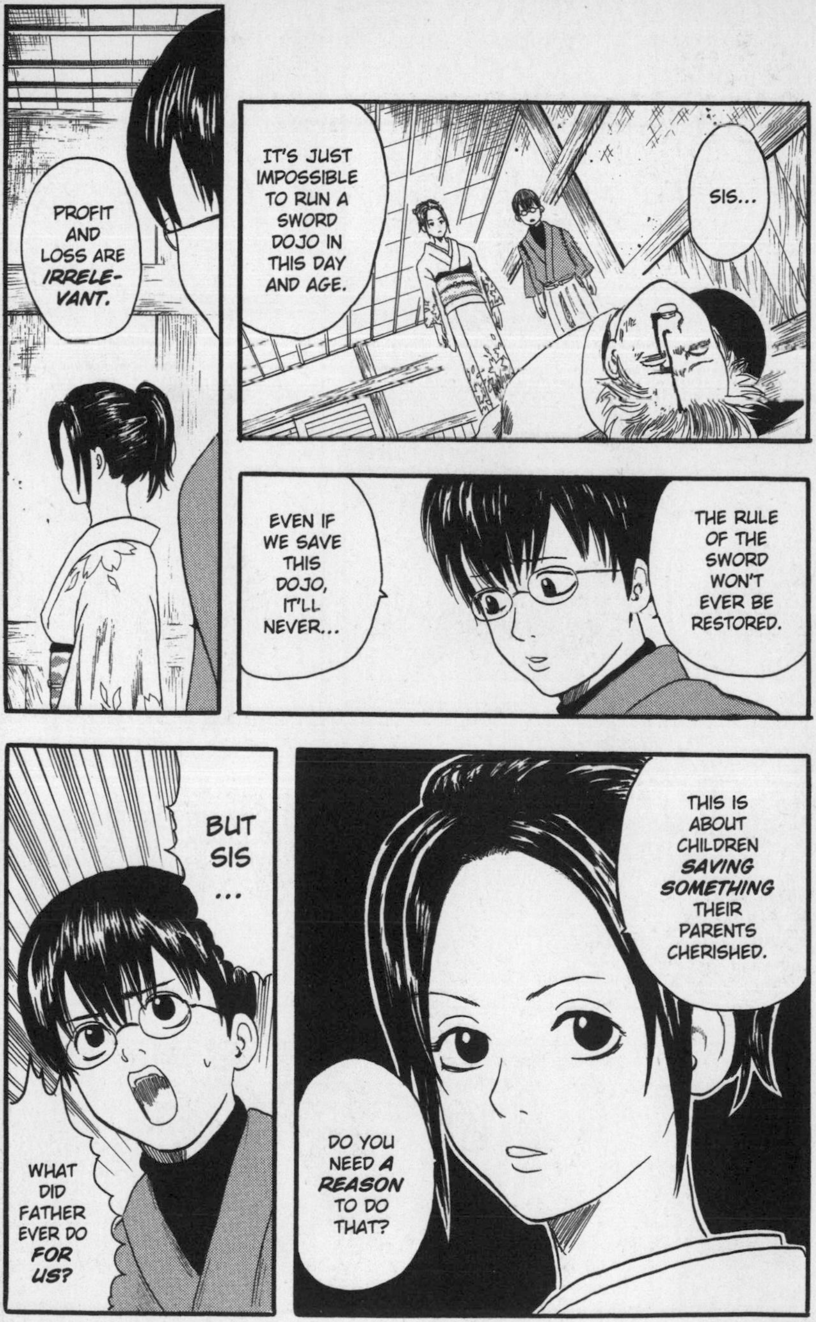
SIS...
IT'S JUST IMPOSSIBLE TO RUN A SWORD DOJO IN THIS DAY AND AGE.
THE RULE OF THE SWORD WON'T EVER BE RESTORED.
EVEN IF WE SAVE THIS DOJO, IT'LL NEVER...
PROFIT AND LOSS ARE *IRRELEVANT.*
THIS IS ABOUT CHILDREN *SAVING SOMETHING* THEIR PARENTS CHERISHED.
DO YOU NEED *A REASON* TO DO THAT?
BUT SIS ...
WHAT DID FATHER EVER DO *FOR US?*

READ THIS WAY

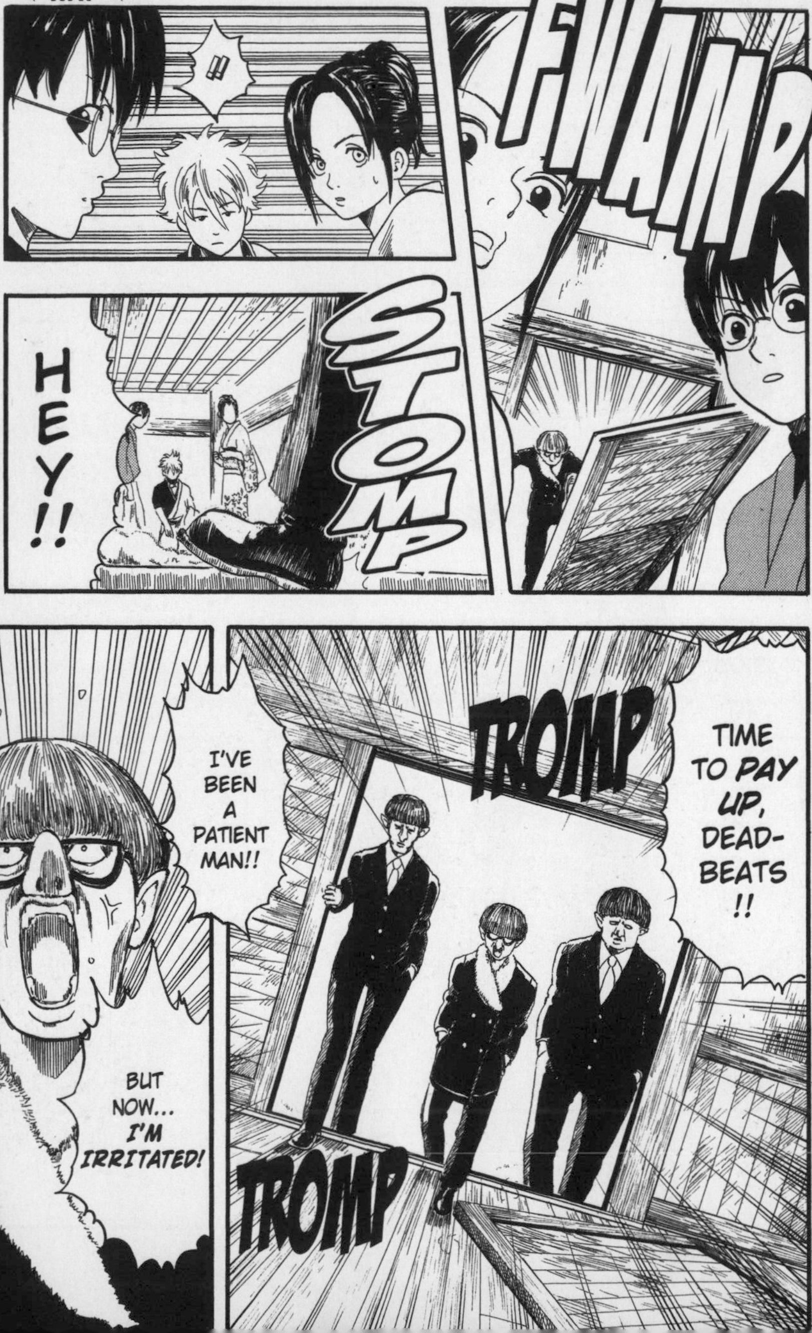
FWAMP
!!
HEY!!
STOMP
TROMP
TIME TO PAY UP, DEAD-BEATS!!
TROMP
I'VE BEEN A PATIENT MAN!!
BUT NOW... I'M IRRITATED!

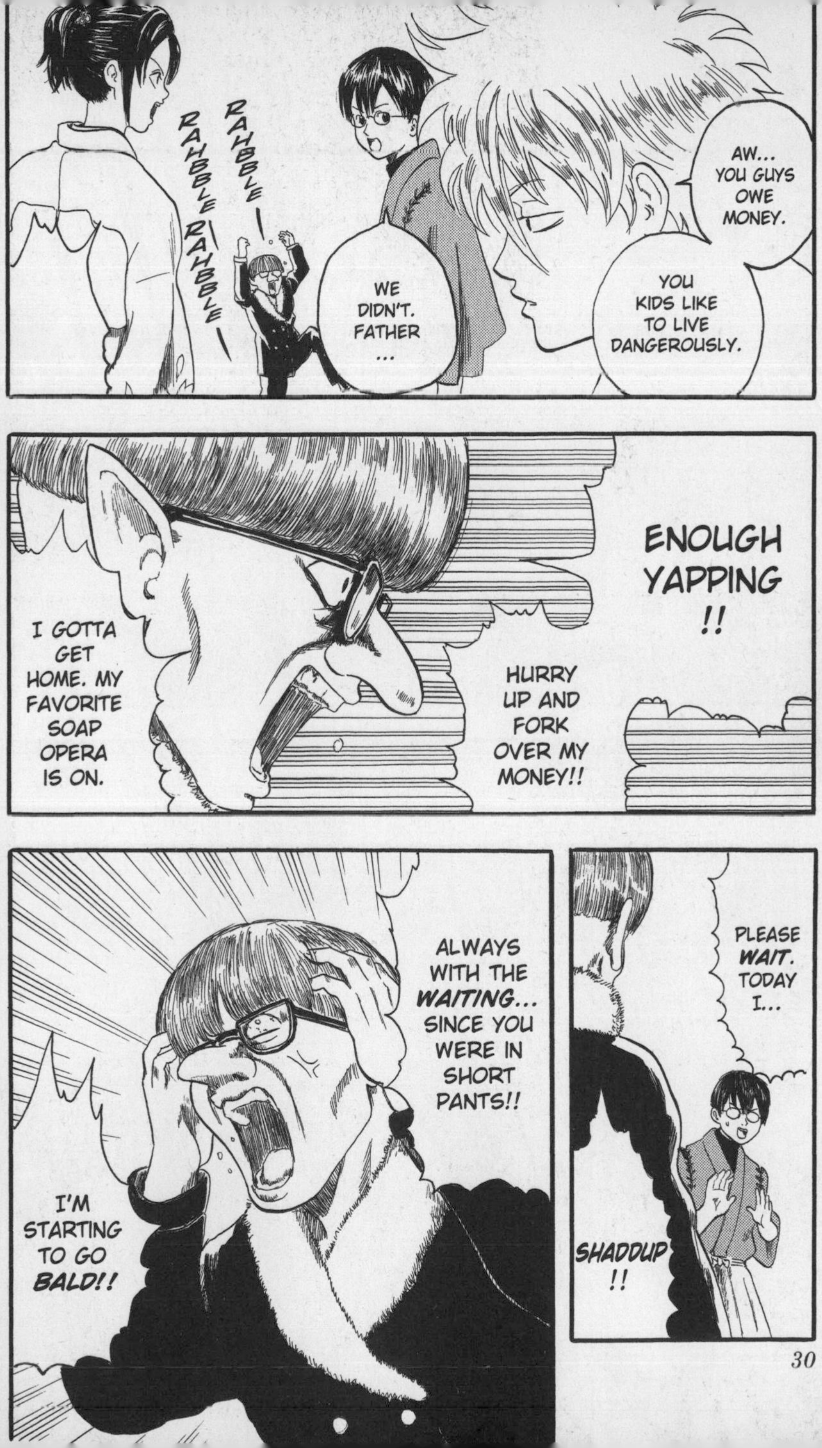
AW... YOU GUYS OWE MONEY.
YOU KIDS LIKE TO LIVE DANGEROUSLY.
WE DIDN'T. FATHER ...
RAHBBLE RAHBBLE
RAHBBLE RAHBBLE
ENOUGH YAPPING !!
HURRY UP AND FORK OVER MY MONEY!!
I GOTTA GET HOME. MY FAVORITE SOAP OPERA IS ON.
PLEASE *WAIT*. TODAY I...
SHADDUP !!
ALWAYS WITH THE *WAITING*... SINCE YOU WERE IN SHORT PANTS!!
I'M STARTING TO GO *BALD!!*

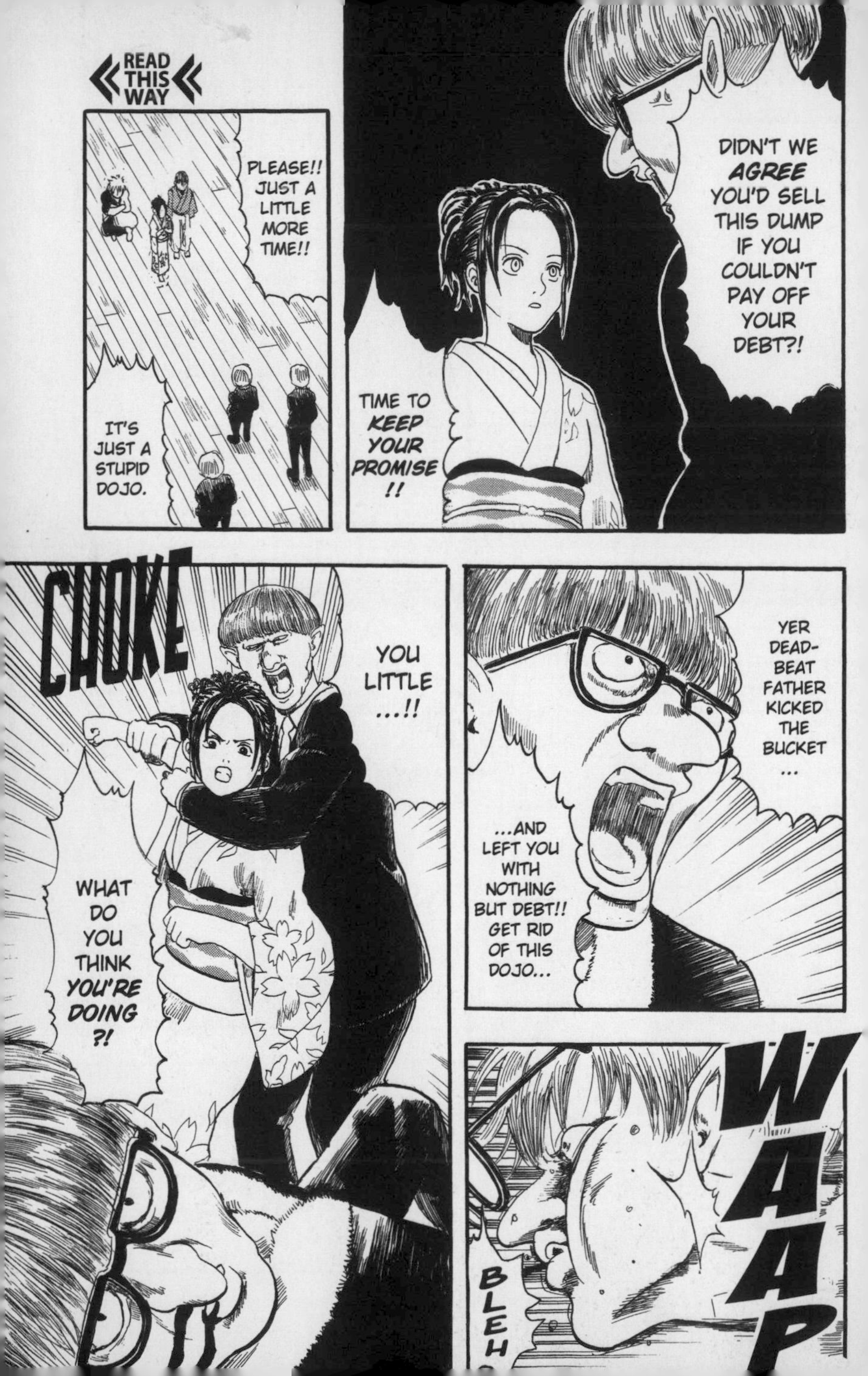
READ THIS WAY
DIDN'T WE AGREE YOU'D SELL THIS DUMP IF YOU COULDN'T PAY OFF YOUR DEBT?!
TIME TO KEEP YOUR PROMISE!!
PLEASE!! JUST A LITTLE MORE TIME!!
IT'S JUST A STUPID DOJO.
YER DEAD-BEAT FATHER KICKED THE BUCKET...
...AND LEFT YOU WITH NOTHING BUT DEBT!! GET RID OF THIS DOJO...
WAAP
BLEH
CHOKE
YOU LITTLE...!!
WHAT DO YOU THINK YOU'RE DOING?!

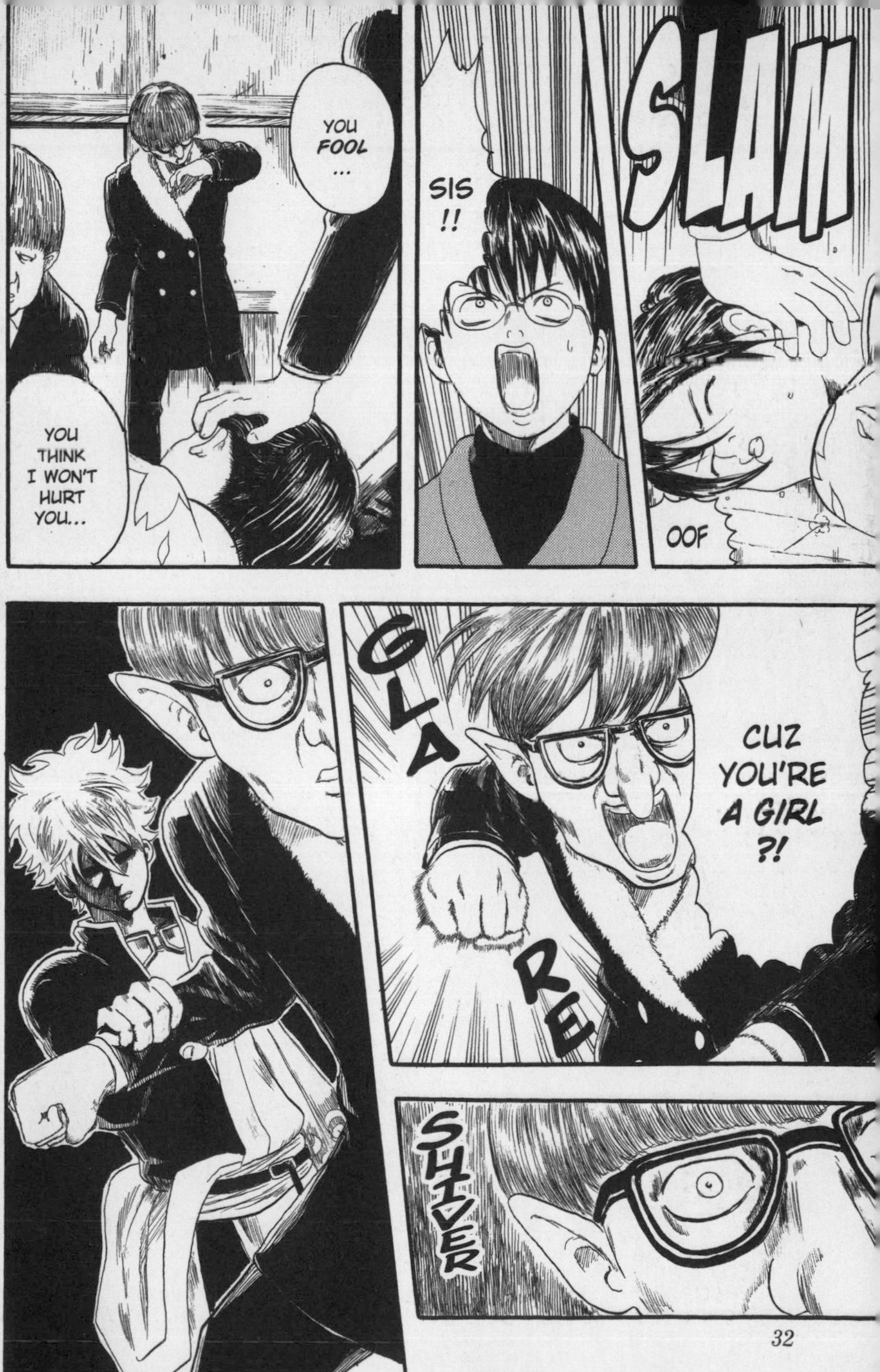
SLAM
OOF
SIS !!
YOU FOOL ...
YOU THINK I WON'T HURT YOU...
GLARE
CUZ YOU'RE A GIRL ?!
SHIVER

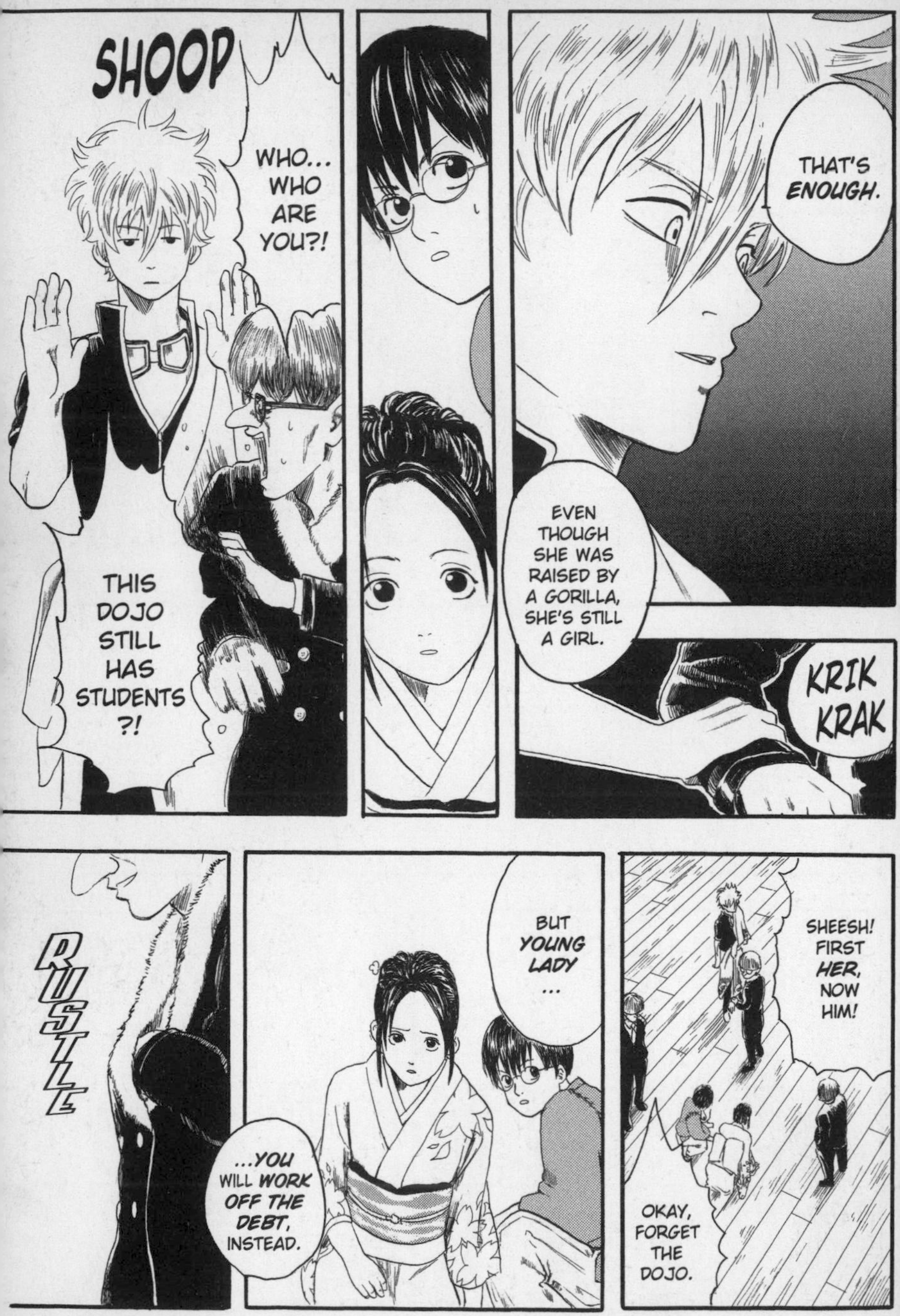
THAT'S ENOUGH.
EVEN THOUGH SHE WAS RAISED BY A GORILLA, SHE'S STILL A GIRL.
KRIK KRAK
SHOOP
WHO... WHO ARE YOU?!
THIS DOJO STILL HAS STUDENTS?!
SHEESH! FIRST HER, NOW HIM!
OKAY, FORGET THE DOJO.
BUT YOUNG LADY...
...YOU WILL WORK OFF THE DEBT, INSTEAD.
RUSTLE

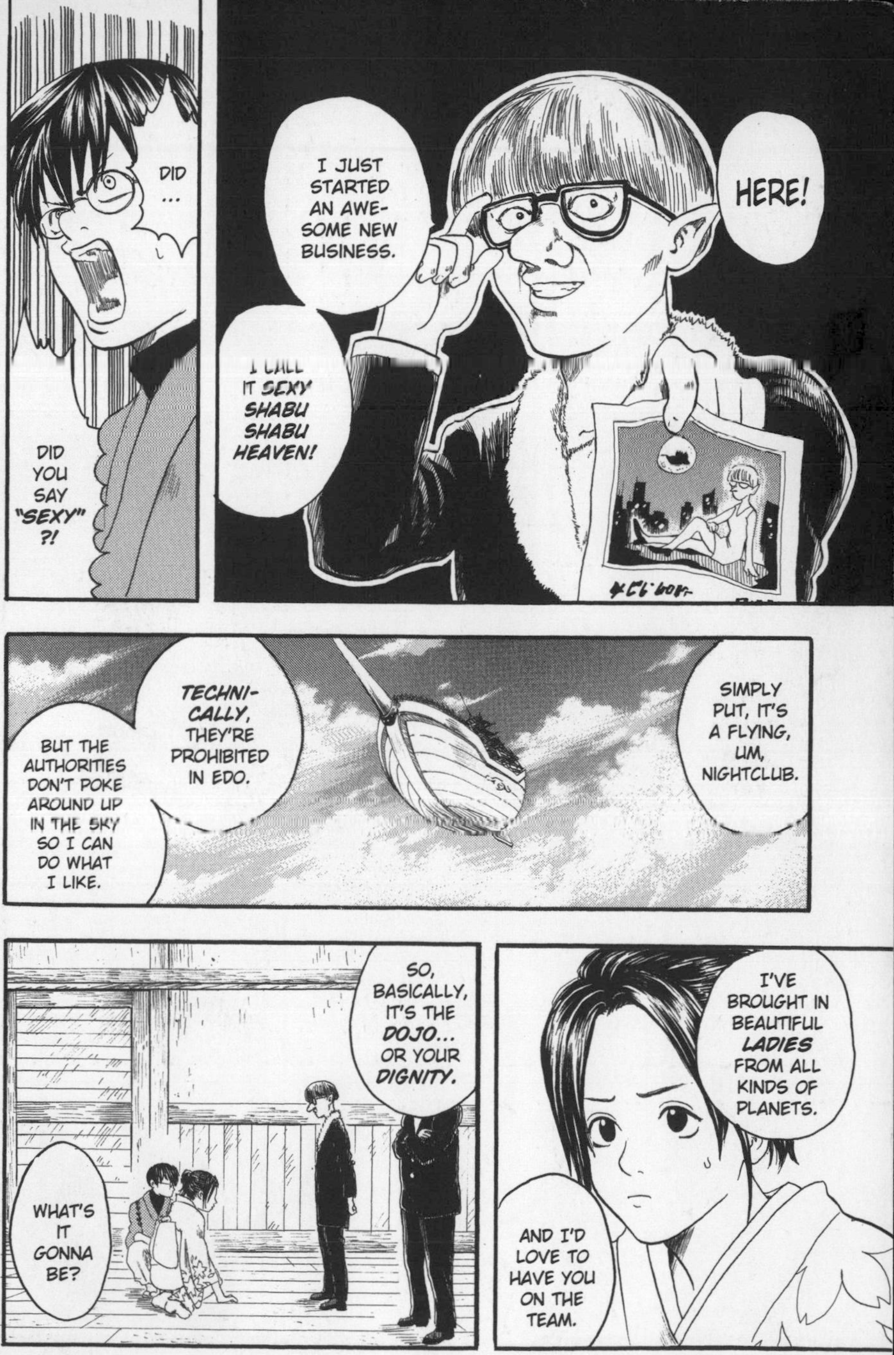
HERE!
I JUST STARTED AN AWESOME NEW BUSINESS.
I CALL IT SEXY SHABU SHABU HEAVEN!
DID...
DID YOU SAY "SEXY"?!
SIMPLY PUT, IT'S A FLYING, UM, NIGHTCLUB.
TECHNICALLY, THEY'RE PROHIBITED IN EDO.
BUT THE AUTHORITIES DON'T POKE AROUND UP IN THE SKY SO I CAN DO WHAT I LIKE.
I'VE BROUGHT IN BEAUTIFUL LADIES FROM ALL KINDS OF PLANETS.
AND I'D LOVE TO HAVE YOU ON THE TEAM.
SO, BASICALLY, IT'S THE DOJO... OR YOUR DIGNITY.
WHAT'S IT GONNA BE?

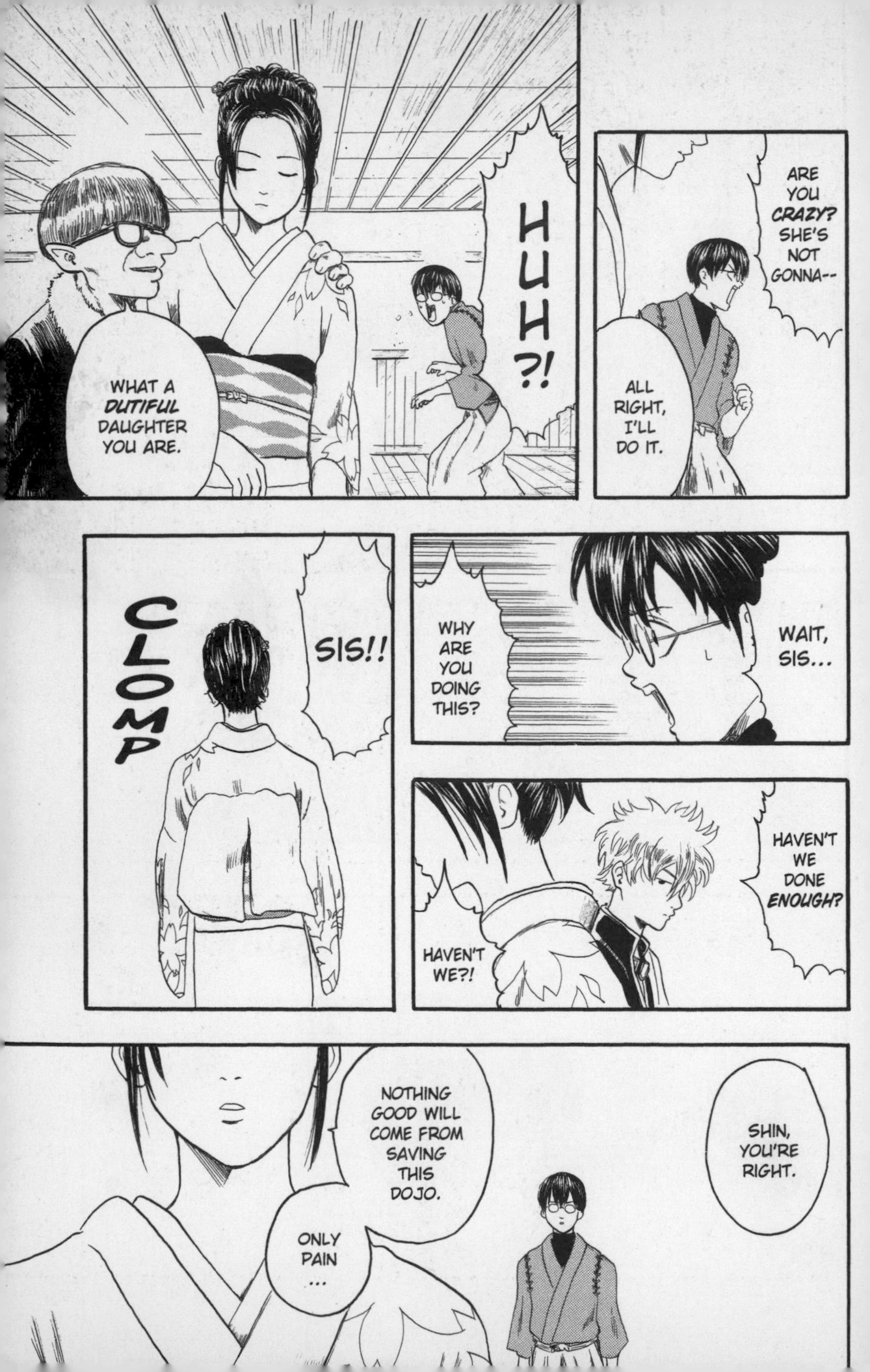
ARE YOU CRAZY? SHE'S NOT GONNA--
ALL RIGHT, I'LL DO IT.
HUH?!
WHAT A DUTIFUL DAUGHTER YOU ARE.
WAIT, SIS...
WHY ARE YOU DOING THIS?
HAVEN'T WE DONE ENOUGH?
HAVEN'T WE?!
SIS!!
CLOMP
SHIN, YOU'RE RIGHT.
NOTHING GOOD WILL COME FROM SAVING THIS DOJO.
ONLY PAIN ...

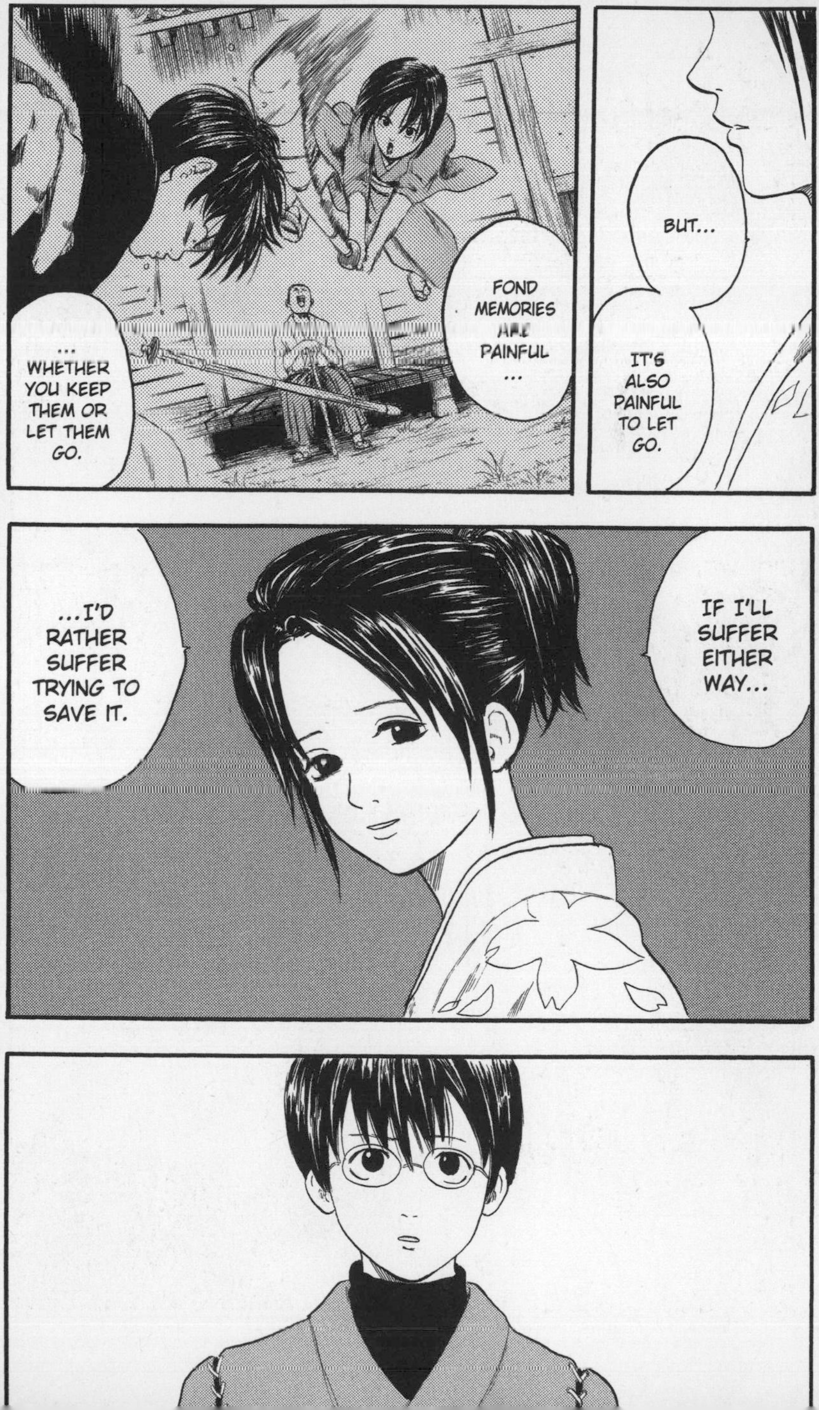
BUT...
IT'S ALSO PAINFUL TO LET GO.
FOND MEMORIES ARE PAINFUL ...
...WHETHER YOU KEEP THEM OR LET THEM GO.
IF I'LL SUFFER EITHER WAY...
...I'D RATHER SUFFER TRYING TO SAVE IT.

READ THIS WAY

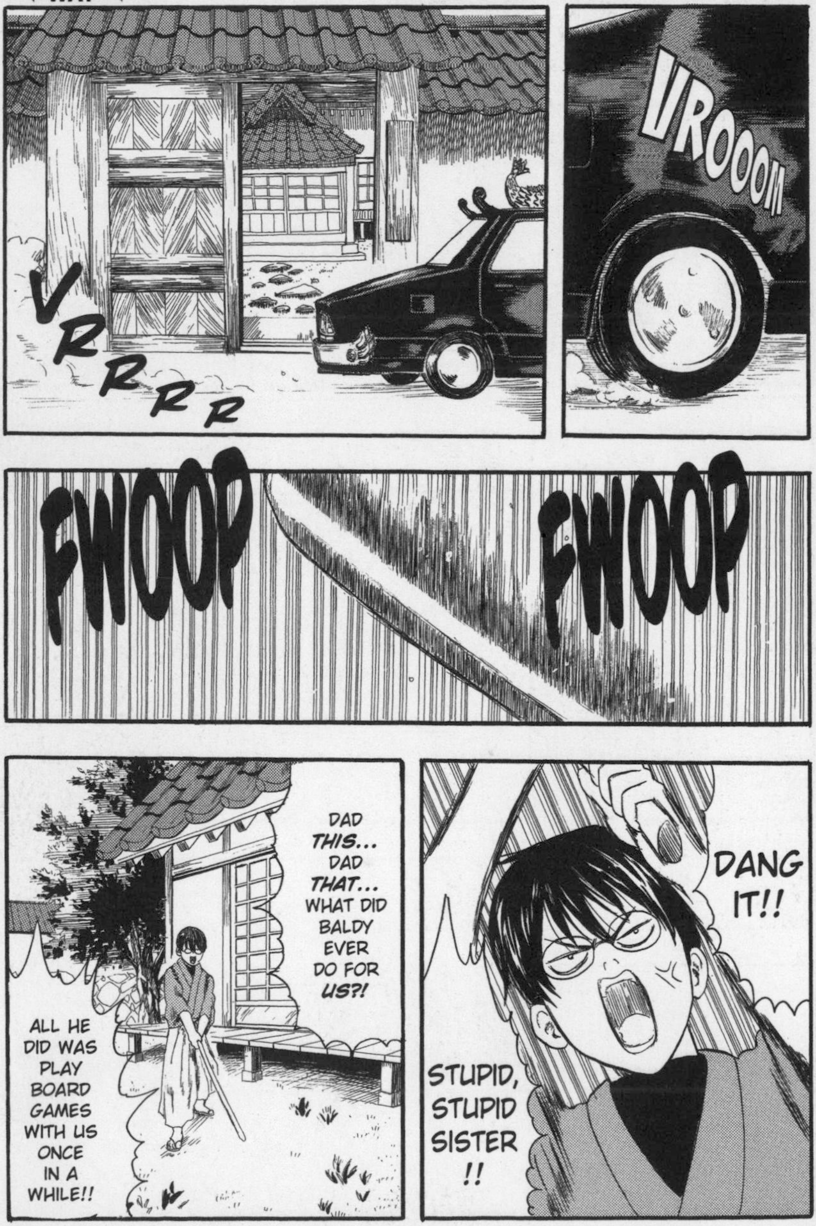
VROOOM
VRRRRR
FWOOP
FWOOP
DANG IT!!
STUPID, STUPID SISTER!!
DAD THIS... DAD THAT... WHAT DID BALDY EVER DO FOR US?!
ALL HE DID WAS PLAY BOARD GAMES WITH US ONCE IN A WHILE!!

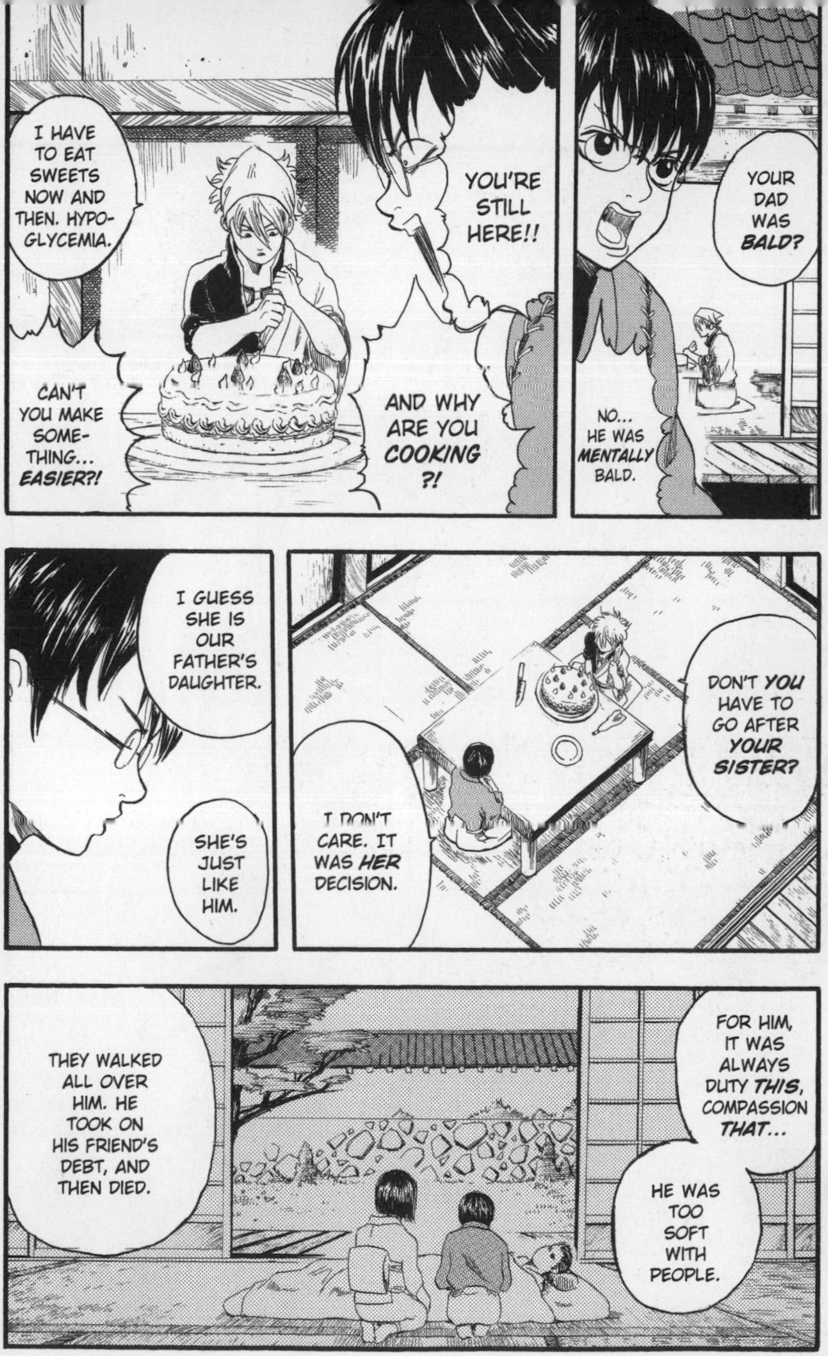
YOUR DAD WAS BALD?
NO... HE WAS MENTALLY BALD.
YOU'RE STILL HERE!!
AND WHY ARE YOU COOKING?!
I HAVE TO EAT SWEETS NOW AND THEN. HYPO-GLYCEMIA.
CAN'T YOU MAKE SOME-THING... EASIER?!
DON'T YOU HAVE TO GO AFTER YOUR SISTER?
I DON'T CARE. IT WAS HER DECISION.
I GUESS SHE IS OUR FATHER'S DAUGHTER.
SHE'S JUST LIKE HIM.
FOR HIM, IT WAS ALWAYS DUTY THIS, COMPASSION THAT...
HE WAS TOO SOFT WITH PEOPLE.
THEY WALKED ALL OVER HIM. HE TOOK ON HIS FRIEND'S DEBT, AND THEN DIED.

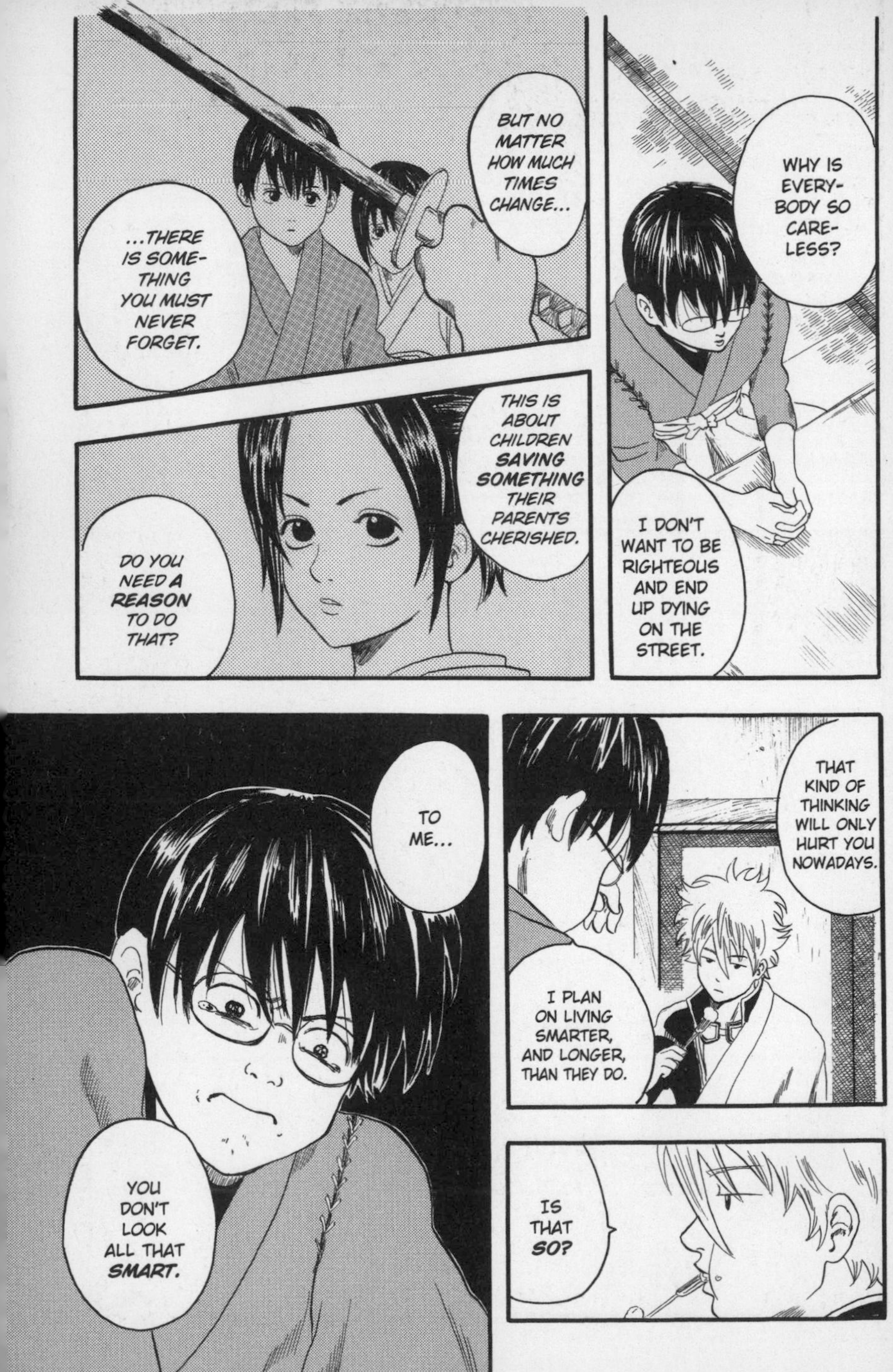
WHY IS EVERY-BODY SO CARE-LESS?
I DON'T WANT TO BE RIGHTEOUS AND END UP DYING ON THE STREET.
BUT NO MATTER HOW MUCH TIMES CHANGE...
...THERE IS SOME-THING YOU MUST NEVER FORGET.
THIS IS ABOUT CHILDREN SAVING SOMETHING THEIR PARENTS CHERISHED.
DO YOU NEED A REASON TO DO THAT?
THAT KIND OF THINKING WILL ONLY HURT YOU NOWADAYS.
I PLAN ON LIVING SMARTER, AND LONGER, THAN THEY DO.
IS THAT SO?
TO ME...
YOU DON'T LOOK ALL THAT SMART.

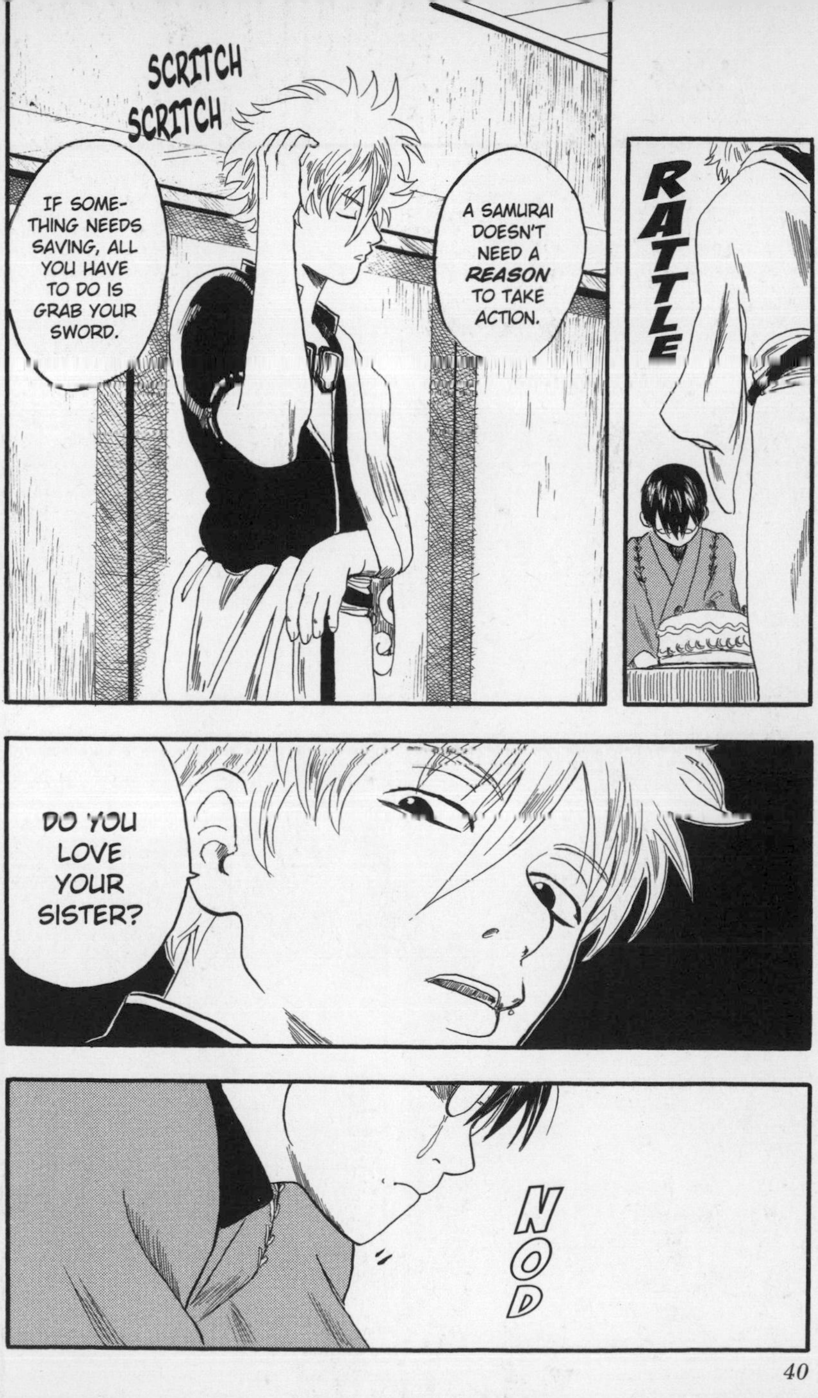
RATTLE
SCRITCH SCRITCH
A SAMURAI DOESN'T NEED A REASON TO TAKE ACTION.
IF SOME-THING NEEDS SAVING, ALL YOU HAVE TO DO IS GRAB YOUR SWORD.
DO YOU LOVE YOUR SISTER?
NOD

READ THIS WAY

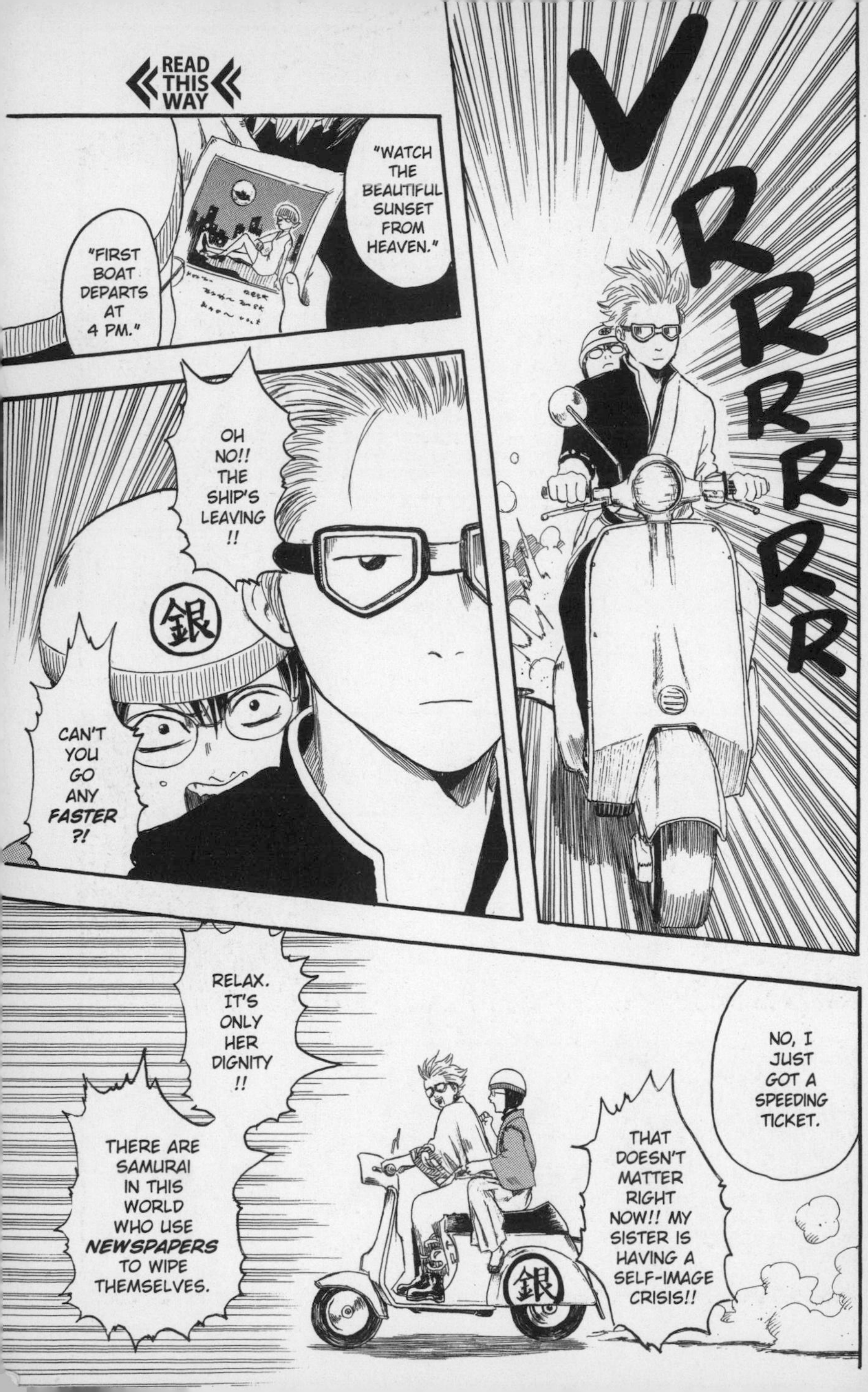
VRRRRRR
"WATCH THE BEAUTIFUL SUNSET FROM HEAVEN."
"FIRST BOAT DEPARTS AT 4 PM."
OH NO!! THE SHIP'S LEAVING!!
CAN'T YOU GO ANY FASTER?!
NO, I JUST GOT A SPEEDING TICKET.
THAT DOESN'T MATTER RIGHT NOW!! MY SISTER IS HAVING A SELF-IMAGE CRISIS!!
RELAX. IT'S ONLY HER DIGNITY!!
THERE ARE SAMURAI IN THIS WORLD WHO USE NEWSPAPERS TO WIPE THEMSELVES.

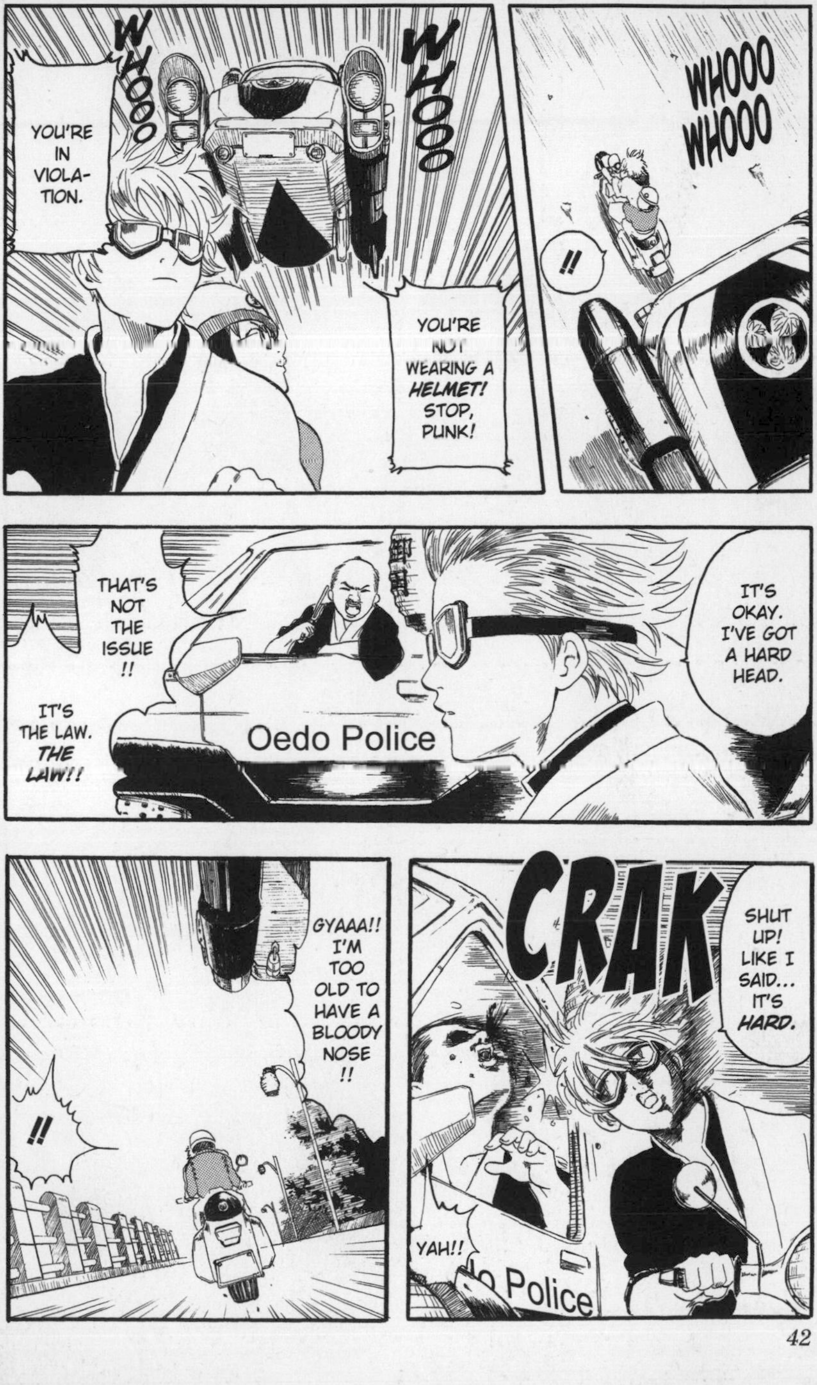
WHOOO WHOOO
!!
WHOOO
WHOOO
YOU'RE NOT WEARING A HELMET! STOP, PUNK!
YOU'RE IN VIOLATION.
IT'S OKAY. I'VE GOT A HARD HEAD.
THAT'S NOT THE ISSUE!!
IT'S THE LAW. THE LAW!!
Oedo Police
CRAK
SHUT UP! LIKE I SAID... IT'S HARD.
YAH!!
GYAAA!! I'M TOO OLD TO HAVE A BLOODY NOSE!!
!!

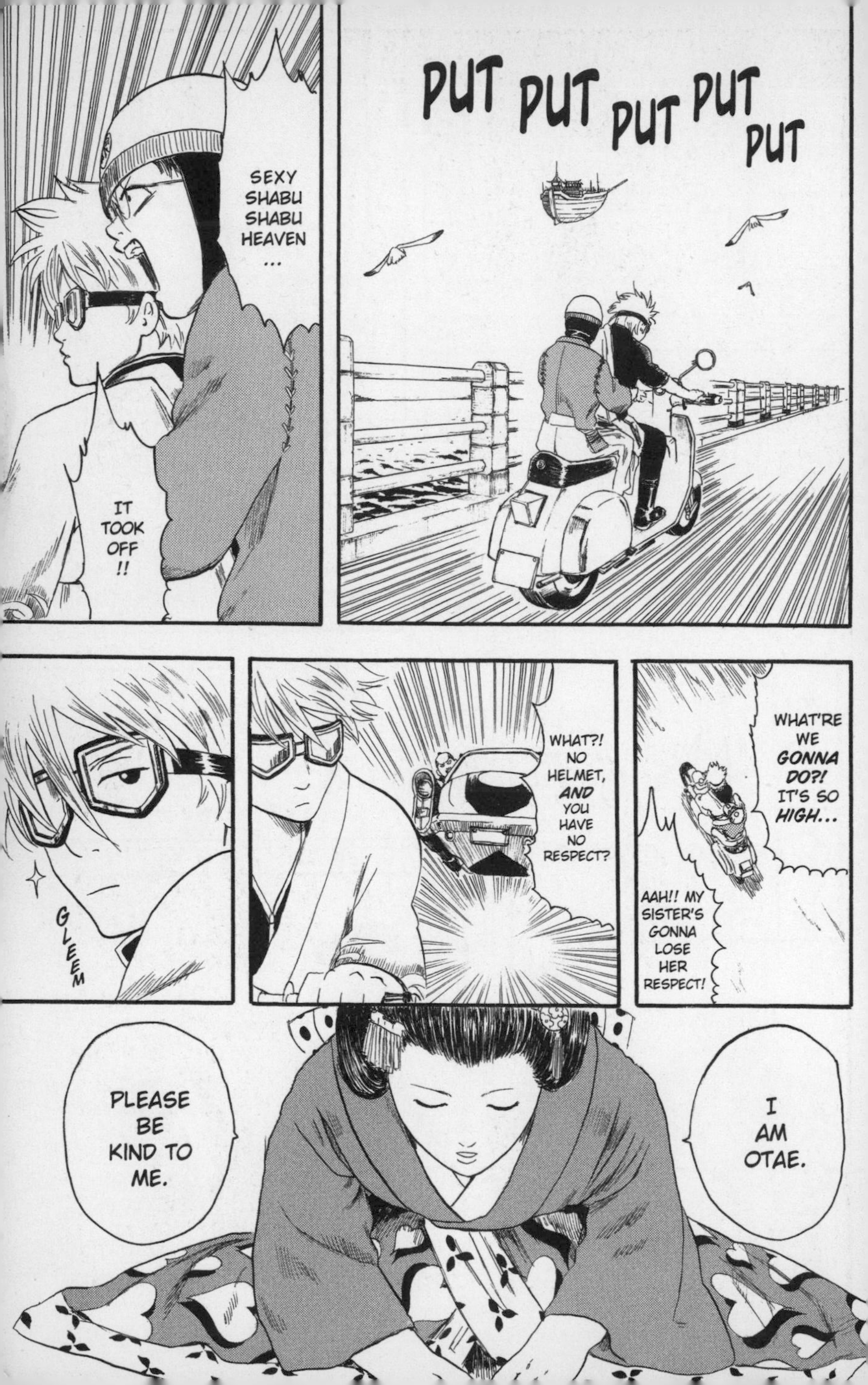
PUT PUT PUT PUT PUT
SEXY SHABU SHABU HEAVEN ...
IT TOOK OFF !!
WHAT'RE WE GONNA DO?! IT'S SO HIGH...
AAH!! MY SISTER'S GONNA LOSE HER RESPECT!
WHAT?! NO HELMET, AND YOU HAVE NO RESPECT?
GLEEM
I AM OTAE.
PLEASE BE KIND TO ME.

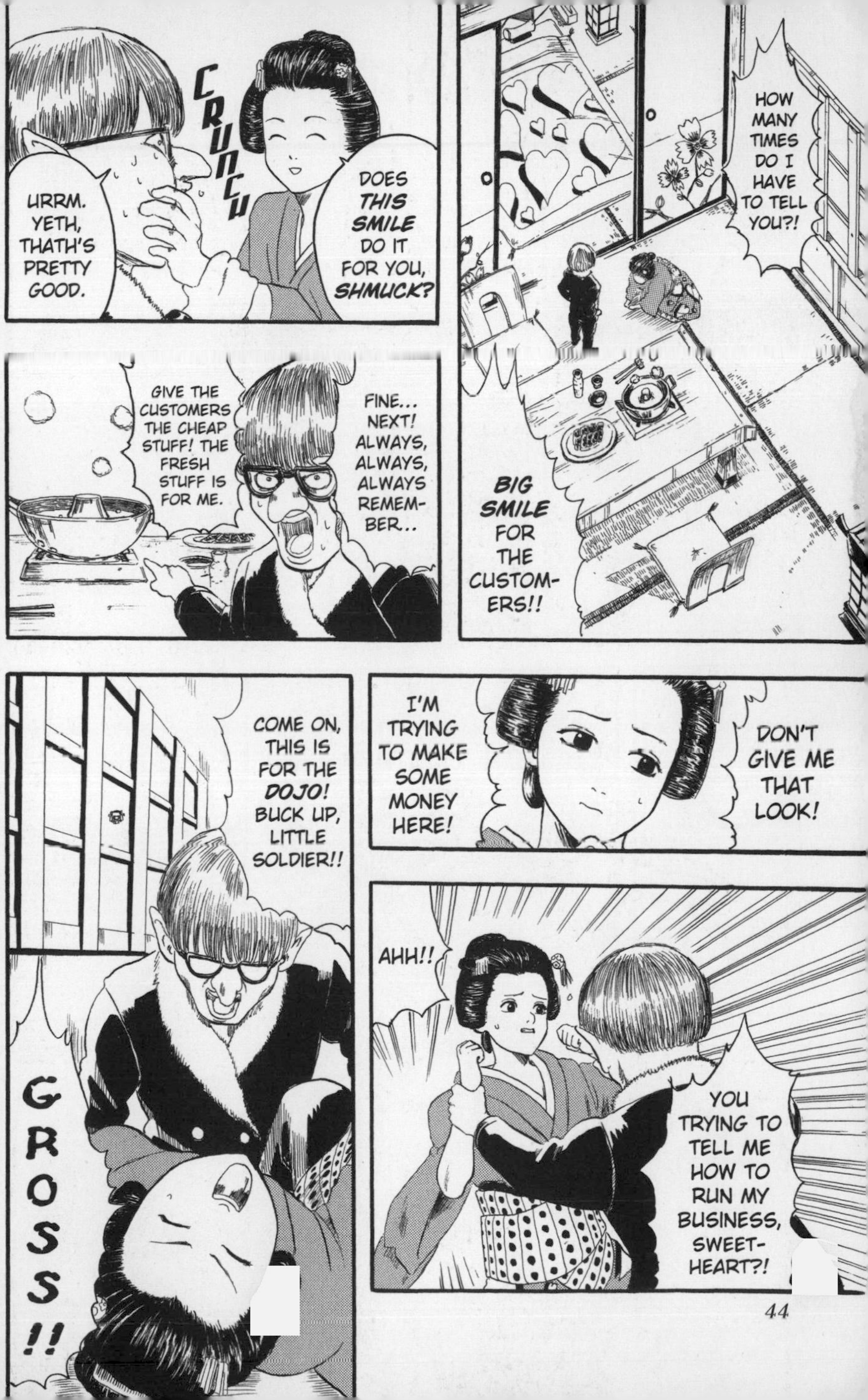
HOW MANY TIMES DO I HAVE TO TELL YOU?!
BIG SMILE FOR THE CUSTOM-ERS!!
DOES THIS SMILE DO IT FOR YOU, SHMUCK?
CRUNCH
URRM. YETH, THATH'S PRETTY GOOD.
FINE... NEXT! ALWAYS, ALWAYS, ALWAYS REMEM-BER...
GIVE THE CUSTOMERS THE CHEAP STUFF! THE FRESH STUFF IS FOR ME.
DON'T GIVE ME THAT LOOK!
I'M TRYING TO MAKE SOME MONEY HERE!
YOU TRYING TO TELL ME HOW TO RUN MY BUSINESS, SWEET-HEART?!
AHH!!
COME ON, THIS IS FOR THE DOJO! BUCK UP, LITTLE SOLDIER!!
GROSS!!

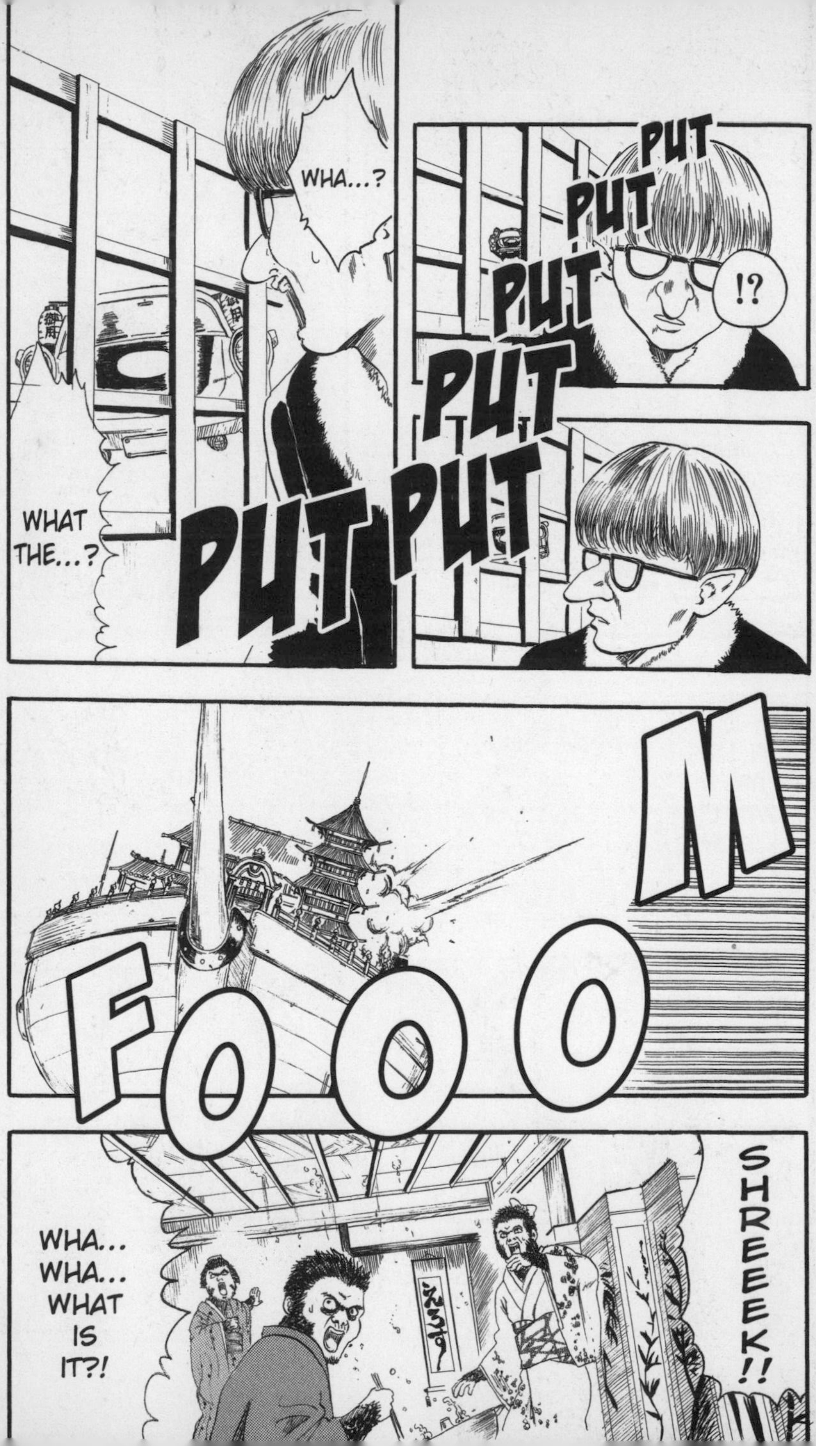
PUT PUT
!?
PUT PUT PUT PUT
WHA...?
WHAT THE...?
FOOOM
SHREEEK!!
WHA... WHA... WHAT IS IT?!

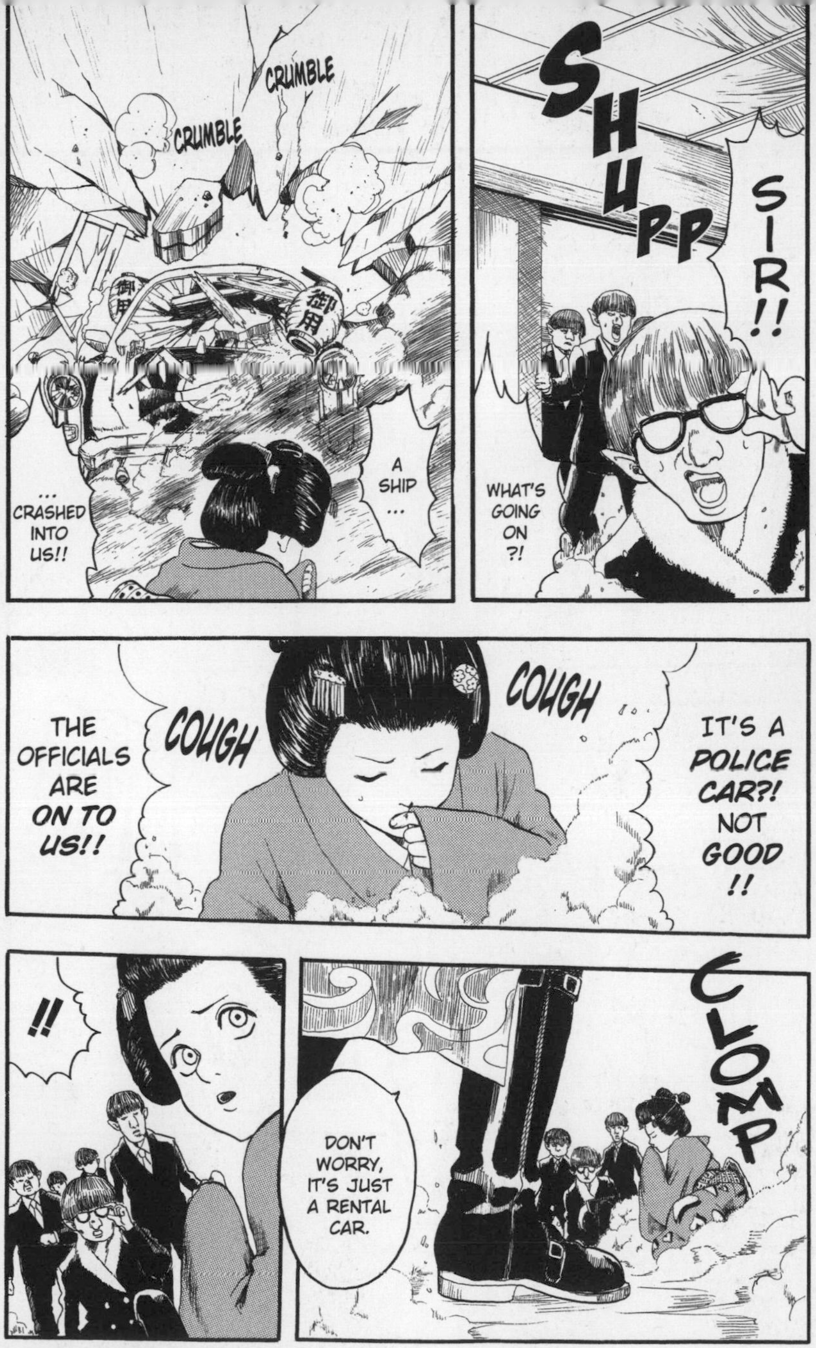
SHUPP
SIR!!
WHAT'S GOING ON ?!
CRUMBLE
CRUMBLE
A SHIP...
...CRASHED INTO US!!
IT'S A POLICE CAR?! NOT GOOD!!
COUGH
COUGH
THE OFFICIALS ARE ON TO US!!
CLOMP
DON'T WORRY, IT'S JUST A RENTAL CAR.
!!

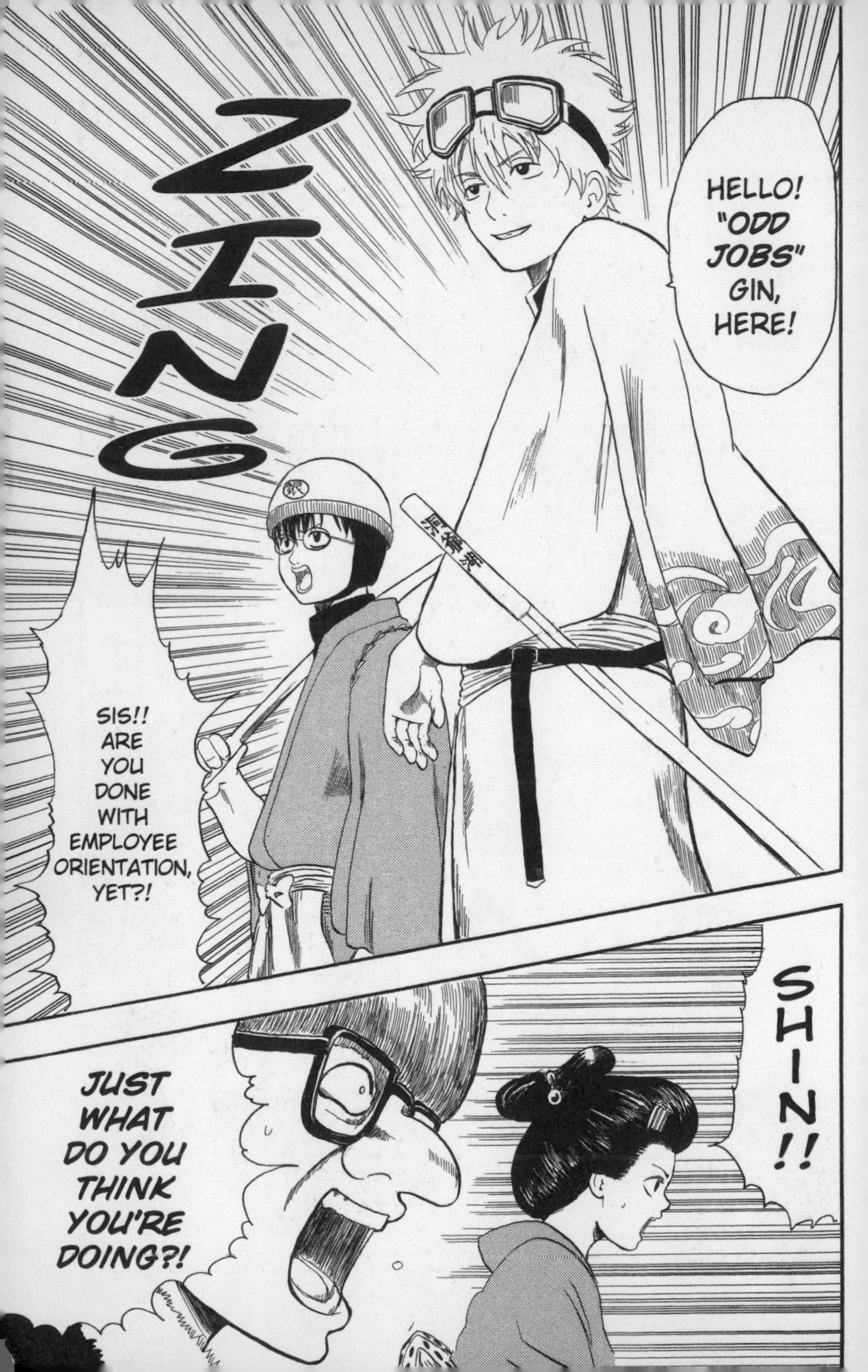
HELLO! "ODD JOBS" GIN, HERE!
ZING
SIS!! ARE YOU DONE WITH EMPLOYEE ORIENTATION, YET?!
SHIN!!
JUST WHAT DO YOU THINK YOU'RE DOING?!

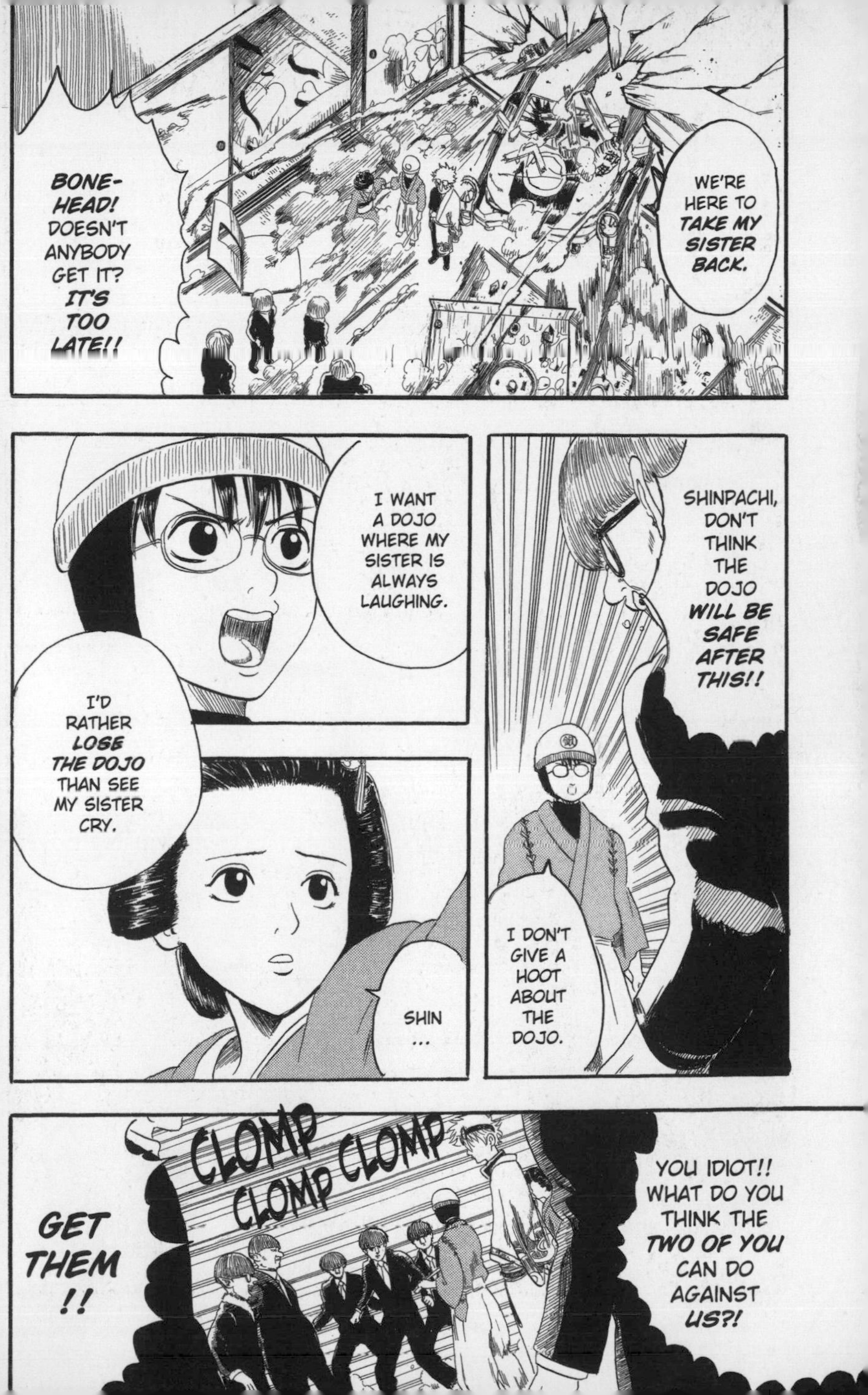
WE'RE HERE TO TAKE MY SISTER BACK.
BONE-HEAD! DOESN'T ANYBODY GET IT? IT'S TOO LATE!!
SHINPACHI, DON'T THINK THE DOJO WILL BE SAFE AFTER THIS!!
I DON'T GIVE A HOOT ABOUT THE DOJO.
I WANT A DOJO WHERE MY SISTER IS ALWAYS LAUGHING.
I'D RATHER LOSE THE DOJO THAN SEE MY SISTER CRY.
SHIN...
YOU IDIOT!! WHAT DO YOU THINK THE TWO OF YOU CAN DO AGAINST US?!
CLOMP CLOMP CLOMP
GET THEM!!

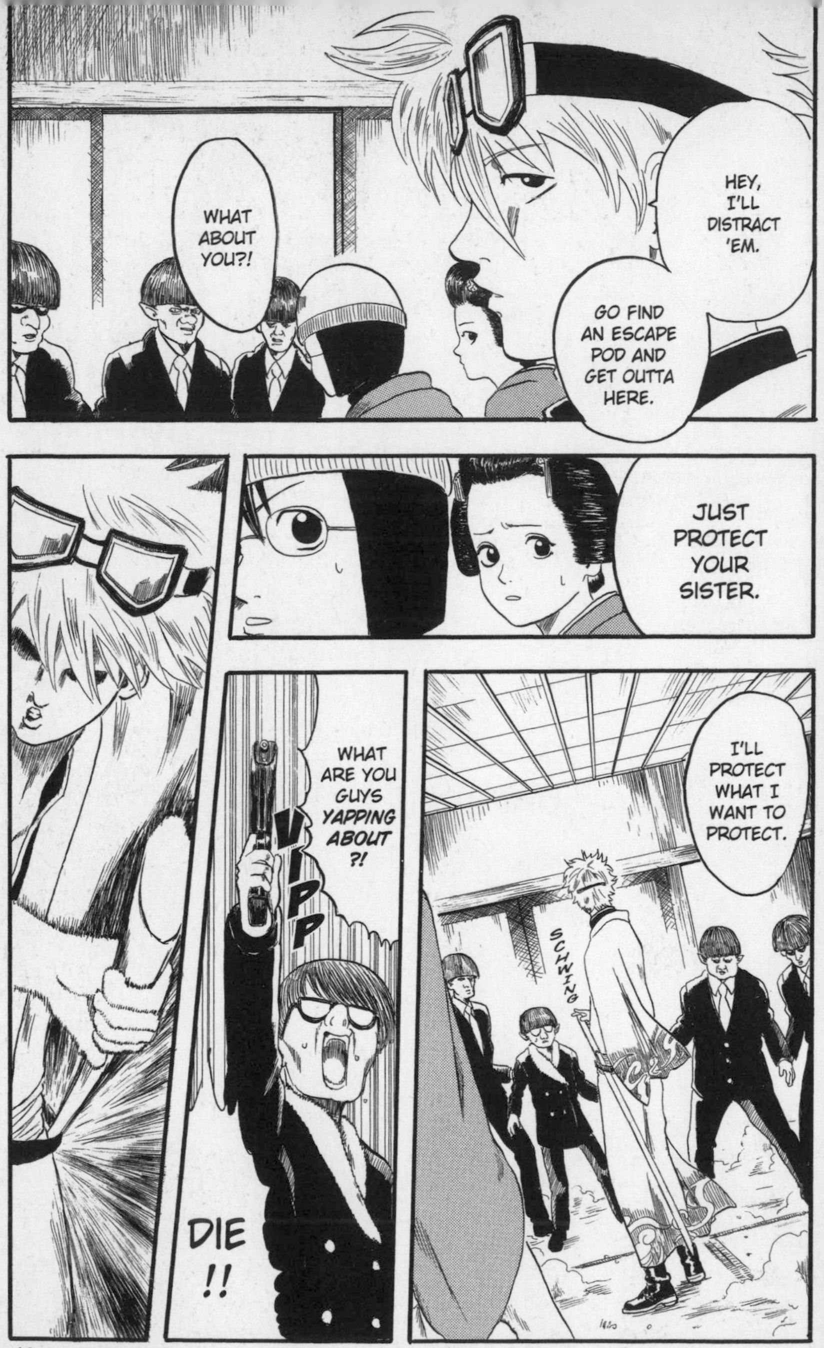
HEY, I'LL DISTRACT 'EM.
GO FIND AN ESCAPE POD AND GET OUTTA HERE.
WHAT ABOUT YOU?!
JUST PROTECT YOUR SISTER.
I'LL PROTECT WHAT I WANT TO PROTECT.
SCHWING
WHAT ARE YOU GUYS YAPPING ABOUT?!
VIPP
DIE !!

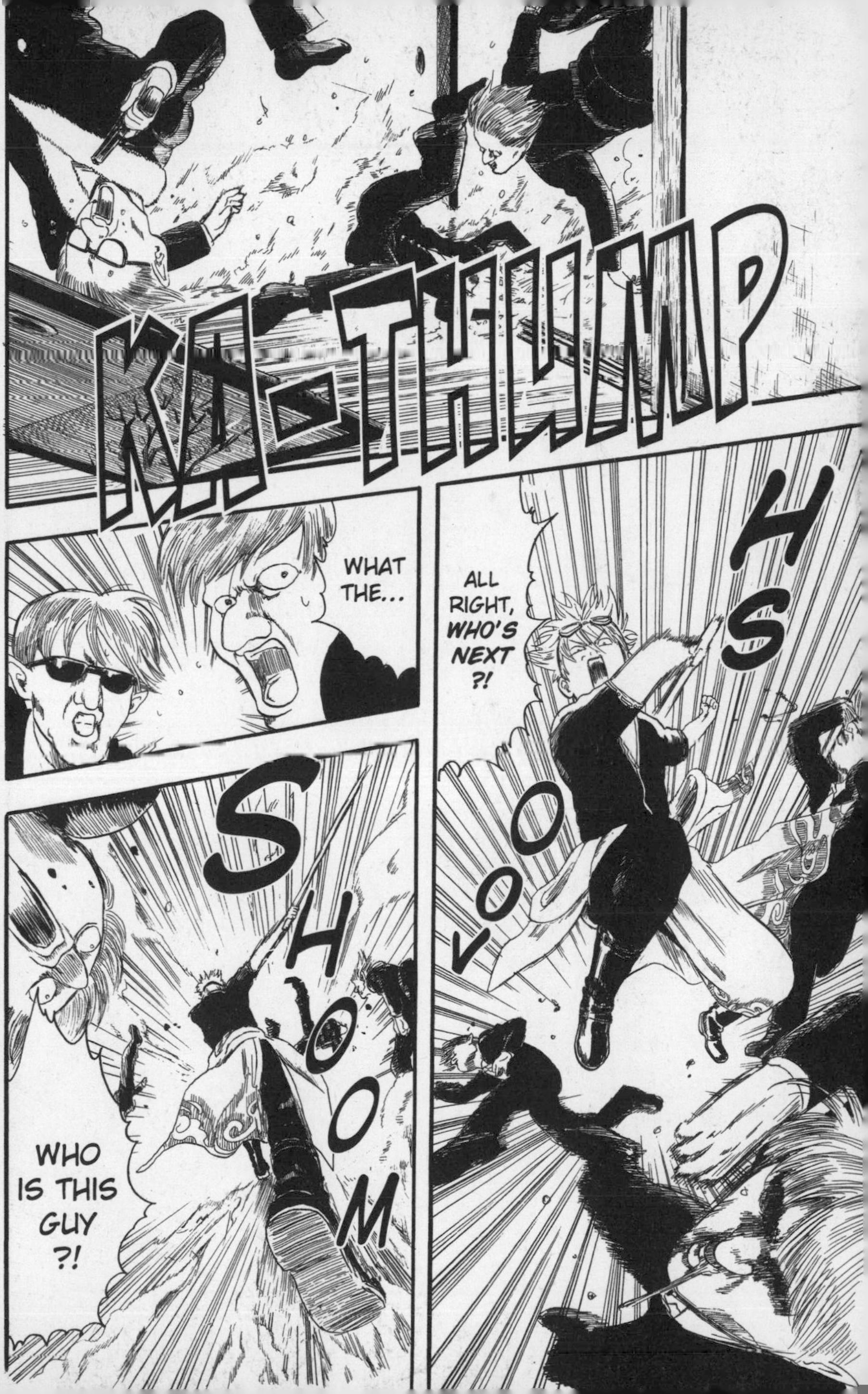
KA-THUMP
ALL RIGHT, WHO'S NEXT?!
VOOOSH
WHAT THE...
SHOOOM
WHO IS THIS GUY?!

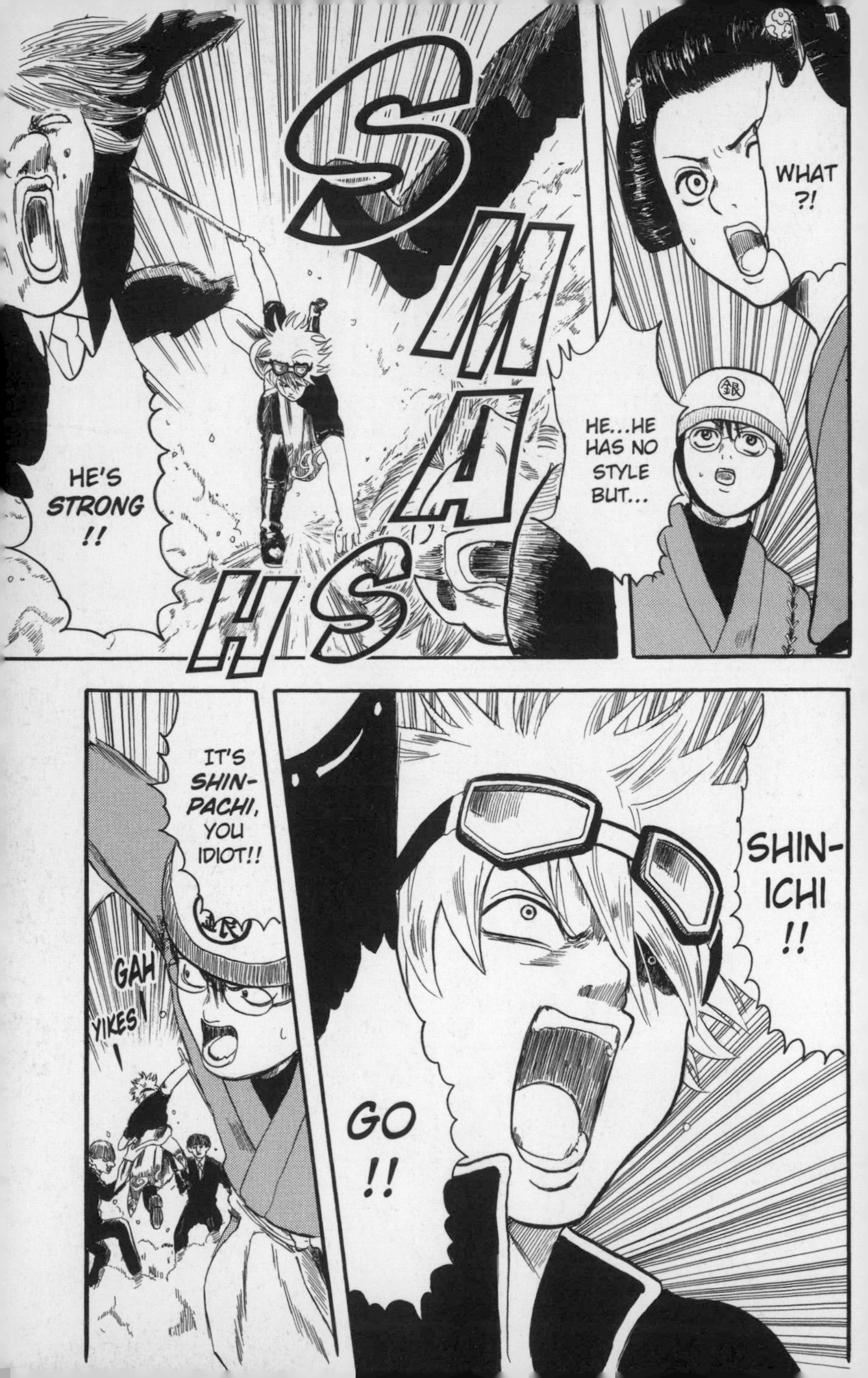
WHAT ?!
HE...HE HAS NO STYLE BUT...
SMASH
HE'S STRONG !!
SHIN-ICHI !!
GO !!
IT'S SHIN-PACHI, YOU IDIOT!!
GAH
YIKES

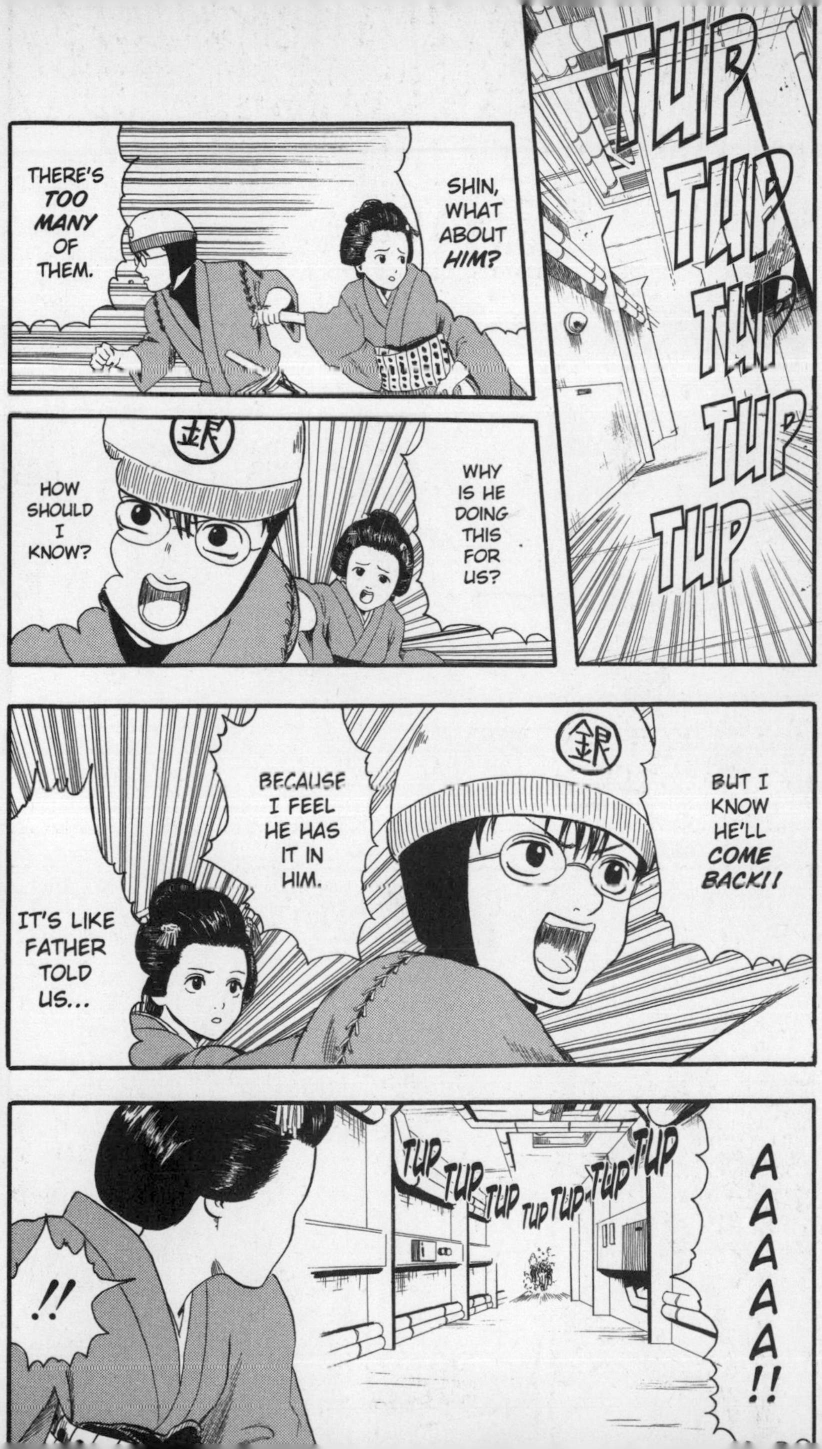
TUP
TUP
TUP
TUP
TUP
SHIN, WHAT ABOUT *HIM?*
THERE'S *TOO MANY* OF THEM.
WHY IS HE DOING THIS FOR US?
HOW SHOULD I KNOW?
BUT I KNOW HE'LL *COME BACK!!*
BECAUSE I FEEL HE HAS IT IN HIM.
IT'S LIKE FATHER TOLD US...
AAAAAA!!
TUP TUP TUP TUP TUP-TUP-TUP
!!

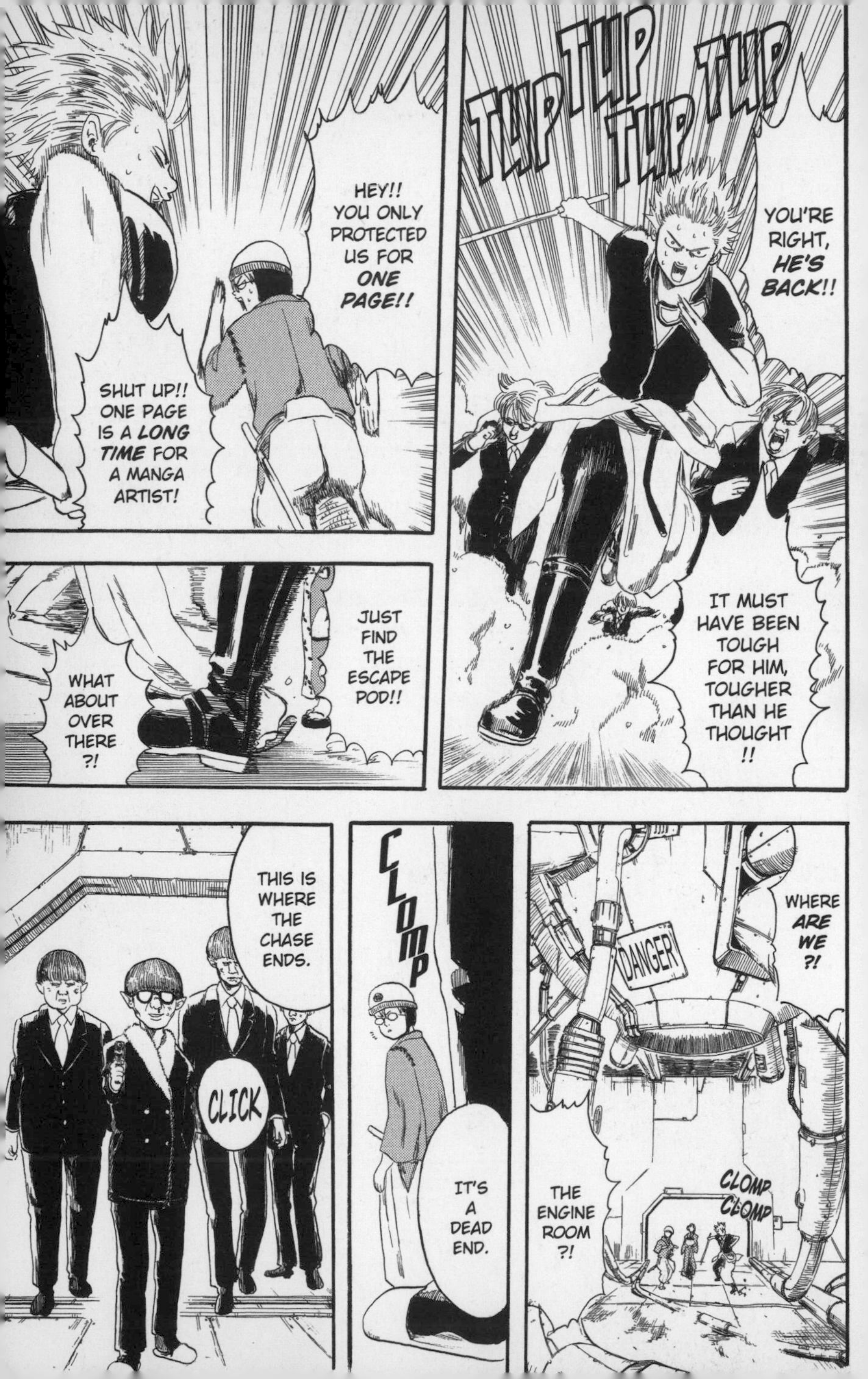
TUP TUP TUP TUP
YOU'RE RIGHT, *HE'S BACK!!*
IT MUST HAVE BEEN TOUGH FOR HIM, TOUGHER THAN HE THOUGHT!!
HEY!! YOU ONLY PROTECTED US FOR *ONE PAGE!!*
SHUT UP!! ONE PAGE IS A *LONG TIME* FOR A MANGA ARTIST!
JUST FIND THE ESCAPE POD!!
WHAT ABOUT OVER THERE?!
WHERE *ARE WE?!*
DANGER
CLOMP CLOMP
THE ENGINE ROOM?!
CLOMP
IT'S A DEAD END.
THIS IS WHERE THE CHASE ENDS.
CLICK

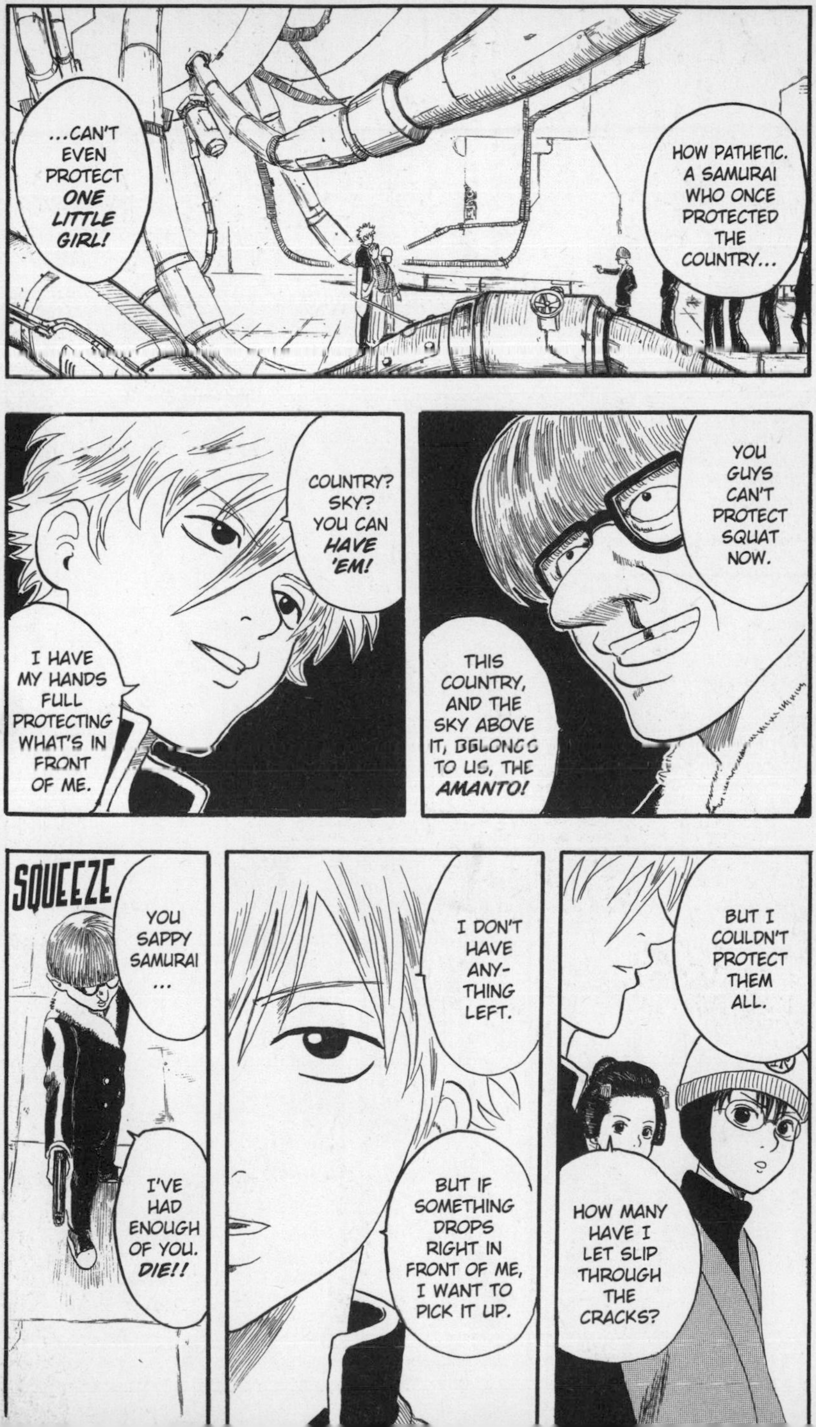
HOW PATHETIC. A SAMURAI WHO ONCE PROTECTED THE COUNTRY...
...CAN'T EVEN PROTECT *ONE LITTLE GIRL!*
YOU GUYS CAN'T PROTECT SQUAT NOW.
THIS COUNTRY, AND THE SKY ABOVE IT, BELONGS TO US, THE *AMANTO!*
COUNTRY? SKY? YOU CAN *HAVE 'EM!*
I HAVE MY HANDS FULL PROTECTING WHAT'S IN FRONT OF ME.
BUT I COULDN'T PROTECT THEM ALL.
HOW MANY HAVE I LET SLIP THROUGH THE CRACKS?
I DON'T HAVE ANYTHING LEFT.
BUT IF SOMETHING DROPS RIGHT IN FRONT OF ME, I WANT TO PICK IT UP.
SQUEEZE
YOU SAPPY SAMURAI...
I'VE HAD ENOUGH OF YOU. *DIE!!*

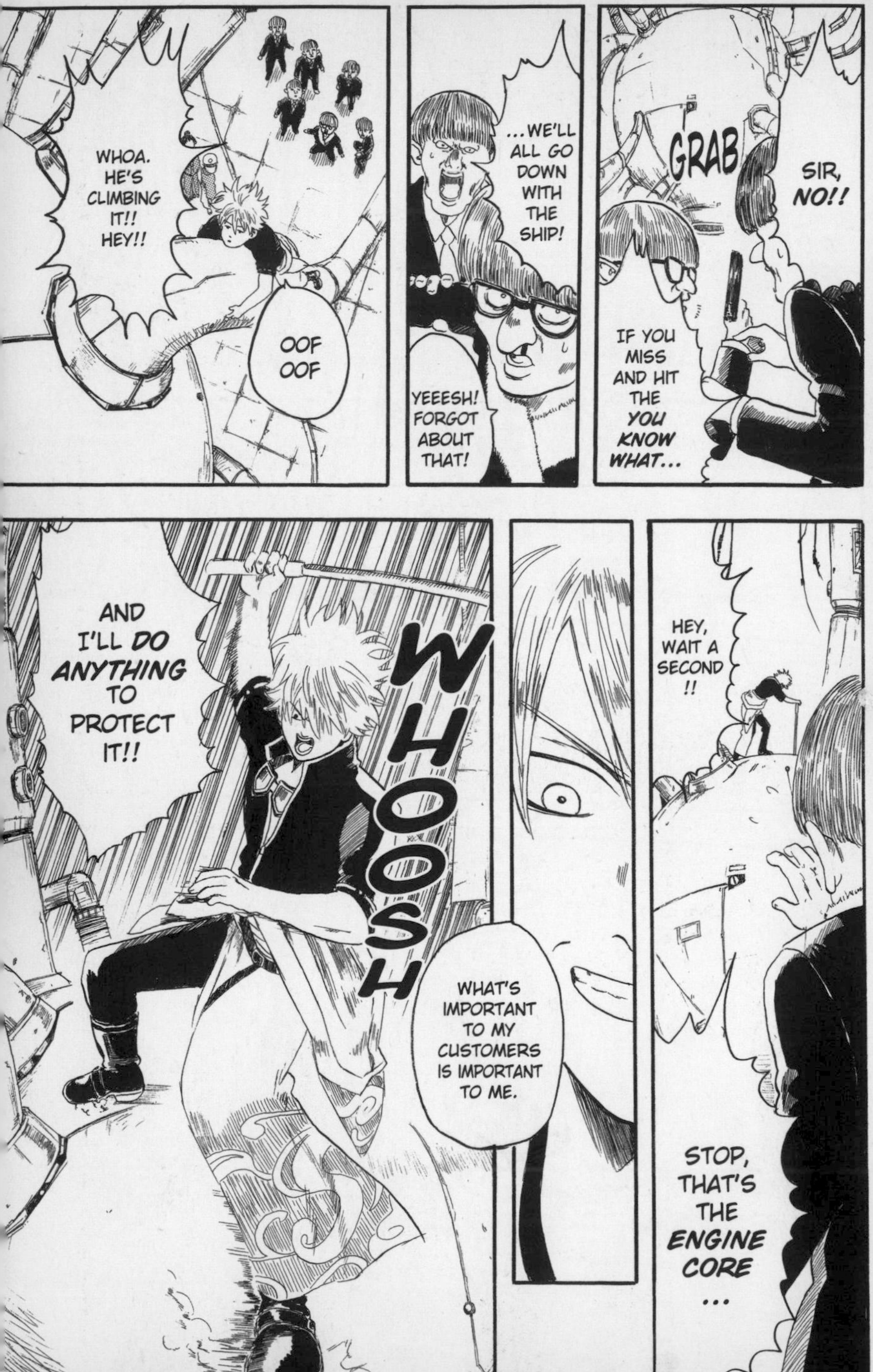
SIR, NO!!
GRAB
IF YOU MISS AND HIT THE YOU KNOW WHAT...
...WE'LL ALL GO DOWN WITH THE SHIP!
YEEESH! FORGOT ABOUT THAT!
WHOA. HE'S CLIMBING IT!! HEY!!
OOF OOF
HEY, WAIT A SECOND!!
STOP, THAT'S THE ENGINE CORE...
WHAT'S IMPORTANT TO MY CUSTOMERS IS IMPORTANT TO ME.
AND I'LL DO ANYTHING TO PROTECT IT!!
WHOOOSH

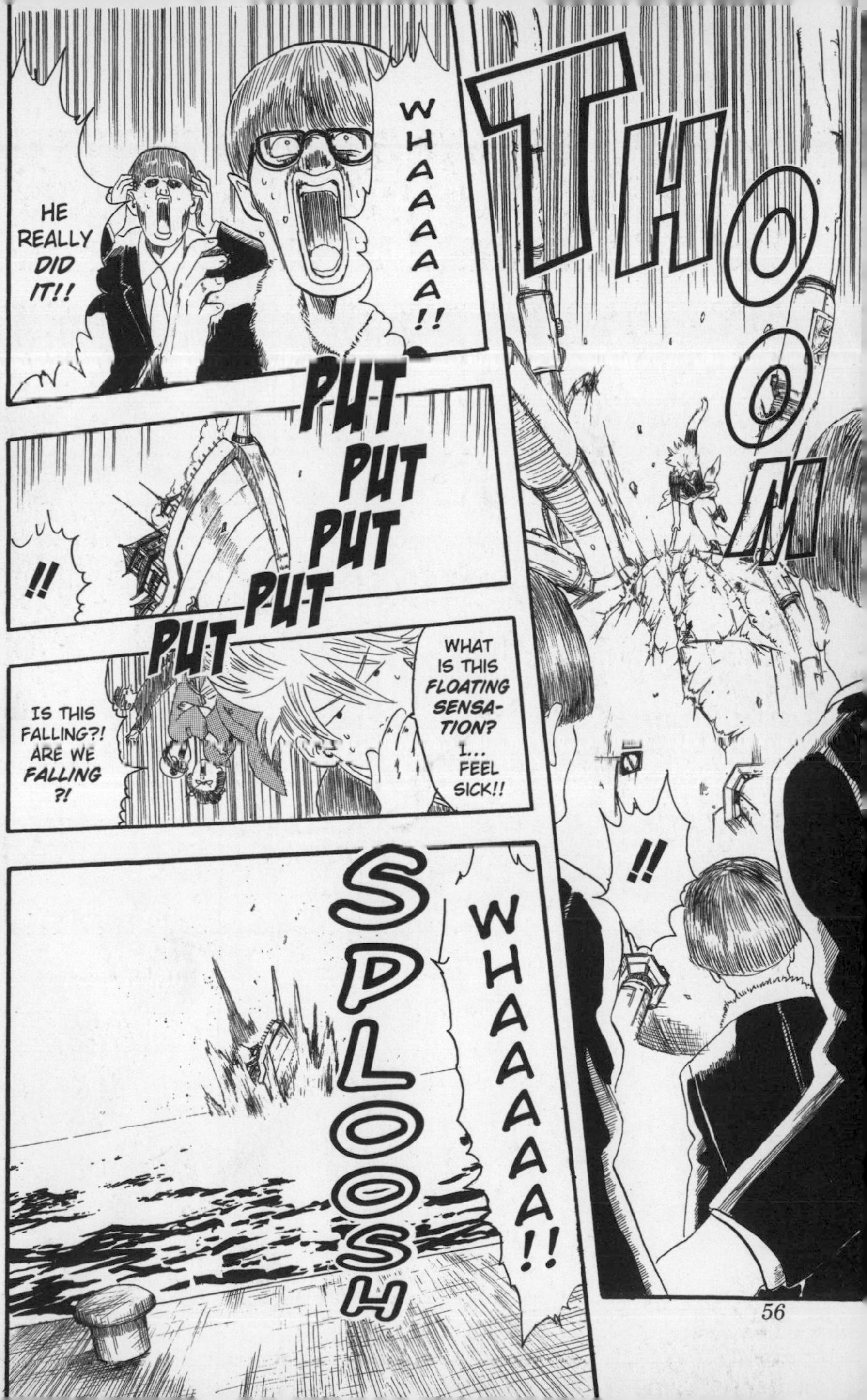
THOOOM
!!
WHAAAAA!!
HE REALLY DID IT!!
PUT PUT PUT PUT PUT
!!
WHAT IS THIS FLOATING SENSATION? I... FEEL SICK!!
IS THIS FALLING?! ARE WE FALLING?!
SPLOOOSH
WHAAAAA!!

READ THIS WAY

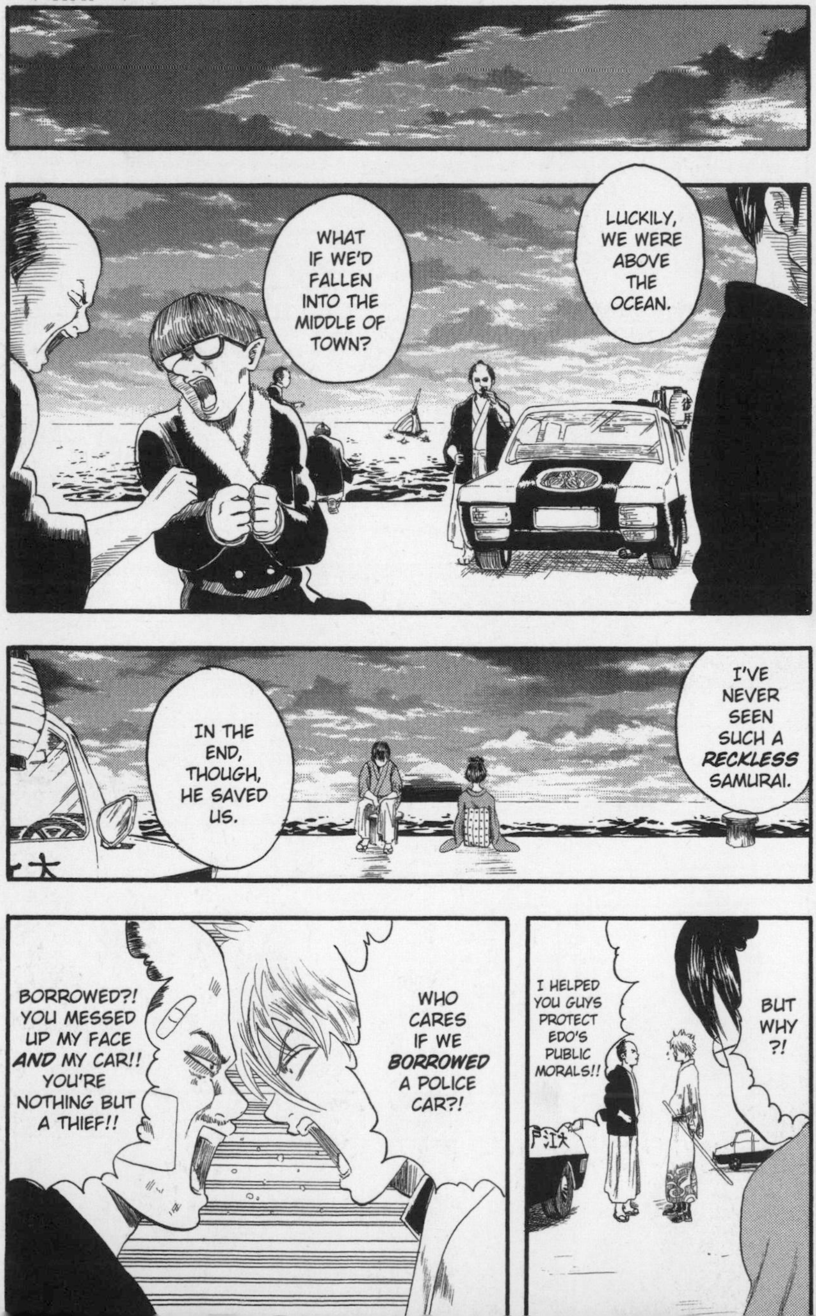
LUCKILY, WE WERE ABOVE THE OCEAN.
WHAT IF WE'D FALLEN INTO THE MIDDLE OF TOWN?
I'VE NEVER SEEN SUCH A *RECKLESS* SAMURAI.
IN THE END, THOUGH, HE SAVED US.
BUT WHY?!
I HELPED YOU GUYS PROTECT EDO'S PUBLIC MORALS!!
WHO CARES IF WE *BORROWED* A POLICE CAR?!
BORROWED?! YOU MESSED UP MY FACE *AND* MY CAR!! YOU'RE NOTHING BUT A THIEF!!

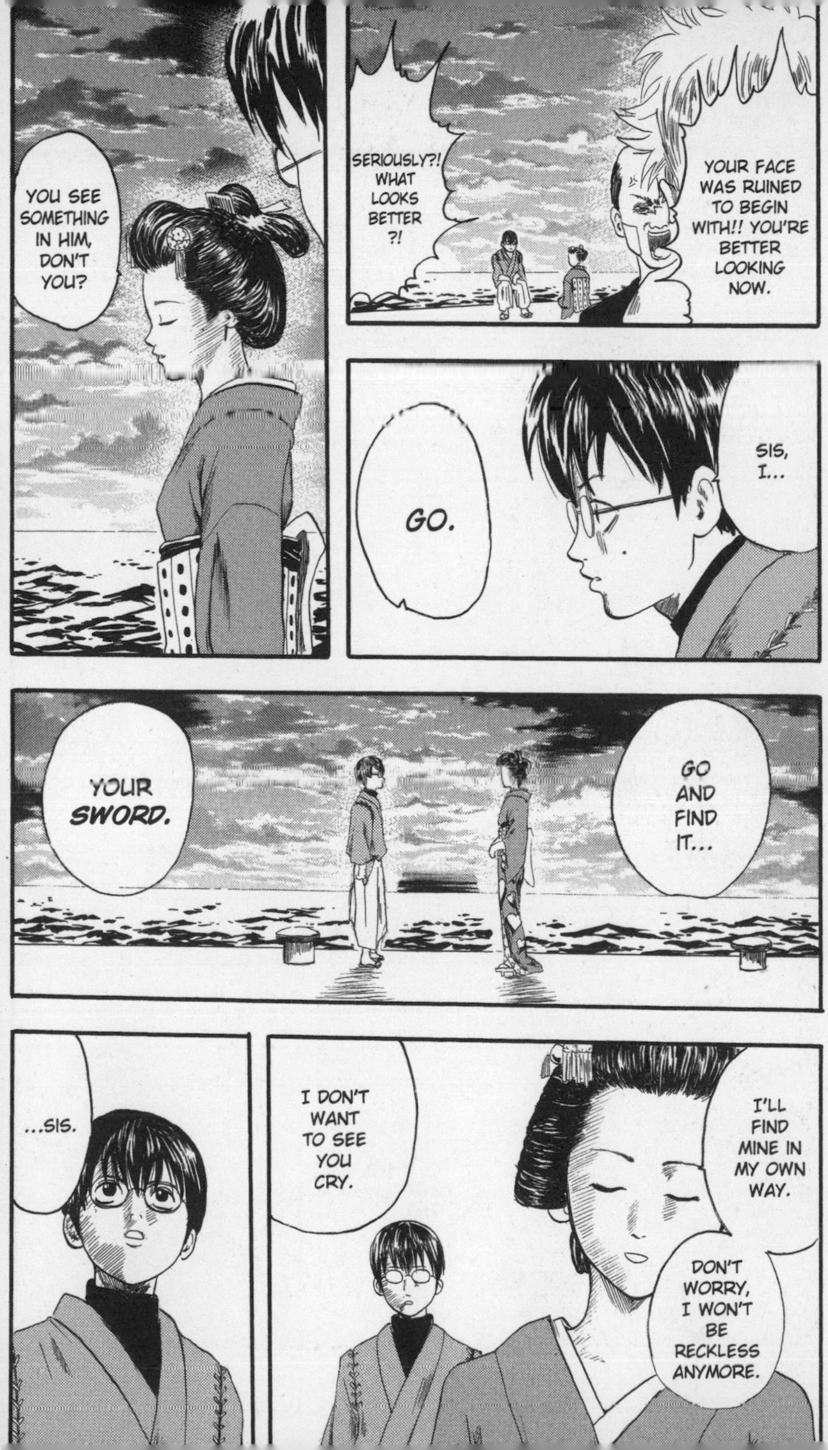
YOUR FACE WAS RUINED TO BEGIN WITH!! YOU'RE BETTER LOOKING NOW.
SERIOUSLY?! WHAT LOOKS BETTER ?!
SIS, I...
GO.
YOU SEE SOMETHING IN HIM, DON'T YOU?
GO AND FIND IT...
YOUR SWORD.
I'LL FIND MINE IN MY OWN WAY.
DON'T WORRY, I WON'T BE RECKLESS ANYMORE.
I DON'T WANT TO SEE YOU CRY.
...SIS.

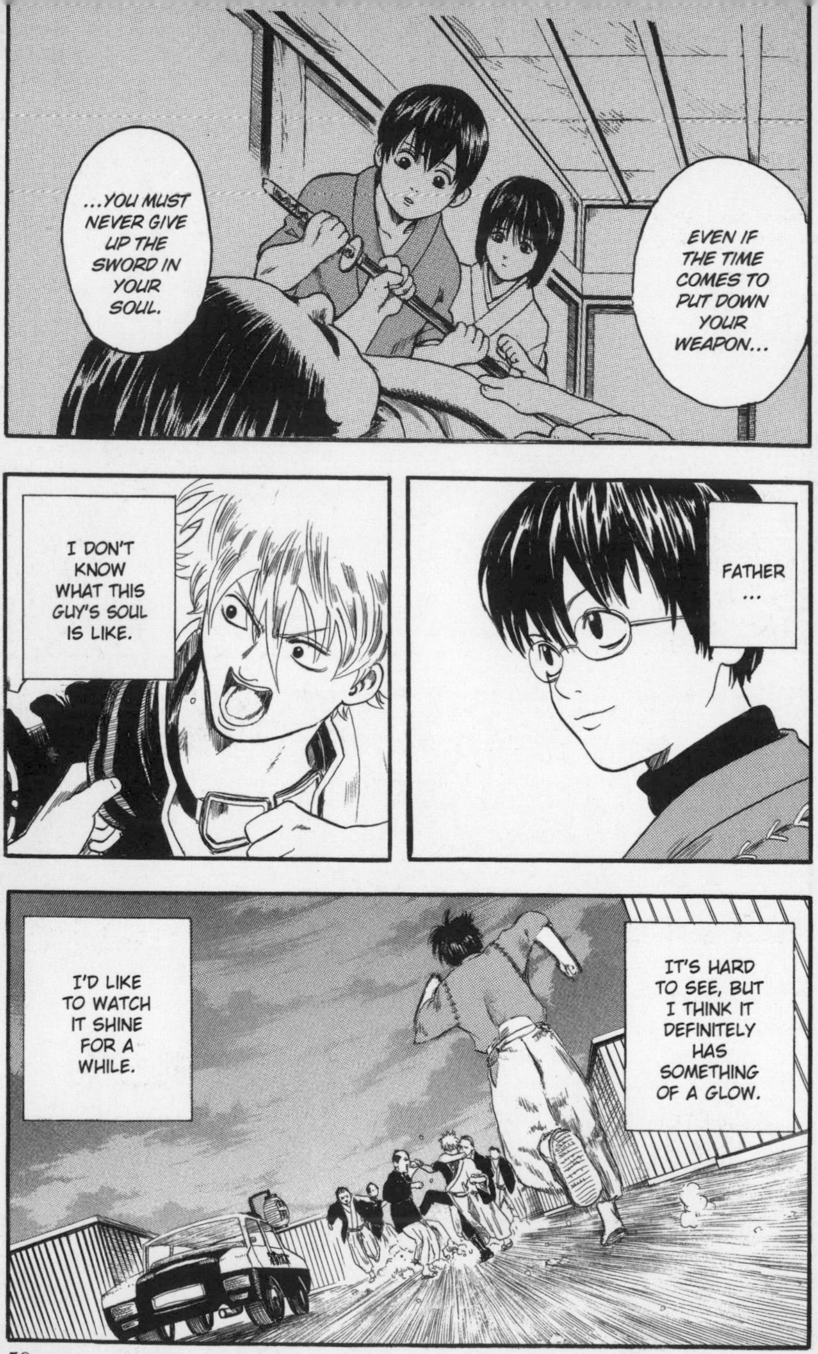
EVEN IF THE TIME COMES TO PUT DOWN YOUR WEAPON...
...YOU MUST NEVER GIVE UP THE SWORD IN YOUR SOUL.
FATHER ...
I DON'T KNOW WHAT THIS GUY'S SOUL IS LIKE.
IT'S HARD TO SEE, BUT I THINK IT DEFINITELY HAS SOMETHING OF A GLOW.
I'D LIKE TO WATCH IT SHINE FOR A WHILE.

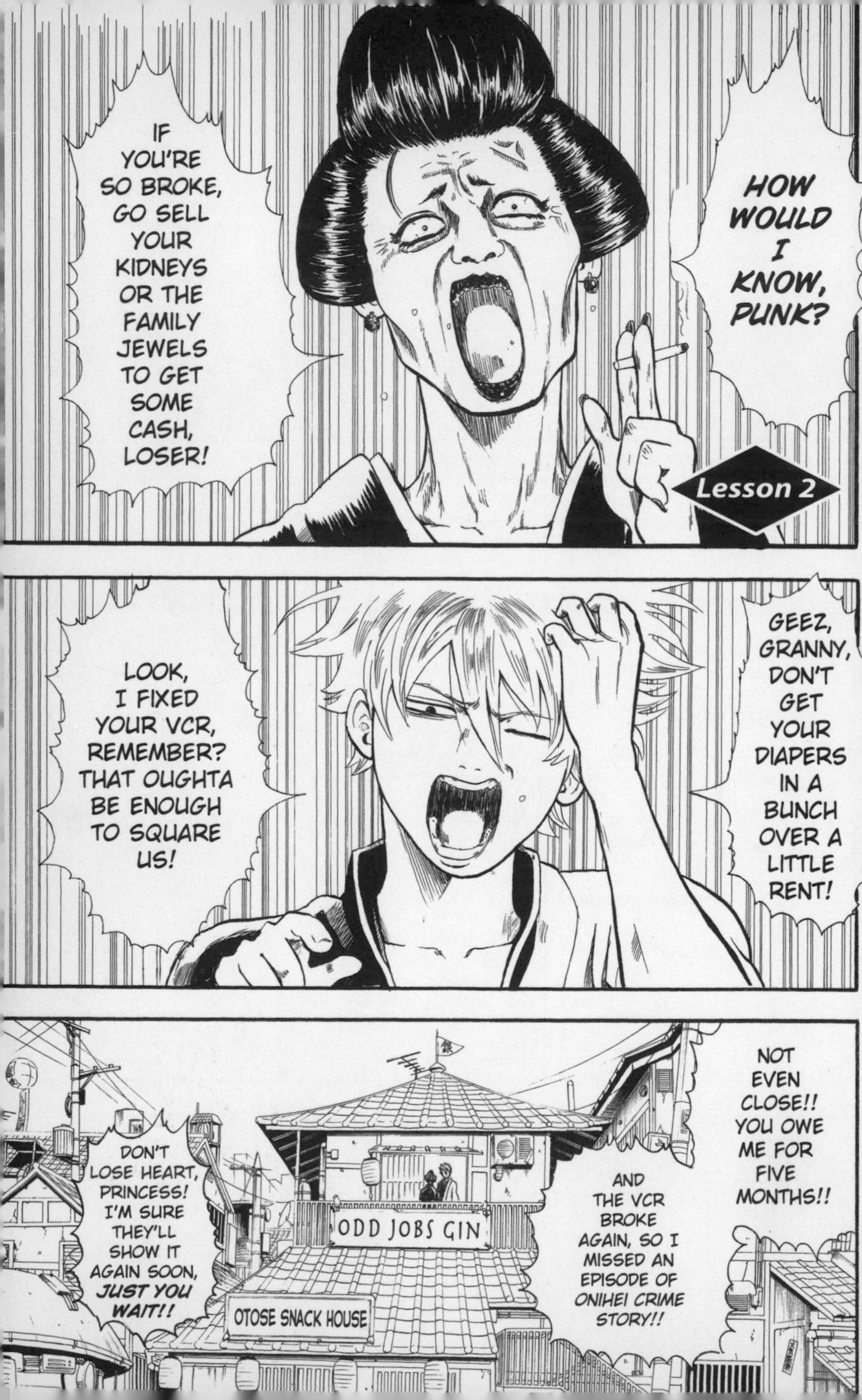
HOW WOULD I KNOW, PUNK?
IF YOU'RE SO BROKE, GO SELL YOUR KIDNEYS OR THE FAMILY JEWELS TO GET SOME CASH, LOSER!
Lesson 2
GEEZ, GRANNY, DON'T GET YOUR DIAPERS IN A BUNCH OVER A LITTLE RENT!
LOOK, I FIXED YOUR VCR, REMEMBER? THAT OUGHTA BE ENOUGH TO SQUARE US!
NOT EVEN CLOSE!! YOU OWE ME FOR FIVE MONTHS!!
AND THE VCR BROKE AGAIN, SO I MISSED AN EPISODE OF ONIHEI CRIME STORY!!
ODD JOBS GIN
OTOSE SNACK HOUSE
DON'T LOSE HEART, PRINCESS! I'M SURE THEY'LL SHOW IT AGAIN SOON, JUST YOU WAIT!!

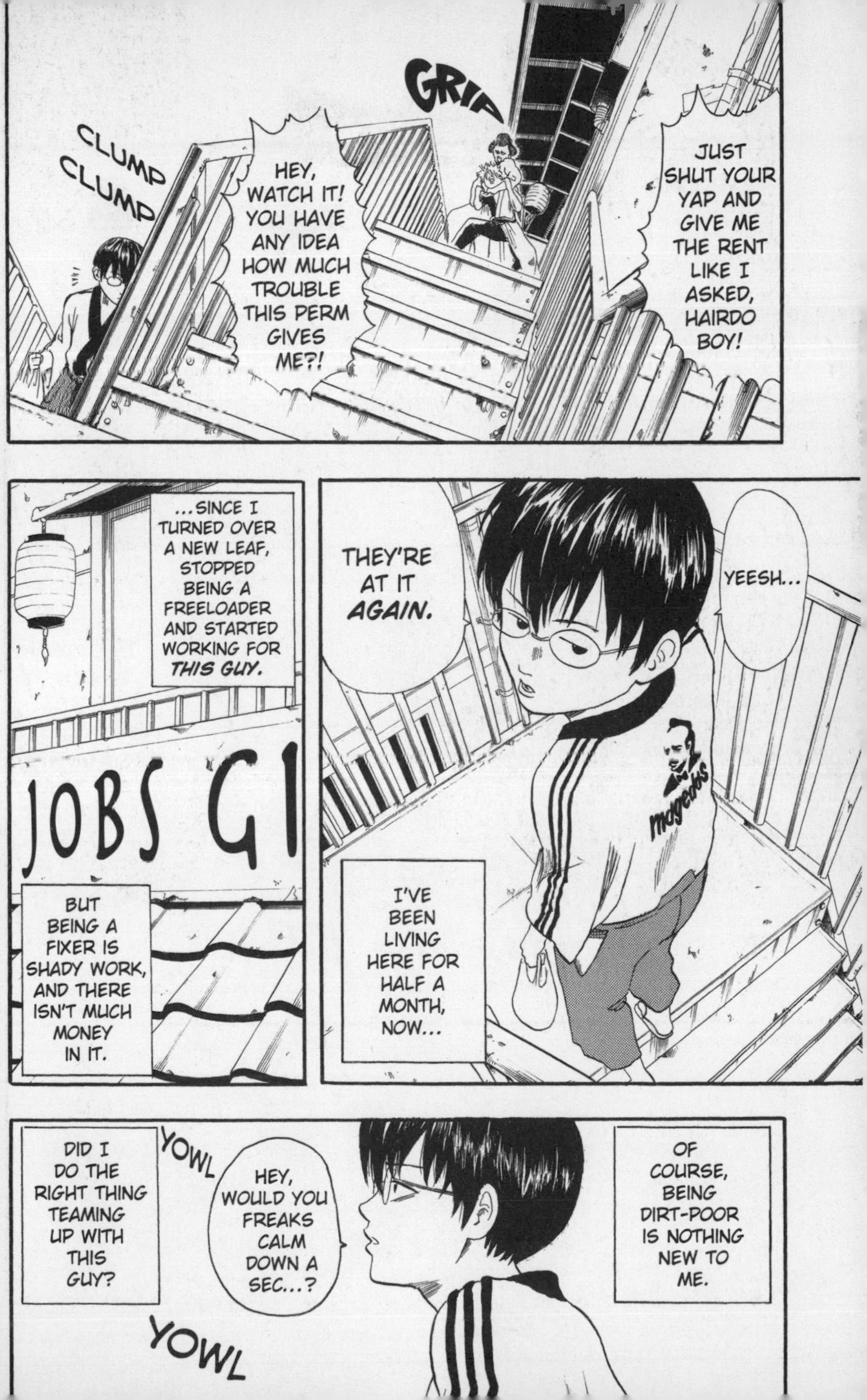
JUST SHUT YOUR YAP AND GIVE ME THE RENT LIKE I ASKED, HAIRDO BOY!
GRIP
HEY, WATCH IT! YOU HAVE ANY IDEA HOW MUCH TROUBLE THIS PERM GIVES ME?!
CLUMP CLUMP
YEESH...
THEY'RE AT IT AGAIN.
I'VE BEEN LIVING HERE FOR HALF A MONTH, NOW...
...SINCE I TURNED OVER A NEW LEAF, STOPPED BEING A FREELOADER AND STARTED WORKING FOR THIS GUY.
JOBS GI
BUT BEING A FIXER IS SHADY WORK, AND THERE ISN'T MUCH MONEY IN IT.
OF COURSE, BEING DIRT-POOR IS NOTHING NEW TO ME.
HEY, WOULD YOU FREAKS CALM DOWN A SEC...?
YOWL
DID I DO THE RIGHT THING TEAMING UP WITH THIS GUY?
YOWL

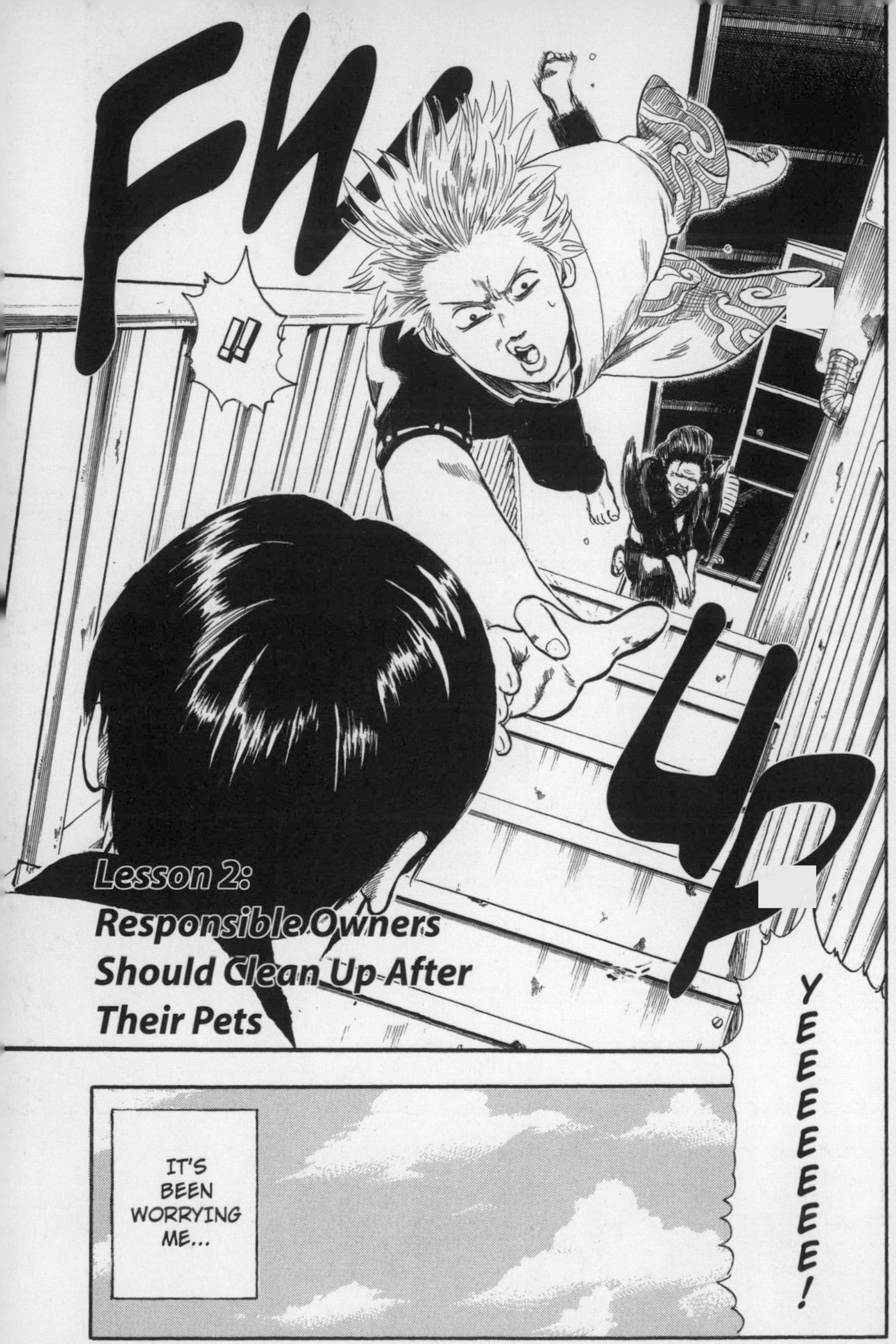
FW
UP
!!
YEEEEEEEE!
Lesson 2:
Responsible Owners Should Clean Up After Their Pets
IT'S BEEN WORRYING ME...

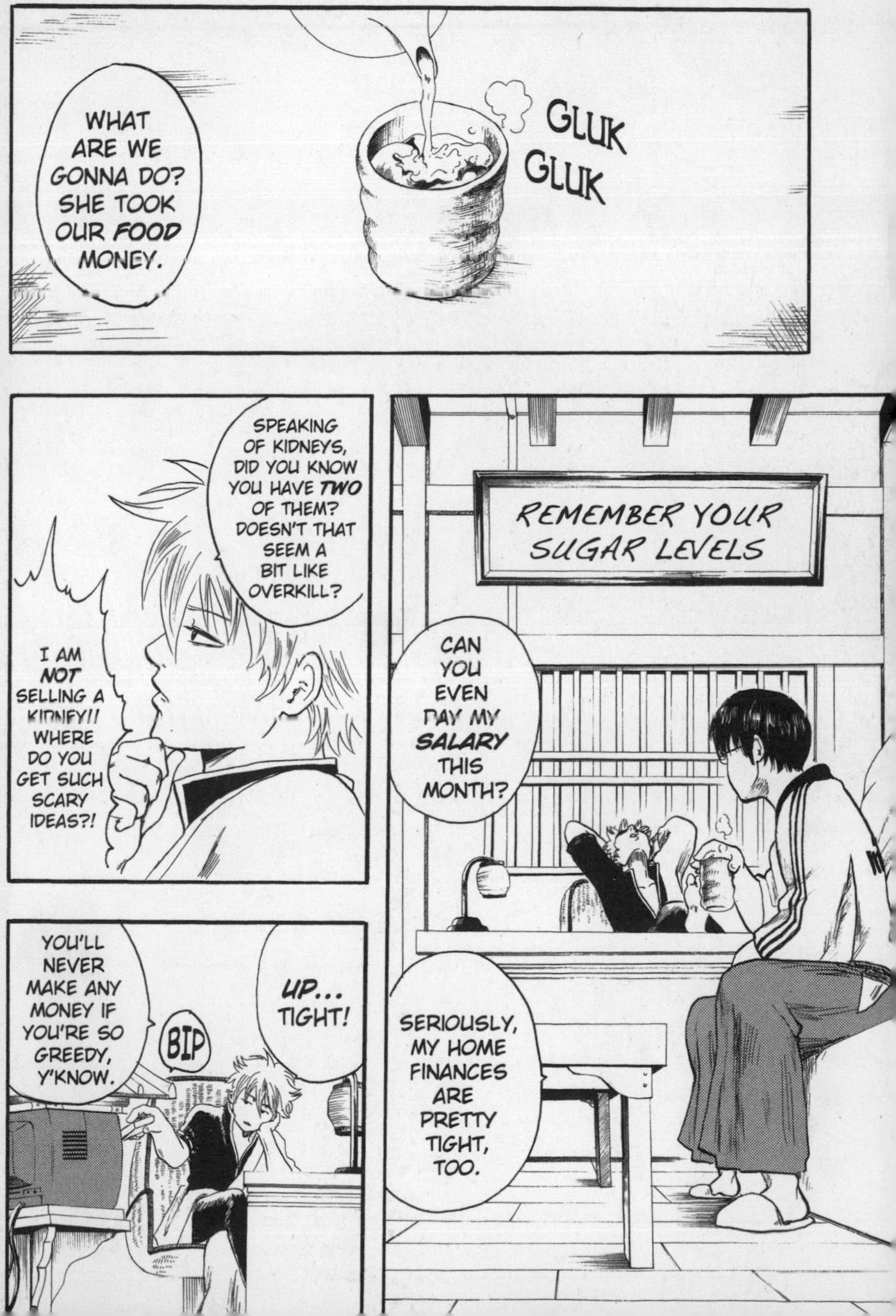
GLUK
GLUK
WHAT ARE WE GONNA DO? SHE TOOK OUR *FOOD* MONEY.
REMEMBER YOUR SUGAR LEVELS
CAN YOU EVEN PAY MY *SALARY* THIS MONTH?
SERIOUSLY, MY HOME FINANCES ARE PRETTY TIGHT, TOO.
SPEAKING OF KIDNEYS, DID YOU KNOW YOU HAVE *TWO* OF THEM? DOESN'T THAT SEEM A BIT LIKE OVERKILL?
I AM *NOT* SELLING A KIDNEY!! WHERE DO YOU GET SUCH SCARY IDEAS?!
UP... TIGHT!
YOU'LL NEVER MAKE ANY MONEY IF YOU'RE SO GREEDY, Y'KNOW.
BIP

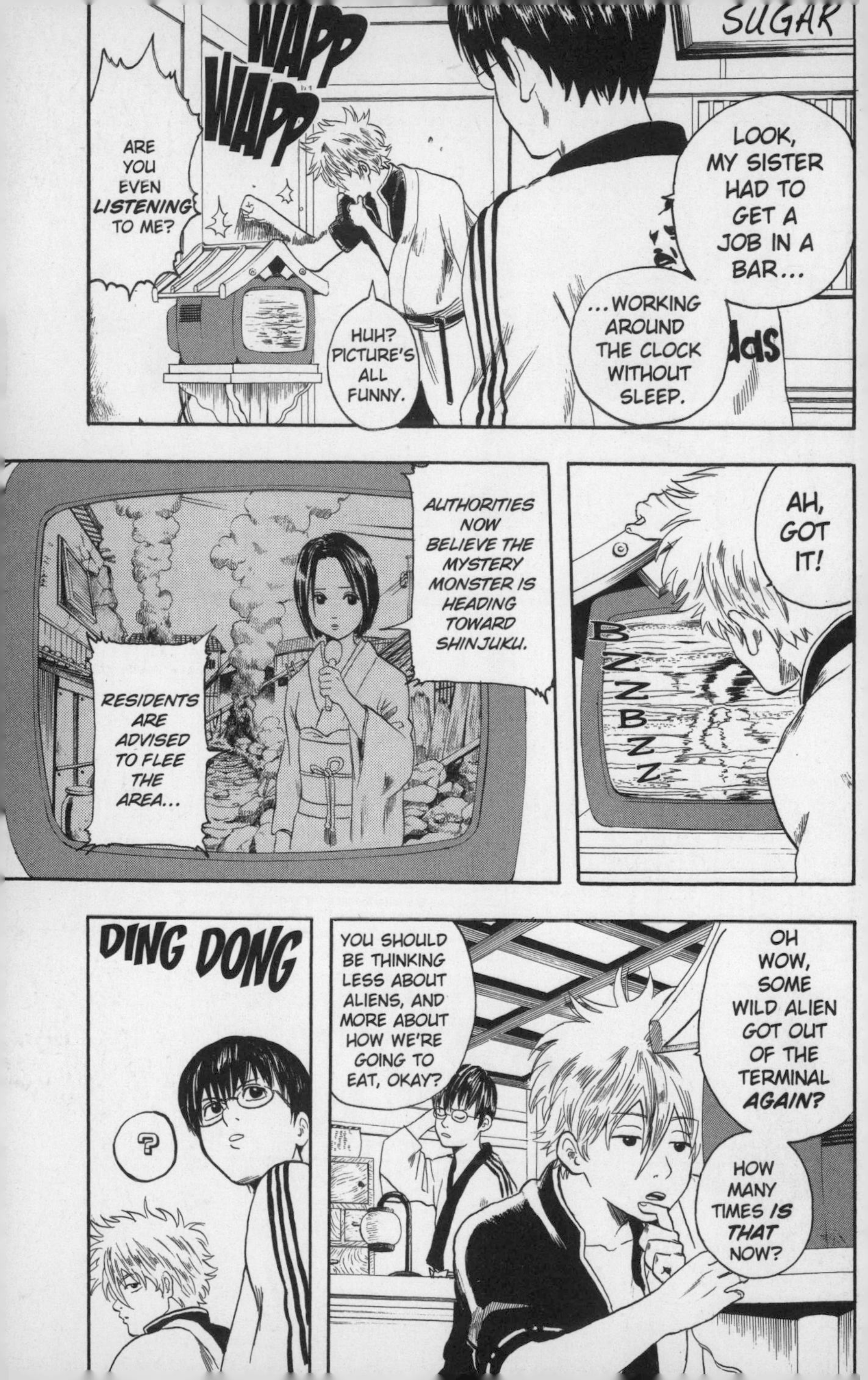
SUGAR
LOOK, MY SISTER HAD TO GET A JOB IN A BAR...
...WORKING AROUND THE CLOCK WITHOUT SLEEP.
HUH? PICTURE'S ALL FUNNY.
WAPP WAPP
ARE YOU EVEN *LISTENING* TO ME?
AH, GOT IT!
BZZBZZ
AUTHORITIES NOW BELIEVE THE MYSTERY MONSTER IS HEADING TOWARD SHINJUKU.
RESIDENTS ARE ADVISED TO FLEE THE AREA...
OH WOW, SOME WILD ALIEN GOT OUT OF THE TERMINAL *AGAIN?*
HOW MANY TIMES *IS THAT* NOW?
YOU SHOULD BE THINKING LESS ABOUT ALIENS, AND MORE ABOUT HOW WE'RE GOING TO EAT, OKAY?
DING DONG
?

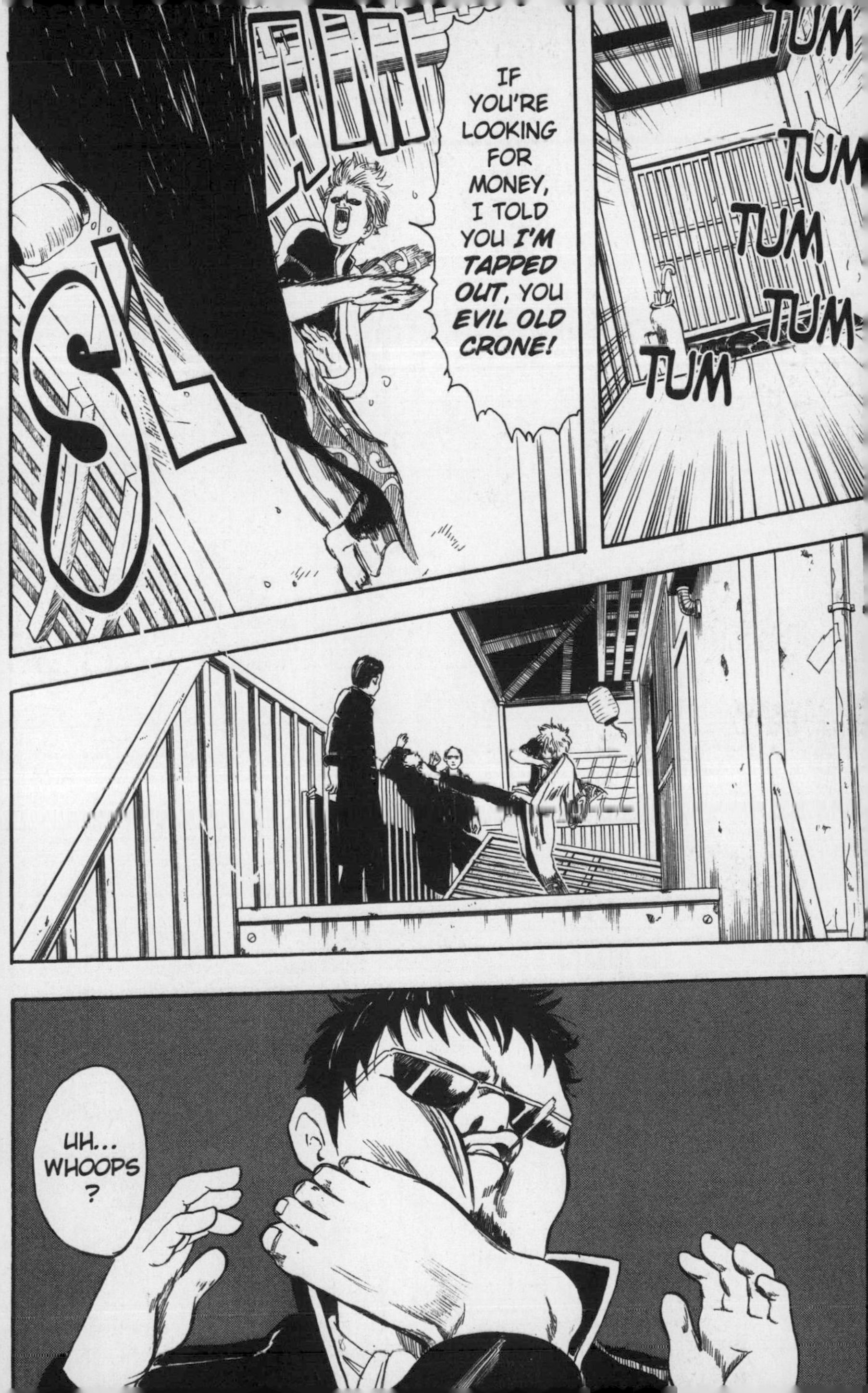
TUM
TUM
TUM
TUM
TUM
SLAM
IF YOU'RE LOOKING FOR MONEY, I TOLD YOU *I'M TAPPED OUT*, YOU *EVIL OLD CRONE!*
UH... WHOOPS?

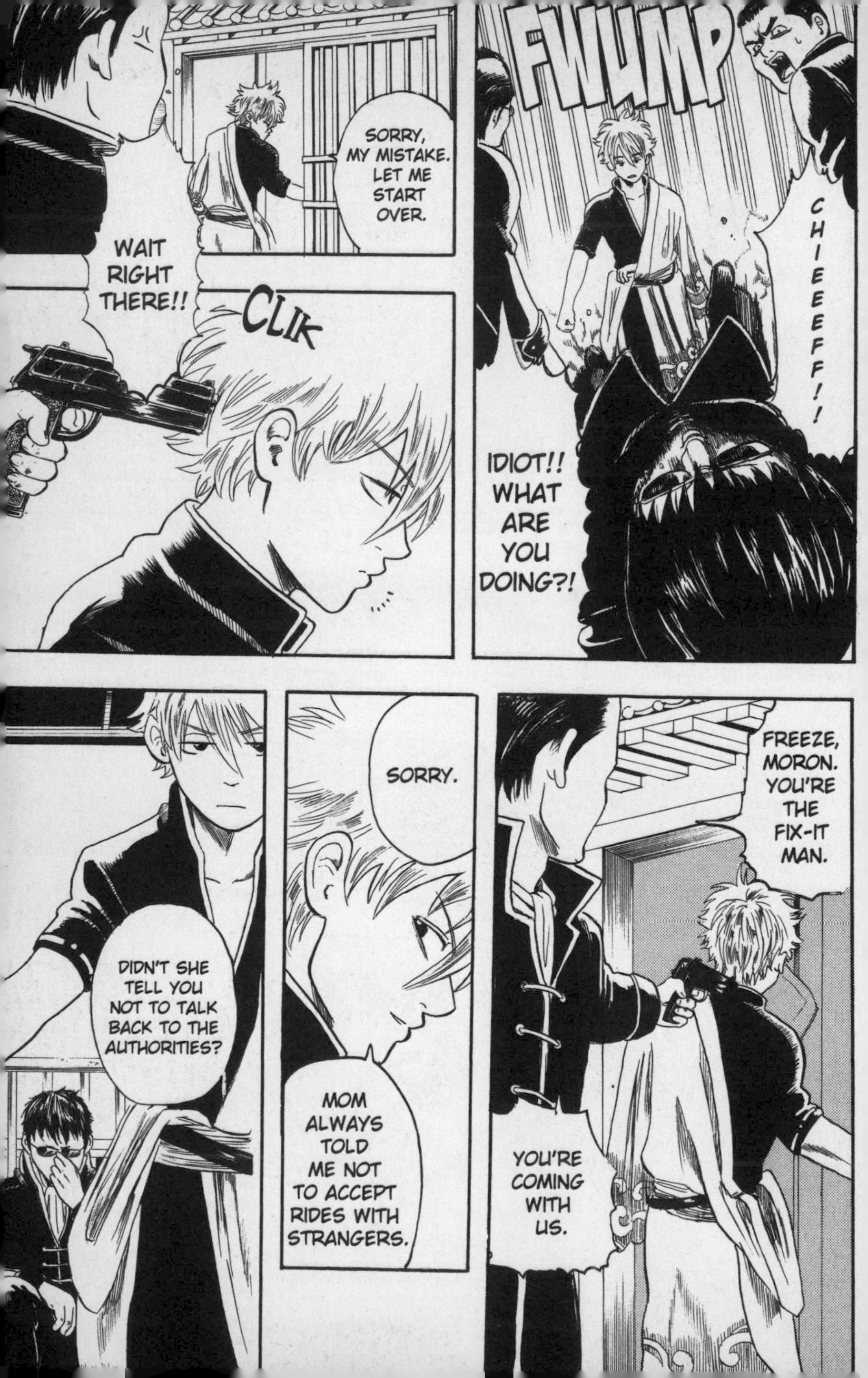
FWUMP
CHIEEEFF!!
IDIOT!! WHAT ARE YOU DOING?!
SORRY, MY MISTAKE. LET ME START OVER.
WAIT RIGHT THERE!!
CLIK
FREEZE, MORON. YOU'RE THE FIX-IT MAN.
YOU'RE COMING WITH US.
SORRY.
MOM ALWAYS TOLD ME NOT TO ACCEPT RIDES WITH STRANGERS.
DIDN'T SHE TELL YOU NOT TO TALK BACK TO THE AUTHORITIES?

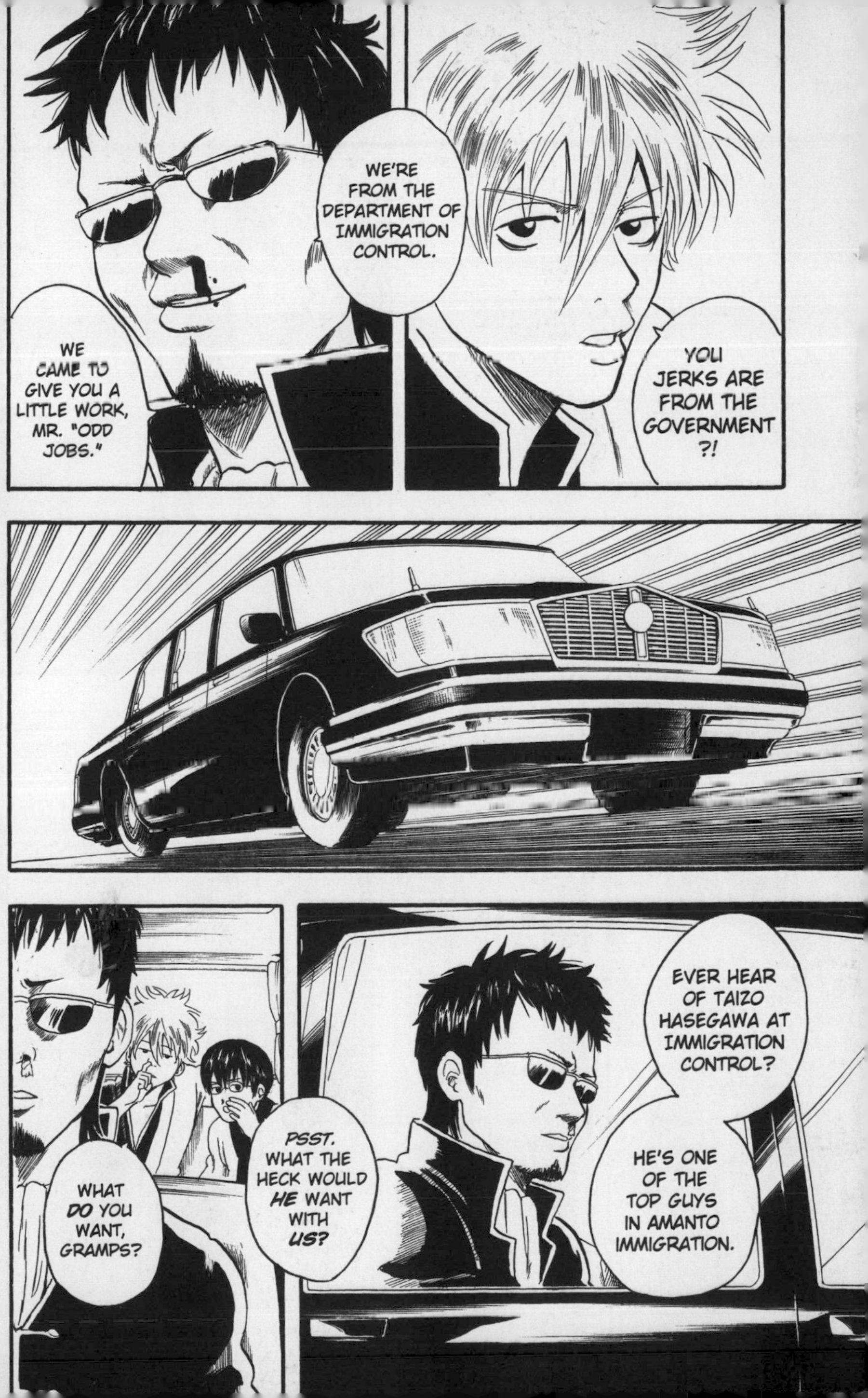
YOU JERKS ARE FROM THE GOVERNMENT?!
WE'RE FROM THE DEPARTMENT OF IMMIGRATION CONTROL.
WE CAME TO GIVE YOU A LITTLE WORK, MR. "ODD JOBS."
EVER HEAR OF TAIZO HASEGAWA AT IMMIGRATION CONTROL?
HE'S ONE OF THE TOP GUYS IN AMANTO IMMIGRATION.
PSST. WHAT THE HECK WOULD HE WANT WITH US?
WHAT DO YOU WANT, GRAMPS?

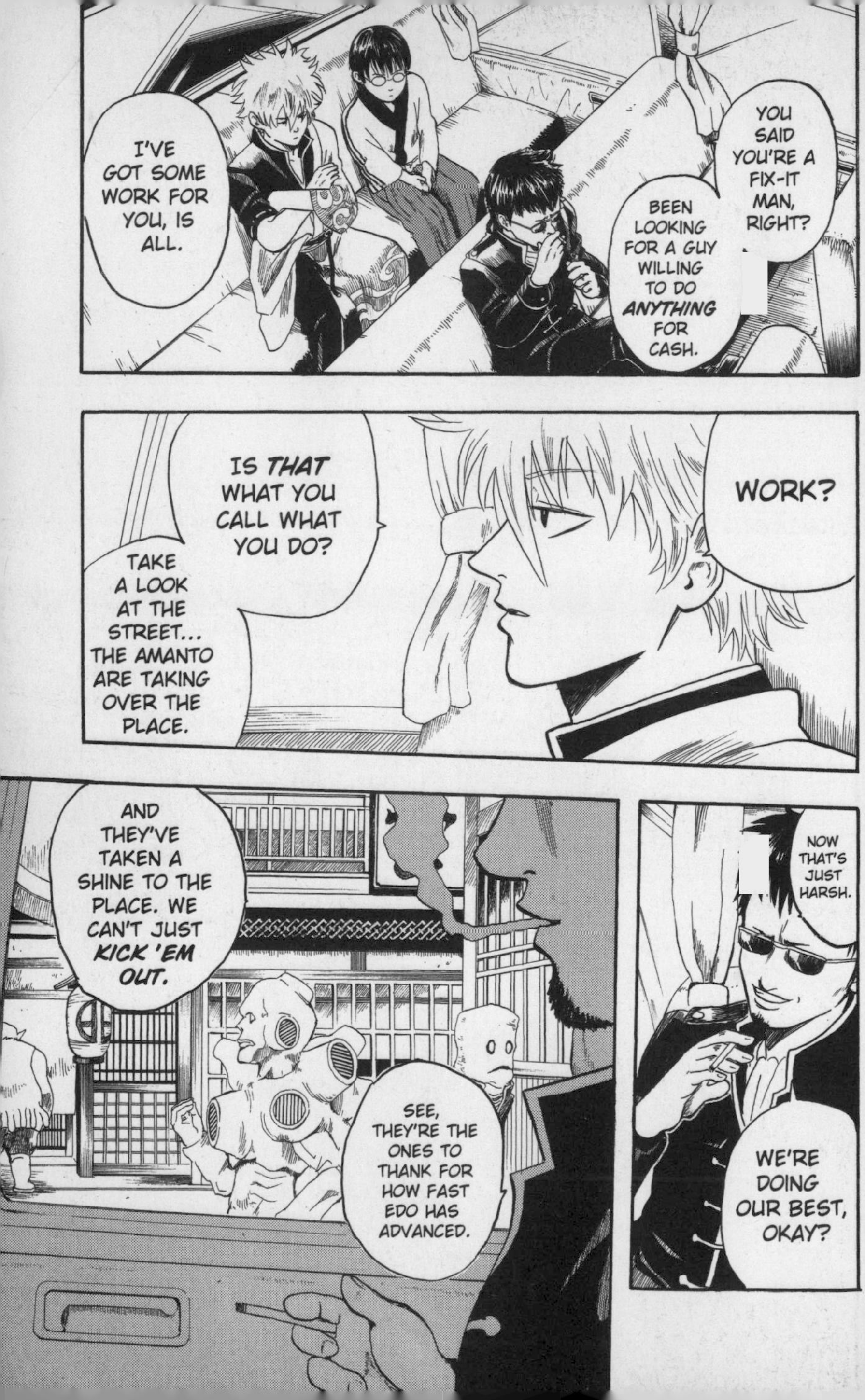
YOU SAID YOU'RE A FIX-IT MAN, RIGHT?
BEEN LOOKING FOR A GUY WILLING TO DO *ANYTHING* FOR CASH.
I'VE GOT SOME WORK FOR YOU, IS ALL.
WORK?
IS *THAT* WHAT YOU CALL WHAT YOU DO?
TAKE A LOOK AT THE STREET... THE AMANTO ARE TAKING OVER THE PLACE.
NOW THAT'S JUST HARSH.
WE'RE DOING OUR BEST, OKAY?
AND THEY'VE TAKEN A SHINE TO THE PLACE. WE CAN'T JUST *KICK 'EM OUT.*
SEE, THEY'RE THE ONES TO THANK FOR HOW FAST EDO HAS ADVANCED.

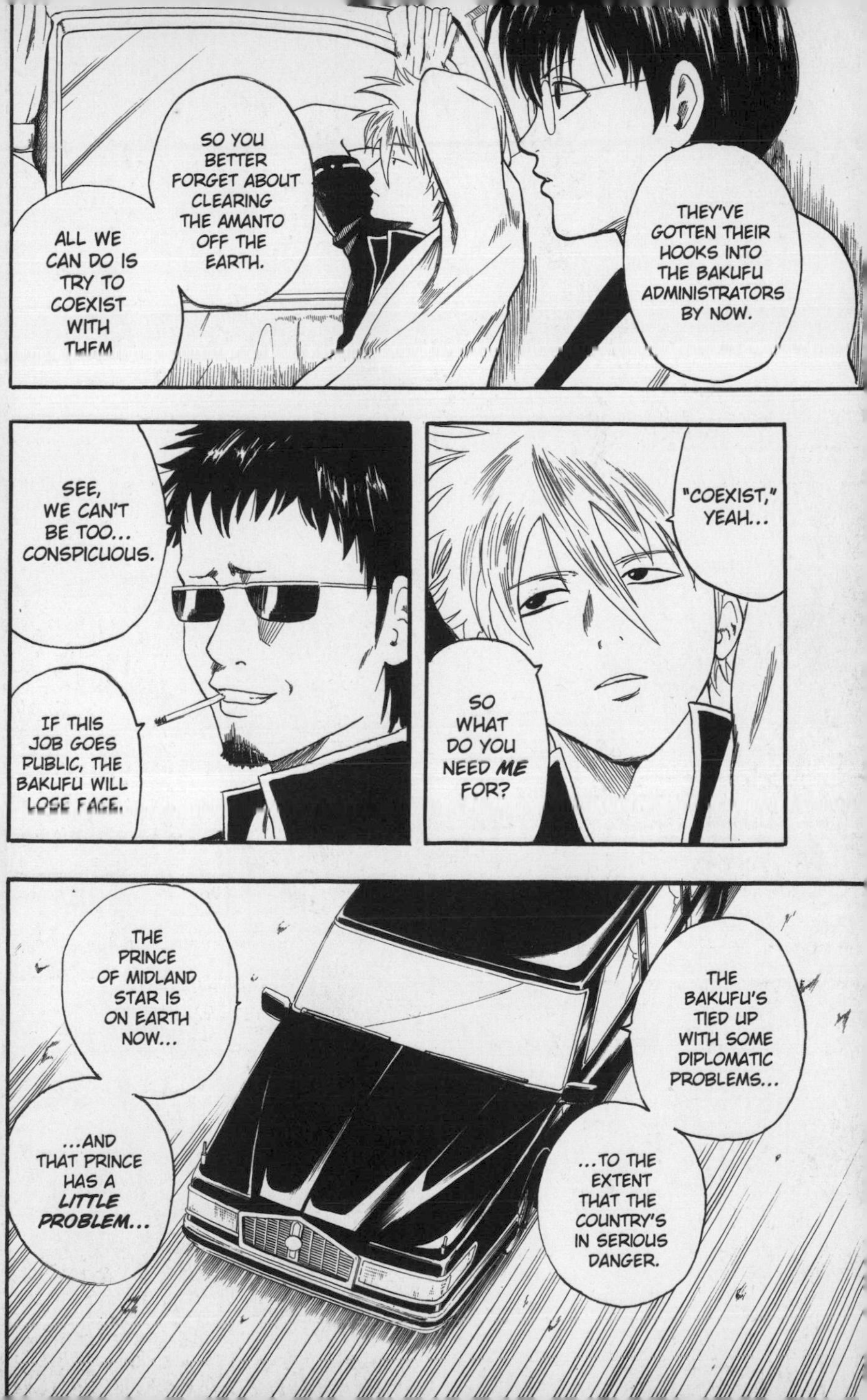
THEY'VE GOTTEN THEIR HOOKS INTO THE BAKUFU ADMINISTRATORS BY NOW.
SO YOU BETTER FORGET ABOUT CLEARING THE AMANTO OFF THE EARTH.
ALL WE CAN DO IS TRY TO COEXIST WITH THEM
"COEXIST," YEAH...
SO WHAT DO YOU NEED *ME* FOR?
SEE, WE CAN'T BE TOO... CONSPICUOUS.
IF THIS JOB GOES PUBLIC, THE BAKUFU WILL LOSE FACE.
THE BAKUFU'S TIED UP WITH SOME DIPLOMATIC PROBLEMS...
...TO THE EXTENT THAT THE COUNTRY'S IN SERIOUS DANGER.
THE PRINCE OF MIDLAND STAR IS ON EARTH NOW...
...AND THAT PRINCE HAS A *LITTLE PROBLEM*...

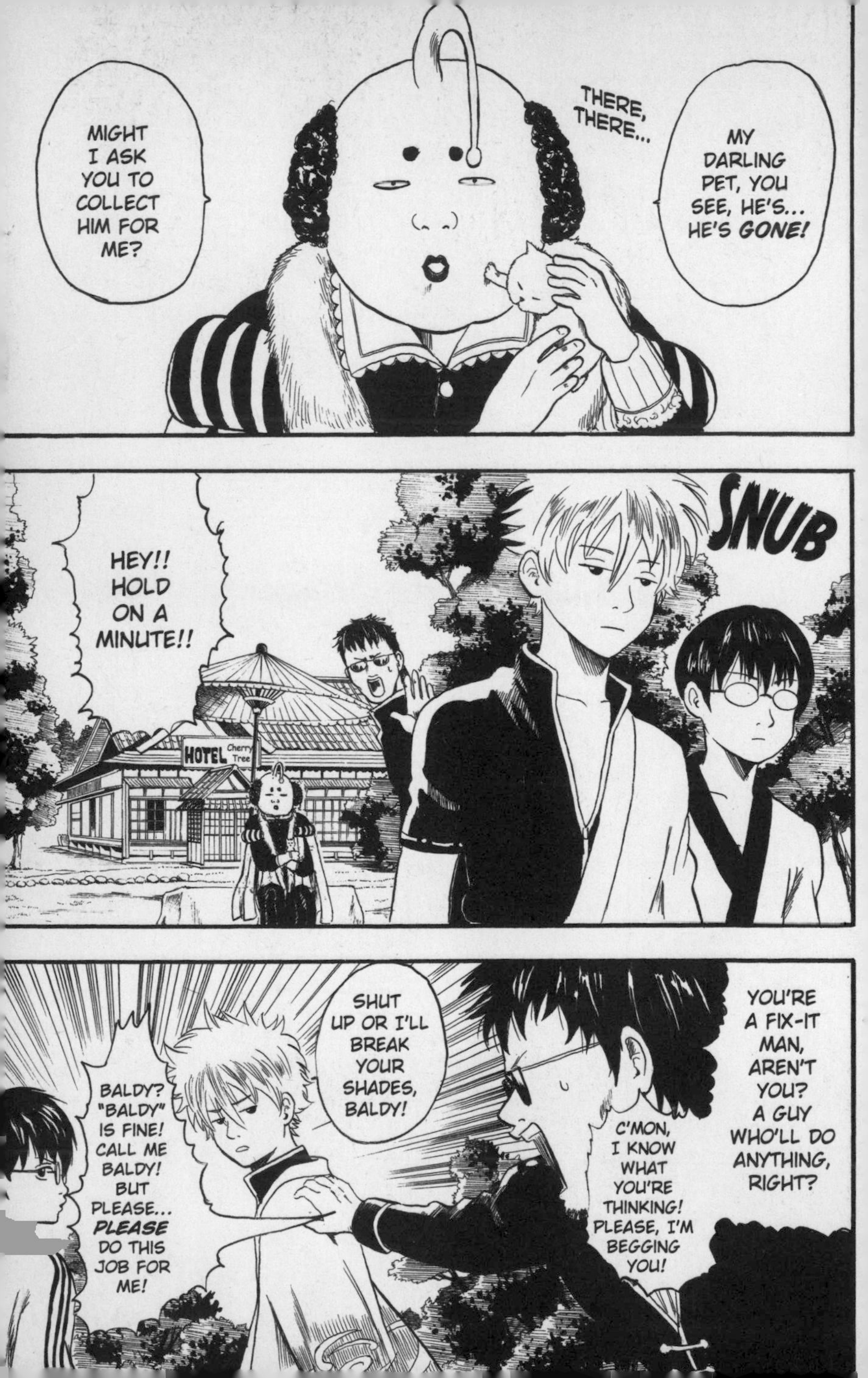
MY DARLING PET, YOU SEE, HE'S... HE'S *GONE!*
THERE, THERE...
MIGHT I ASK YOU TO COLLECT HIM FOR ME?
SNUB
HEY!! HOLD ON A MINUTE!!
HOTEL
Cherry Tree
YOU'RE A FIX-IT MAN, AREN'T YOU? A GUY WHO'LL DO ANYTHING, RIGHT?
C'MON, I KNOW WHAT YOU'RE THINKING! PLEASE, I'M BEGGING YOU!
SHUT UP OR I'LL BREAK YOUR SHADES, BALDY!
BALDY? "BALDY" IS FINE! CALL ME BALDY! BUT PLEASE... *PLEASE* DO THIS JOB FOR ME!

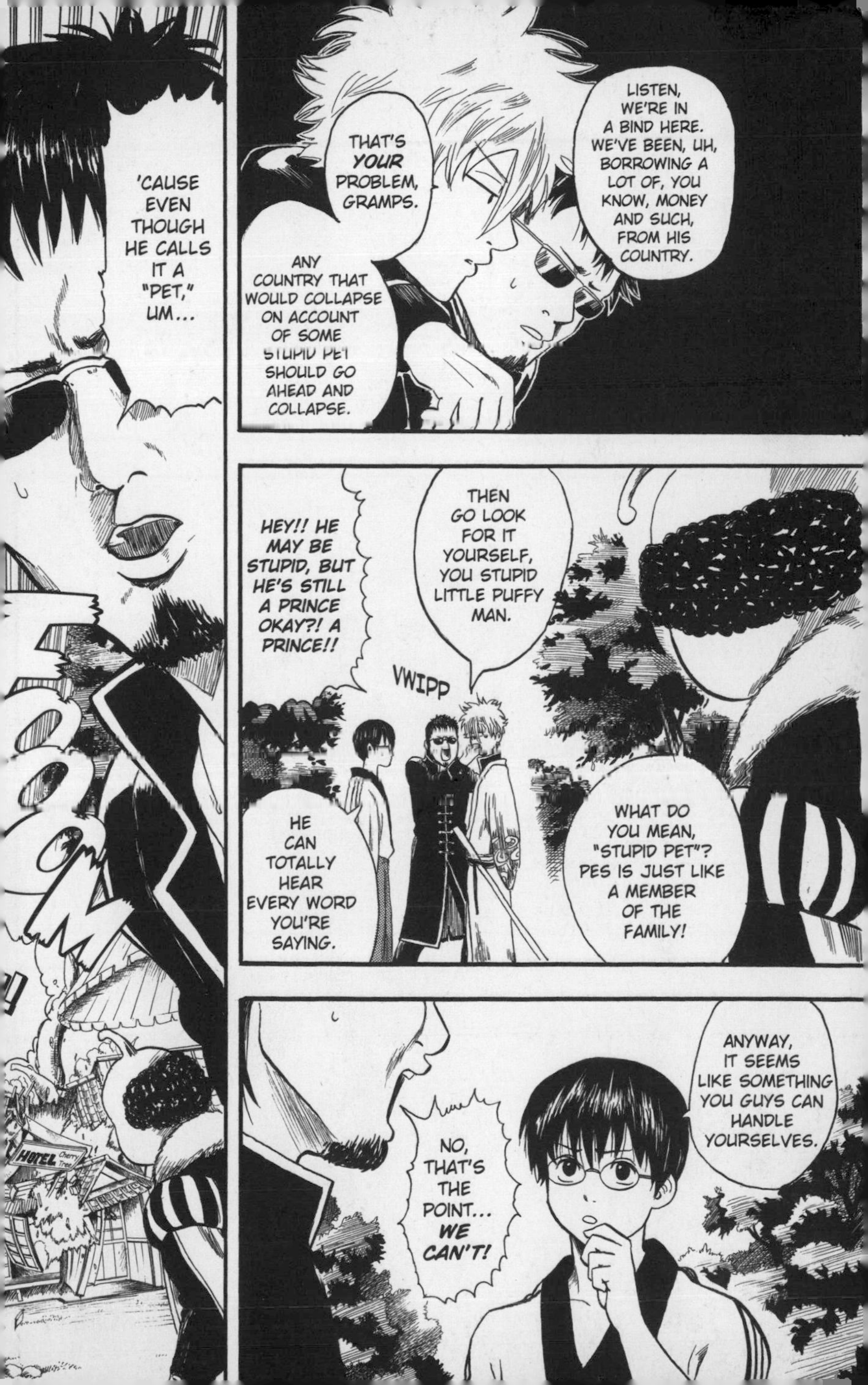
LISTEN, WE'RE IN A BIND HERE. WE'VE BEEN, UH, BORROWING A LOT OF, YOU KNOW, MONEY AND SUCH, FROM HIS COUNTRY.
THAT'S *YOUR* PROBLEM, GRAMPS.
ANY COUNTRY THAT WOULD COLLAPSE ON ACCOUNT OF SOME STUPID PET SHOULD GO AHEAD AND COLLAPSE.
WHAT DO YOU MEAN, "STUPID PET"? PES IS JUST LIKE A MEMBER OF THE FAMILY!
THEN GO LOOK FOR IT YOURSELF, YOU STUPID LITTLE PUFFY MAN.
VWIPP
HEY!! HE MAY BE STUPID, BUT HE'S STILL A PRINCE OKAY?! A PRINCE!!
HE CAN TOTALLY HEAR EVERY WORD YOU'RE SAYING.
ANYWAY, IT SEEMS LIKE SOMETHING YOU GUYS CAN HANDLE YOURSELVES.
NO, THAT'S THE POINT... *WE CAN'T!*
'CAUSE EVEN THOUGH HE CALLS IT A "PET," UM...
HOTEL Cherry Tree

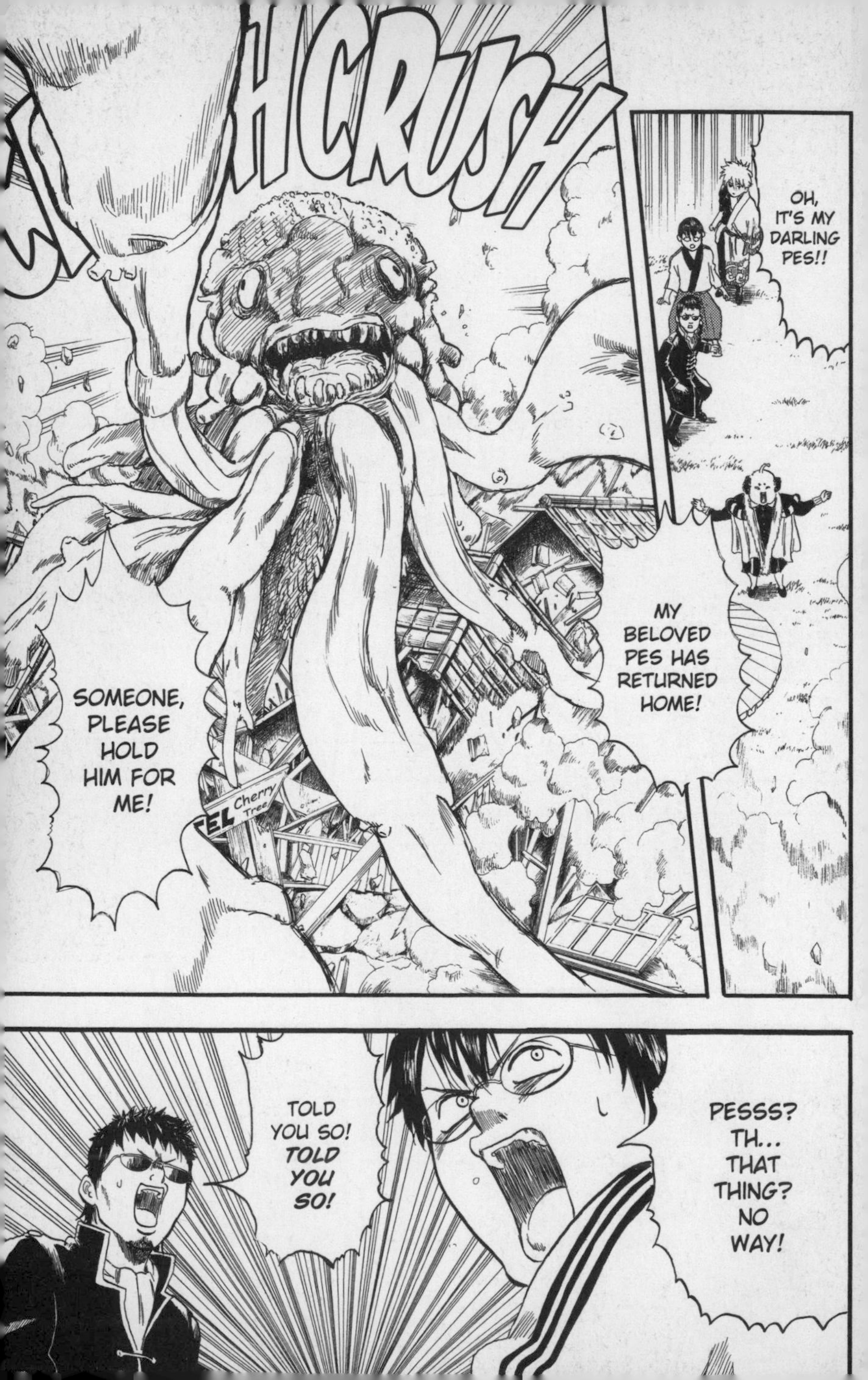
OH, IT'S MY DARLING PES!!
MY BELOVED PES HAS RETURNED HOME!
HCRUSH
TEL Cherry Tree
SOMEONE, PLEASE HOLD HIM FOR ME!
PESSS? TH... THAT THING? NO WAY!
TOLD YOU SO! *TOLD YOU SO!*

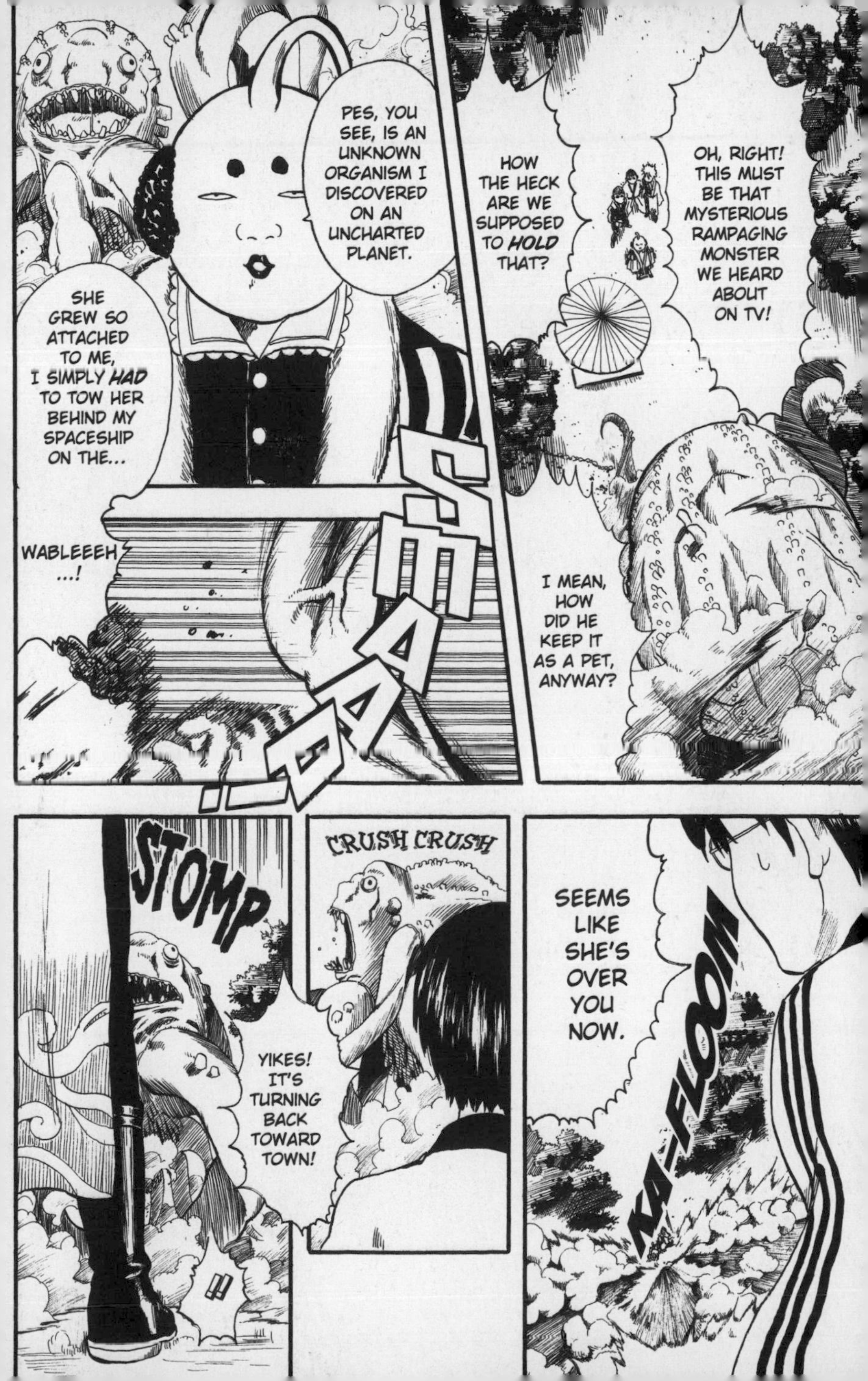

OH, RIGHT! THIS MUST BE THAT MYSTERIOUS RAMPAGING MONSTER WE HEARD ABOUT ON TV!
HOW THE HECK ARE WE SUPPOSED TO *HOLD* THAT?
I MEAN, HOW DID HE KEEP IT AS A PET, ANYWAY?
PES, YOU SEE, IS AN UNKNOWN ORGANISM I DISCOVERED ON AN UNCHARTED PLANET.
SHE GREW SO ATTACHED TO ME, I SIMPLY *HAD* TO TOW HER BEHIND MY SPACESHIP ON THE...
SMAAG...!
WABLEEEH...!
SEEMS LIKE SHE'S OVER YOU NOW.
KA-FLOOM
CRUSH CRUSH
YIKES! IT'S TURNING BACK TOWARD TOWN!
STOMP
!!

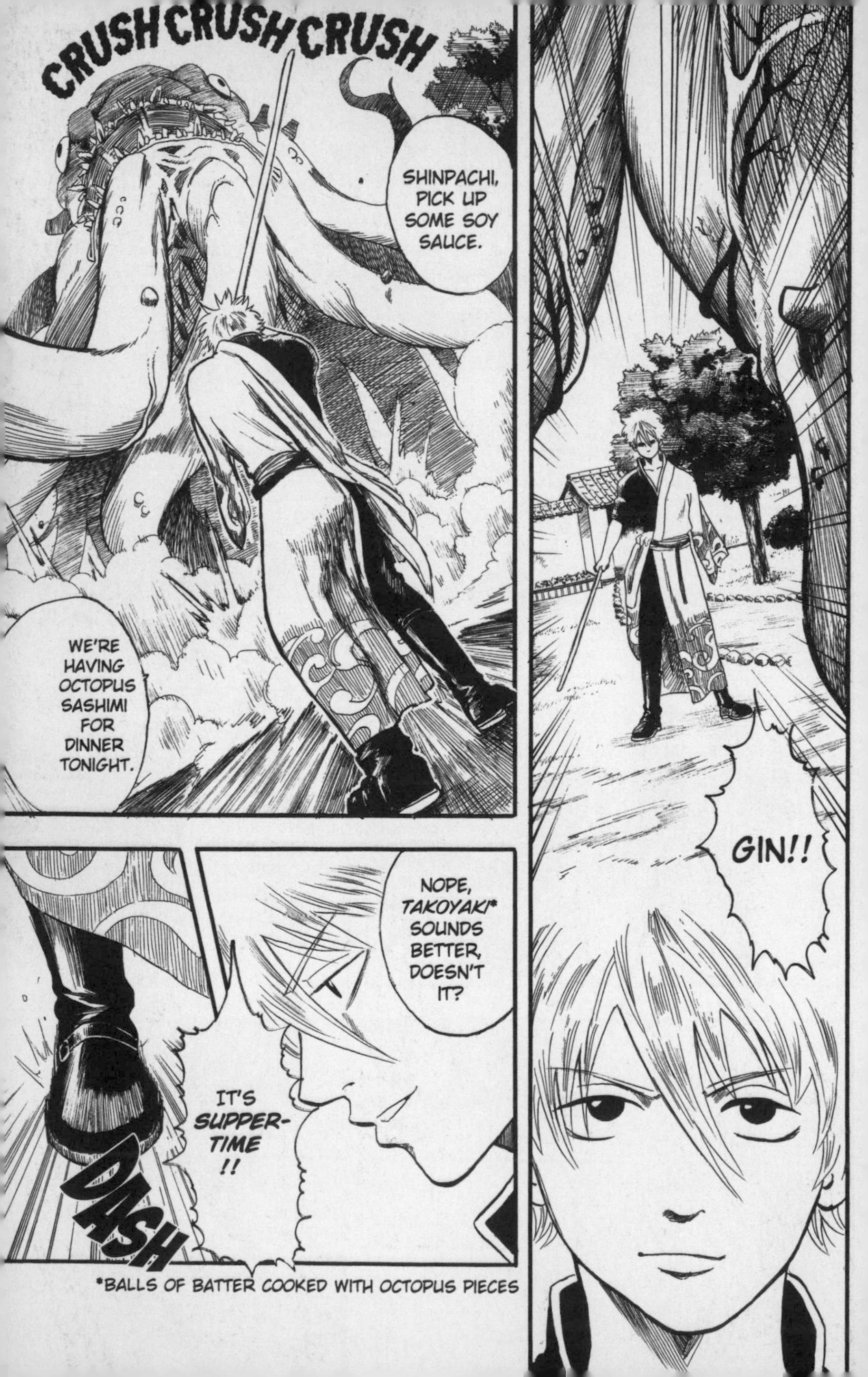
GIN!!
CRUSH CRUSH CRUSH
SHINPACHI, PICK UP SOME SOY SAUCE.
WE'RE HAVING OCTOPUS SASHIMI FOR DINNER TONIGHT.
NOPE, *TAKOYAKI** SOUNDS BETTER, DOESN'T IT?
IT'S *SUPPER-TIME* !!
DASH

*BALLS OF BATTER COOKED WITH OCTOPUS PIECES

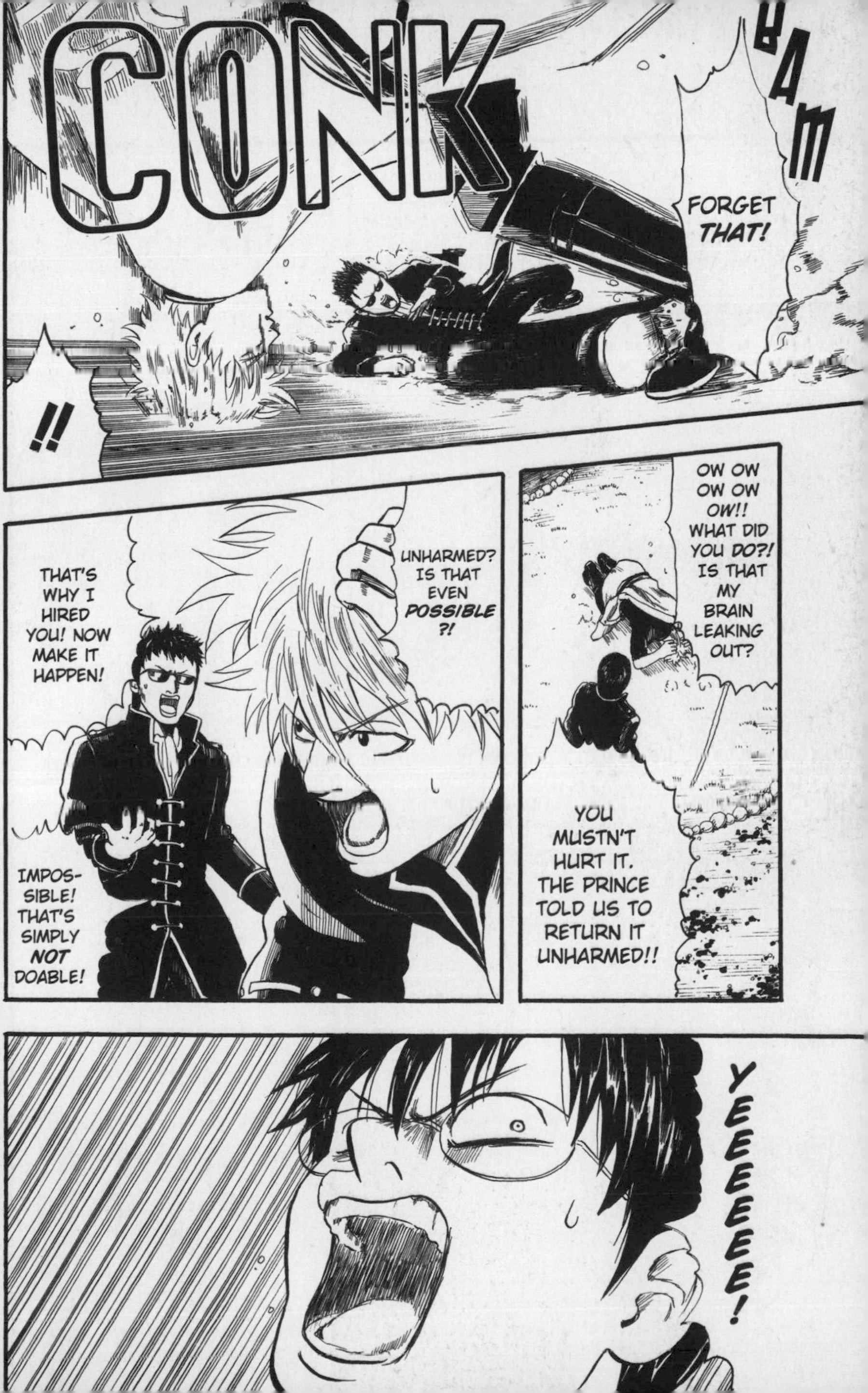
BAM
FORGET THAT!
CONK
!!
OW OW OW OW OW!! WHAT DID YOU DO?! IS THAT MY BRAIN LEAKING OUT?
YOU MUSTN'T HURT IT. THE PRINCE TOLD US TO RETURN IT UNHARMED!!
UNHARMED? IS THAT EVEN POSSIBLE?!
THAT'S WHY I HIRED YOU! NOW MAKE IT HAPPEN!
IMPOSSIBLE! THAT'S SIMPLY NOT DOABLE!
YEEEEEEE!

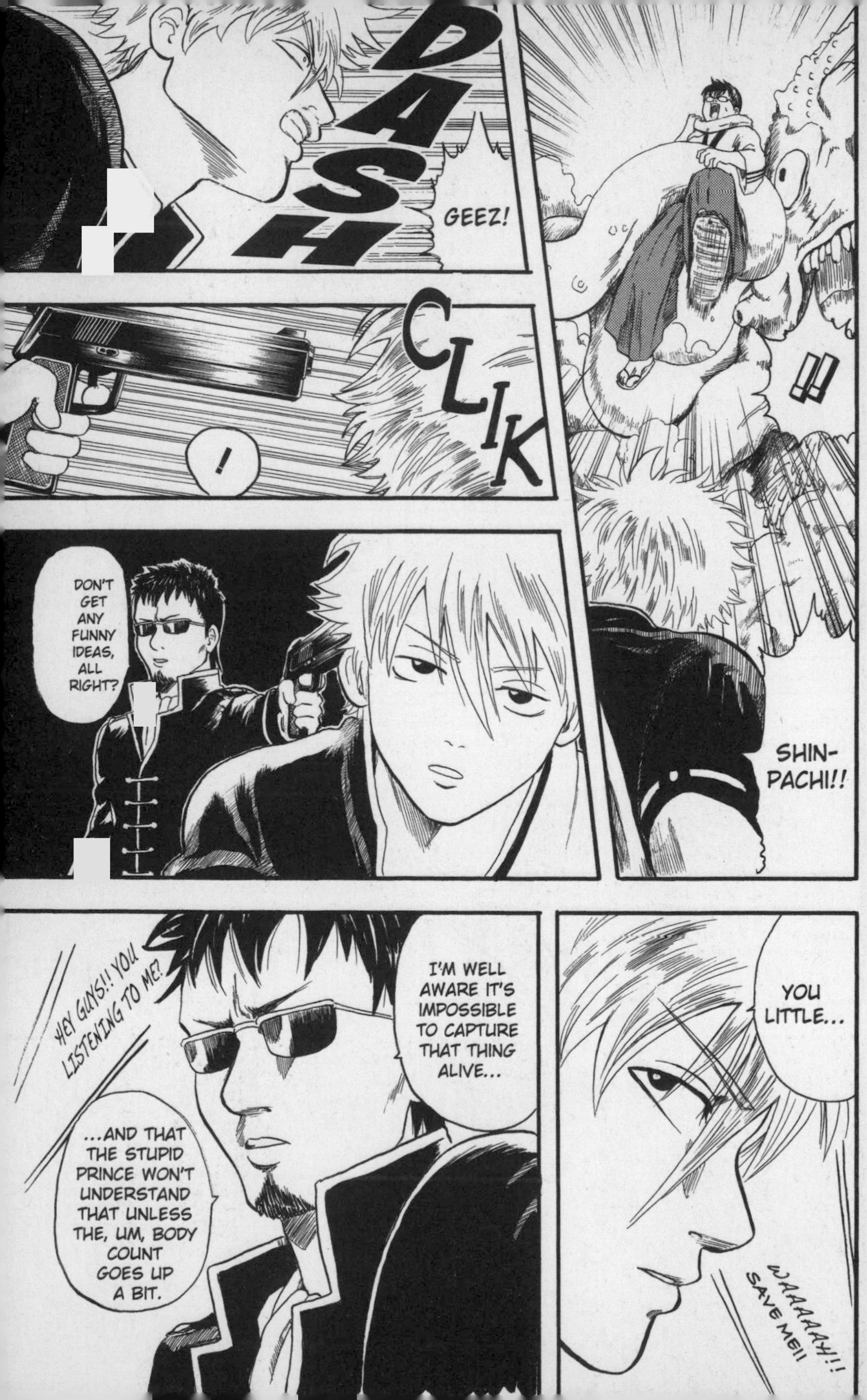
!!
SHIN-PACHI!!
GEEZ!
DASH
CLIK
!
DON'T GET ANY FUNNY IDEAS, ALL RIGHT?
YOU LITTLE...
WAAAAAH!! SAVE ME!!
I'M WELL AWARE IT'S IMPOSSIBLE TO CAPTURE THAT THING ALIVE...
HEY GUYS!! YOU LISTENING TO ME?
...AND THAT THE STUPID PRINCE WON'T UNDERSTAND THAT UNLESS THE, UM, BODY COUNT GOES UP A BIT.

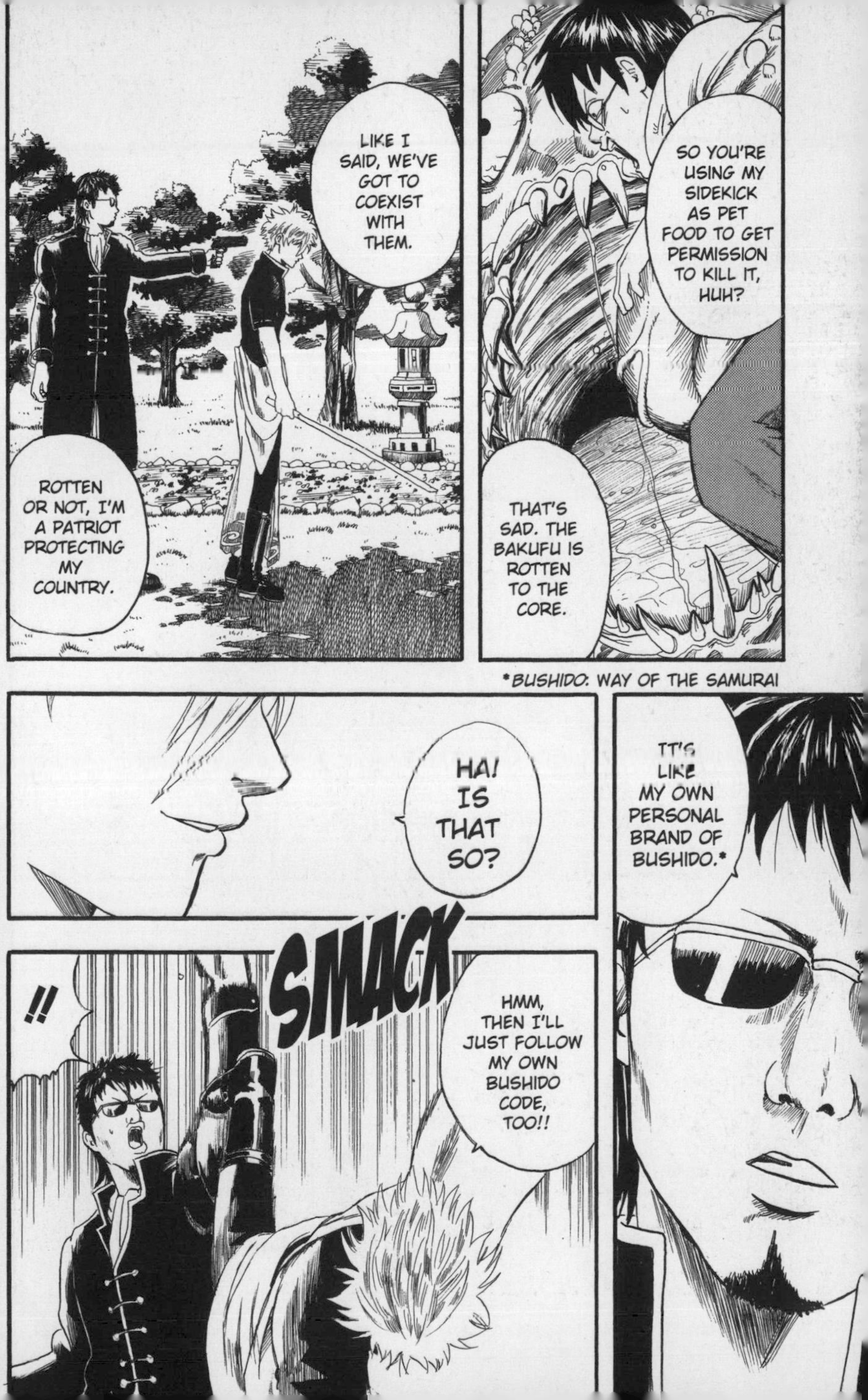
SO YOU'RE USING MY SIDEKICK AS PET FOOD TO GET PERMISSION TO KILL IT, HUH?
THAT'S SAD. THE BAKUFU IS ROTTEN TO THE CORE.
LIKE I SAID, WE'VE GOT TO COEXIST WITH THEM.
ROTTEN OR NOT, I'M A PATRIOT PROTECTING MY COUNTRY.
IT'S LIKE MY OWN PERSONAL BRAND OF BUSHIDO.*
HA! IS THAT SO?
SMACK
HMM, THEN I'LL JUST FOLLOW MY OWN BUSHIDO CODE, TOO!!
!!

*BUSHIDO: WAY OF THE SAMURAI

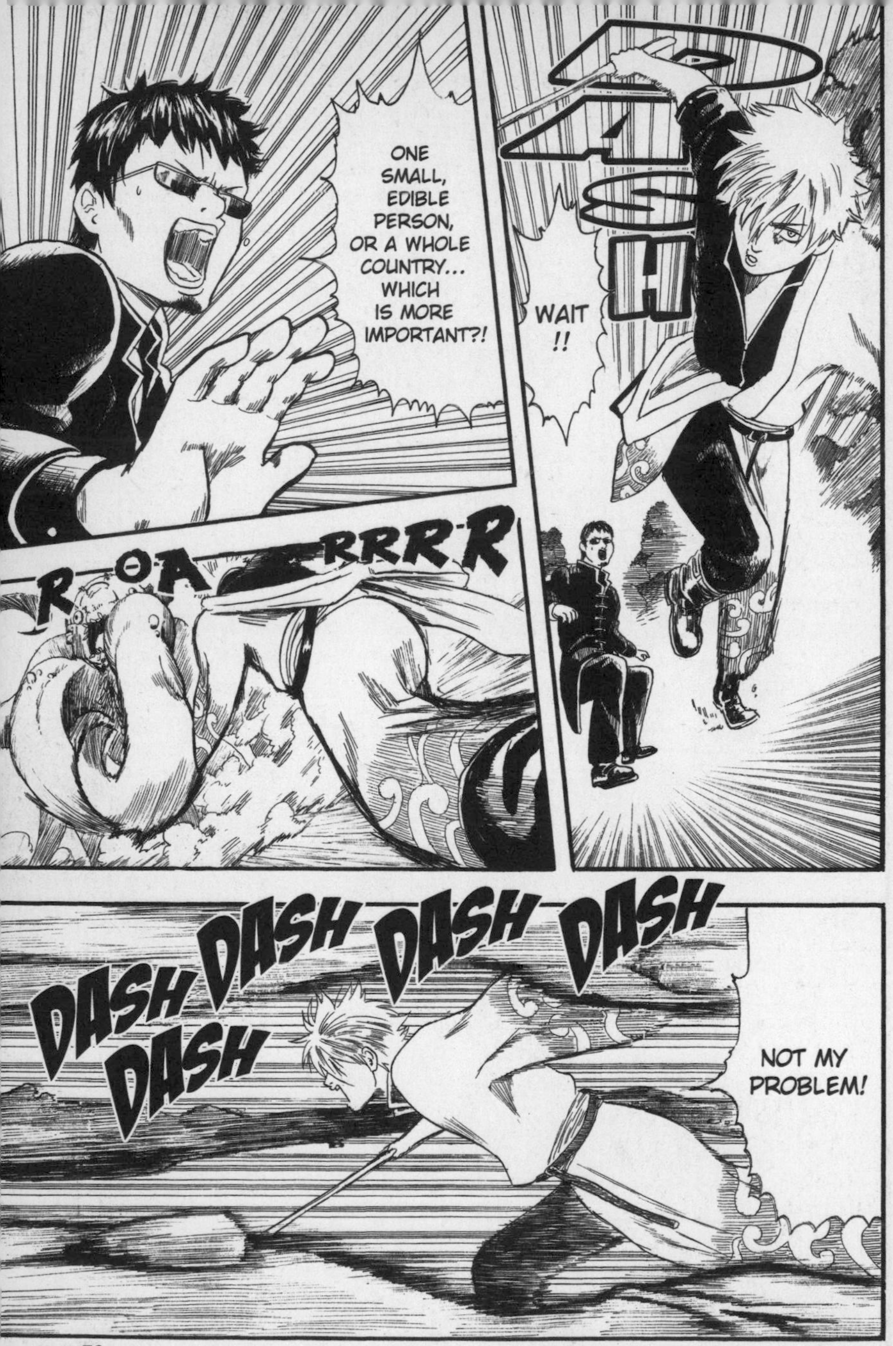
DASH
WAIT !!
ONE SMALL, EDIBLE PERSON, OR A WHOLE COUNTRY... WHICH IS MORE IMPORTANT?!
R-O-A-RRRRR
DASH DASH DASH DASH DASH
NOT MY PROBLEM!

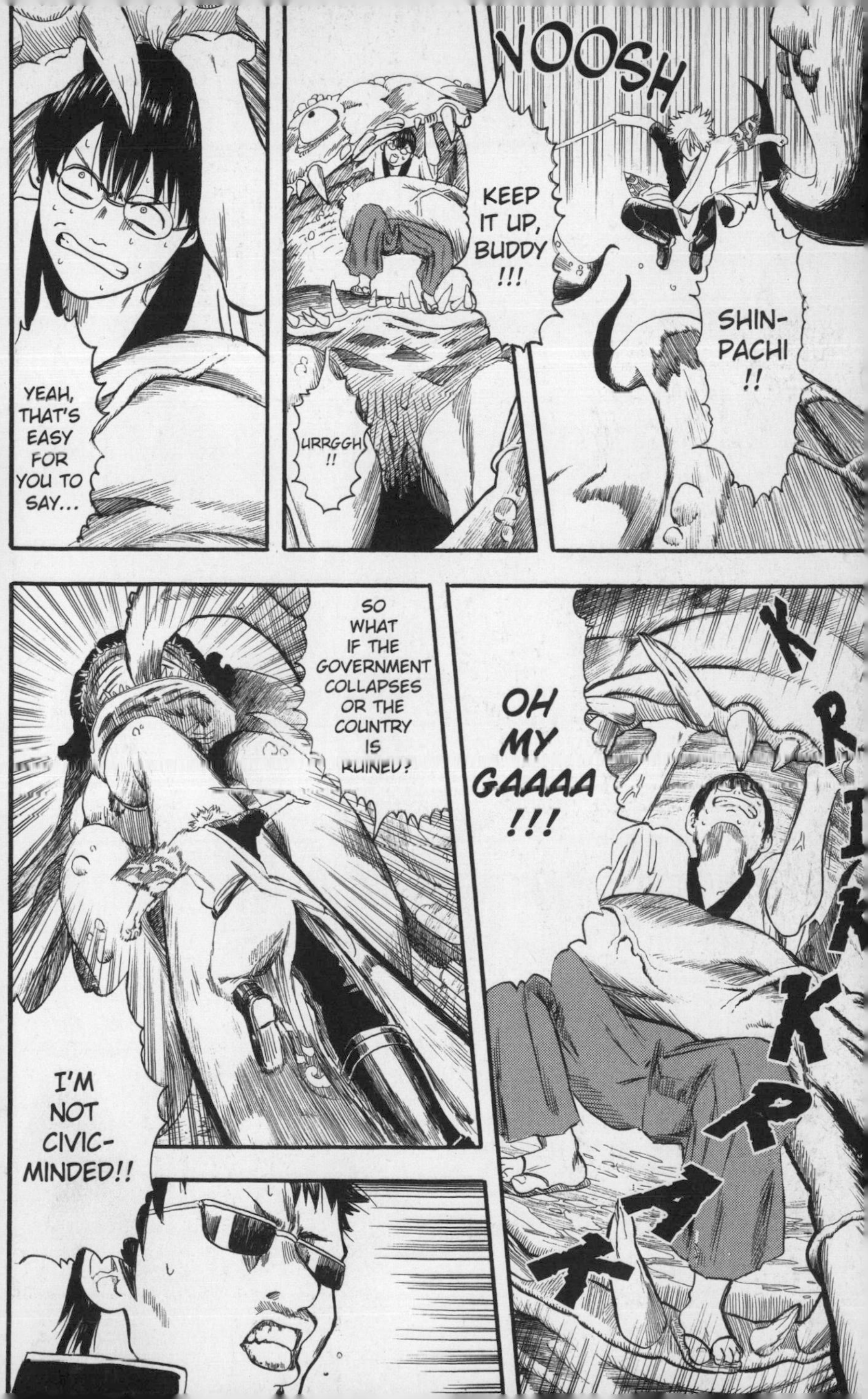
VOOSH
SHIN-PACHI!!
KEEP IT UP, BUDDY!!!
URRGGH!!
YEAH, THAT'S EASY FOR YOU TO SAY...
KRIKKRAK
OH MY GAAAA!!!
SO WHAT IF THE GOVERNMENT COLLAPSES OR THE COUNTRY IS RUINED?
I'M NOT CIVIC-MINDED!!

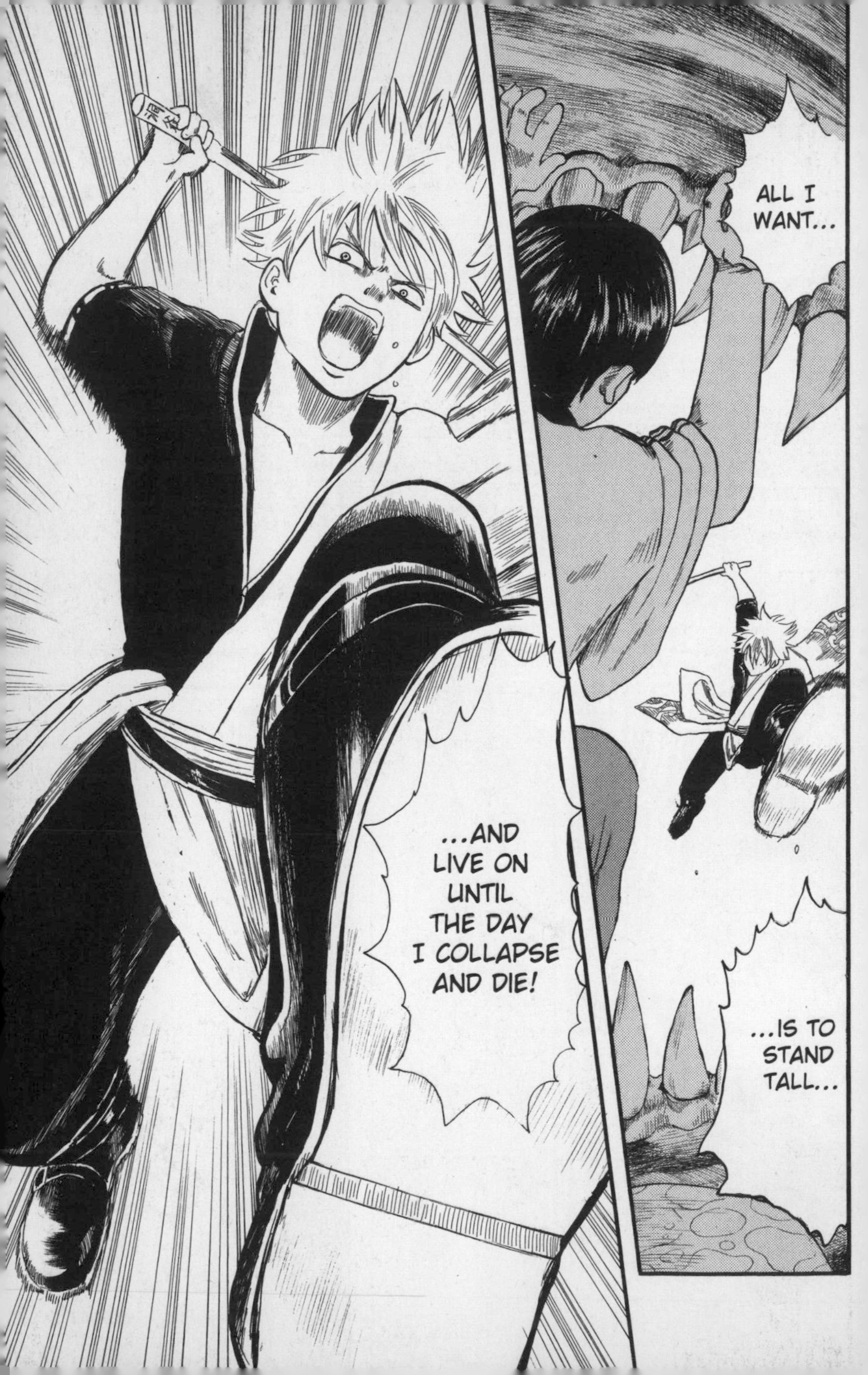
ALL I WANT...
...IS TO STAND TALL...
...AND LIVE ON UNTIL THE DAY I COLLAPSE AND DIE!

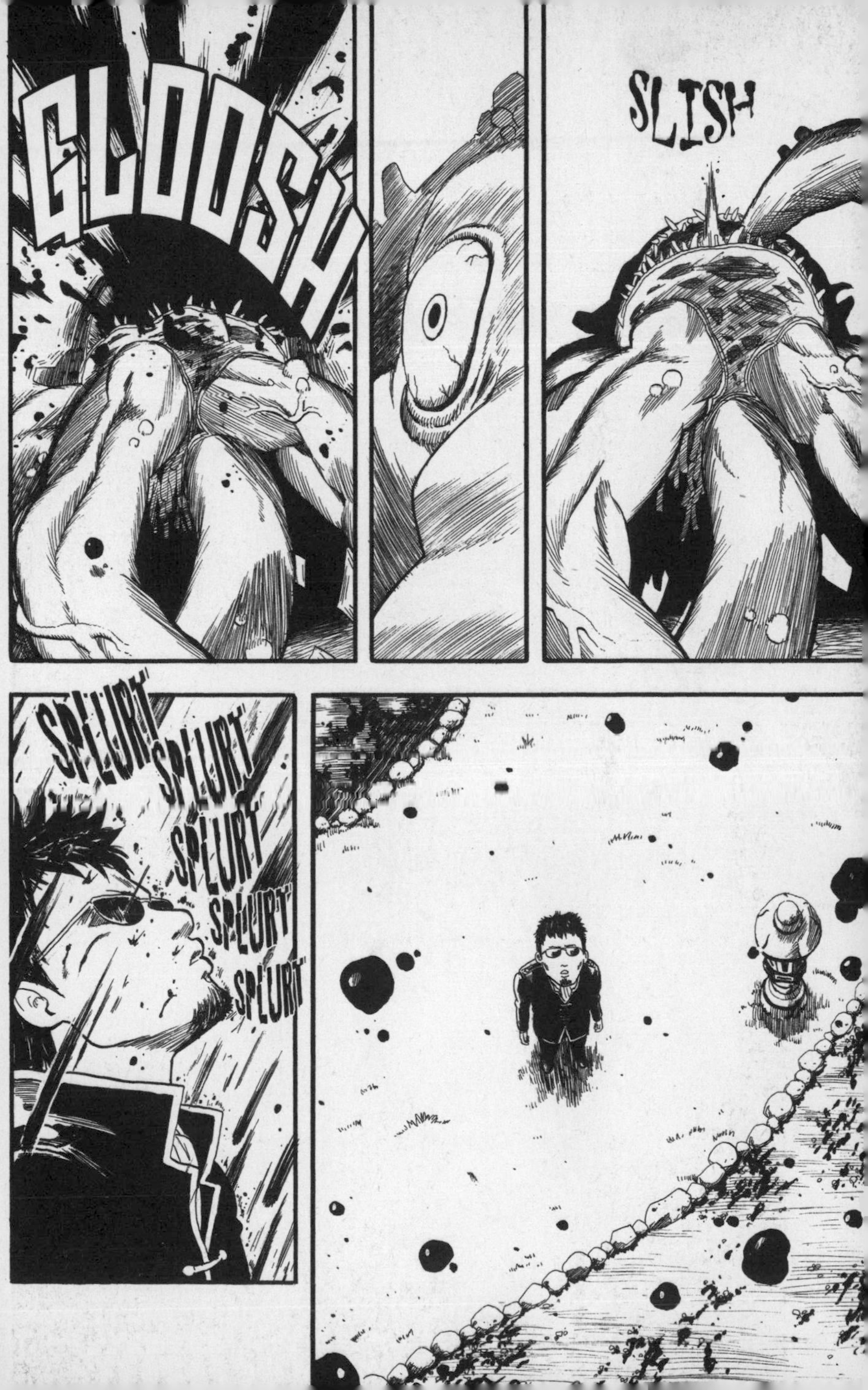
SLISH
GLOOSH
SPLURT
SPLURT
SPLURT
SPLURT
SPLURT
SPLURT

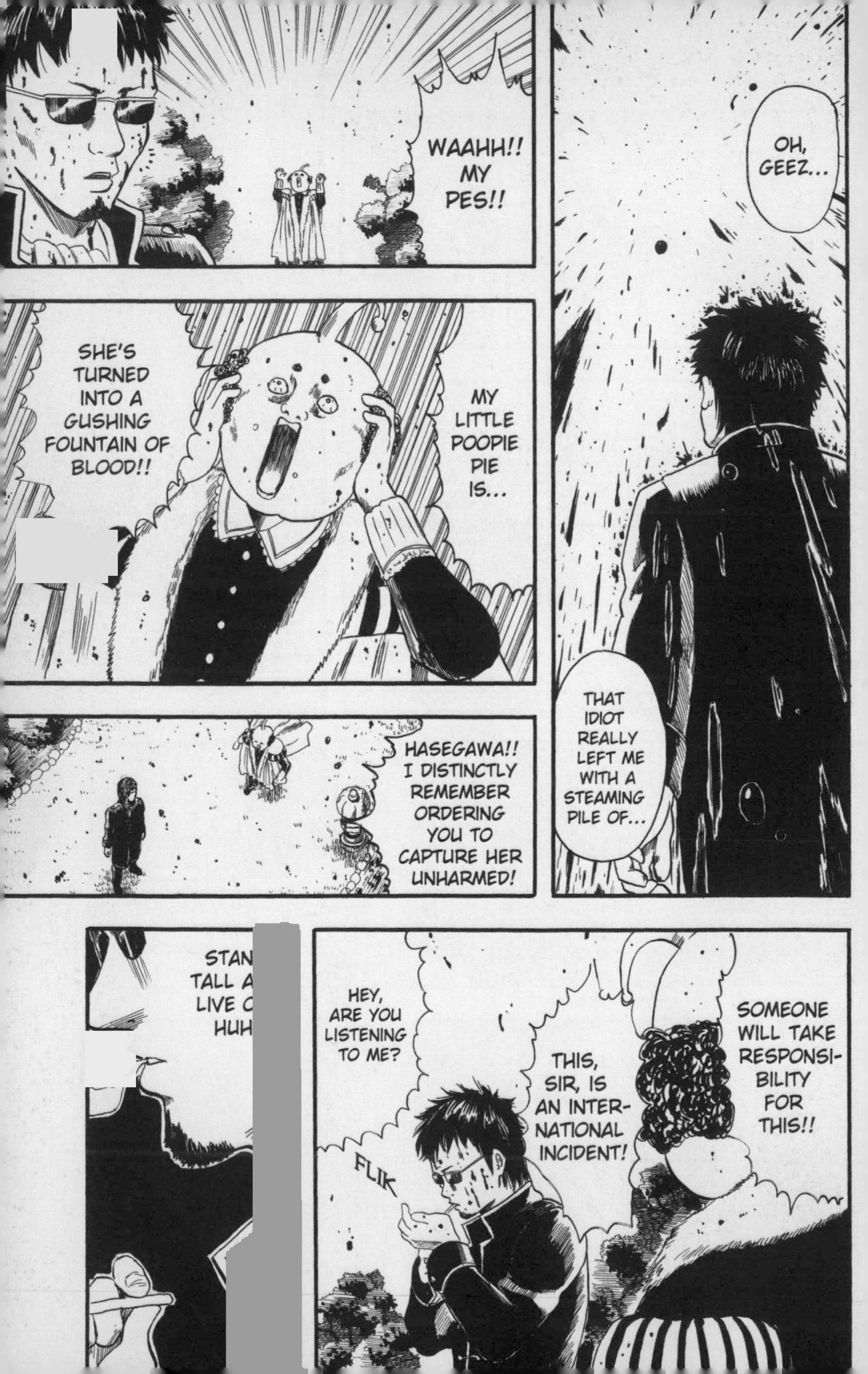
OH, GEEZ...
THAT IDIOT REALLY LEFT ME WITH A STEAMING PILE OF...
WAAHH!! MY PES!!
MY LITTLE POOPIE PIE IS...
SHE'S TURNED INTO A GUSHING FOUNTAIN OF BLOOD!!
HASEGAWA!! I DISTINCTLY REMEMBER ORDERING YOU TO CAPTURE HER UNHARMED!
SOMEONE WILL TAKE RESPONSIBILITY FOR THIS!!
THIS, SIR, IS AN INTERNATIONAL INCIDENT!
HEY, ARE YOU LISTENING TO ME?
FLIK
STAN
TALL A
LIVE O
HUH

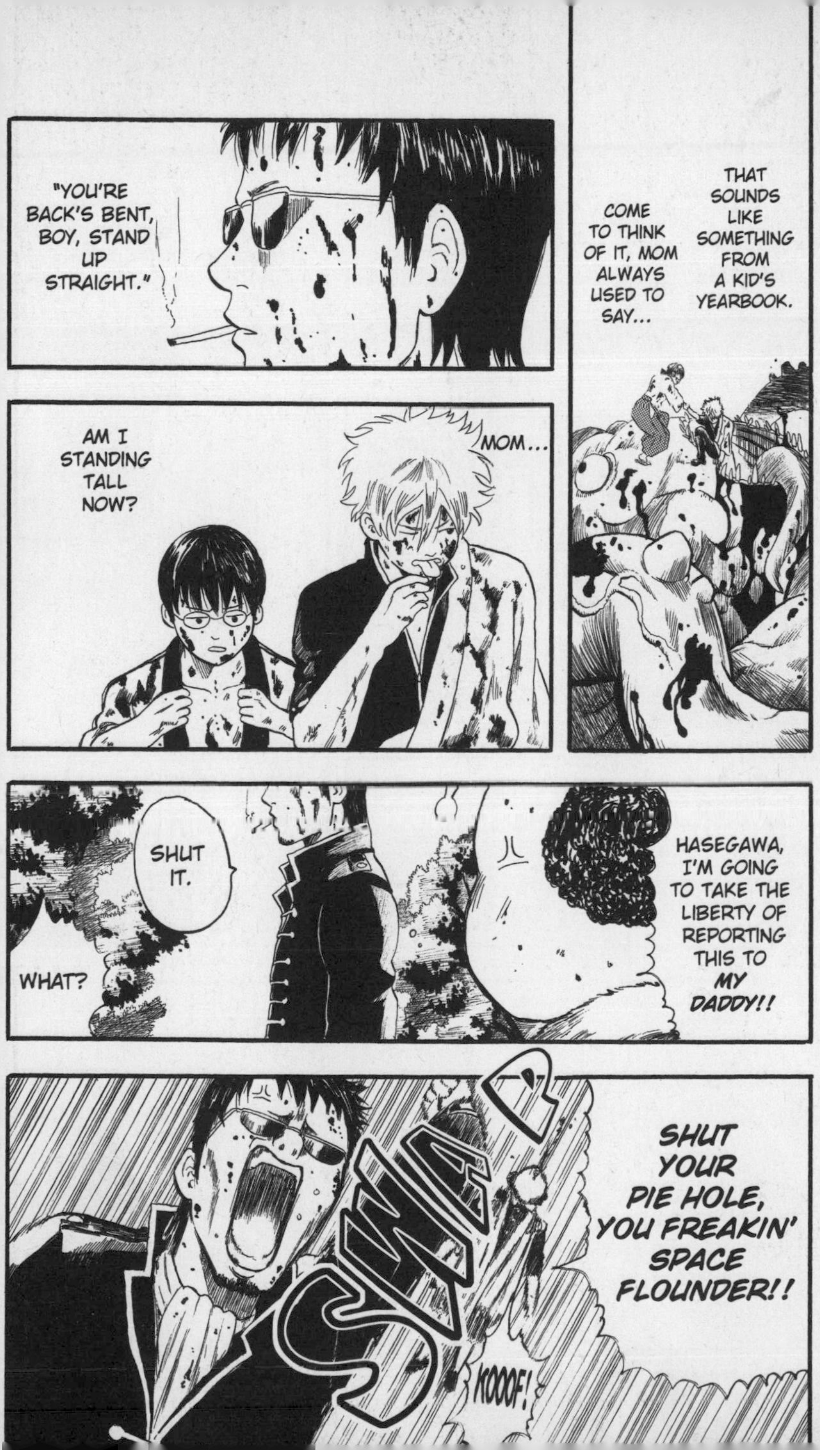
THAT SOUNDS LIKE SOMETHING FROM A KID'S YEARBOOK.
COME TO THINK OF IT, MOM ALWAYS USED TO SAY...
"YOU'RE BACK'S BENT, BOY, STAND UP STRAIGHT."
MOM...
AM I STANDING TALL NOW?
HASEGAWA, I'M GOING TO TAKE THE LIBERTY OF REPORTING THIS TO *MY DADDY!!*
SHUT IT.
WHAT?
SHUT YOUR PIE HOLE, YOU FREAKIN' SPACE FLOUNDER!!
SMACK
KOOOF!

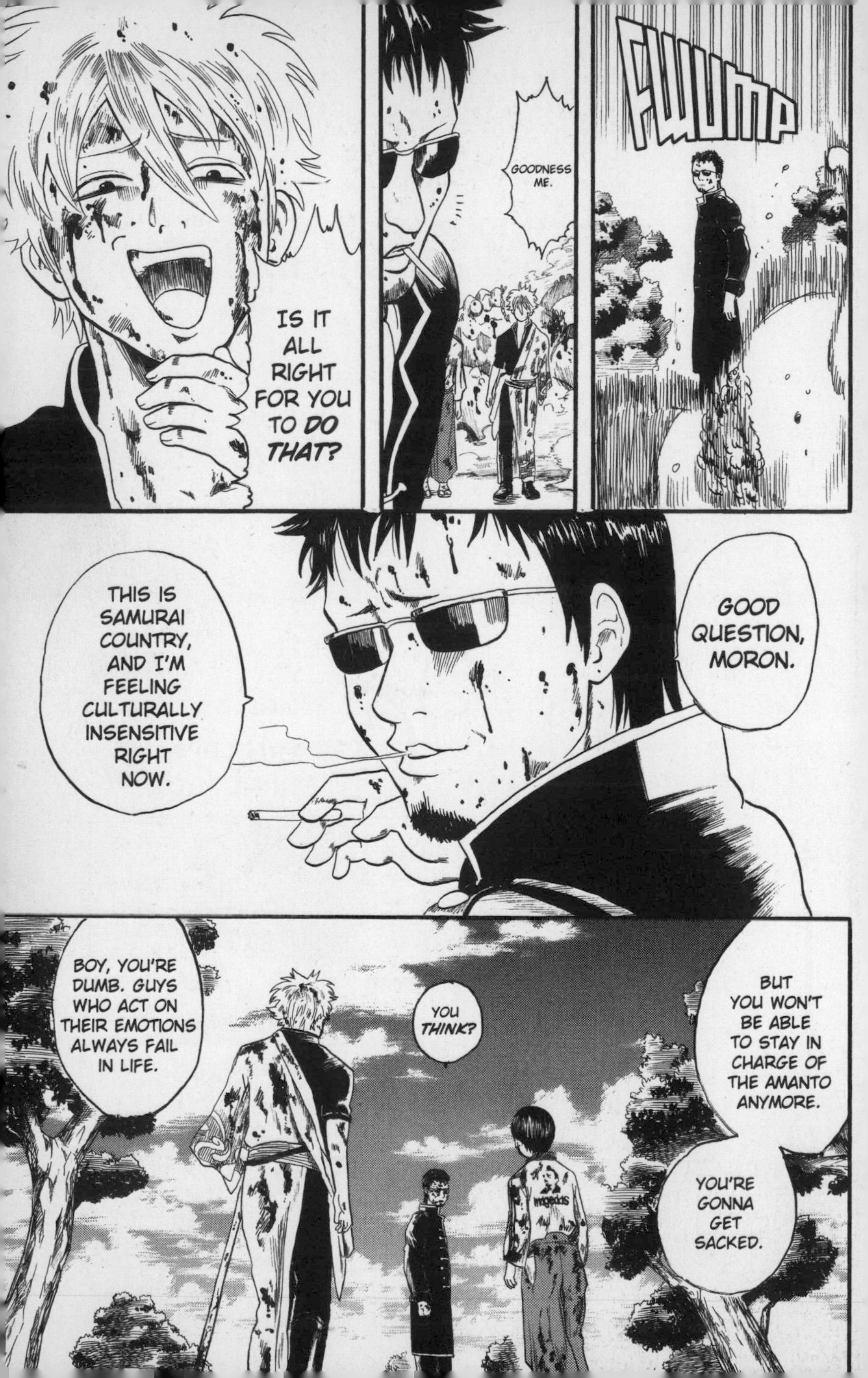
FWUMP
GOODNESS ME.
IS IT ALL RIGHT FOR YOU TO *DO THAT?*
GOOD QUESTION, MORON.
THIS IS SAMURAI COUNTRY, AND I'M FEELING CULTURALLY INSENSITIVE RIGHT NOW.
BUT YOU WON'T BE ABLE TO STAY IN CHARGE OF THE AMANTO ANYMORE.
YOU'RE GONNA GET SACKED.
YOU *THINK?*
BOY, YOU'RE DUMB. GUYS WHO ACT ON THEIR EMOTIONS ALWAYS FAIL IN LIFE.

Sorachi

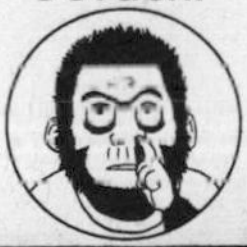

Sorachi's Mumblings 1

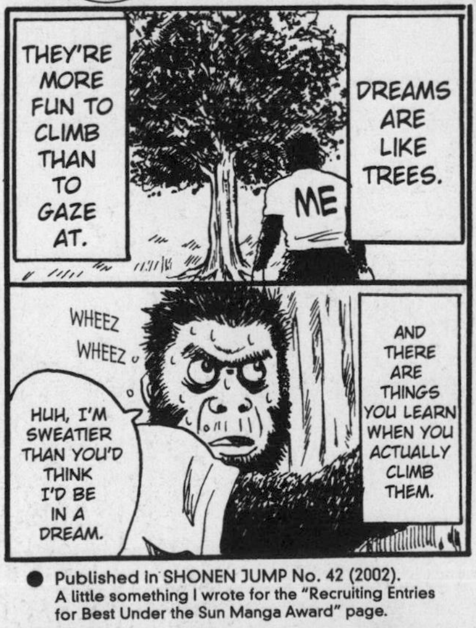
DREAMS ARE LIKE TREES.
ME
THEY'RE MORE FUN TO CLIMB THAN TO GAZE AT.
AND THERE ARE THINGS YOU LEARN WHEN YOU ACTUALLY CLIMB THEM.
WHEEZ
WHEEZ
HUH, I'M SWEATIER THAN YOU'D THINK I'D BE IN A DREAM.

- **Published in SHONEN JUMP No. 42 (2002).**
A little something I wrote for the "Recruiting Entries for Best Under the Sun Manga Award" page.

Lesson 3: Watch Out! Weekly Shonen Jump Sometimes Comes Out on Saturdays!*

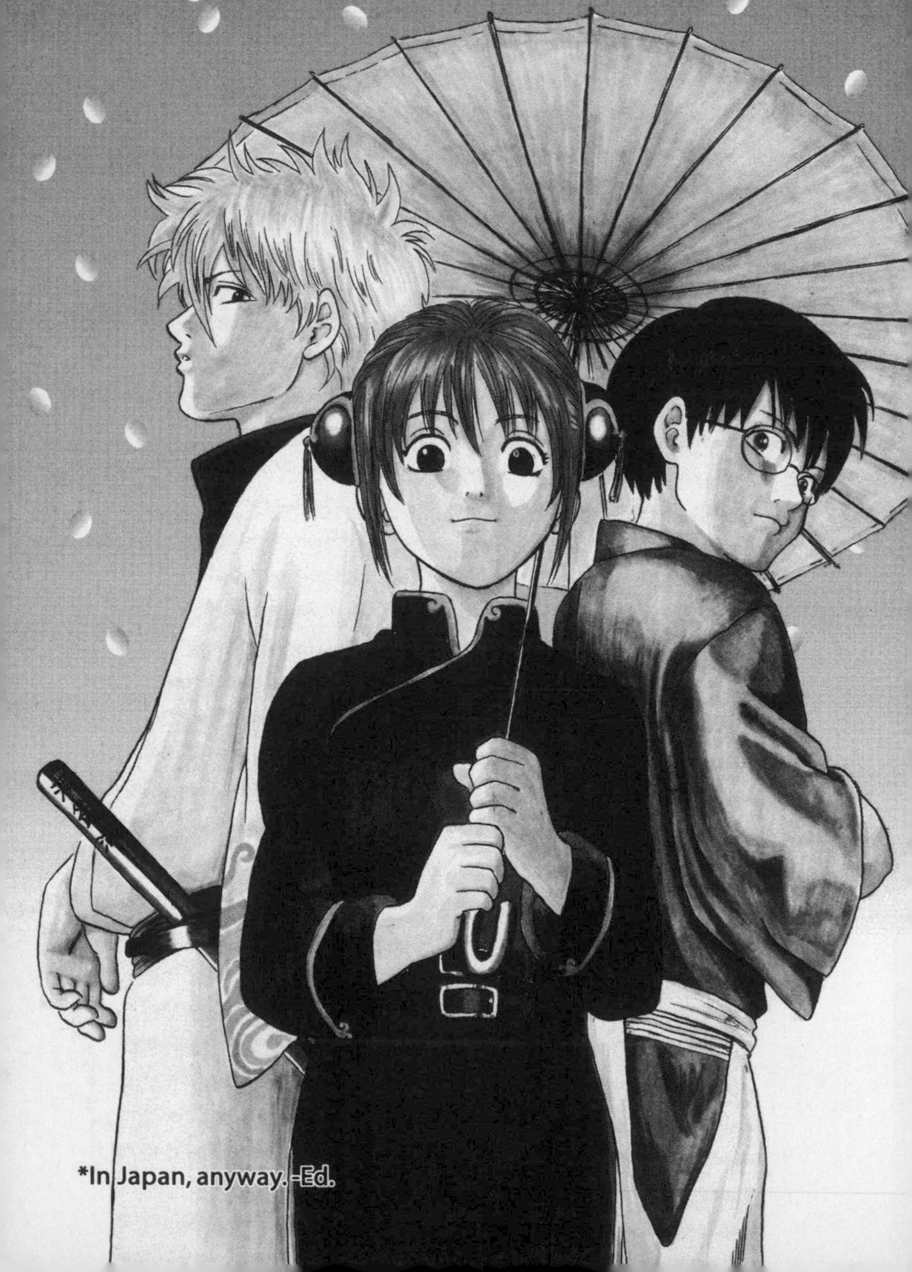

*In Japan, anyway. -Ed.

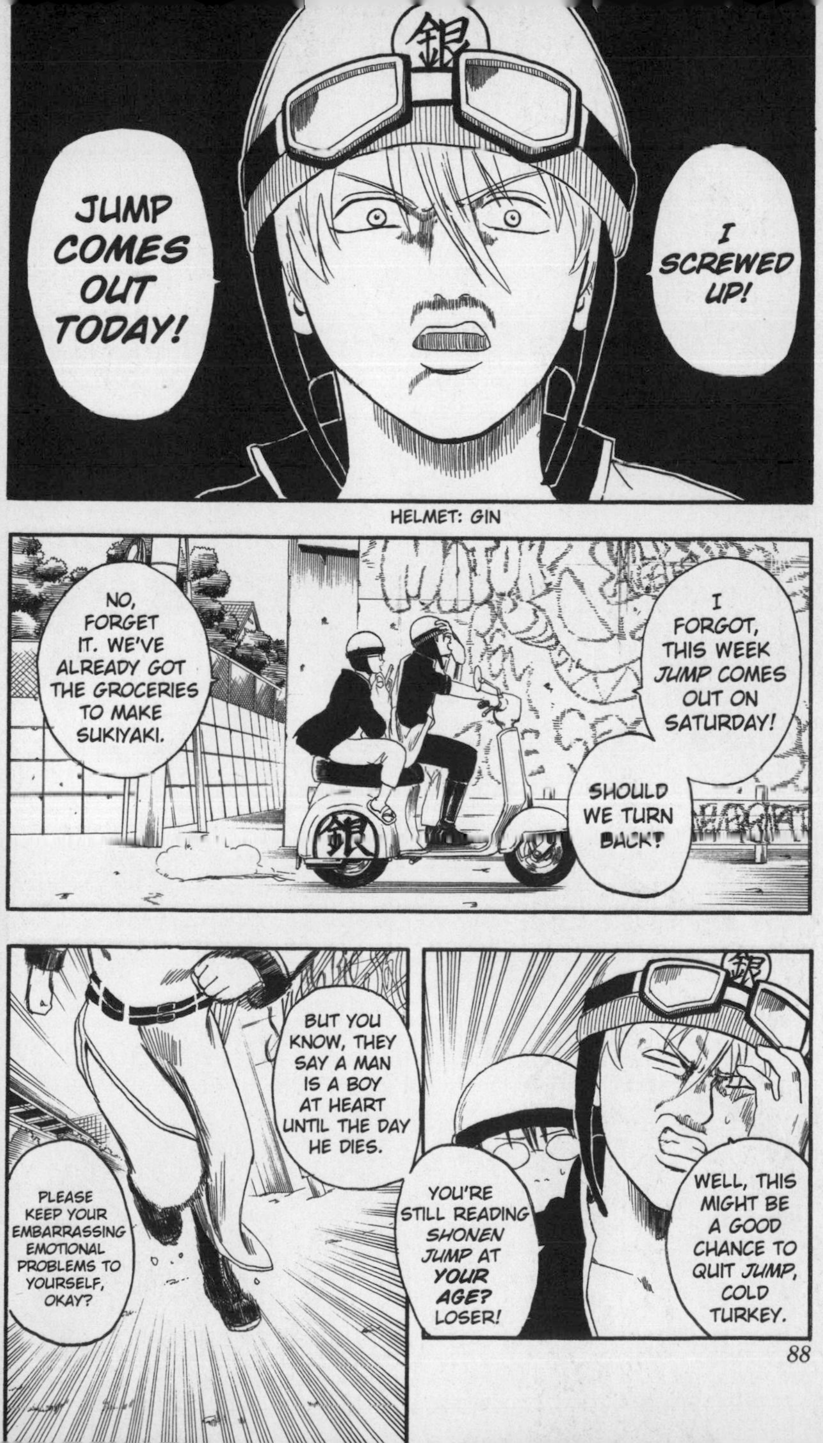
I SCREWED UP!
JUMP COMES OUT TODAY!
HELMET: GIN
I FORGOT, THIS WEEK JUMP COMES OUT ON SATURDAY!
SHOULD WE TURN BACK?
NO, FORGET IT. WE'VE ALREADY GOT THE GROCERIES TO MAKE SUKIYAKI.
WELL, THIS MIGHT BE A GOOD CHANCE TO QUIT JUMP, COLD TURKEY.
YOU'RE STILL READING SHONEN JUMP AT YOUR AGE? LOSER!
BUT YOU KNOW, THEY SAY A MAN IS A BOY AT HEART UNTIL THE DAY HE DIES.
PLEASE KEEP YOUR EMBARRASSING EMOTIONAL PROBLEMS TO YOURSELF, OKAY?

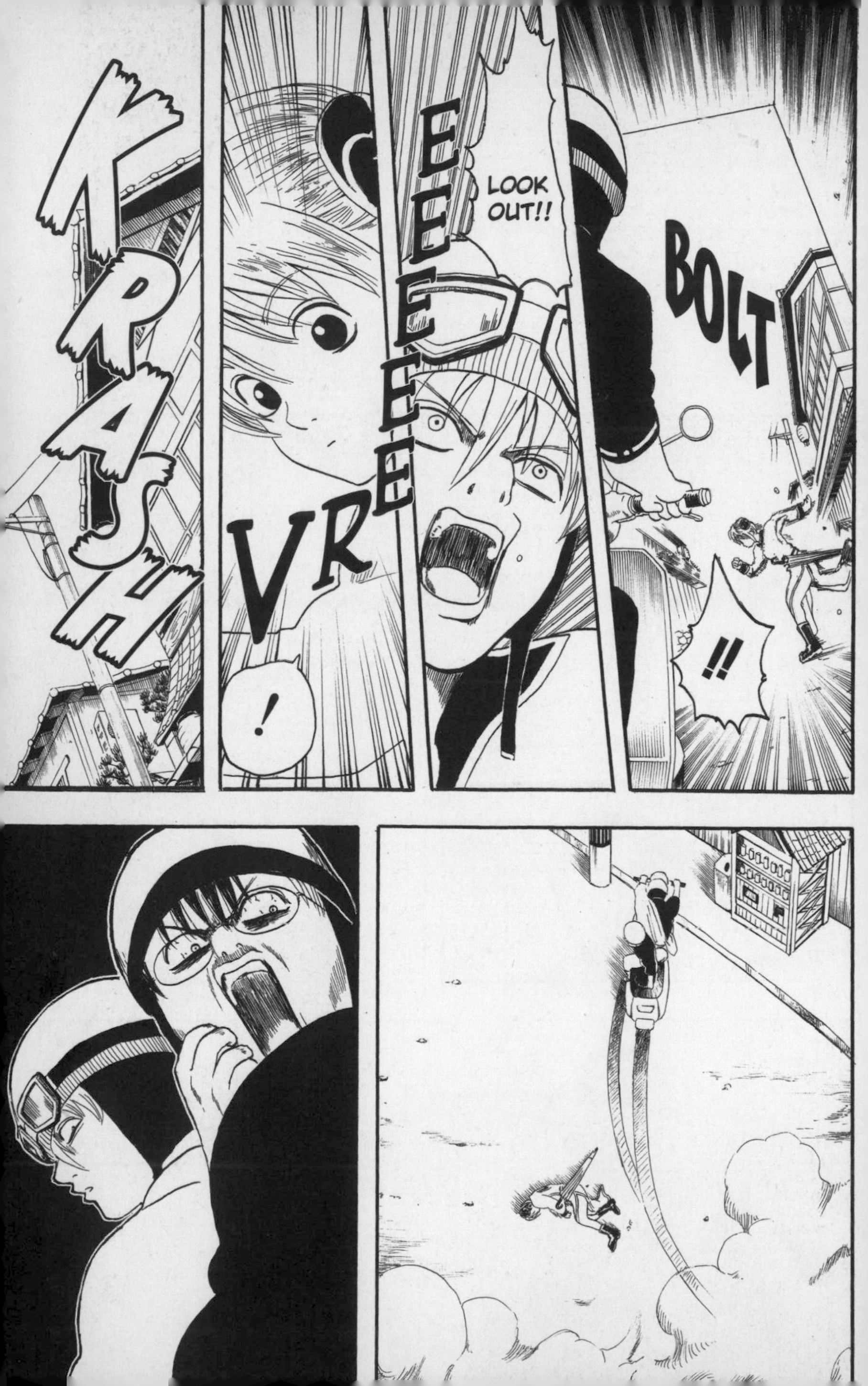
BOLT
!!
LOOK OUT!!
VREEEEEE
!
KRASH

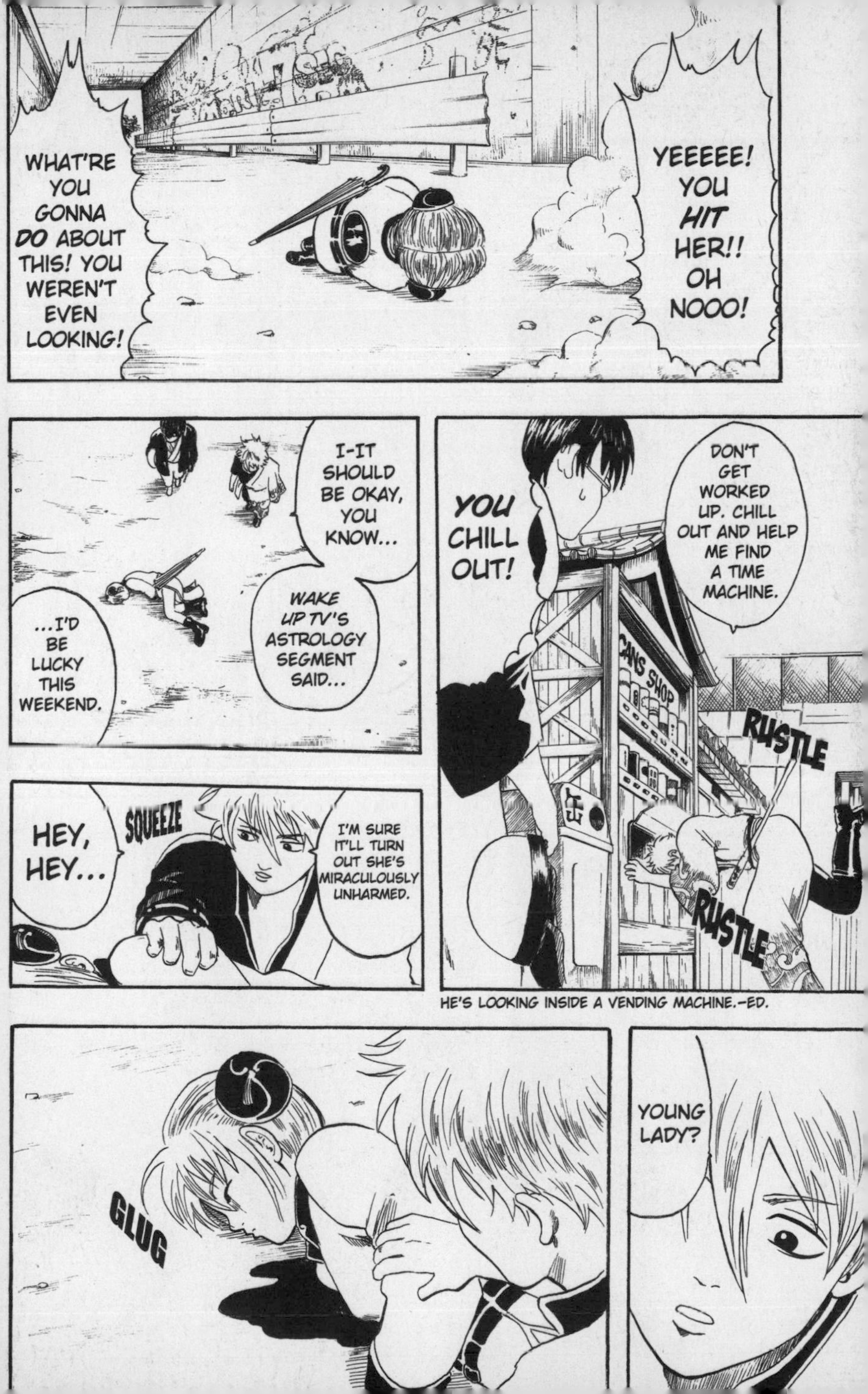
YEEEEE! YOU HIT HER!! OH NOOO!
WHAT'RE YOU GONNA DO ABOUT THIS! YOU WEREN'T EVEN LOOKING!
DON'T GET WORKED UP. CHILL OUT AND HELP ME FIND A TIME MACHINE.
YOU CHILL OUT!
CANS SHOP
RUSTLE
RUSTLE
HE'S LOOKING INSIDE A VENDING MACHINE.-ED.
I-IT SHOULD BE OKAY, YOU KNOW...
WAKE UP TV'S ASTROLOGY SEGMENT SAID...
...I'D BE LUCKY THIS WEEKEND.
I'M SURE IT'LL TURN OUT SHE'S MIRACULOUSLY UNHARMED.
SQUEEZE
HEY, HEY...
YOUNG LADY?
GLUG

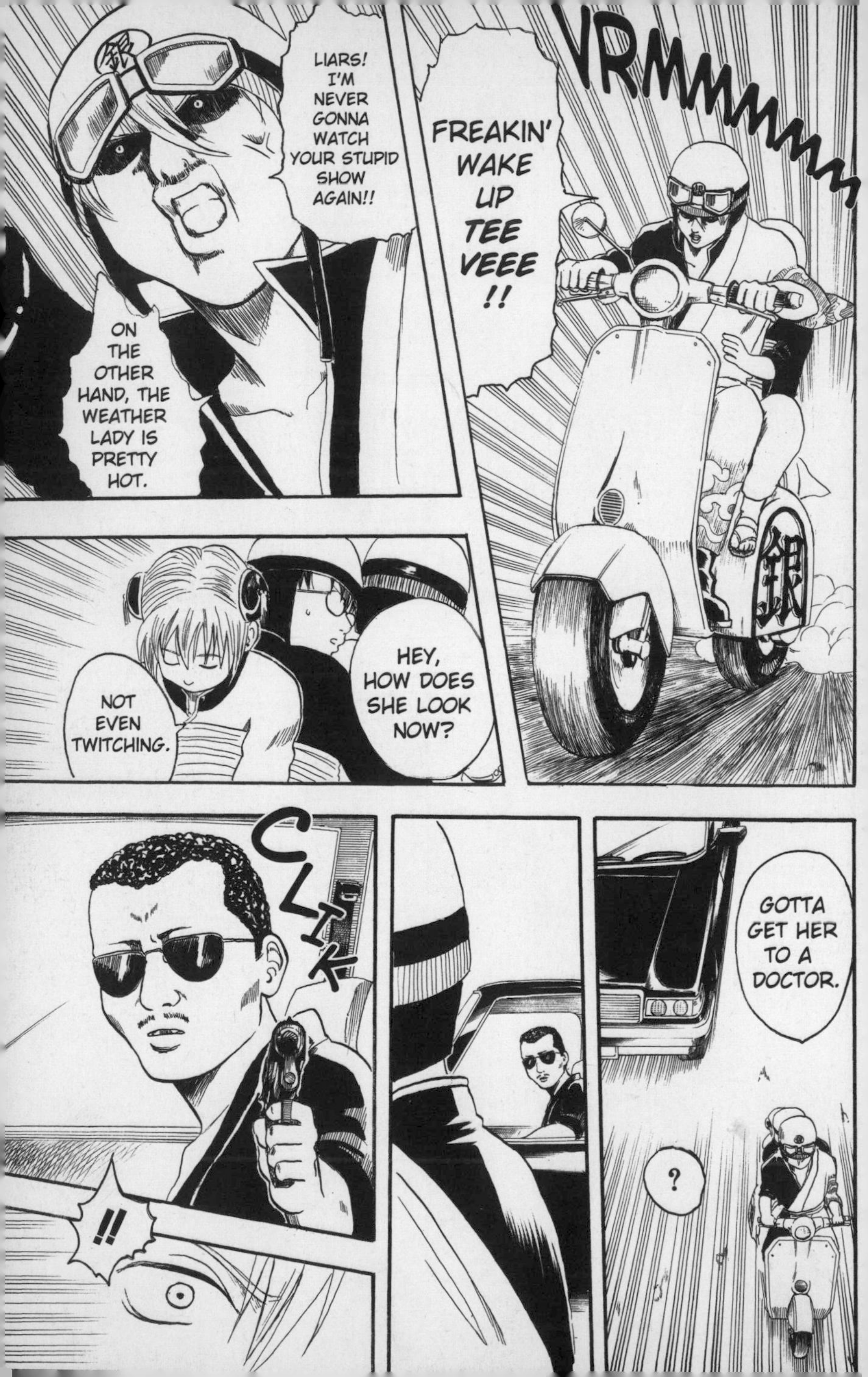
VRMMMMMM
FREAKIN' WAKE UP TEE VEEE!!
LIARS! I'M NEVER GONNA WATCH YOUR STUPID SHOW AGAIN!!
ON THE OTHER HAND, THE WEATHER LADY IS PRETTY HOT.
HEY, HOW DOES SHE LOOK NOW?
NOT EVEN TWITCHING.
GOTTA GET HER TO A DOCTOR.
?
CLIK
!!

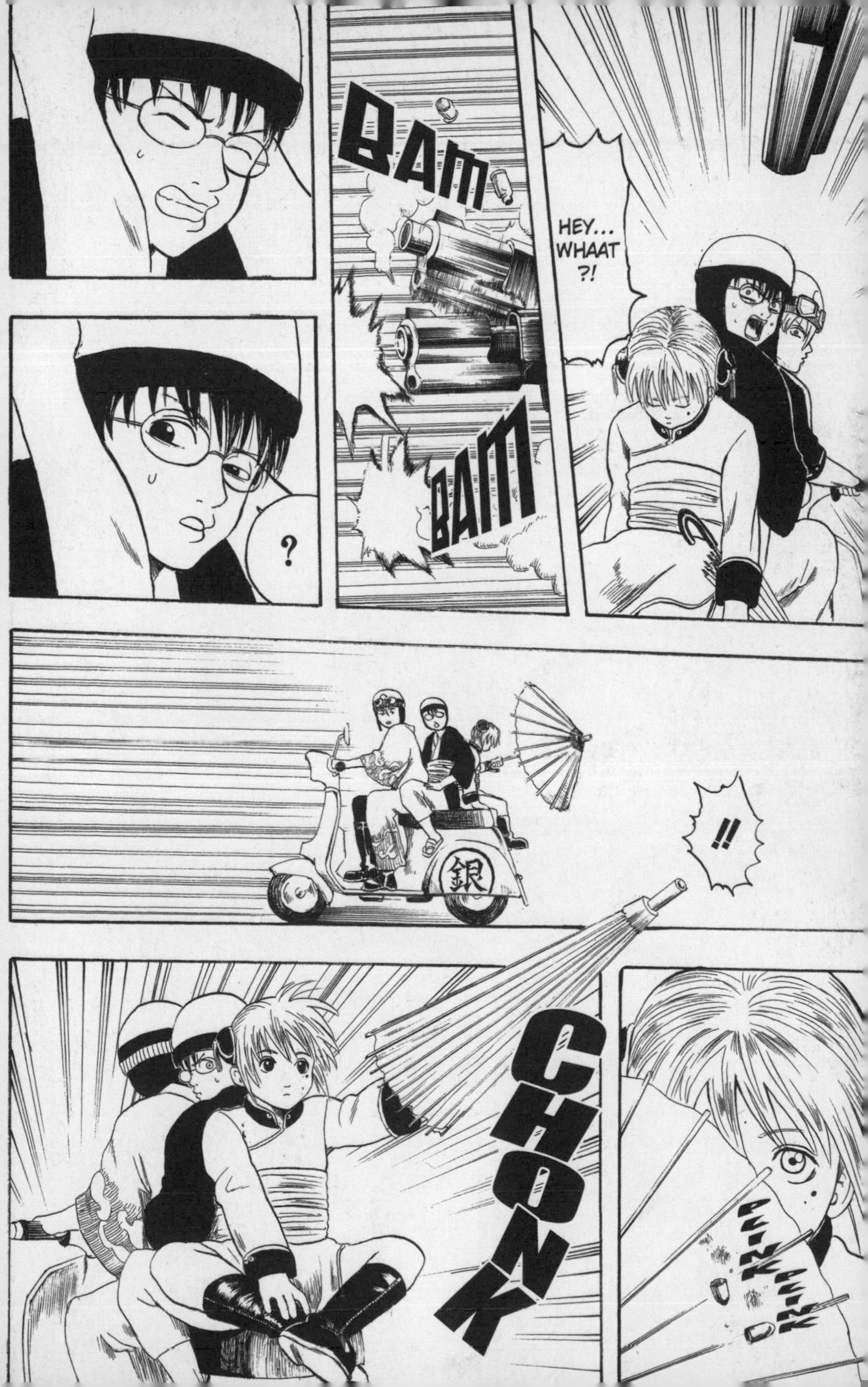
HEY... WHAAT ?!
BAM
BAM
?
!!
PLINK PLINK
CHONK

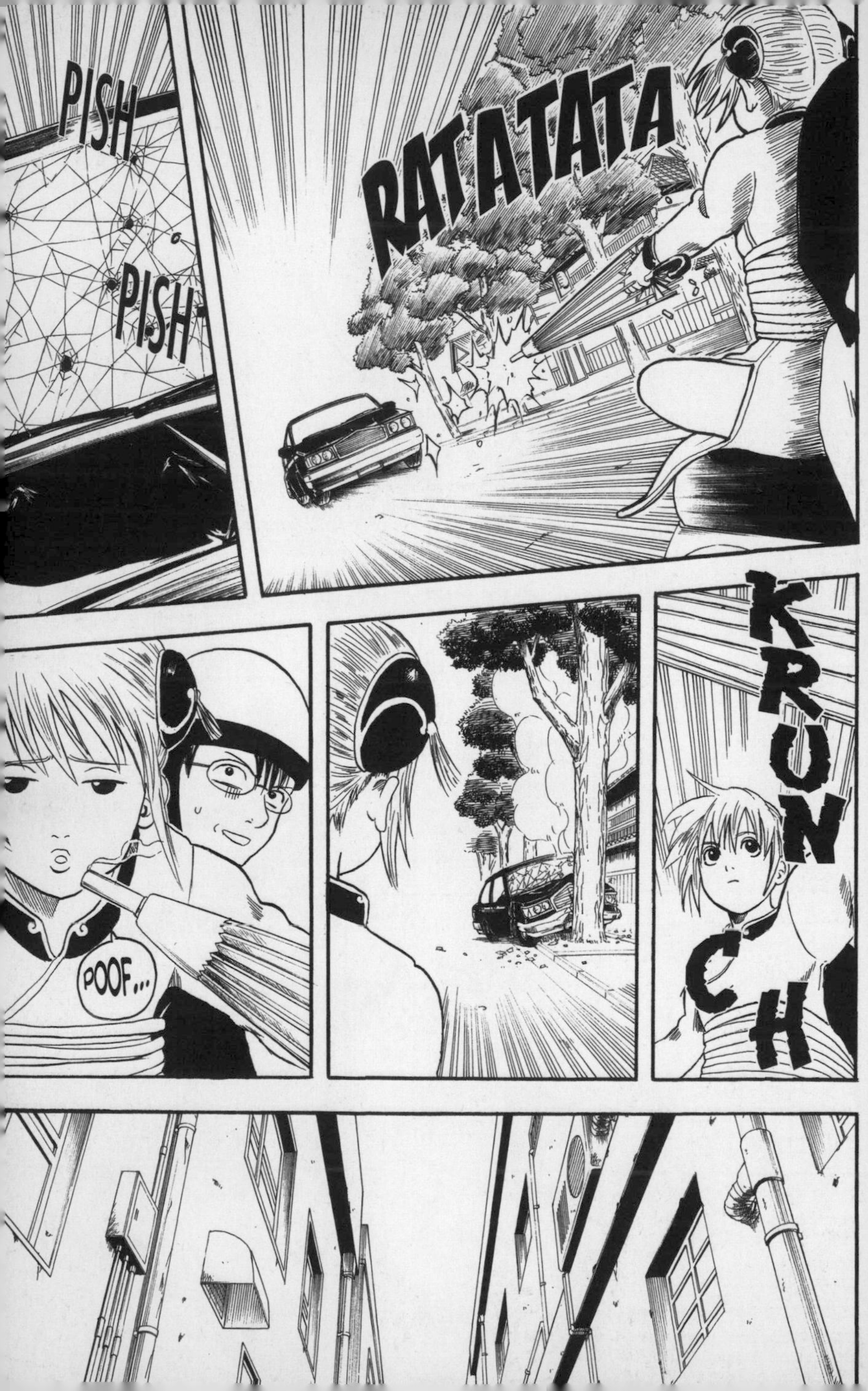
RATATATA
PISH
PISH
KRUNCH
POOF...

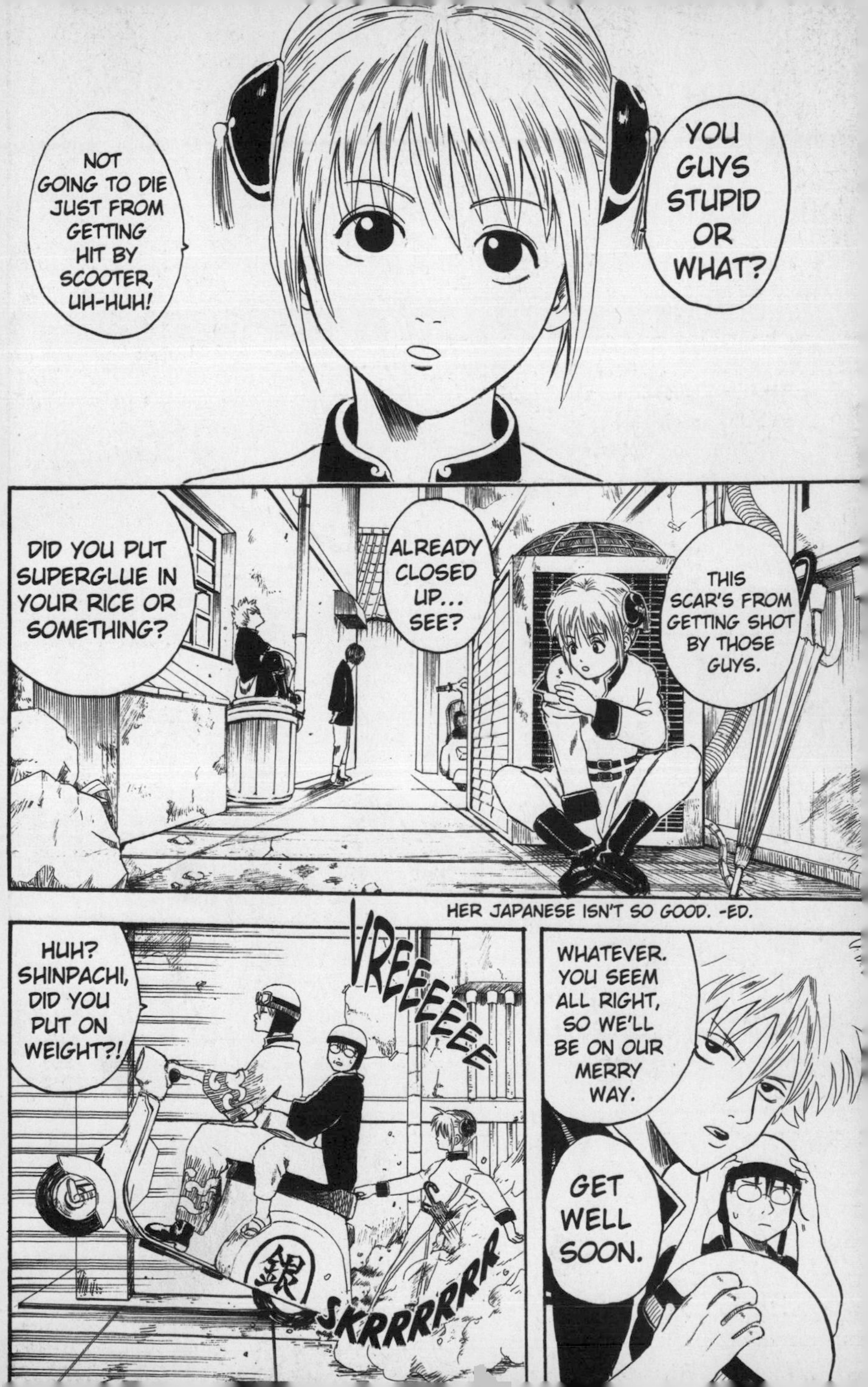
YOU GUYS STUPID OR WHAT?
NOT GOING TO DIE JUST FROM GETTING HIT BY SCOOTER, UH-HUH!
THIS SCAR'S FROM GETTING SHOT BY THOSE GUYS.
ALREADY CLOSED UP... SEE?
DID YOU PUT SUPERGLUE IN YOUR RICE OR SOMETHING?
HER JAPANESE ISN'T SO GOOD. -ED.
WHATEVER. YOU SEEM ALL RIGHT, SO WE'LL BE ON OUR MERRY WAY.
GET WELL SOON.
VREEEEEEE
HUH? SHINPACHI, DID YOU PUT ON WEIGHT?!
SKRRRRRR

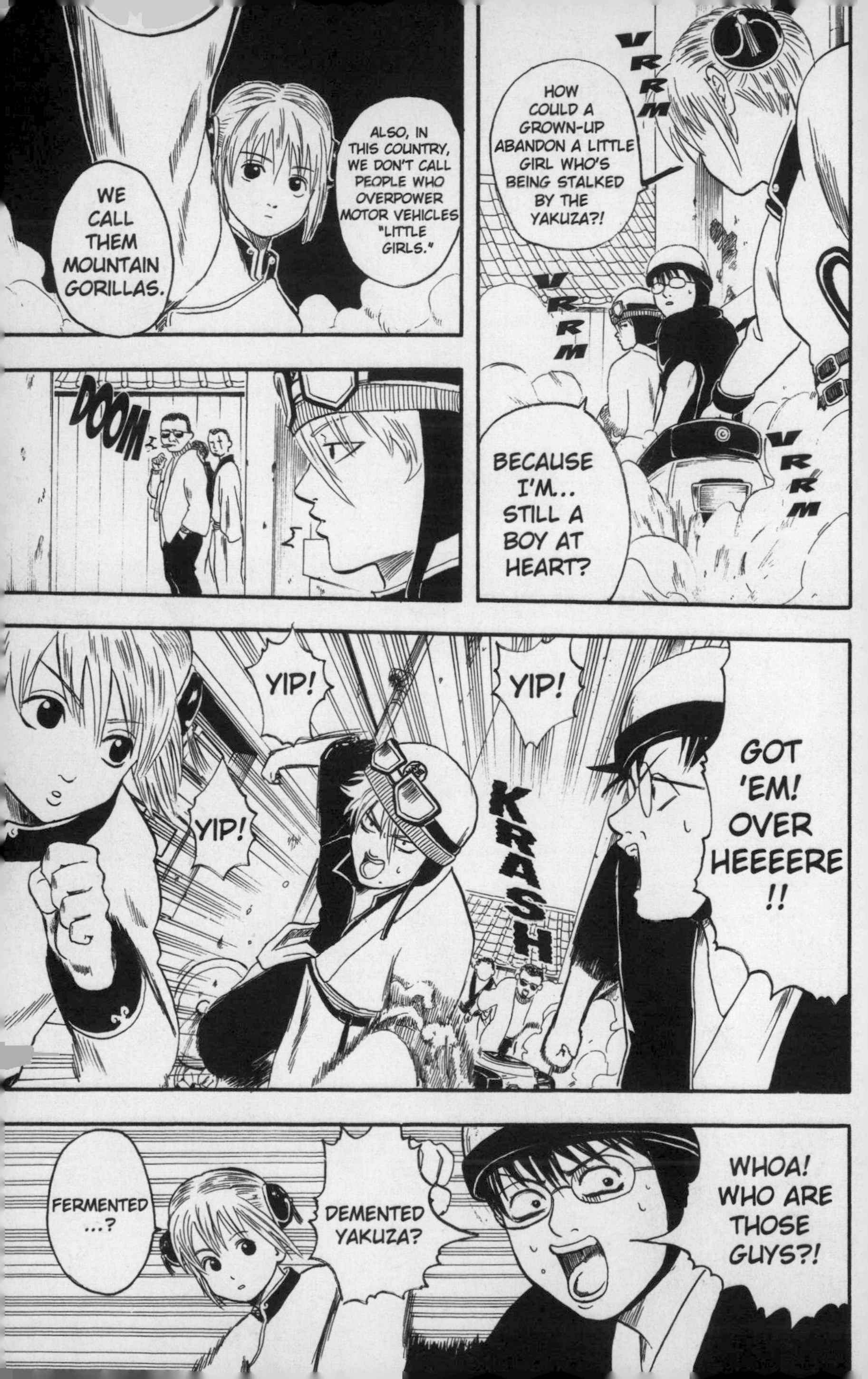
VRRM
HOW COULD A GROWN-UP ABANDON A LITTLE GIRL WHO'S BEING STALKED BY THE YAKUZA?!
VRRM
VRRM
BECAUSE I'M... STILL A BOY AT HEART?
ALSO, IN THIS COUNTRY, WE DON'T CALL PEOPLE WHO OVERPOWER MOTOR VEHICLES "LITTLE GIRLS."
WE CALL THEM MOUNTAIN GORILLAS.
DOOM
GOT 'EM! OVER HEEEEERE!!
YIP!
KRASH
YIP!
YIP!
WHOA! WHO ARE THOSE GUYS?!
DEMENTED YAKUZA?
FERMENTED ...?

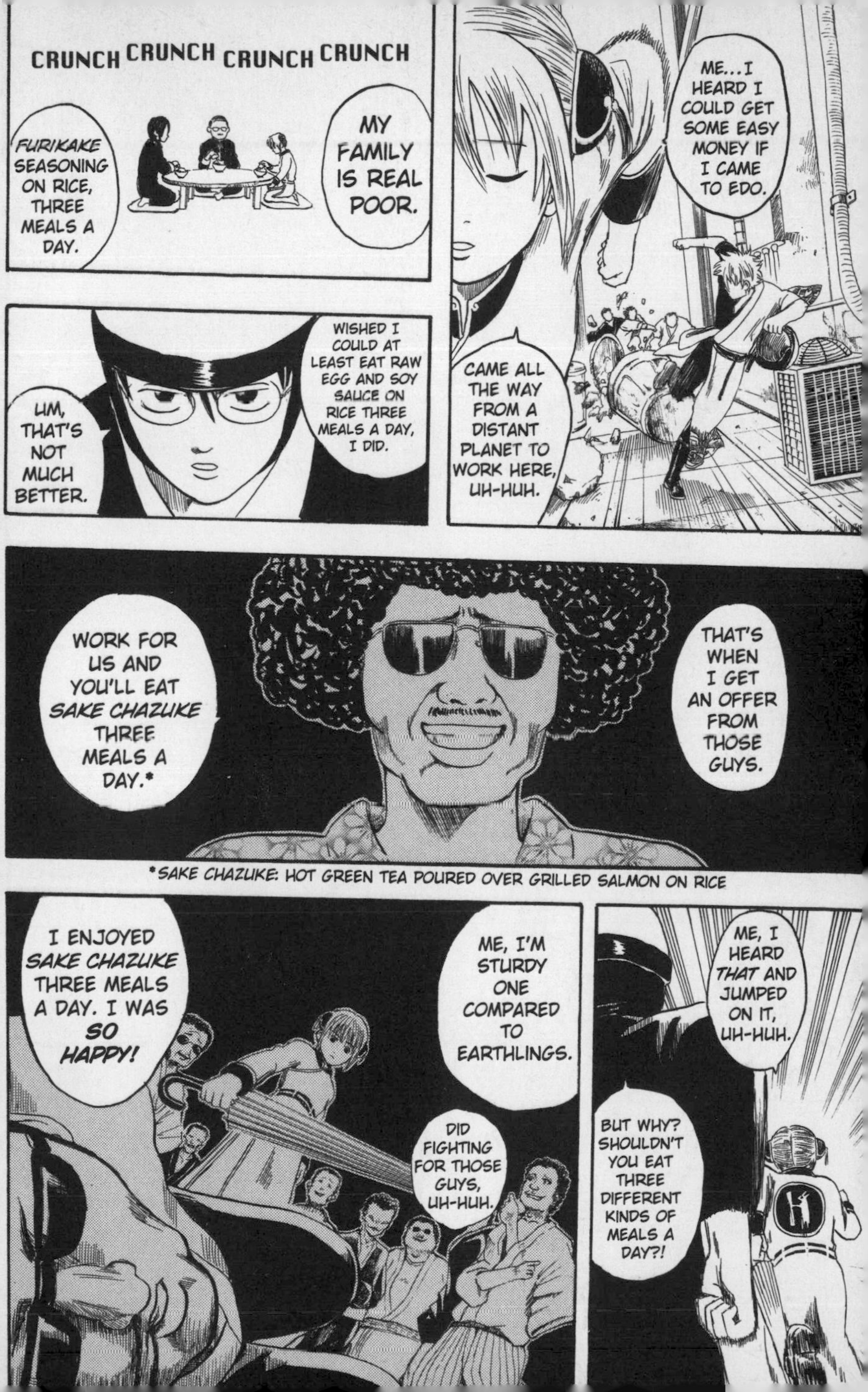
ME...I HEARD I COULD GET SOME EASY MONEY IF I CAME TO EDO.
CAME ALL THE WAY FROM A DISTANT PLANET TO WORK HERE, UH-HUH.
CRUNCH CRUNCH CRUNCH CRUNCH
MY FAMILY IS REAL POOR.
FURIKAKE SEASONING ON RICE, THREE MEALS A DAY.
WISHED I COULD AT LEAST EAT RAW EGG AND SOY SAUCE ON RICE THREE MEALS A DAY, I DID.
UM, THAT'S NOT MUCH BETTER.
THAT'S WHEN I GET AN OFFER FROM THOSE GUYS.
WORK FOR US AND YOU'LL EAT *SAKE CHAZUKE* THREE MEALS A DAY.*
ME, I HEARD *THAT* AND JUMPED ON IT, UH-HUH.
BUT WHY? SHOULDN'T YOU EAT THREE DIFFERENT KINDS OF MEALS A DAY?!
ME, I'M STURDY ONE COMPARED TO EARTHLINGS.
I ENJOYED *SAKE CHAZUKE* THREE MEALS A DAY. I WAS **SO HAPPY!**
DID FIGHTING FOR THOSE GUYS, UH-HUH.

*SAKE CHAZUKE: HOT GREEN TEA POURED OVER GRILLED SALMON ON RICE

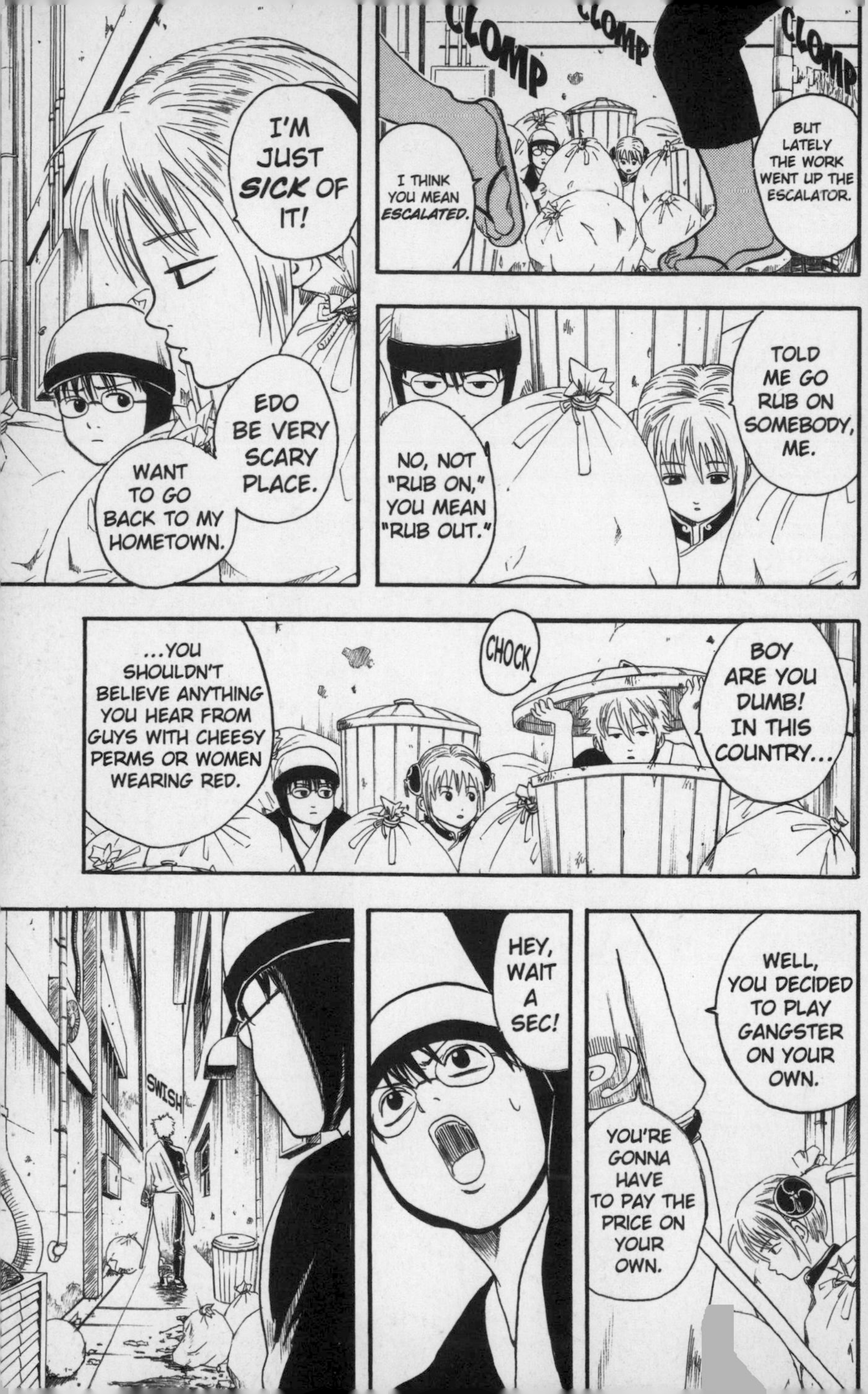
CLOMP
CLOMP
CLOMP
BUT LATELY THE WORK WENT UP THE ESCALATOR.
I THINK YOU MEAN *ESCALATED.*
TOLD ME GO RUB ON SOMEBODY, ME.
NO, NOT "RUB ON," YOU MEAN "RUB OUT."
I'M JUST *SICK* OF IT!
EDO BE VERY SCARY PLACE.
WANT TO GO BACK TO MY HOMETOWN.
BOY ARE YOU DUMB! IN THIS COUNTRY...
CHOCK
...YOU SHOULDN'T BELIEVE ANYTHING YOU HEAR FROM GUYS WITH CHEESY PERMS OR WOMEN WEARING RED.
WELL, YOU DECIDED TO PLAY GANGSTER ON YOUR OWN.
YOU'RE GONNA HAVE TO PAY THE PRICE ON YOUR OWN.
HEY, WAIT A SEC!
SWISH

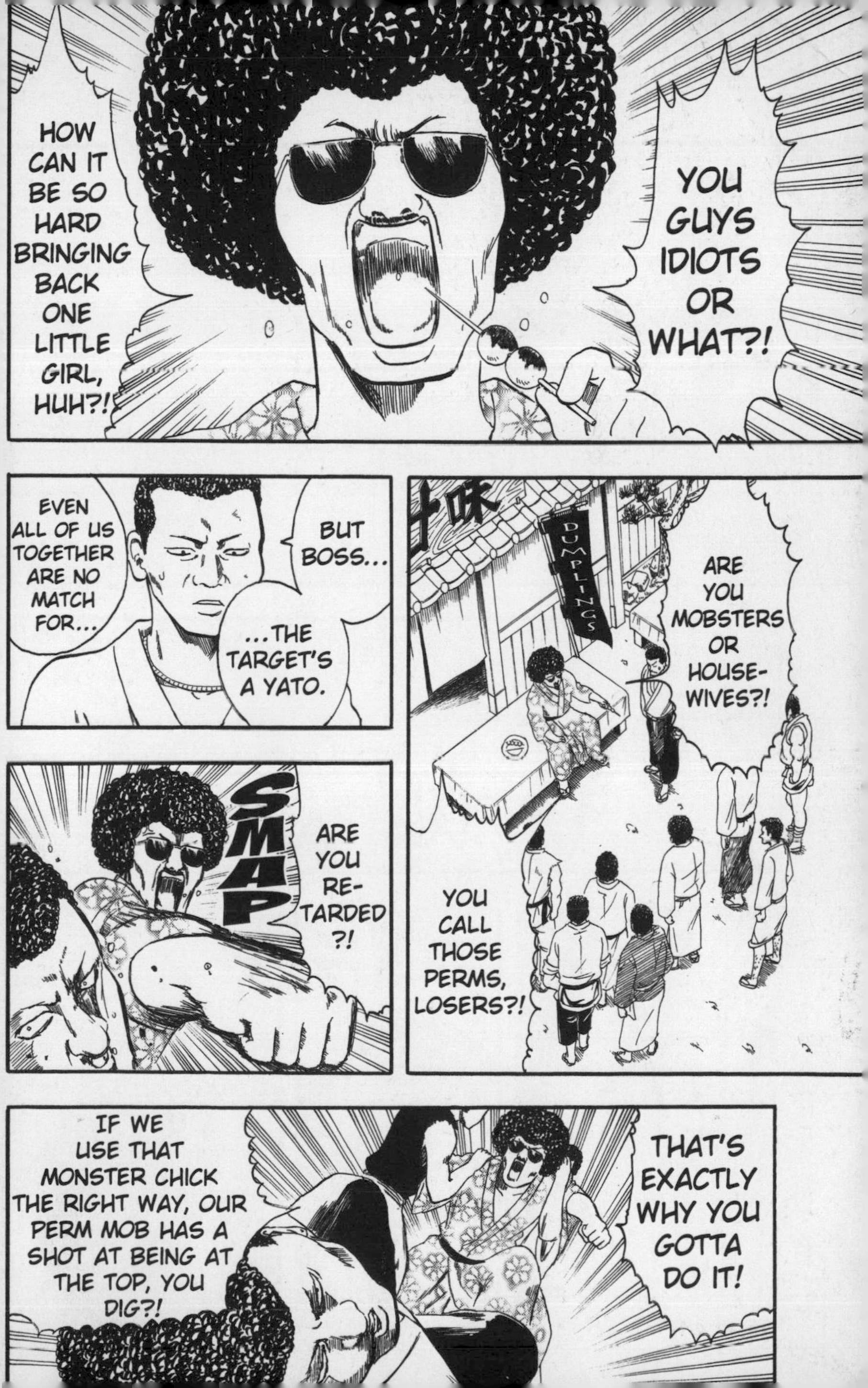
YOU GUYS IDIOTS OR WHAT?!
HOW CAN IT BE SO HARD BRINGING BACK ONE LITTLE GIRL, HUH?!
DUMPLINGS
ARE YOU MOBSTERS OR HOUSE-WIVES?!
YOU CALL THOSE PERMS, LOSERS?!
BUT BOSS...
EVEN ALL OF US TOGETHER ARE NO MATCH FOR...
...THE TARGET'S A YATO.
ARE YOU RE-TARDED?!
SMAP
THAT'S EXACTLY WHY YOU GOTTA DO IT!
IF WE USE THAT MONSTER CHICK THE RIGHT WAY, OUR PERM MOB HAS A SHOT AT BEING AT THE TOP, YOU DIG?!

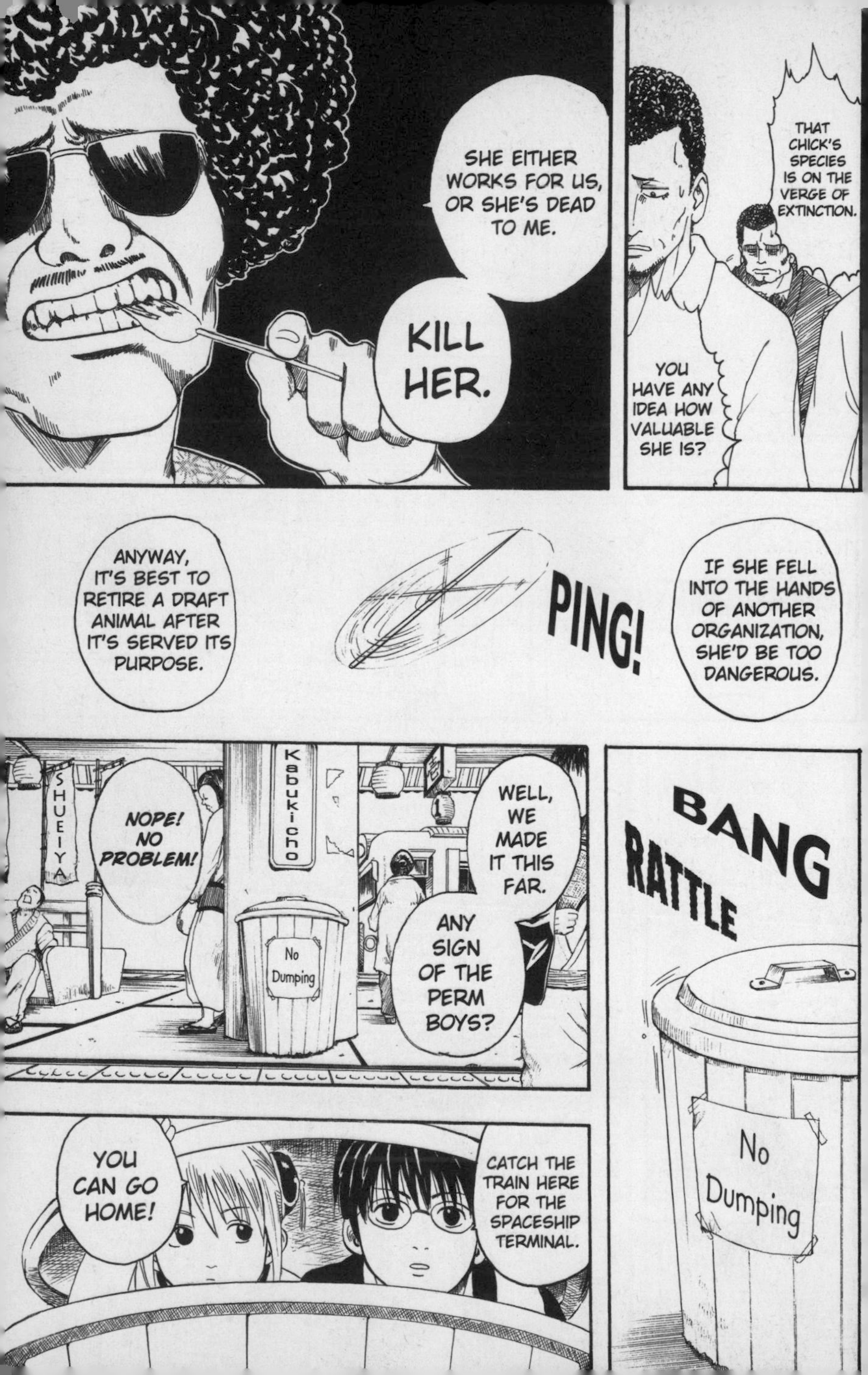
THAT CHICK'S SPECIES IS ON THE VERGE OF EXTINCTION.
YOU HAVE ANY IDEA HOW VALUABLE SHE IS?
SHE EITHER WORKS FOR US, OR SHE'S DEAD TO ME.
KILL HER.
IF SHE FELL INTO THE HANDS OF ANOTHER ORGANIZATION, SHE'D BE TOO DANGEROUS.
PING!
ANYWAY, IT'S BEST TO RETIRE A DRAFT ANIMAL AFTER IT'S SERVED ITS PURPOSE.
BANG
RATTLE
No Dumping
Kabukicho
SHUEIYA
WELL, WE MADE IT THIS FAR.
ANY SIGN OF THE PERM BOYS?
NOPE! NO PROBLEM!
No Dumping
CATCH THE TRAIN HERE FOR THE SPACESHIP TERMINAL.
YOU CAN GO HOME!

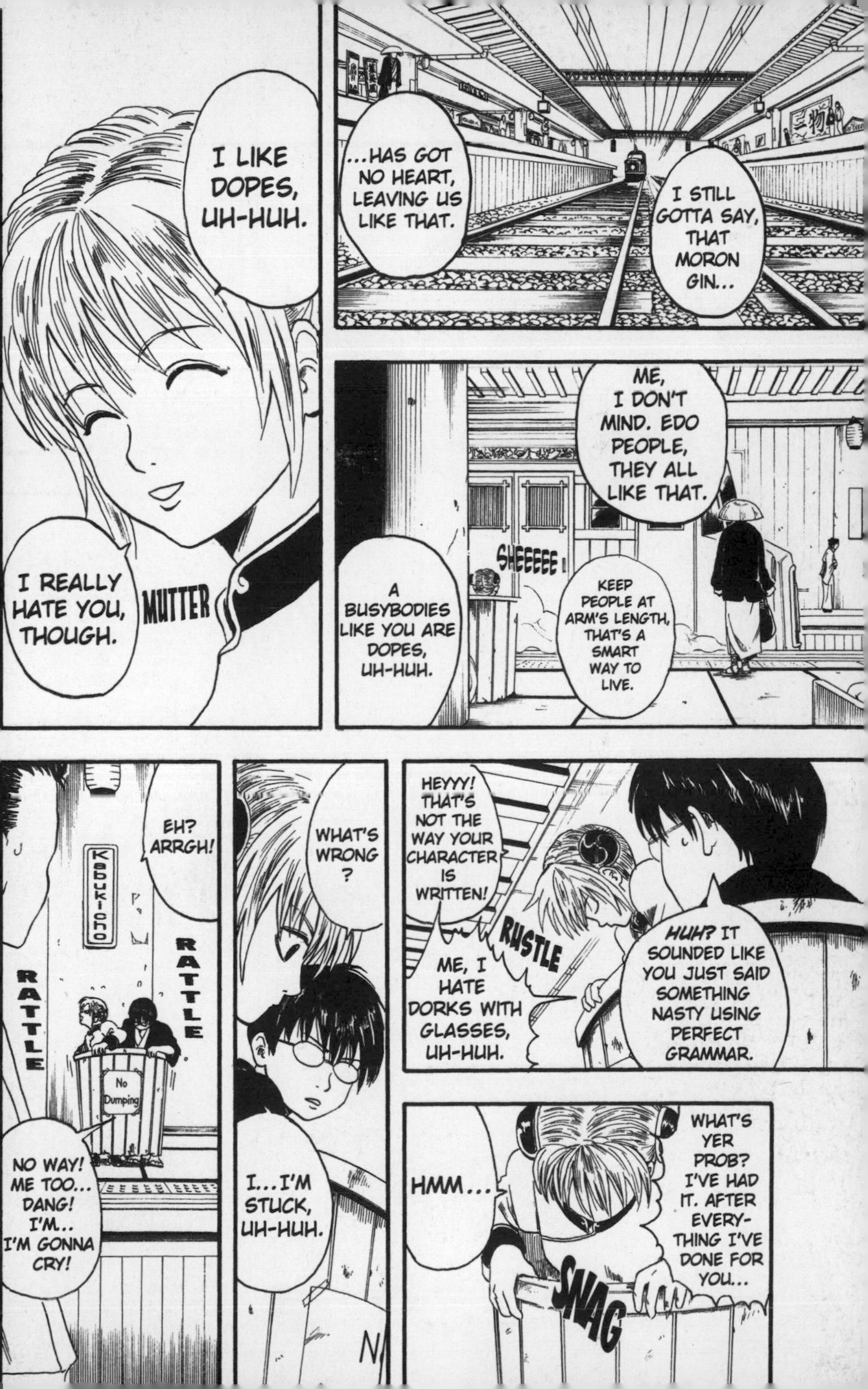
I STILL GOTTA SAY, THAT MORON GIN...
...HAS GOT NO HEART, LEAVING US LIKE THAT.
ME, I DON'T MIND. EDO PEOPLE, THEY ALL LIKE THAT.
KEEP PEOPLE AT ARM'S LENGTH, THAT'S A SMART WAY TO LIVE.
SHEEEEE
A BUSYBODIES LIKE YOU ARE DOPES, UH-HUH.
I LIKE DOPES, UH-HUH.
MUTTER
I REALLY HATE YOU, THOUGH.
HEYYY! THAT'S NOT THE WAY YOUR CHARACTER IS WRITTEN!
RUSTLE
ME, I HATE DORKS WITH GLASSES, UH-HUH.
HUH? IT SOUNDED LIKE YOU JUST SAID SOMETHING NASTY USING PERFECT GRAMMAR.
WHAT'S YER PROB? I'VE HAD IT. AFTER EVERY-THING I'VE DONE FOR YOU...
HMM...
SNAG
WHAT'S WRONG?
I...I'M STUCK, UH-HUH.
EH? ARRGH!
Kabukicho
RATTLE
RATTLE
No Dumping
NO WAY! ME TOO... DANG! I'M.. I'M GONNA CRY!

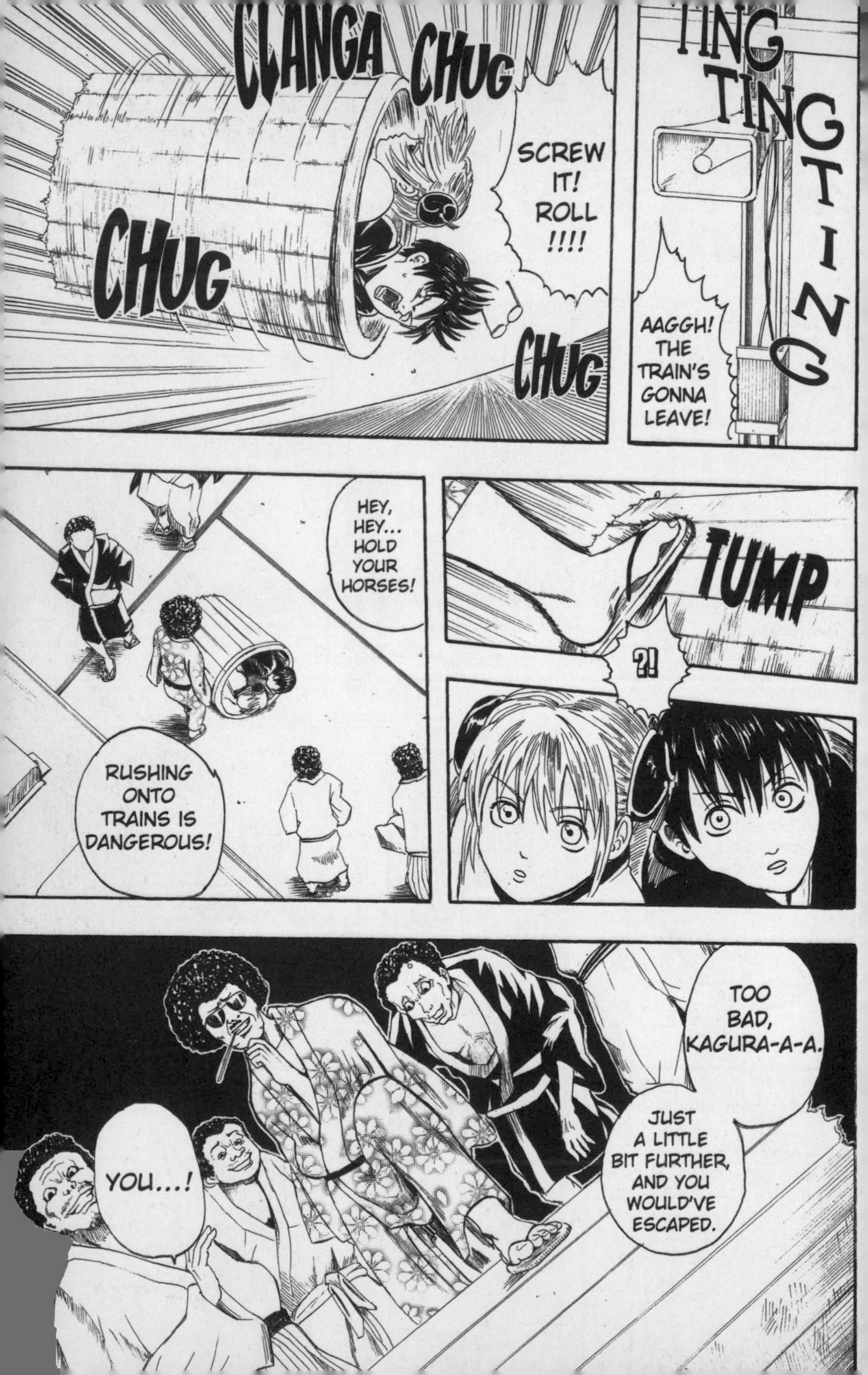
TING TING TING
AAGGH! THE TRAIN'S GONNA LEAVE!
CLANGA CHUG
SCREW IT! ROLL!!!!
CHUG
CHUG
TUMP
?!
HEY, HEY... HOLD YOUR HORSES!
RUSHING ONTO TRAINS IS DANGEROUS!
TOO BAD, KAGURA-A-A.
JUST A LITTLE BIT FURTHER, AND YOU WOULD'VE ESCAPED.
YOU...!

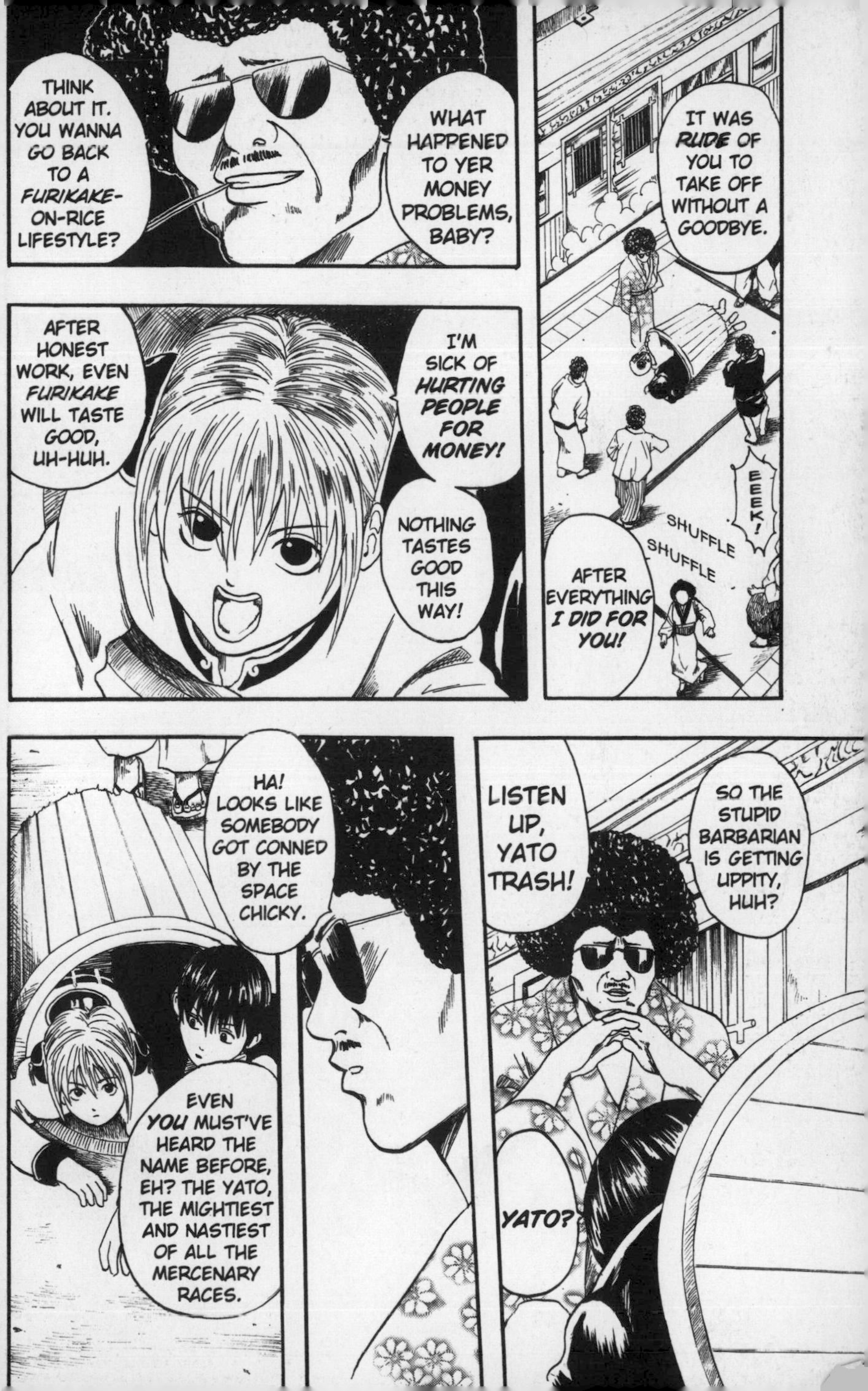
IT WAS RUDE OF YOU TO TAKE OFF WITHOUT A GOODBYE.
EEEK!
SHUFFLE SHUFFLE
AFTER EVERYTHING I DID FOR YOU!
WHAT HAPPENED TO YER MONEY PROBLEMS, BABY?
THINK ABOUT IT. YOU WANNA GO BACK TO A FURIKAKE-ON-RICE LIFESTYLE?
I'M SICK OF HURTING PEOPLE FOR MONEY!
NOTHING TASTES GOOD THIS WAY!
AFTER HONEST WORK, EVEN FURIKAKE WILL TASTE GOOD, UH-HUH.
SO THE STUPID BARBARIAN IS GETTING UPPITY, HUH?
LISTEN UP, YATO TRASH!
YATO?
HA! LOOKS LIKE SOMEBODY GOT CONNED BY THE SPACE CHICKY.
EVEN YOU MUST'VE HEARD THE NAME BEFORE, EH? THE YATO, THE MIGHTIEST AND NASTIEST OF ALL THE MERCENARY RACES.

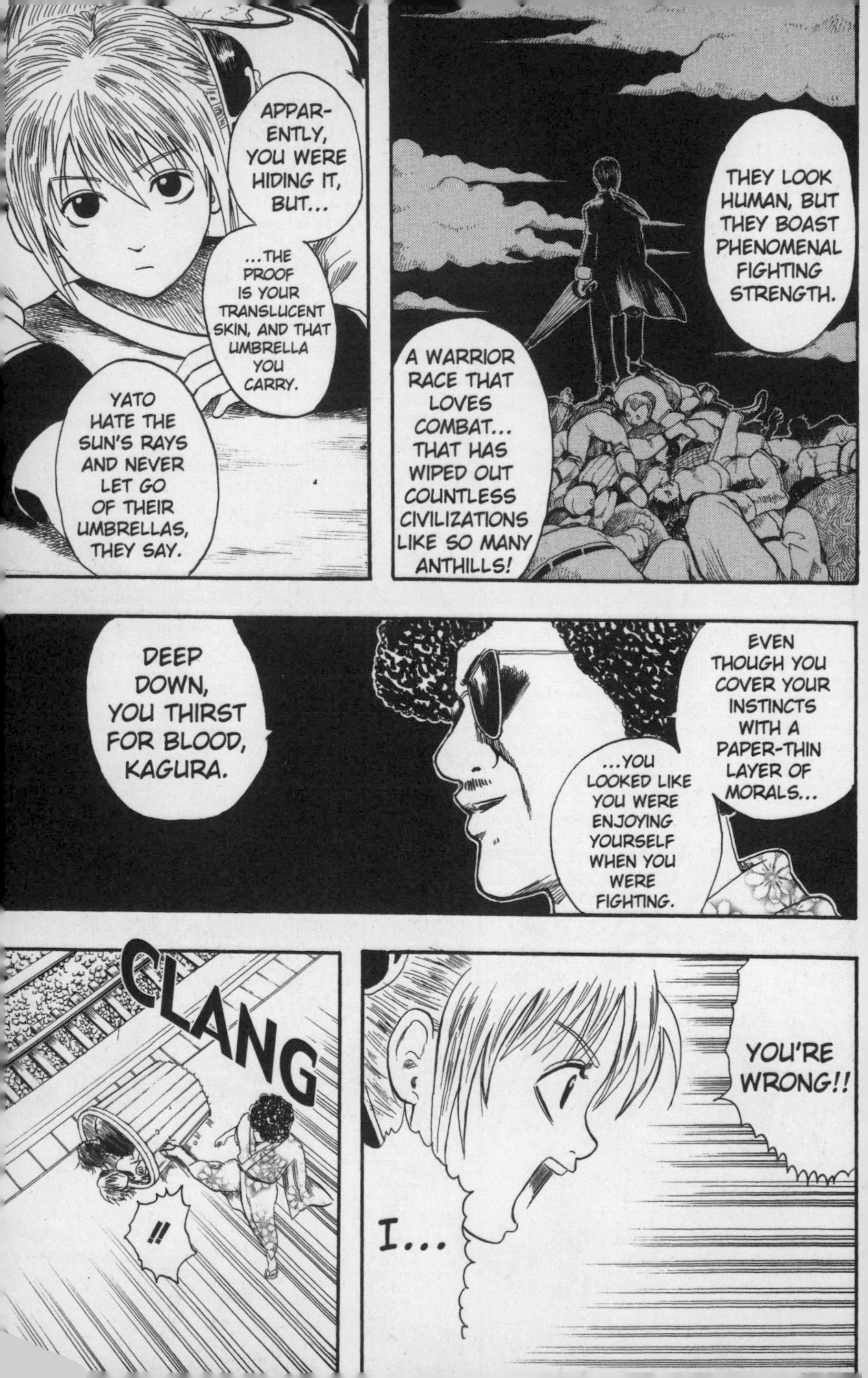
THEY LOOK HUMAN, BUT THEY BOAST PHENOMENAL FIGHTING STRENGTH.
A WARRIOR RACE THAT LOVES COMBAT... THAT HAS WIPED OUT COUNTLESS CIVILIZATIONS LIKE SO MANY ANTHILLS!
APPARENTLY, YOU WERE HIDING IT, BUT...
...THE PROOF IS YOUR TRANSLUCENT SKIN, AND THAT UMBRELLA YOU CARRY.
YATO HATE THE SUN'S RAYS AND NEVER LET GO OF THEIR UMBRELLAS, THEY SAY.
EVEN THOUGH YOU COVER YOUR INSTINCTS WITH A PAPER-THIN LAYER OF MORALS...
...YOU LOOKED LIKE YOU WERE ENJOYING YOURSELF WHEN YOU WERE FIGHTING.
DEEP DOWN, YOU THIRST FOR BLOOD, KAGURA.
YOU'RE WRONG!!
I...
CLANG
!!

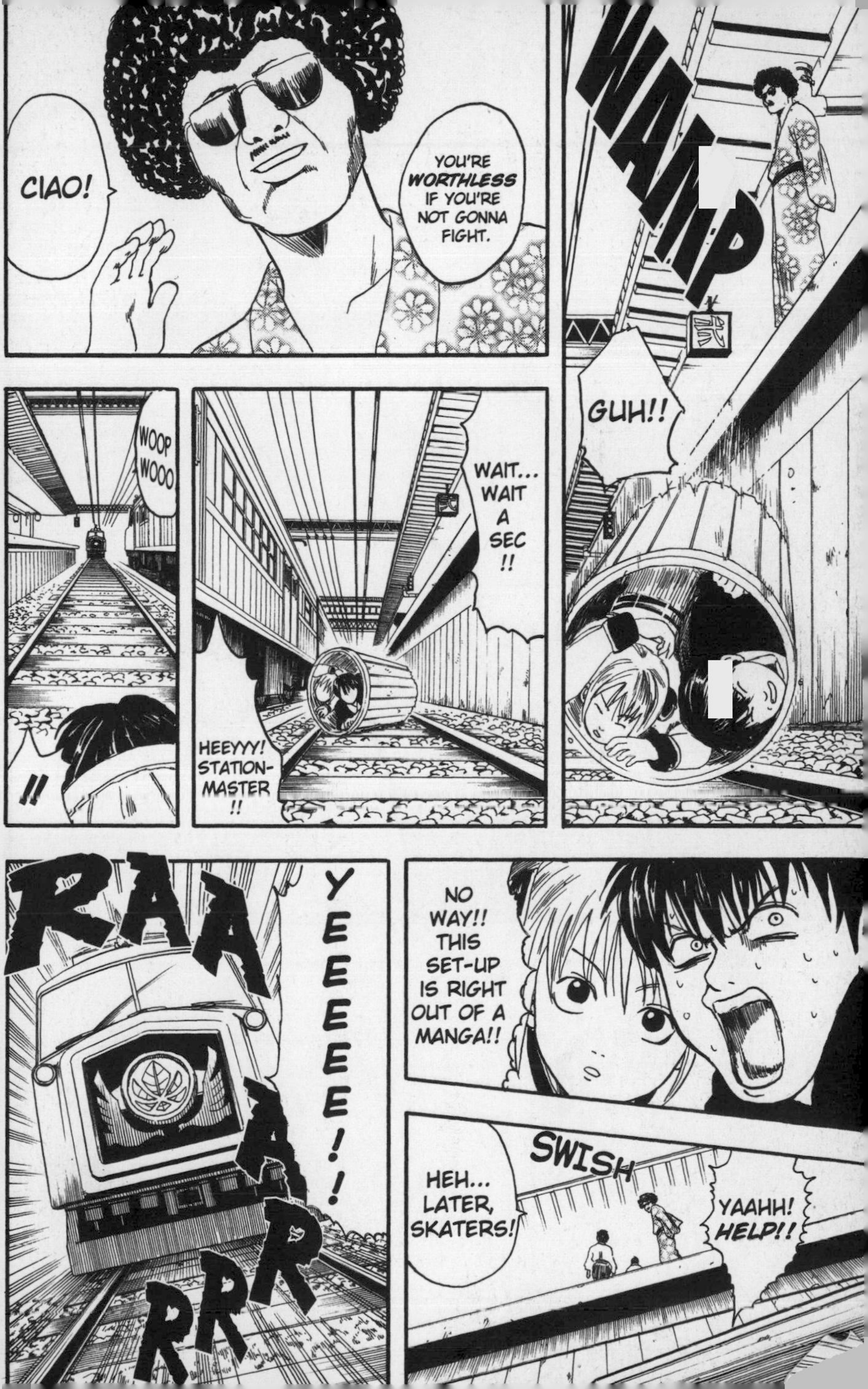
WAMP
GUH!!
YOU'RE *WORTHLESS* IF YOU'RE NOT GONNA FIGHT.
CIAO!
WAIT... WAIT A SEC !!
HEEYYY! STATION-MASTER !!
WOOP WOOO
!!
NO WAY!! THIS SET-UP IS RIGHT OUT OF A MANGA!!
SWISH
YAAHH! *HELP!!*
HEH... LATER, SKATERS!
YEEEEE!!
RAAA
RRRR

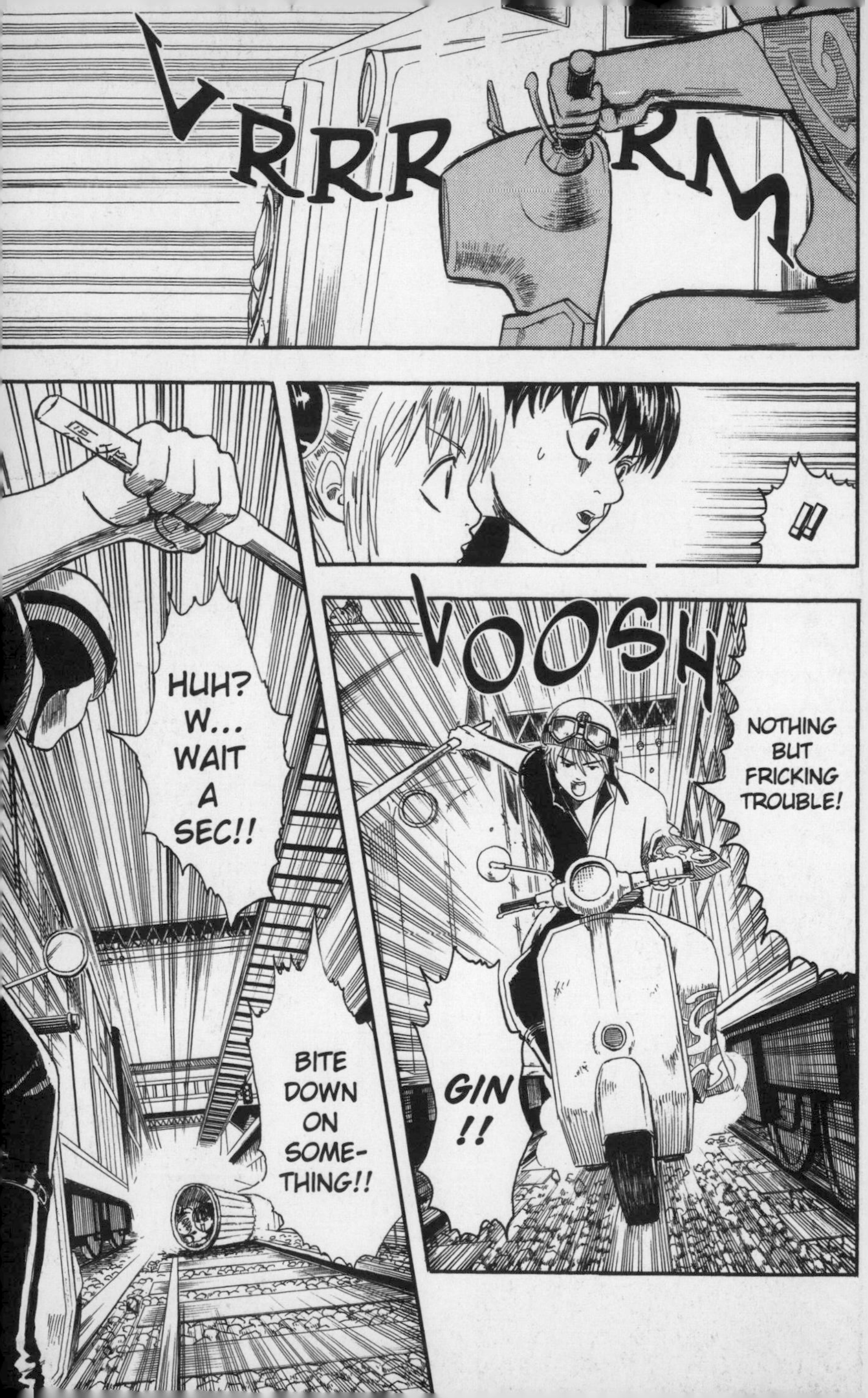
VRRRRM
!!
VOOSH
NOTHING BUT FRICKING TROUBLE!
GIN!!
HUH? W... WAIT A SEC!!
BITE DOWN ON SOMETHING!!

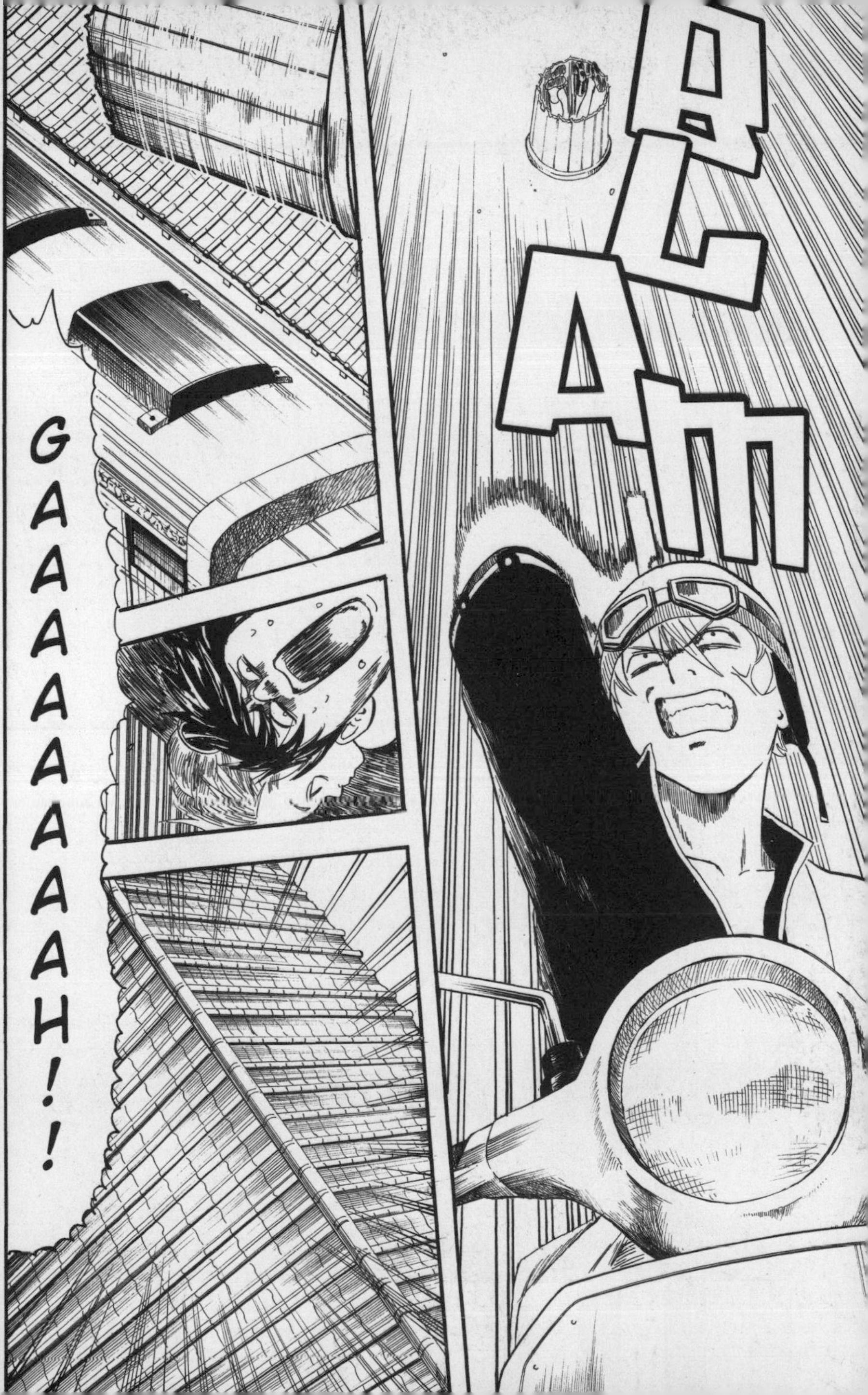
SLAM
GAAAAAAAAH!!

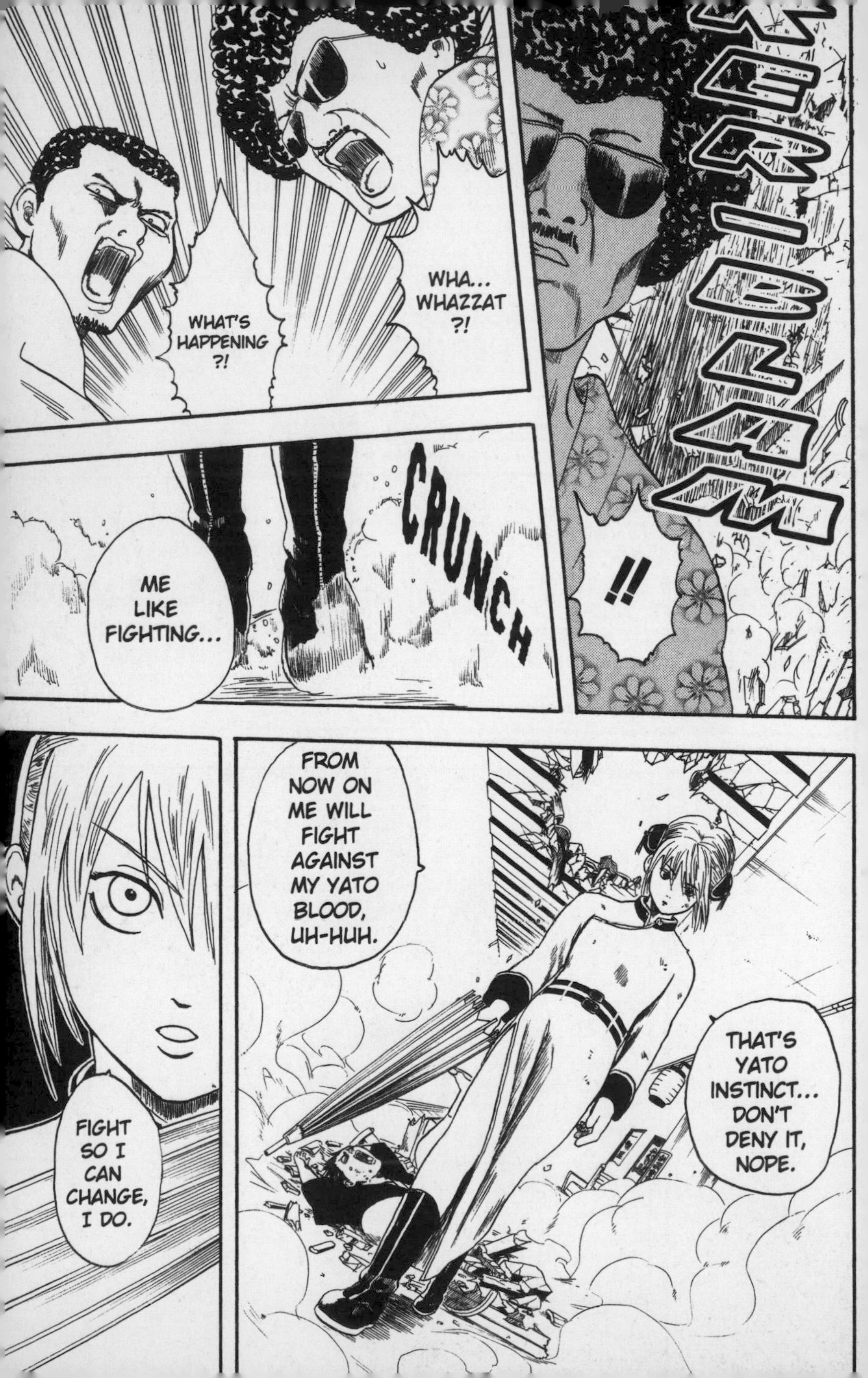
!!
WHA... WHAZZAT ?!
WHAT'S HAPPENING ?!
CRUNCH
ME LIKE FIGHTING...
THAT'S YATO INSTINCT... DON'T DENY IT, NOPE.
FROM NOW ON ME WILL FIGHT AGAINST MY YATO BLOOD, UH-HUH.
FIGHT SO I CAN CHANGE, I DO.

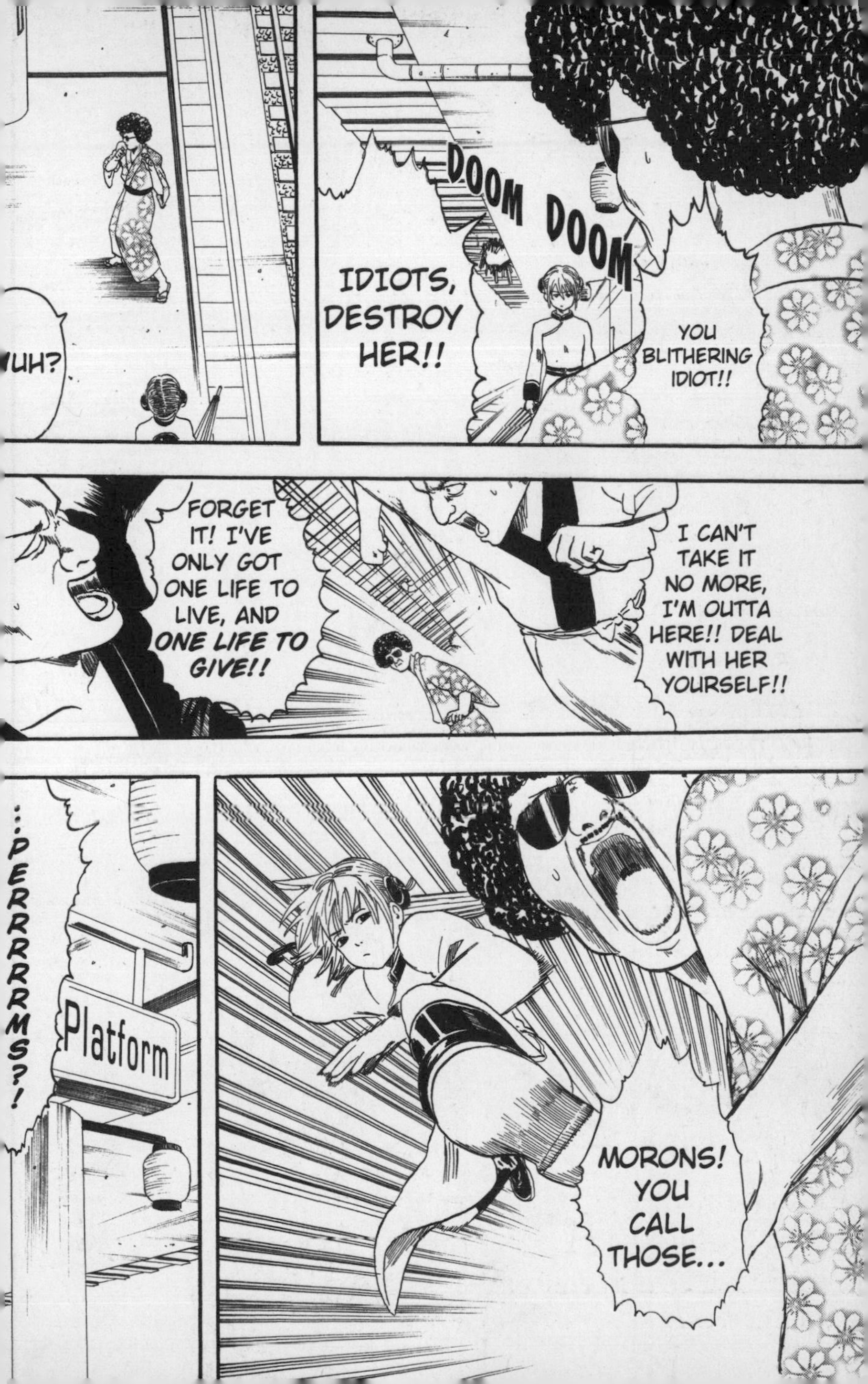
DOOM DOOM
YOU BLITHERING IDIOT!!
IDIOTS, DESTROY HER!!
UH?
I CAN'T TAKE IT NO MORE, I'M OUTTA HERE!! DEAL WITH HER YOURSELF!!
FORGET IT! I'VE ONLY GOT ONE LIFE TO LIVE, AND ONE LIFE TO GIVE!!
MORONS! YOU CALL THOSE...
Platform
...PERRRRRRMS?!

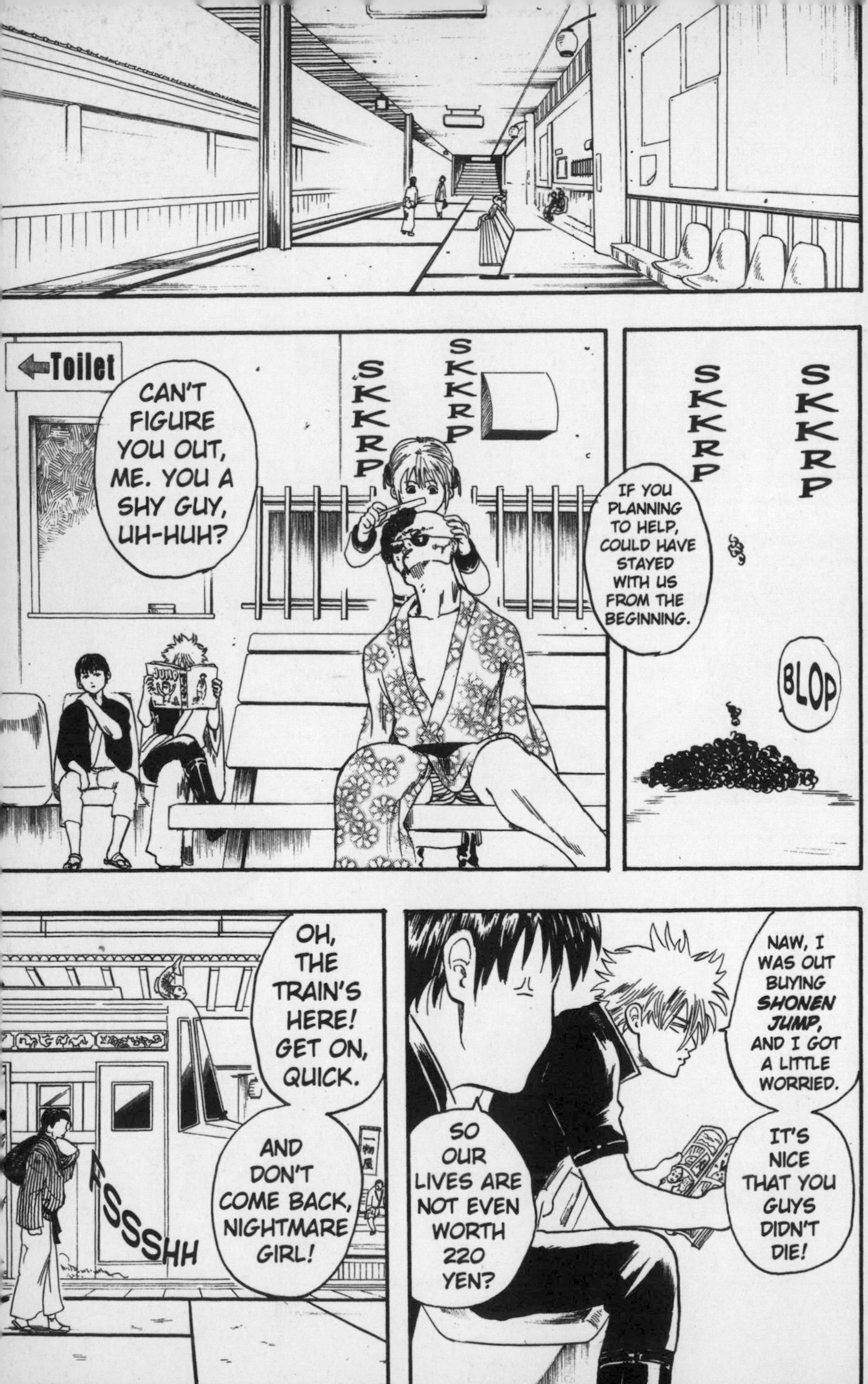
SKKRP
SKKRP
IF YOU PLANNING TO HELP, COULD HAVE STAYED WITH US FROM THE BEGINNING.
BLOP
SKKRP
SKKRP
CAN'T FIGURE YOU OUT, ME. YOU A SHY GUY, UH-HUH?
Toilet
NAW, I WAS OUT BUYING *SHONEN JUMP*, AND I GOT A LITTLE WORRIED.
IT'S NICE THAT YOU GUYS DIDN'T DIE!
SO OUR LIVES ARE NOT EVEN WORTH 220 YEN?
OH, THE TRAIN'S HERE! GET ON, QUICK.
AND DON'T COME BACK, NIGHTMARE GIRL!
FSSSHH

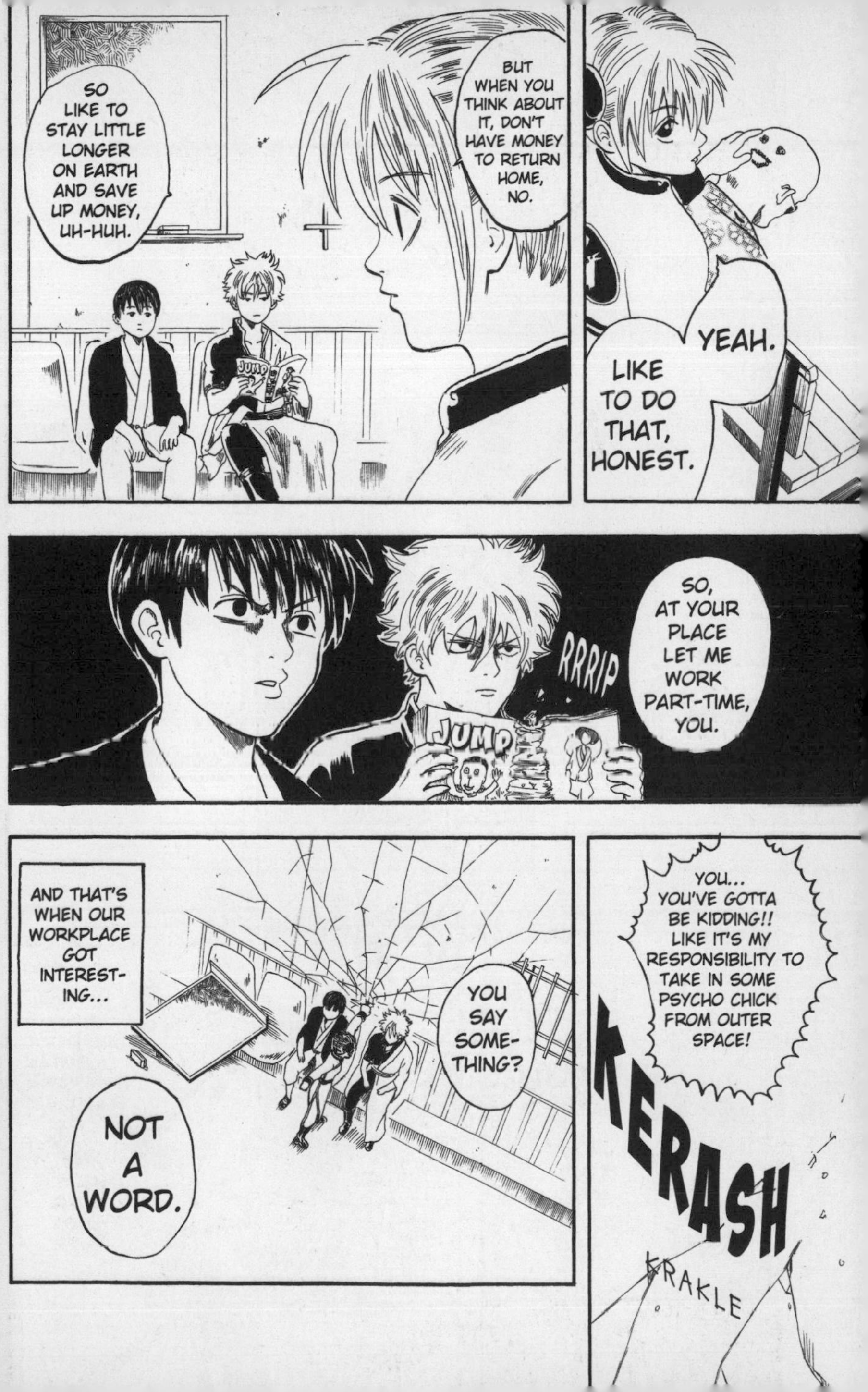
YEAH.
LIKE TO DO THAT, HONEST.
BUT WHEN YOU THINK ABOUT IT, DON'T HAVE MONEY TO RETURN HOME, NO.
SO LIKE TO STAY LITTLE LONGER ON EARTH AND SAVE UP MONEY, UH-HUH.
SO, AT YOUR PLACE LET ME WORK PART-TIME, YOU.
RRRIP
JUMP
YOU... YOU'VE GOTTA BE KIDDING!! LIKE IT'S MY RESPONSIBILITY TO TAKE IN SOME PSYCHO CHICK FROM OUTER SPACE!
KERASH
KRAKLE
YOU SAY SOMETHING?
NOT A WORD.
AND THAT'S WHEN OUR WORKPLACE GOT INTEREST-ING...

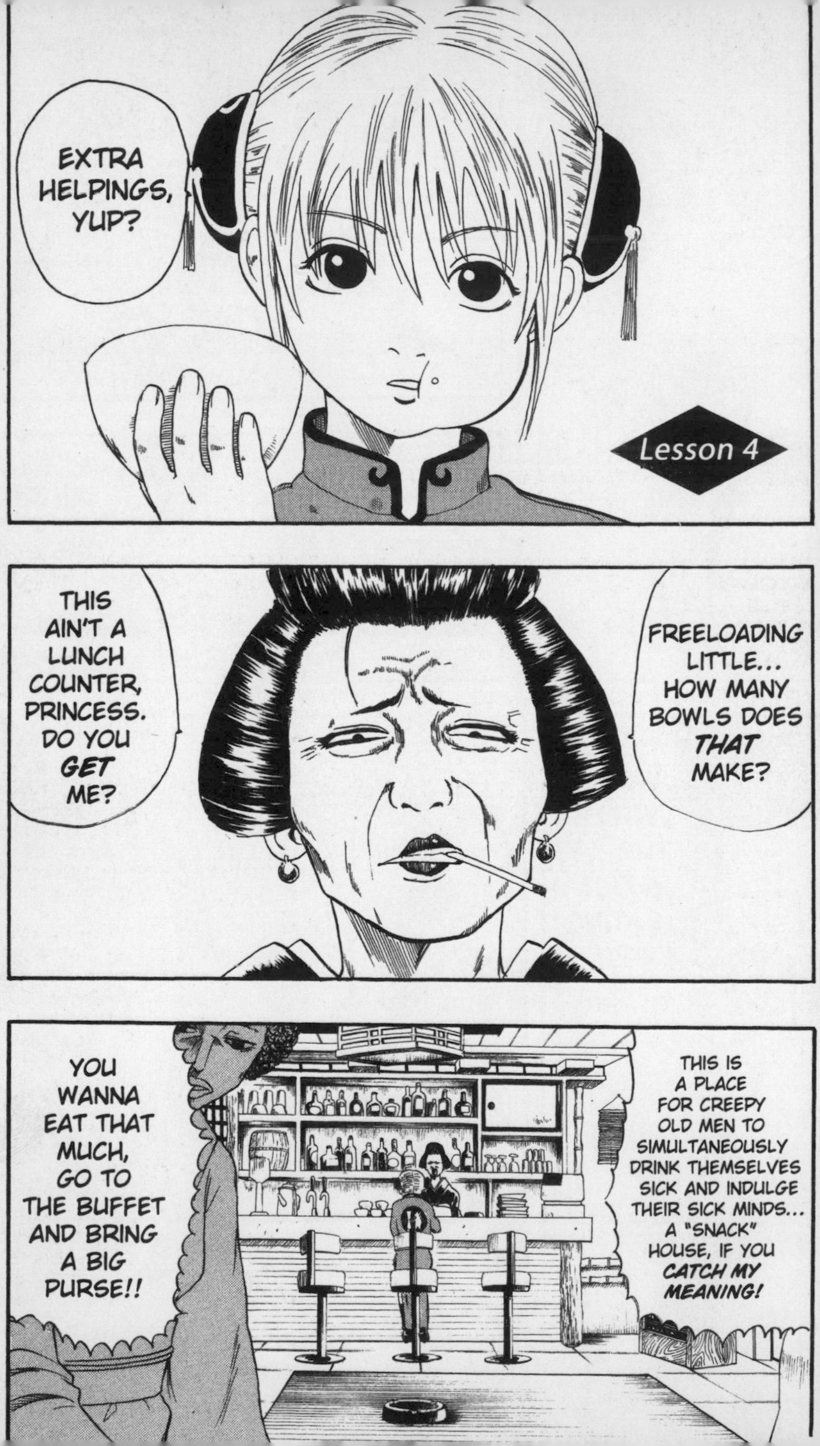
EXTRA HELPINGS, YUP?
Lesson 4
FREELOADING LITTLE... HOW MANY BOWLS DOES *THAT* MAKE?
THIS AIN'T A LUNCH COUNTER, PRINCESS. DO YOU *GET* ME?
THIS IS A PLACE FOR CREEPY OLD MEN TO SIMULTANEOUSLY DRINK THEMSELVES SICK AND INDULGE THEIR SICK MINDS... A "SNACK" HOUSE, IF YOU *CATCH MY MEANING!*
YOU WANNA EAT THAT MUCH, GO TO THE BUFFET AND BRING A BIG PURSE!!

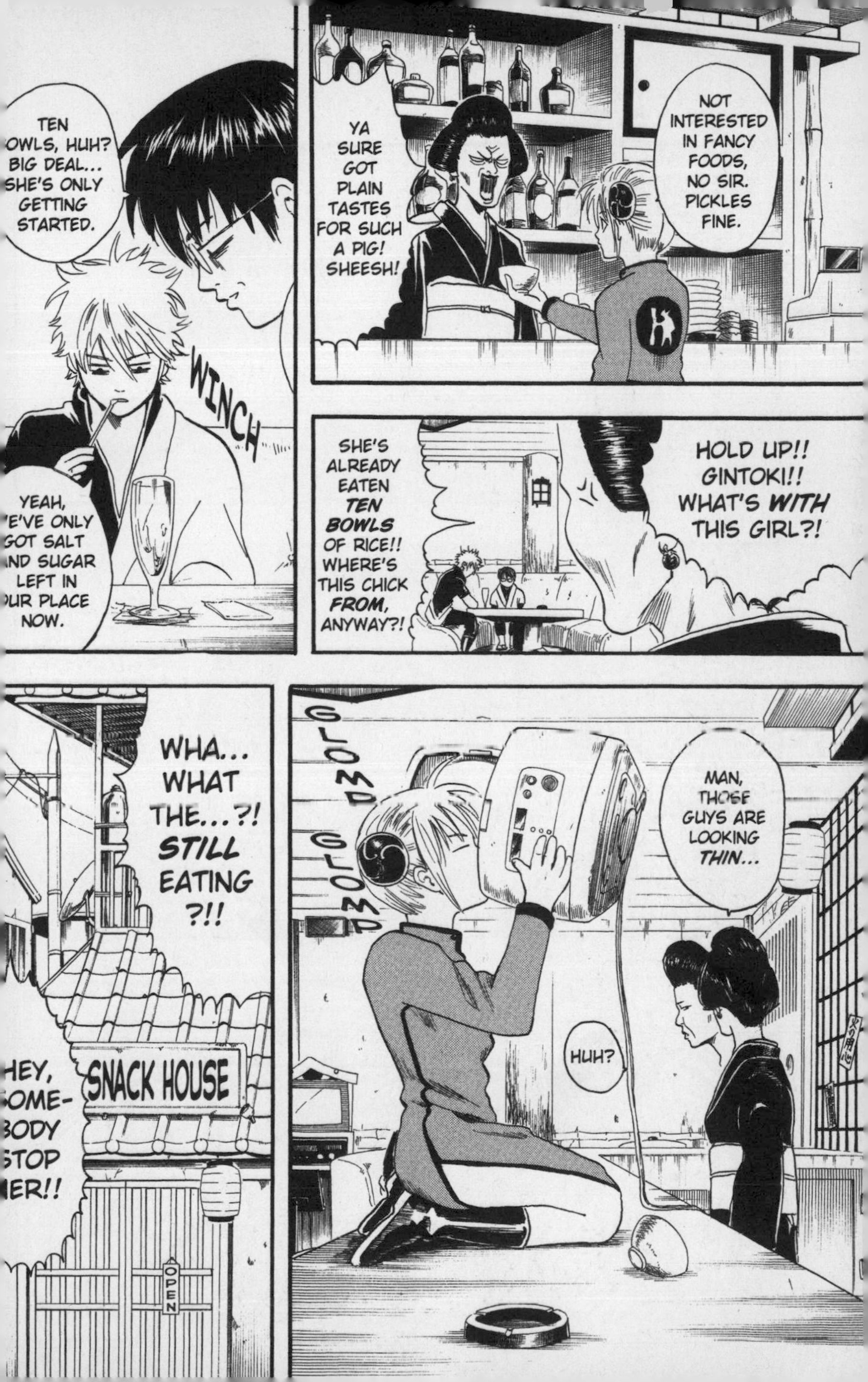
NOT INTERESTED IN FANCY FOODS, NO SIR. PICKLES FINE.
YA SURE GOT PLAIN TASTES FOR SUCH A PIG! SHEESH!
HOLD UP!! GINTOKI!! WHAT'S *WITH* THIS GIRL?!
SHE'S ALREADY EATEN ***TEN BOWLS*** OF RICE!! WHERE'S THIS CHICK ***FROM,*** ANYWAY?!
TEN OWLS, HUH? BIG DEAL... SHE'S ONLY GETTING STARTED.
WINCH
YEAH, E'VE ONLY GOT SALT ND SUGAR LEFT IN UR PLACE NOW.
MAN, THOSE GUYS ARE LOOKING *THIN*...
GLOMP GLOMP GLOMP
火の用心
HUH?
WHA... WHAT THE...?! ***STILL*** EATING ?!!
SNACK HOUSE
HEY, OME- BODY TOP ER!!
OPEN

Lesson 4: People Who Make Good First Impressions Usually Suck

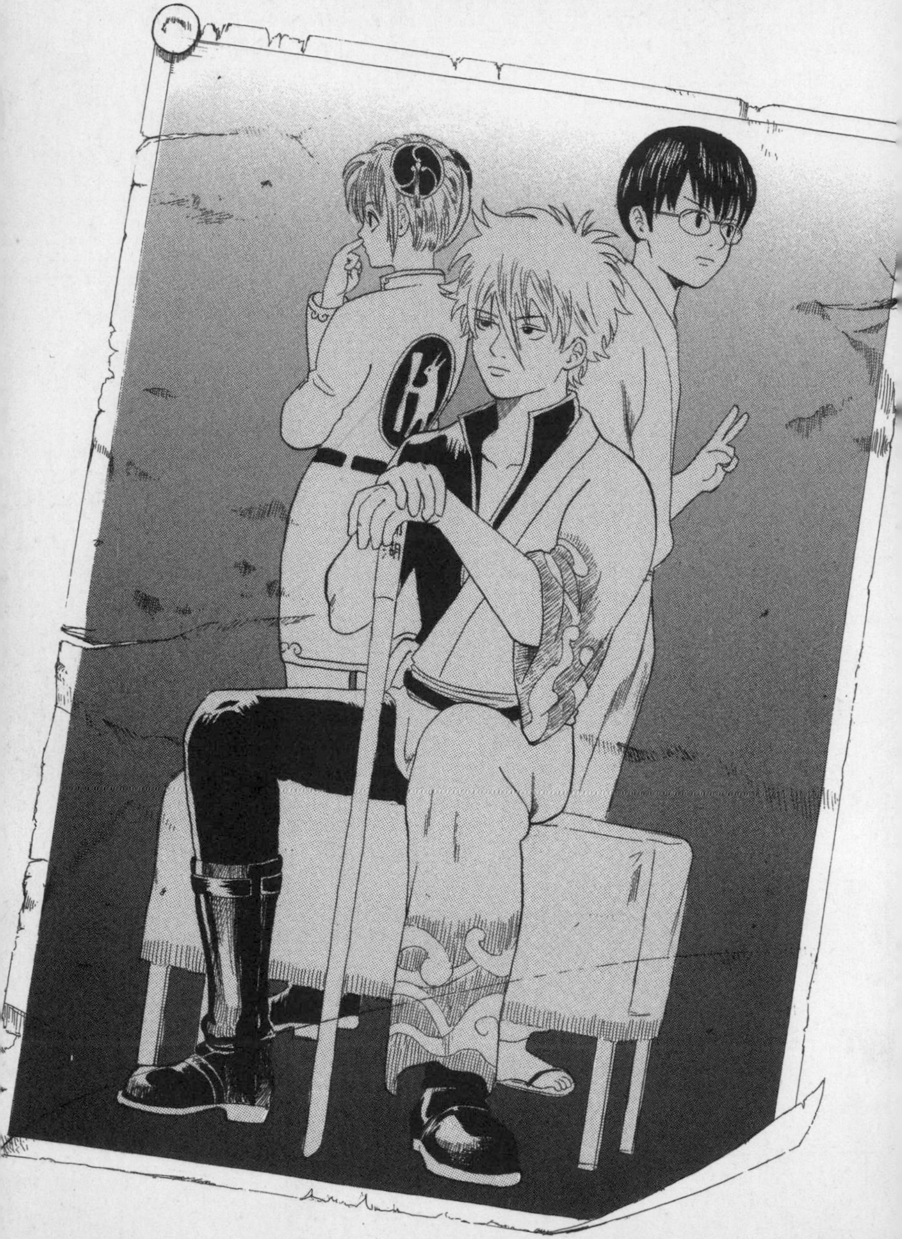

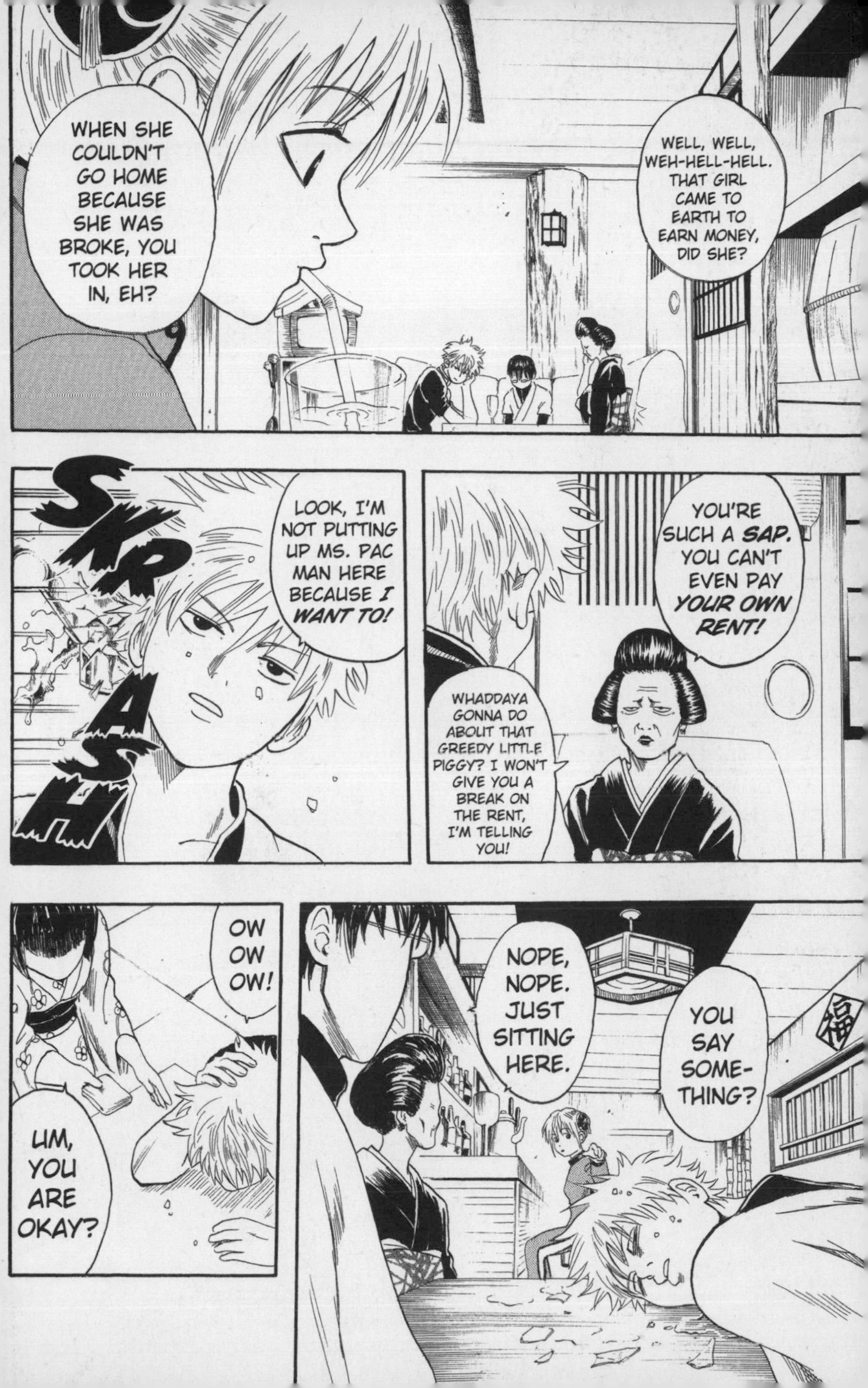
WELL, WELL, WEH-HELL-HELL. THAT GIRL CAME TO EARTH TO EARN MONEY, DID SHE?
WHEN SHE COULDN'T GO HOME BECAUSE SHE WAS BROKE, YOU TOOK HER IN, EH?
YOU'RE SUCH A SAP. YOU CAN'T EVEN PAY YOUR OWN RENT!
WHADDAYA GONNA DO ABOUT THAT GREEDY LITTLE PIGGY? I WON'T GIVE YOU A BREAK ON THE RENT, I'M TELLING YOU!
LOOK, I'M NOT PUTTING UP MS. PAC MAN HERE BECAUSE I WANT TO!
SKRASH
YOU SAY SOME-THING?
NOPE, NOPE. JUST SITTING HERE.
OW OW OW!
UM, YOU ARE OKAY?

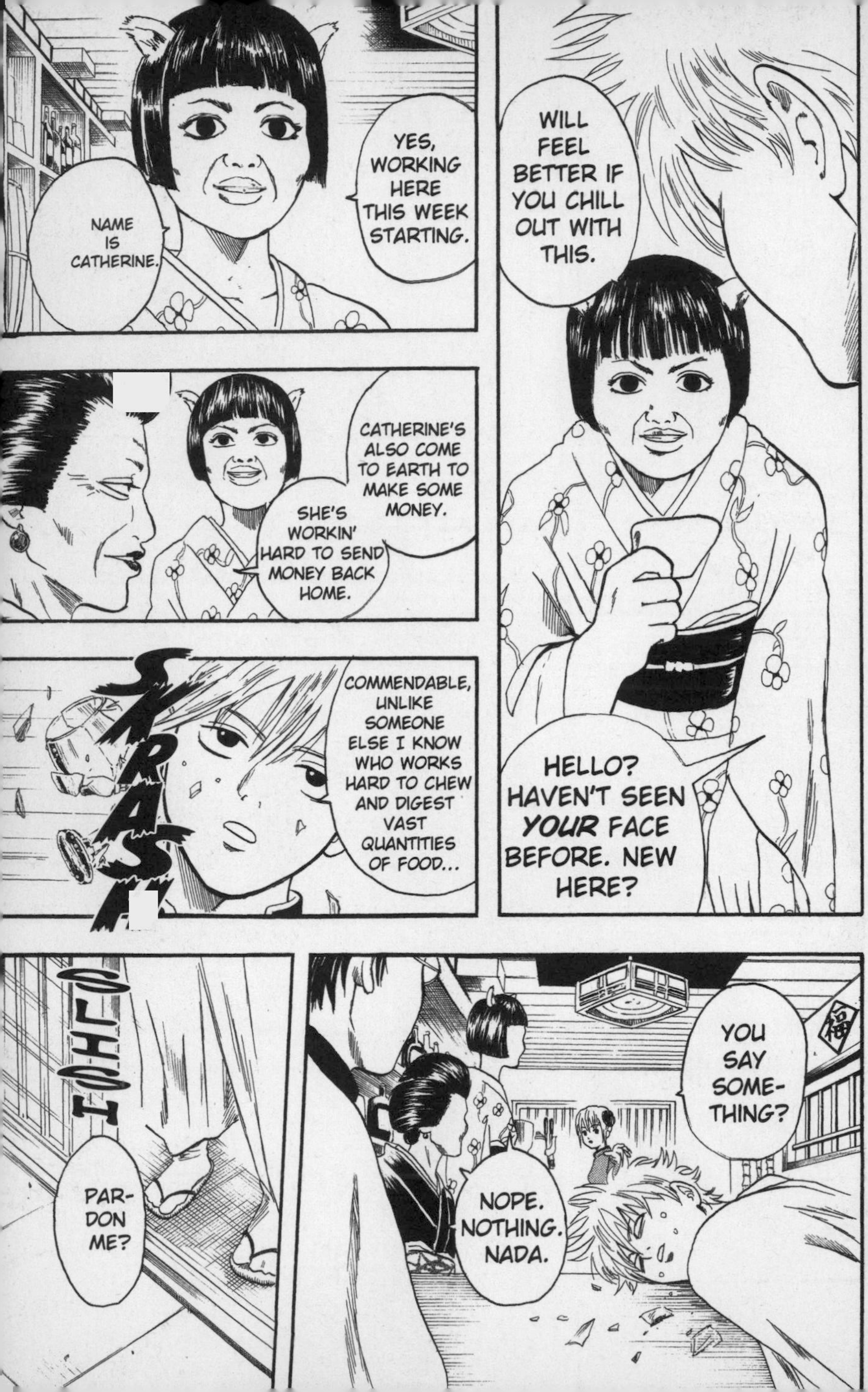
WILL FEEL BETTER IF YOU CHILL OUT WITH THIS.
HELLO? HAVEN'T SEEN *YOUR* FACE BEFORE. NEW HERE?
YES, WORKING HERE THIS WEEK STARTING.
NAME IS CATHERINE.
CATHERINE'S ALSO COME TO EARTH TO MAKE SOME MONEY.
SHE'S WORKIN' HARD TO SEND MONEY BACK HOME.
COMMENDABLE, UNLIKE SOMEONE ELSE I KNOW WHO WORKS HARD TO CHEW AND DIGEST VAST QUANTITIES OF FOOD...
SKRASH
YOU SAY SOME-THING?
NOPE. NOTHING. NADA.
SHISH
PAR-DON ME?

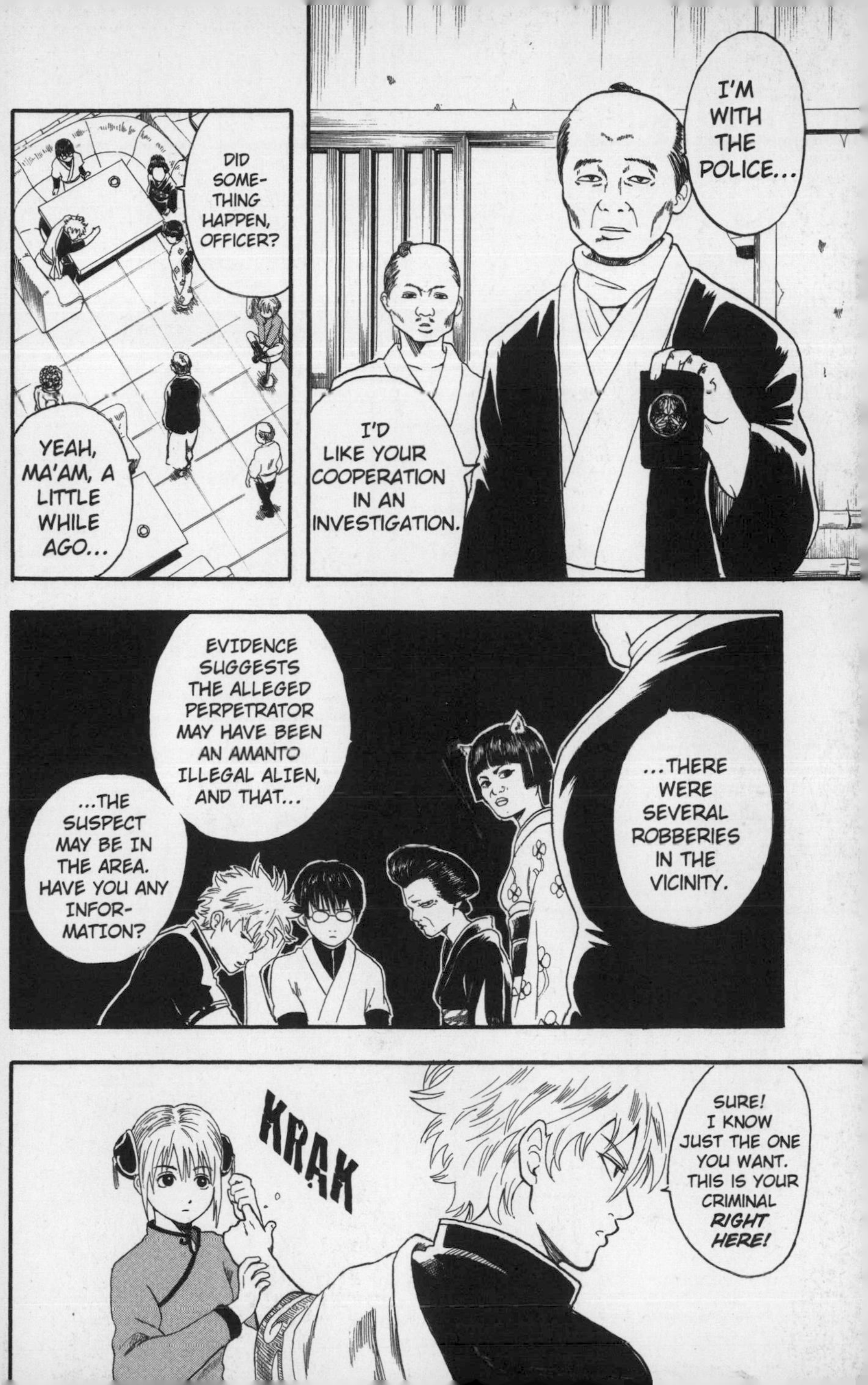
I'M WITH THE POLICE...
I'D LIKE YOUR COOPERATION IN AN INVESTIGATION.
DID SOME-THING HAPPEN, OFFICER?
YEAH, MA'AM, A LITTLE WHILE AGO...
...THERE WERE SEVERAL ROBBERIES IN THE VICINITY.
EVIDENCE SUGGESTS THE ALLEGED PERPETRATOR MAY HAVE BEEN AN AMANTO ILLEGAL ALIEN, AND THAT...
...THE SUSPECT MAY BE IN THE AREA. HAVE YOU ANY INFOR-MATION?
SURE! I KNOW JUST THE ONE YOU WANT. THIS IS YOUR CRIMINAL *RIGHT HERE!*
KRAK

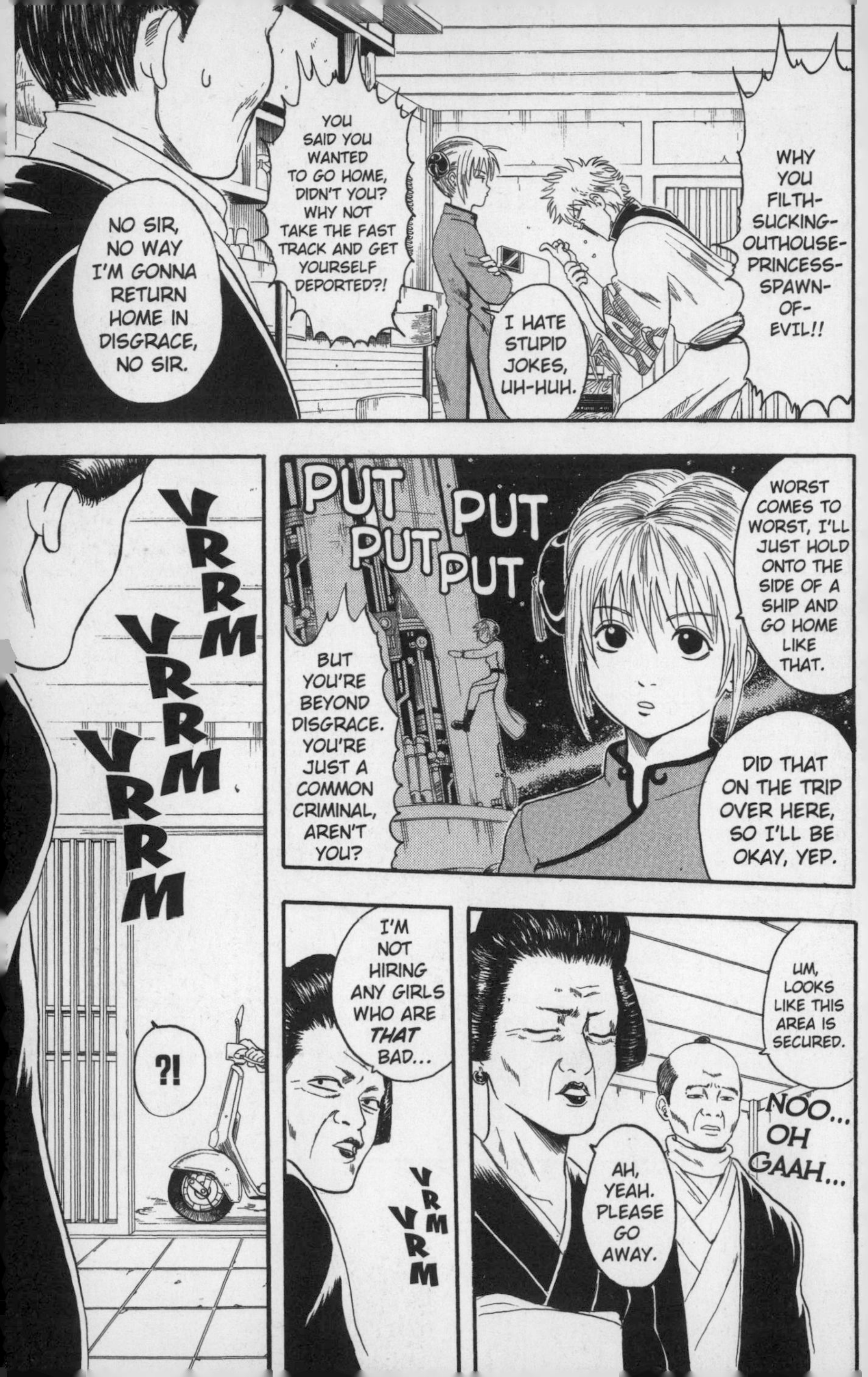
WHY YOU FILTH-SUCKING-OUTHOUSE-PRINCESS-SPAWN-OF-EVIL!!
YOU SAID YOU WANTED TO GO HOME, DIDN'T YOU? WHY NOT TAKE THE FAST TRACK AND GET YOURSELF DEPORTED?!
I HATE STUPID JOKES, UH-HUH.
NO SIR, NO WAY I'M GONNA RETURN HOME IN DISGRACE, NO SIR.
WORST COMES TO WORST, I'LL JUST HOLD ONTO THE SIDE OF A SHIP AND GO HOME LIKE THAT.
DID THAT ON THE TRIP OVER HERE, SO I'LL BE OKAY, YEP.
PUT PUT PUT PUT
BUT YOU'RE BEYOND DISGRACE. YOU'RE JUST A COMMON CRIMINAL, AREN'T YOU?
UM, LOOKS LIKE THIS AREA IS SECURED.
NOO... OH GAAH...
AH, YEAH. PLEASE GO AWAY.
I'M NOT HIRING ANY GIRLS WHO ARE *THAT* BAD...
VRM VRM
VRRM VRRM VRRM
?!

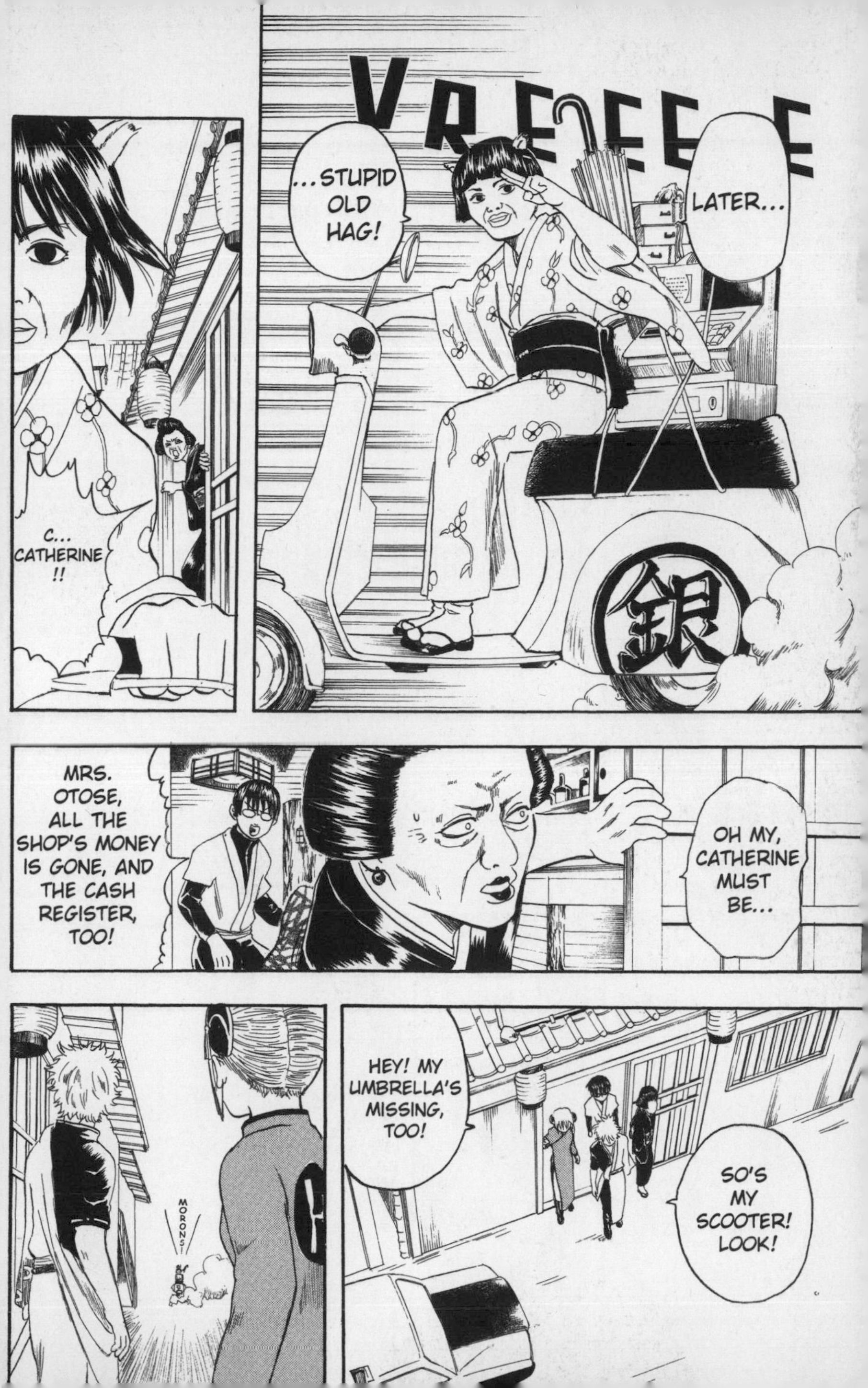
VREEEE
LATER...
...STUPID OLD HAG!
C... CATHERINE !!
OH MY, CATHERINE MUST BE...
MRS. OTOSE, ALL THE SHOP'S MONEY IS GONE, AND THE CASH REGISTER, TOO!
HEY! MY UMBRELLA'S MISSING, TOO!
SO'S MY SCOOTER! LOOK!
MORONS!

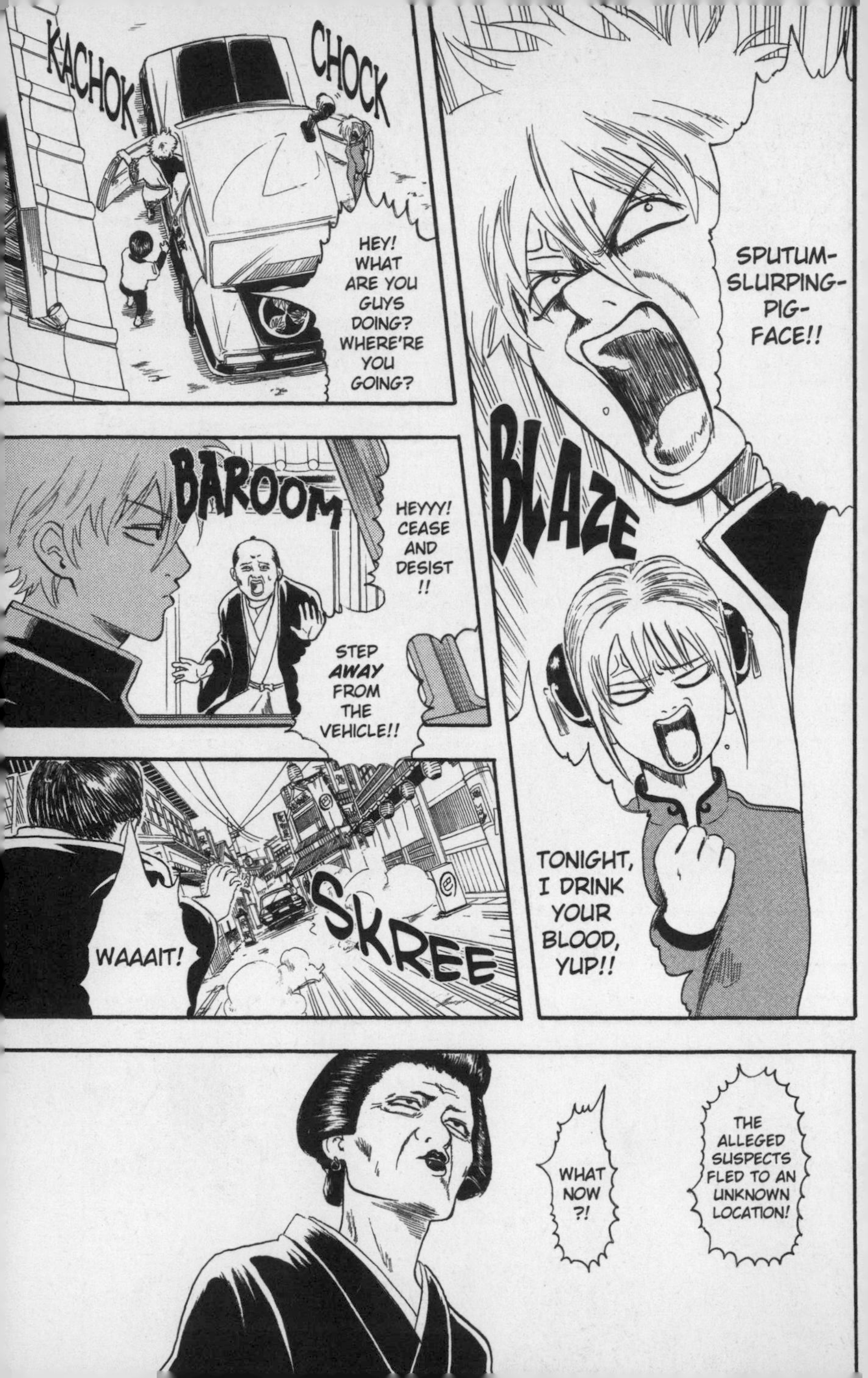
SPUTUM-SLURPING-PIG-FACE!!
BLAZE
TONIGHT, I DRINK YOUR BLOOD, YUP!!
CHOCK
KACHOK
HEY! WHAT ARE YOU GUYS DOING? WHERE'RE YOU GOING?
HEYYY! CEASE AND DESIST!!
BAROOM
STEP AWAY FROM THE VEHICLE!!
SKREE
WAAAIT!
THE ALLEGED SUSPECTS FLED TO AN UNKNOWN LOCATION!
WHAT NOW?!

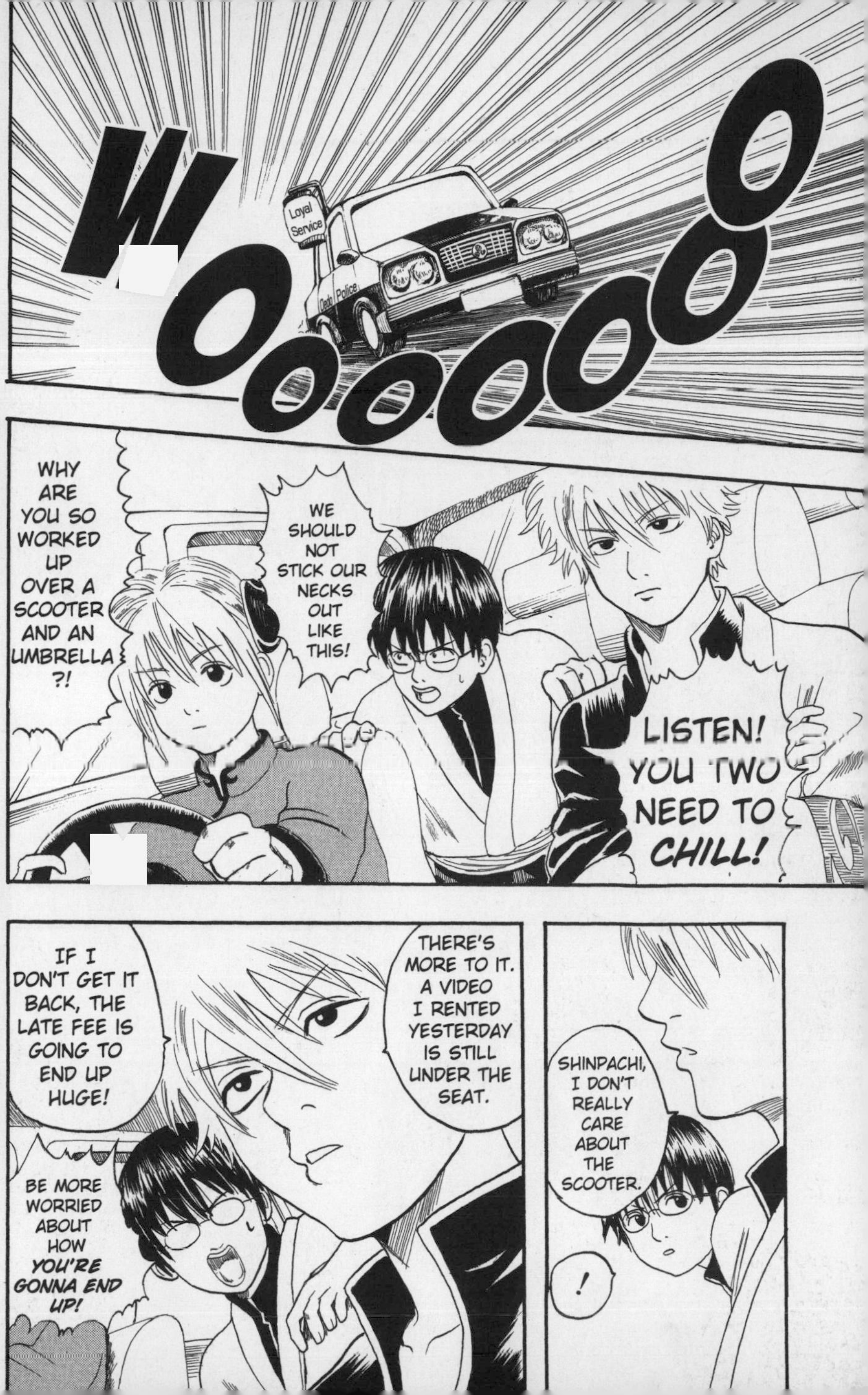
WOOOOOOOO
Loyal Service
Oedo Police
LISTEN! YOU TWO NEED TO CHILL!
WE SHOULD NOT STICK OUR NECKS OUT LIKE THIS!
WHY ARE YOU SO WORKED UP OVER A SCOOTER AND AN UMBRELLA?!
SHINPACHI, I DON'T REALLY CARE ABOUT THE SCOOTER.
!
THERE'S MORE TO IT. A VIDEO I RENTED YESTERDAY IS STILL UNDER THE SEAT.
IF I DON'T GET IT BACK, THE LATE FEE IS GOING TO END UP HUGE!
BE MORE WORRIED ABOUT HOW YOU'RE GONNA END UP!

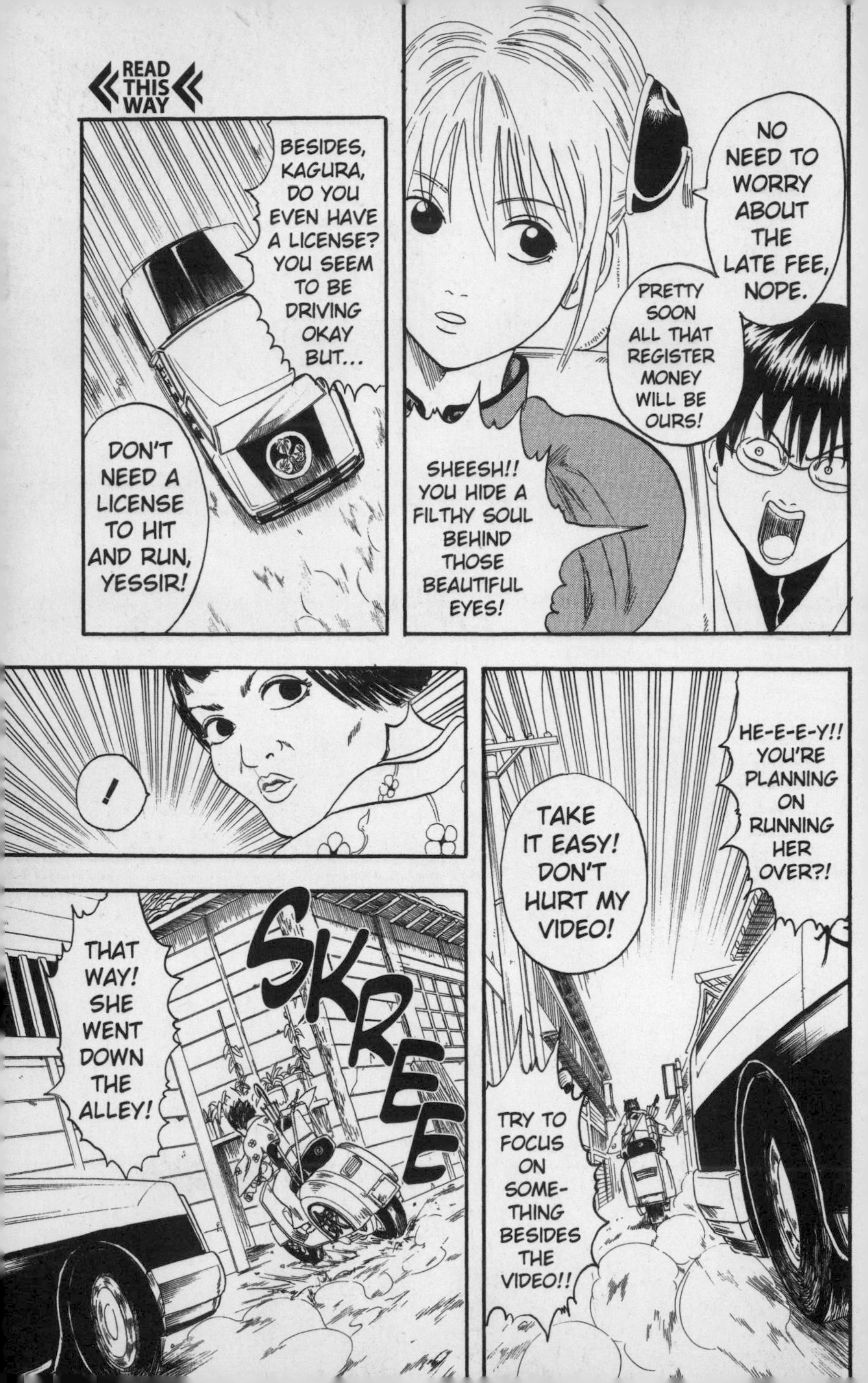
READ THIS WAY
NO NEED TO WORRY ABOUT THE LATE FEE, NOPE.
PRETTY SOON ALL THAT REGISTER MONEY WILL BE OURS!
SHEESH!! YOU HIDE A FILTHY SOUL BEHIND THOSE BEAUTIFUL EYES!
BESIDES, KAGURA, DO YOU EVEN HAVE A LICENSE? YOU SEEM TO BE DRIVING OKAY BUT...
DON'T NEED A LICENSE TO HIT AND RUN, YESSIR!
HE-E-E-Y!! YOU'RE PLANNING ON RUNNING HER OVER?!
TAKE IT EASY! DON'T HURT MY VIDEO!
TRY TO FOCUS ON SOME-THING BESIDES THE VIDEO!!
!
THAT WAY! SHE WENT DOWN THE ALLEY!
SKREE

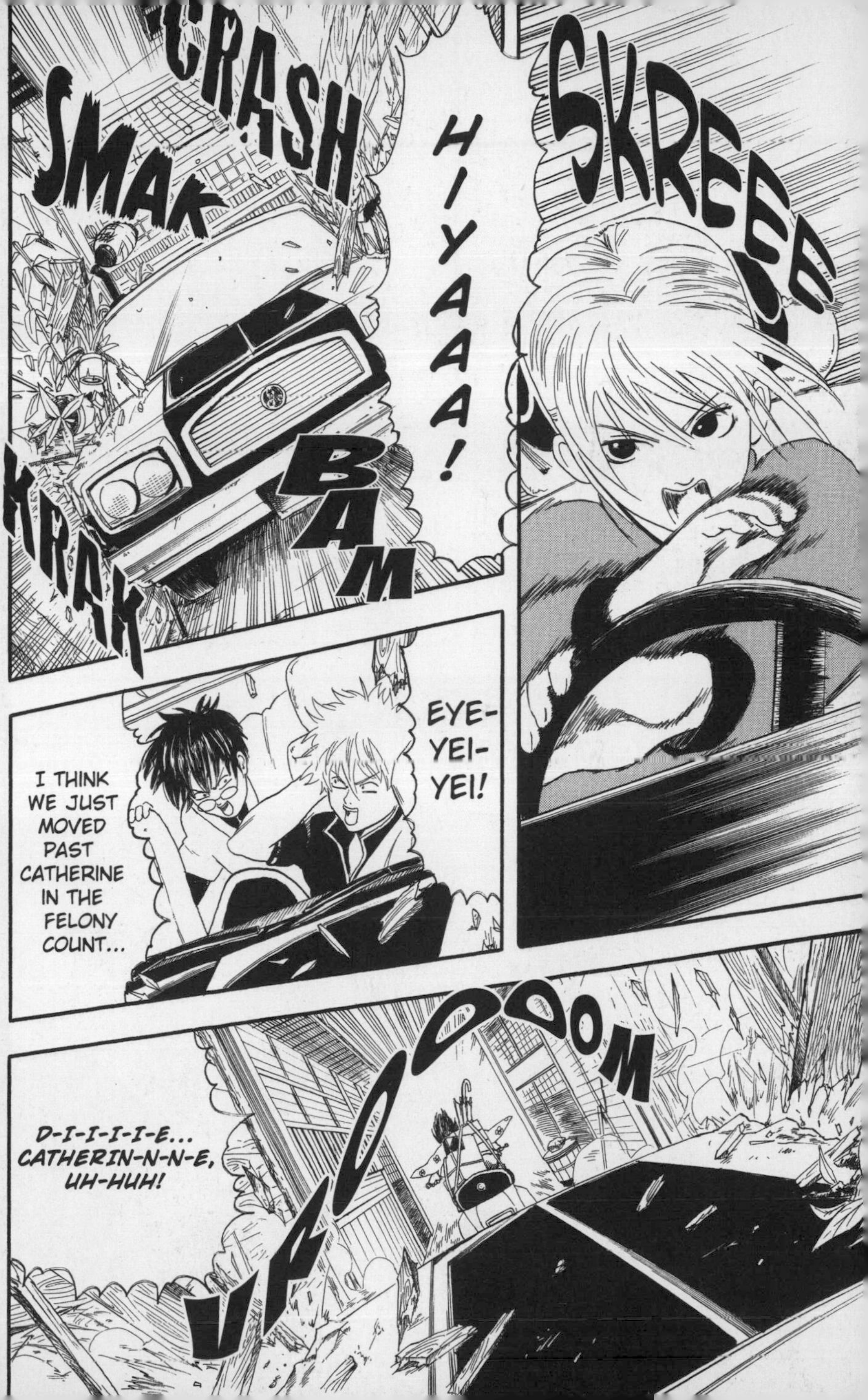
SKREEE
HIYAAAA!
CRASH
SMAK
KRAK
BAM
EYE-YEI-YEI!
I THINK WE JUST MOVED PAST CATHERINE IN THE FELONY COUNT...
VROOOOM
D-I-I-I-I-E... CATHERIN-N-N-E, UH-HUH!

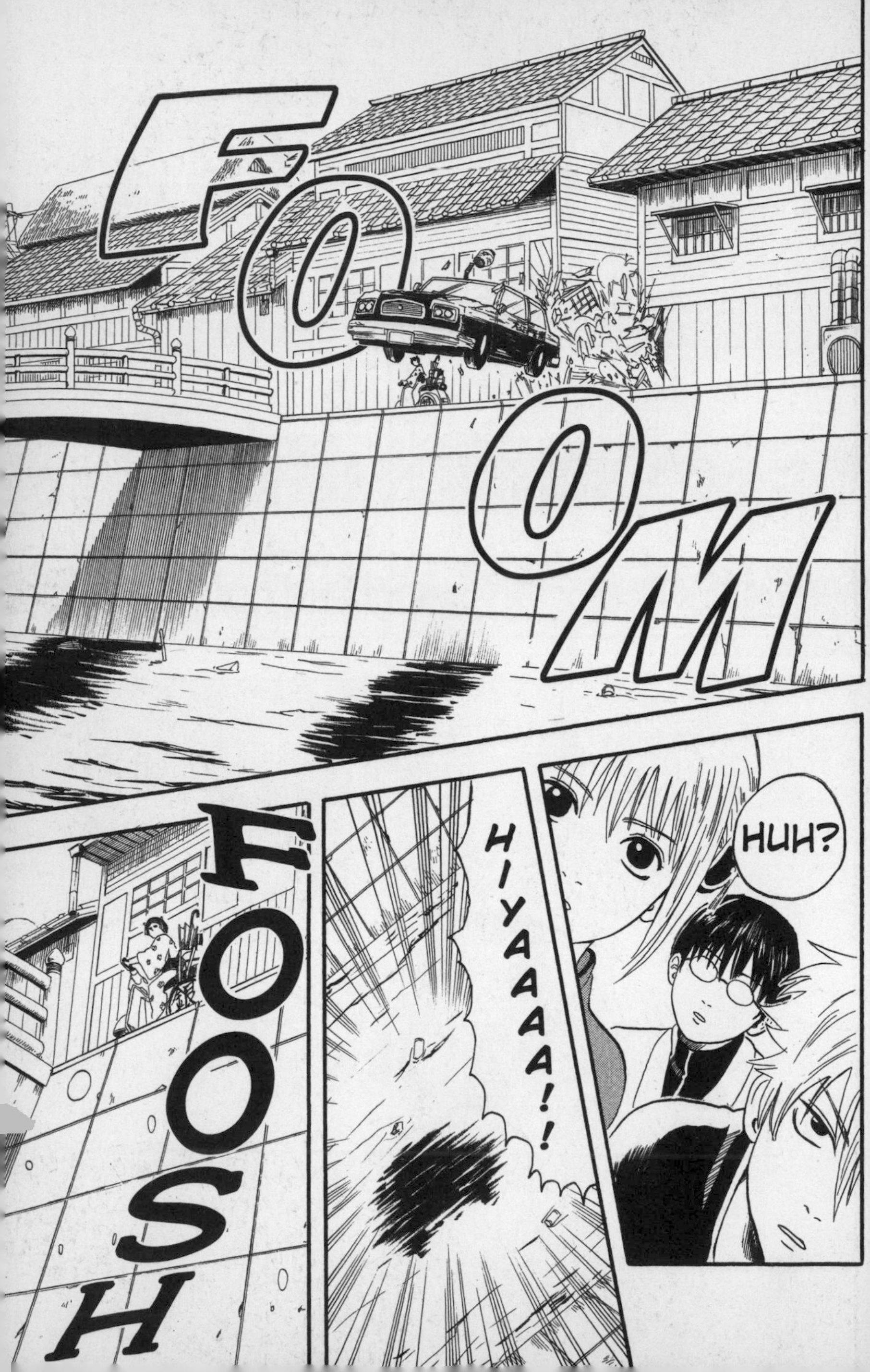
FOOOM
HUH?
HIYAAAA!!
FOOOSH

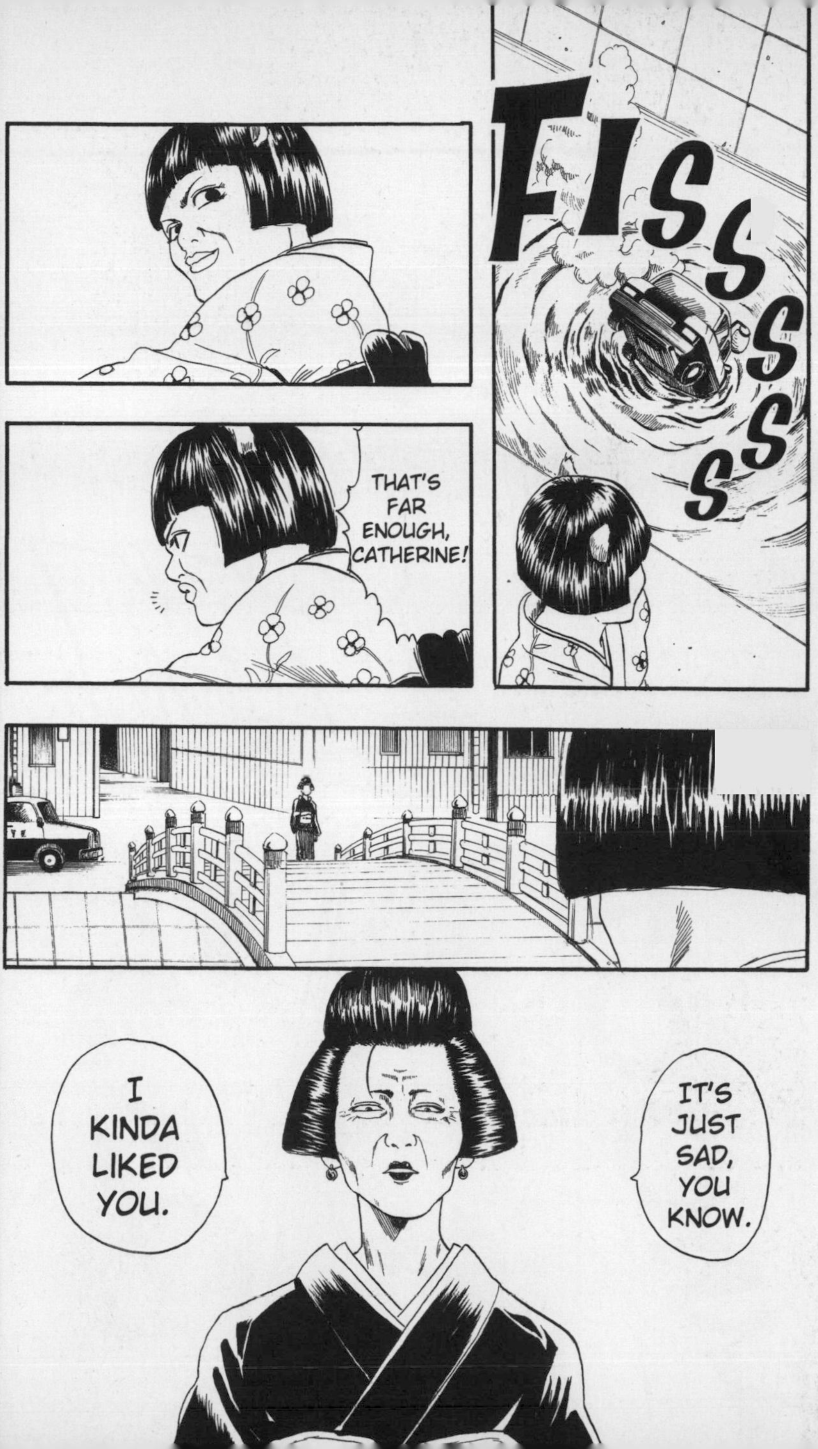
FISSSSS
THAT'S FAR ENOUGH, CATHERINE!
IT'S JUST SAD, YOU KNOW.
I KINDA LIKED YOU.

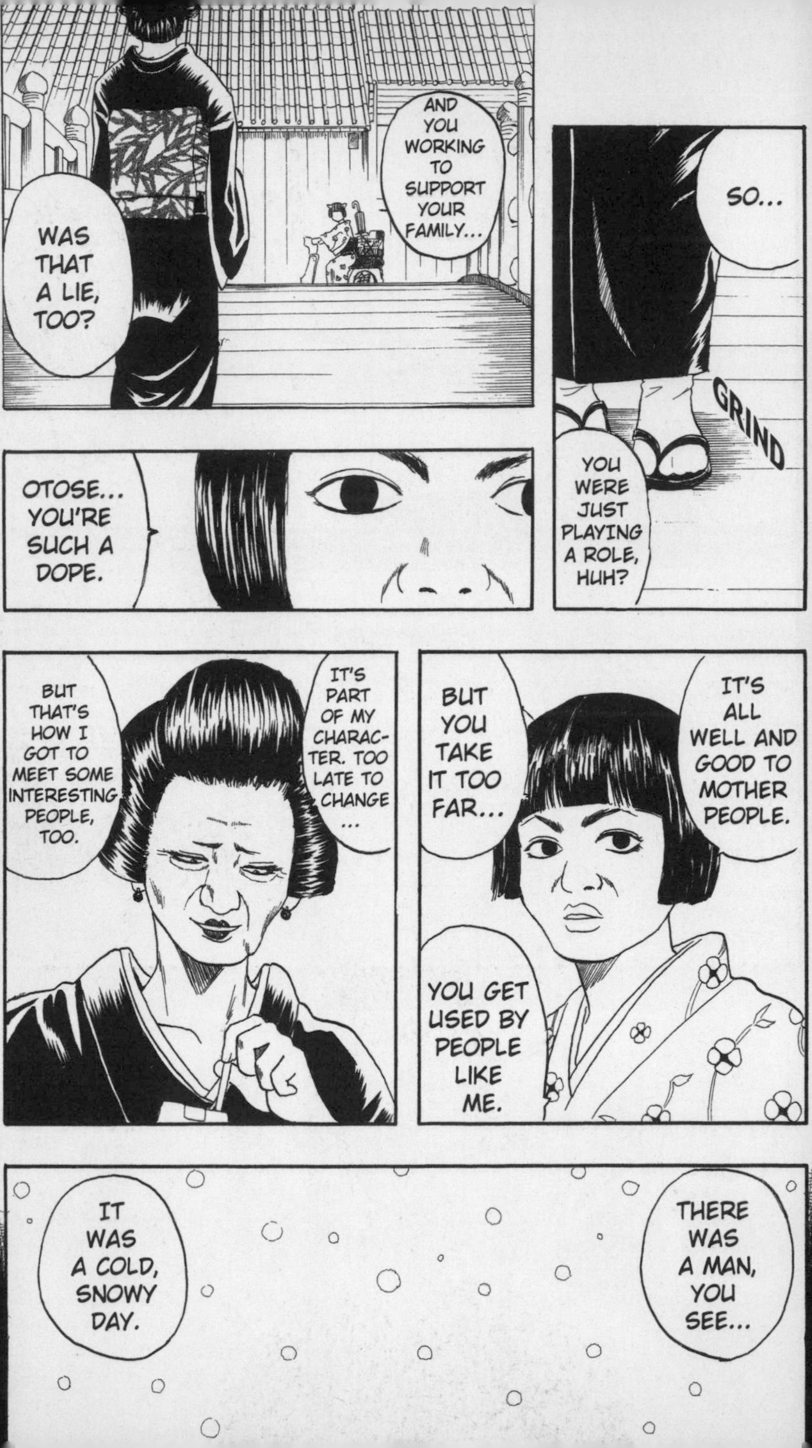
SO...
GRIND
YOU WERE JUST PLAYING A ROLE, HUH?
AND YOU WORKING TO SUPPORT YOUR FAMILY...
WAS THAT A LIE, TOO?
OTOSE... YOU'RE SUCH A DOPE.
IT'S ALL WELL AND GOOD TO MOTHER PEOPLE.
BUT YOU TAKE IT TOO FAR...
YOU GET USED BY PEOPLE LIKE ME.
IT'S PART OF MY CHARACTER. TOO LATE TO CHANGE...
BUT THAT'S HOW I GOT TO MEET SOME INTERESTING PEOPLE, TOO.
THERE WAS A MAN, YOU SEE...
IT WAS A COLD, SNOWY DAY.

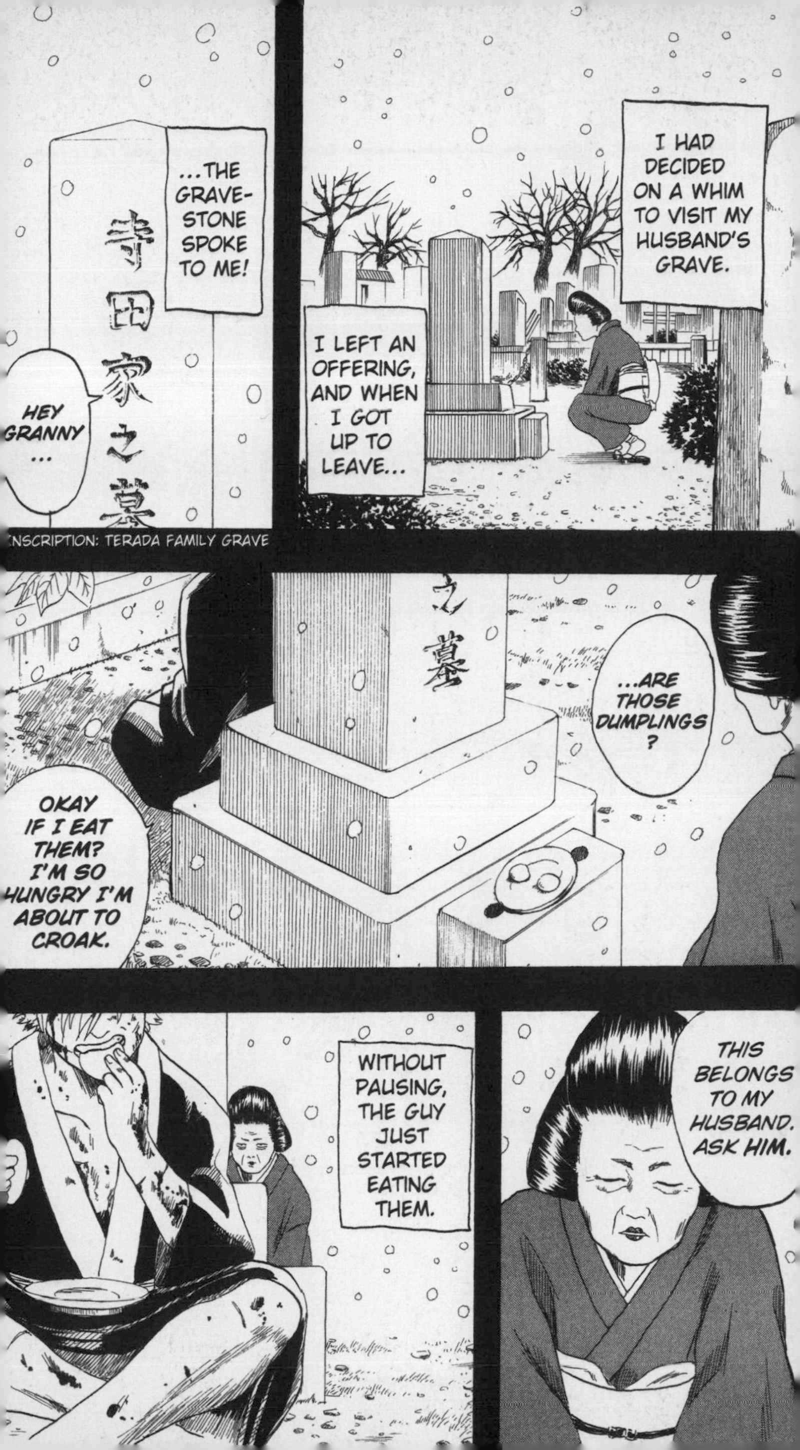
I HAD DECIDED ON A WHIM TO VISIT MY HUSBAND'S GRAVE.
I LEFT AN OFFERING, AND WHEN I GOT UP TO LEAVE...
...THE GRAVE-STONE SPOKE TO ME!
寺田家之墓
HEY GRANNY ...
INSCRIPTION: TERADA FAMILY GRAVE
...ARE THOSE DUMPLINGS?
OKAY IF I EAT THEM? I'M SO HUNGRY I'M ABOUT TO CROAK.
THIS BELONGS TO MY HUSBAND. ASK HIM.
WITHOUT PAUSING, THE GUY JUST STARTED EATING THEM.

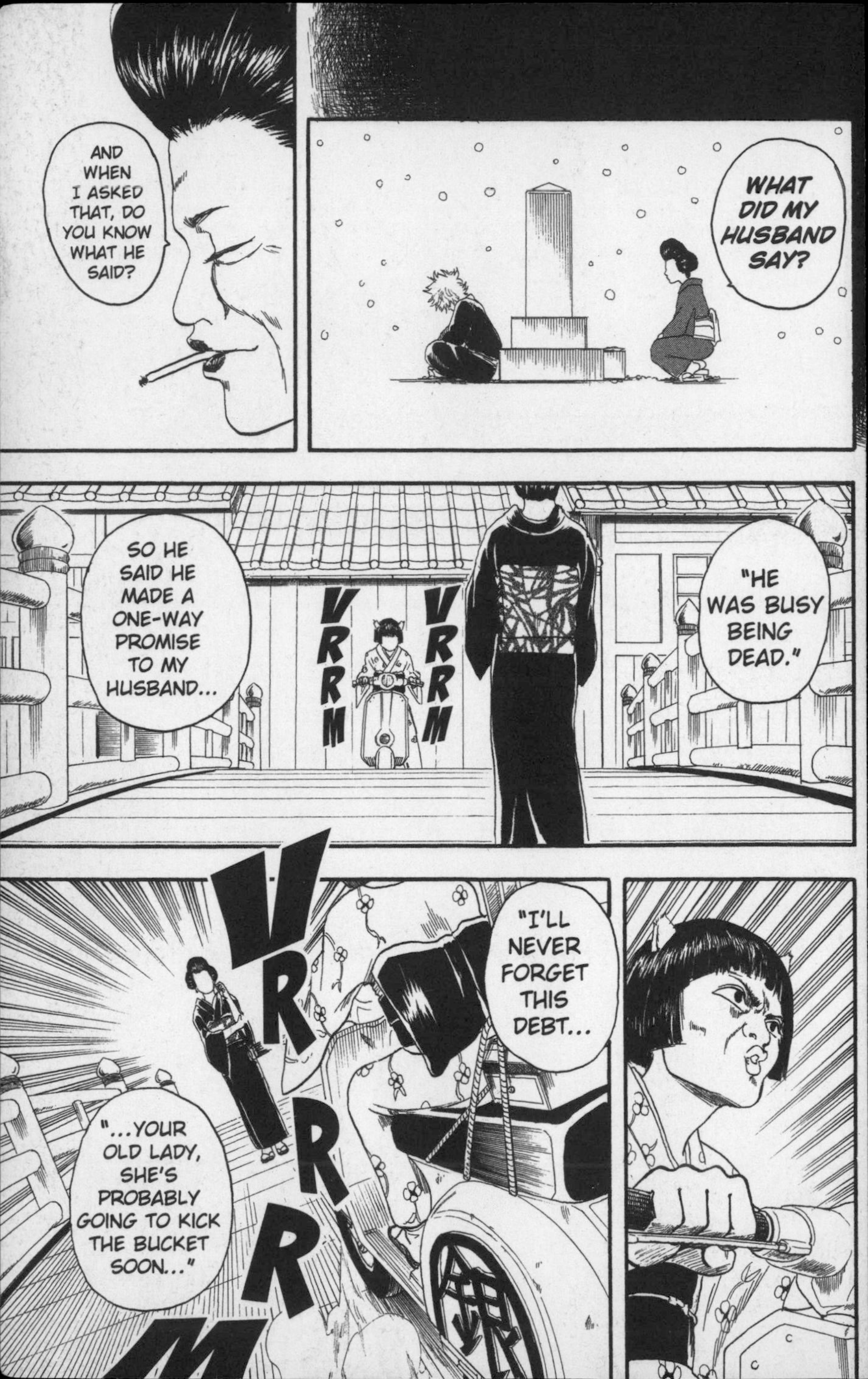
WHAT DID MY HUSBAND SAY?
AND WHEN I ASKED THAT, DO YOU KNOW WHAT HE SAID?
"HE WAS BUSY BEING DEAD."
VRRM
VRRM
SO HE SAID HE MADE A ONE-WAY PROMISE TO MY HUSBAND...
"I'LL NEVER FORGET THIS DEBT...
"...YOUR OLD LADY, SHE'S PROBABLY GOING TO KICK THE BUCKET SOON..."
VRRRM

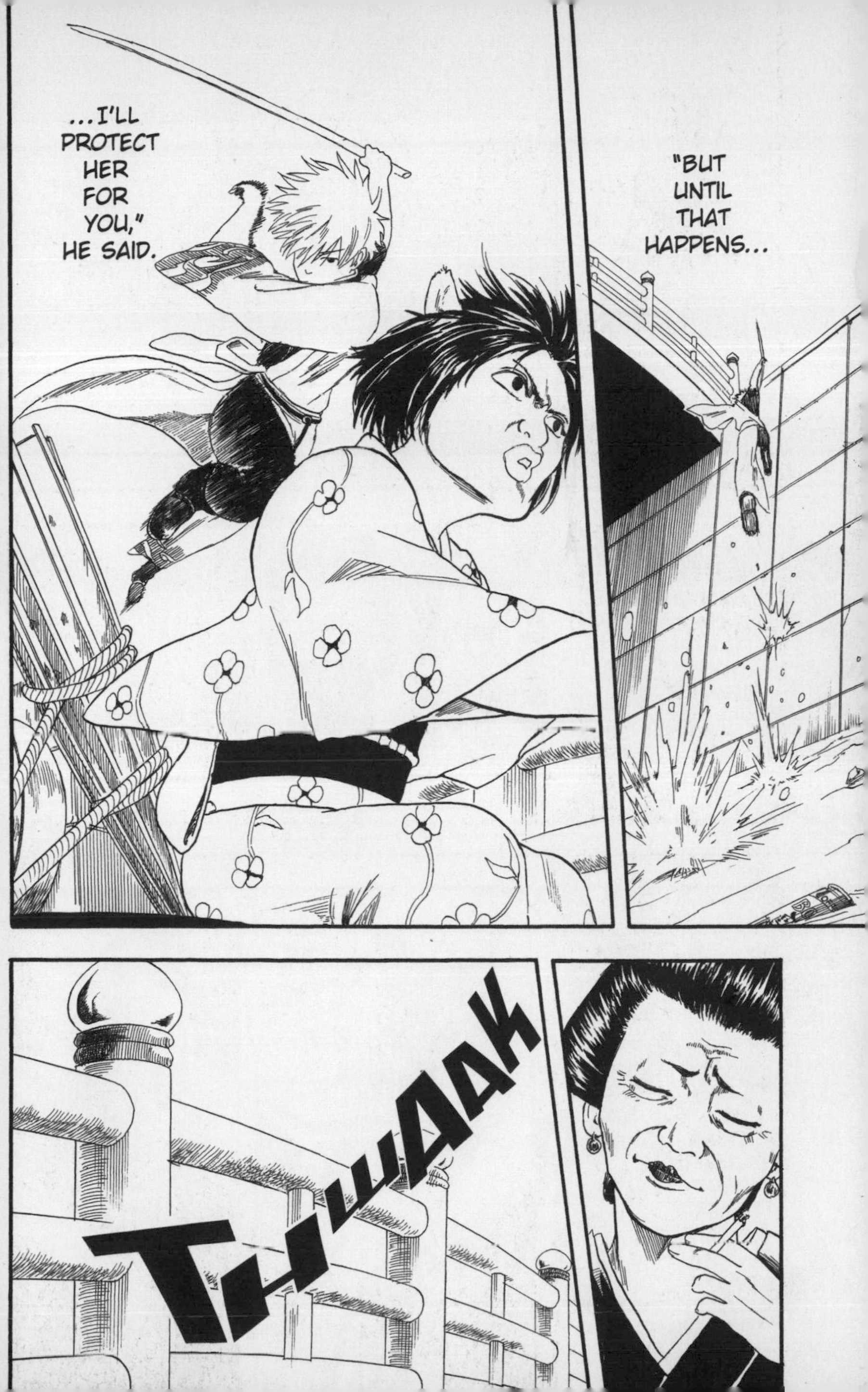
"BUT UNTIL THAT HAPPENS...
...I'LL PROTECT HER FOR YOU," HE SAID.
THWAAK

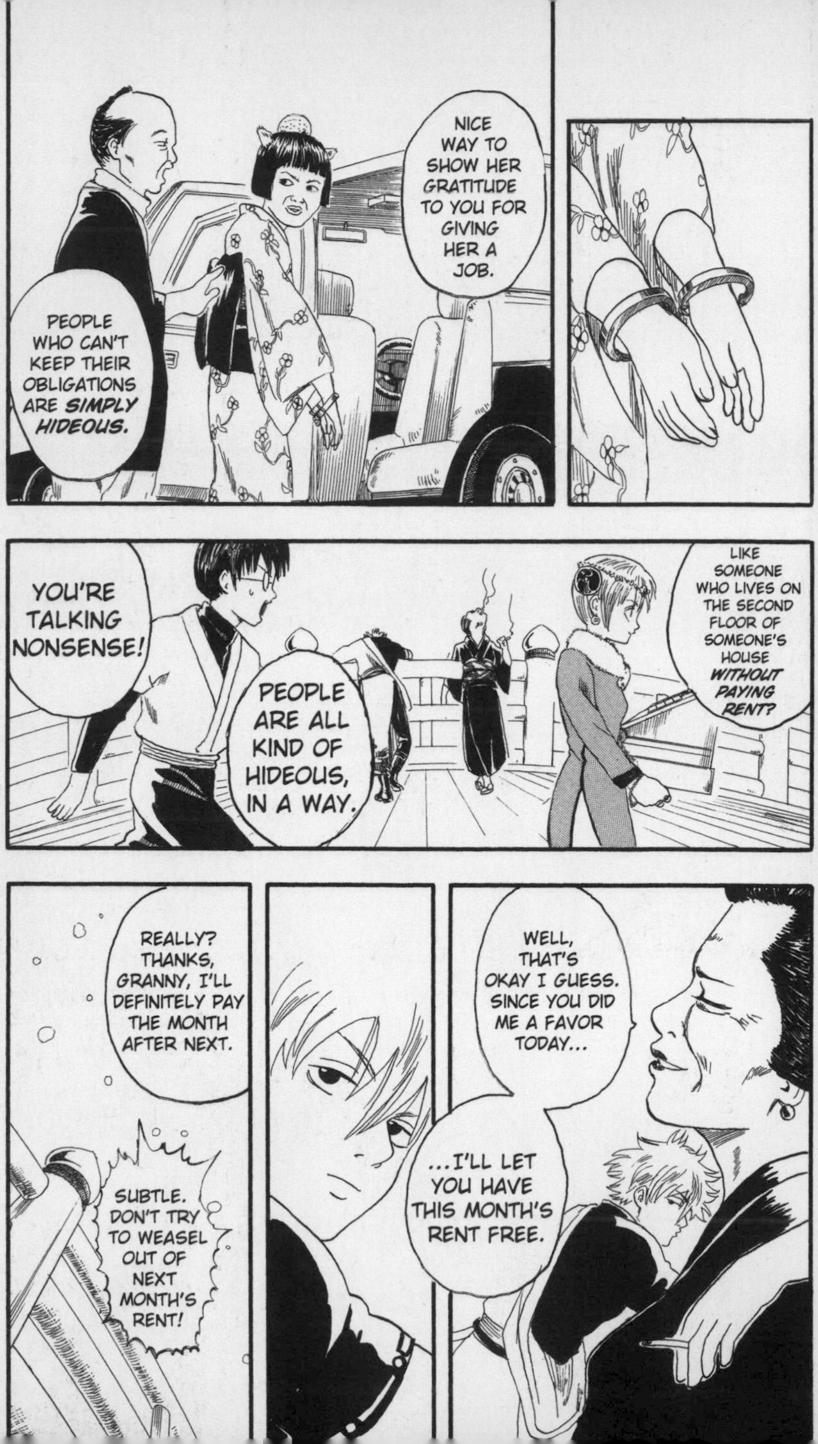
NICE WAY TO SHOW HER GRATITUDE TO YOU FOR GIVING HER A JOB.
PEOPLE WHO CAN'T KEEP THEIR OBLIGATIONS ARE *SIMPLY HIDEOUS.*
LIKE SOMEONE WHO LIVES ON THE SECOND FLOOR OF SOMEONE'S HOUSE *WITHOUT PAYING RENT?*
YOU'RE TALKING NONSENSE!
PEOPLE ARE ALL KIND OF HIDEOUS, IN A WAY.
WELL, THAT'S OKAY I GUESS. SINCE YOU DID ME A FAVOR TODAY...
...I'LL LET YOU HAVE THIS MONTH'S RENT FREE.
REALLY? THANKS, GRANNY, I'LL DEFINITELY PAY THE MONTH AFTER NEXT.
SUBTLE. DON'T TRY TO WEASEL OUT OF NEXT MONTH'S RENT!

Sorachi

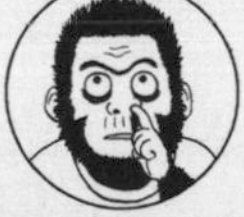

Sorachi's Mumblings ②

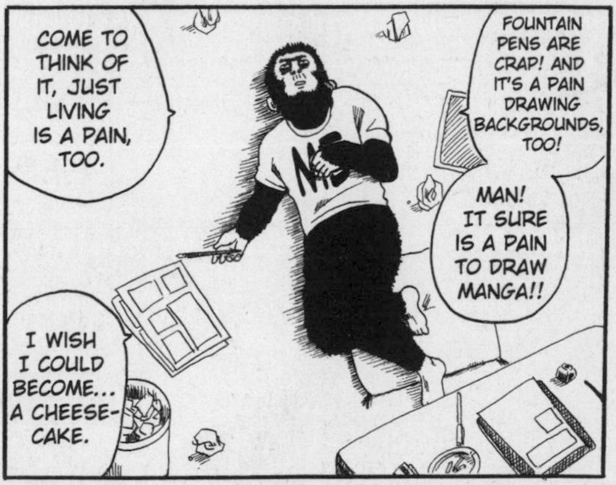
FOUNTAIN PENS ARE CRAP! AND IT'S A PAIN DRAWING BACKGROUNDS, TOO!
MAN! IT SURE IS A PAIN TO DRAW MANGA!!
COME TO THINK OF IT, JUST LIVING IS A PAIN, TOO.
I WISH I COULD BECOME... A CHEESE-CAKE.

● A reply to the question, "What was it like the first time you submitted your work? Published in *Weekly Shonen Jump*, combined issue, nos. 4 and 5 (2004).

READ THIS WAY

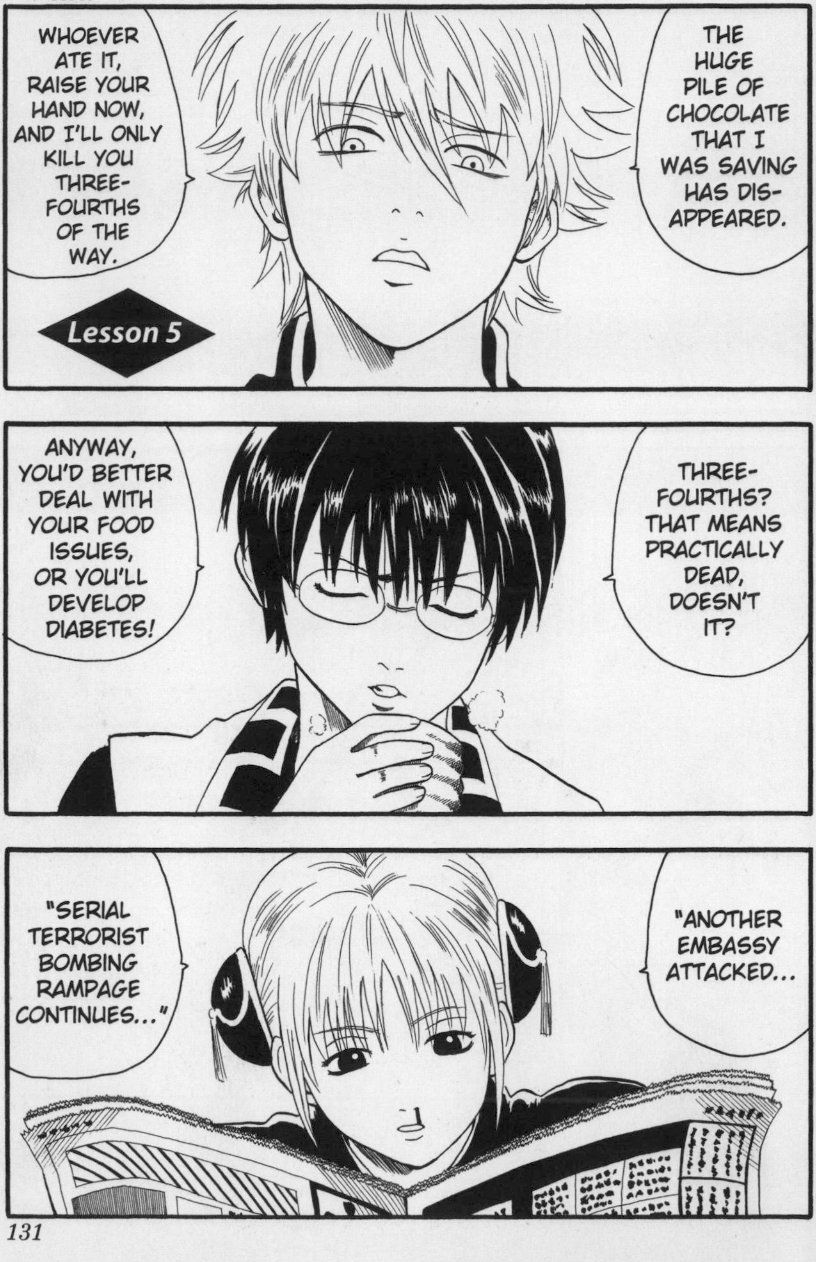
THE HUGE PILE OF CHOCOLATE THAT I WAS SAVING HAS DISAPPEARED.
WHOEVER ATE IT, RAISE YOUR HAND NOW, AND I'LL ONLY KILL YOU THREE-FOURTHS OF THE WAY.
Lesson 5
THREE-FOURTHS? THAT MEANS PRACTICALLY DEAD, DOESN'T IT?
ANYWAY, YOU'D BETTER DEAL WITH YOUR FOOD ISSUES, OR YOU'LL DEVELOP DIABETES!
"ANOTHER EMBASSY ATTACKED...
"SERIAL TERRORIST BOMBING RAMPAGE CONTINUES..."

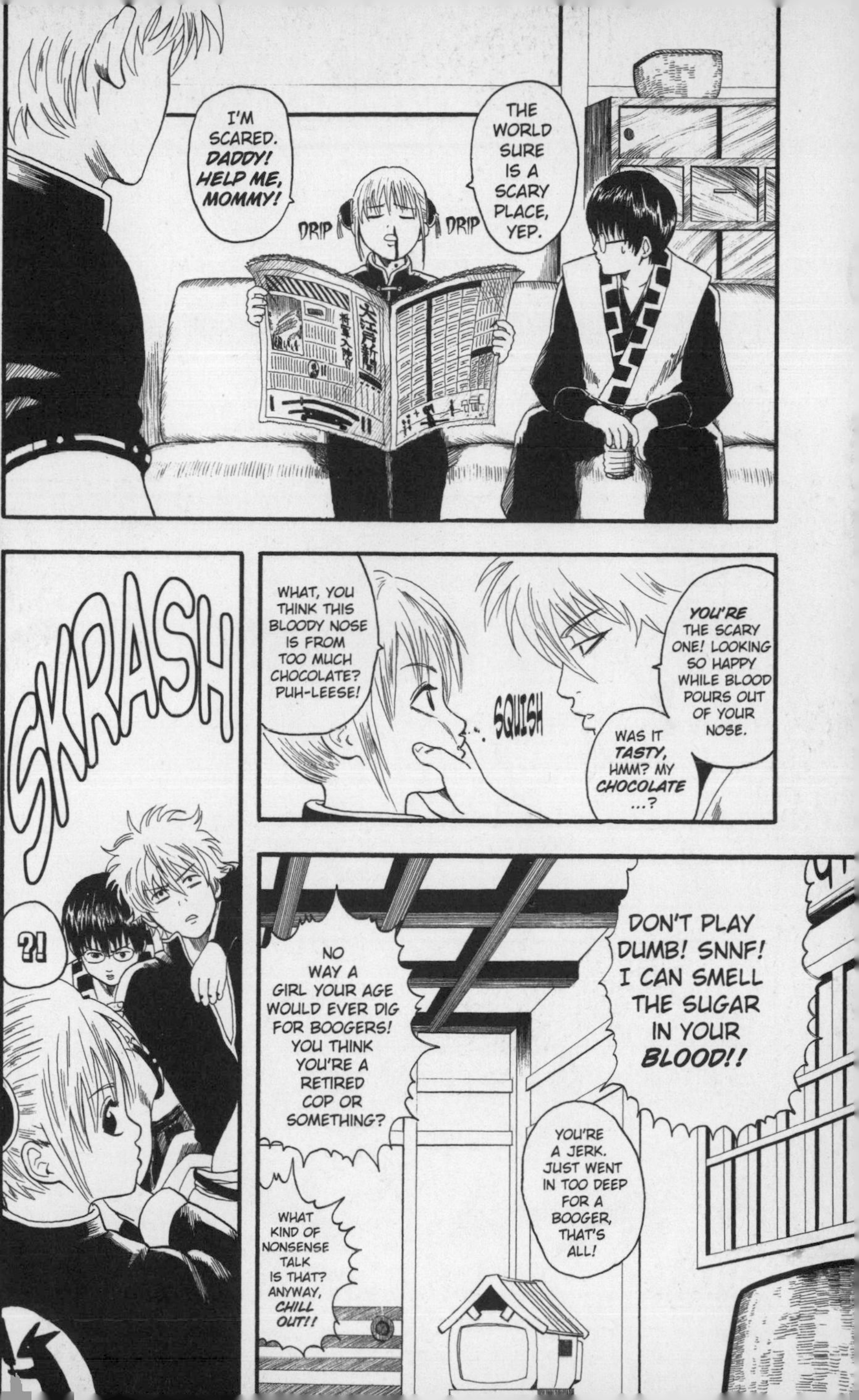
THE WORLD SURE IS A SCARY PLACE, YEP.
DRIP
DRIP
I'M SCARED. DADDY! HELP ME, MOMMY!
大江戸新聞
YOU'RE THE SCARY ONE! LOOKING SO HAPPY WHILE BLOOD POURS OUT OF YOUR NOSE.
WAS IT TASTY, HMM? MY CHOCOLATE ...?
SQUISH
WHAT, YOU THINK THIS BLOODY NOSE IS FROM TOO MUCH CHOCOLATE? PUH-LEESE!
DON'T PLAY DUMB! SNNF! I CAN SMELL THE SUGAR IN YOUR BLOOD!!
NO WAY A GIRL YOUR AGE WOULD EVER DIG FOR BOOGERS! YOU THINK YOU'RE A RETIRED COP OR SOMETHING?
YOU'RE A JERK. JUST WENT IN TOO DEEP FOR A BOOGER, THAT'S ALL!
WHAT KIND OF NONSENSE TALK IS THAT? ANYWAY, CHILL OUT!!
SKRASH
?!

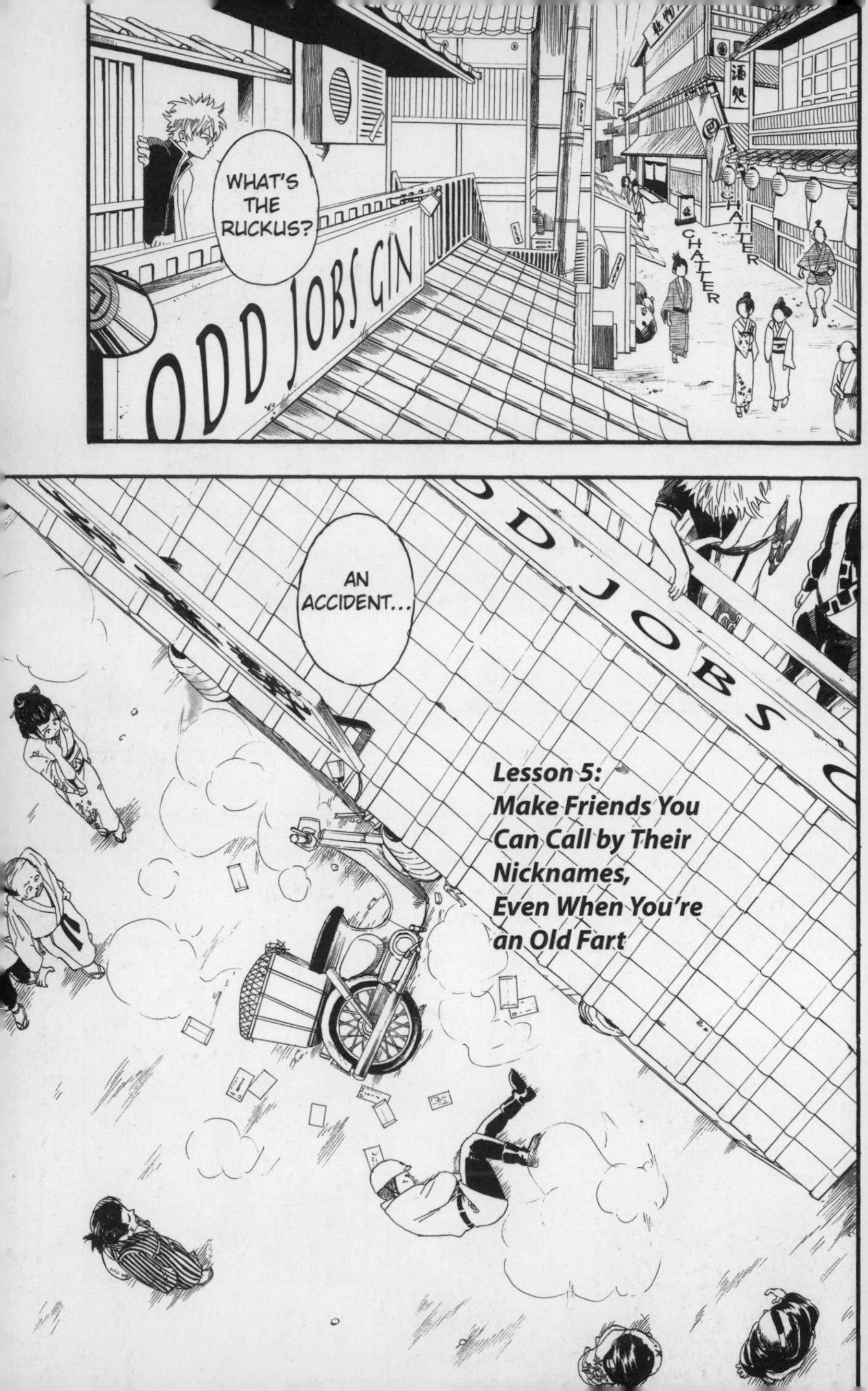
ODD JOBS GIN
WHAT'S THE RUCKUS?
CHATTER
CHATTER
ODD JOBS
AN ACCIDENT…
Lesson 5:
Make Friends You Can Call by Their Nicknames, Even When You're an Old Fart

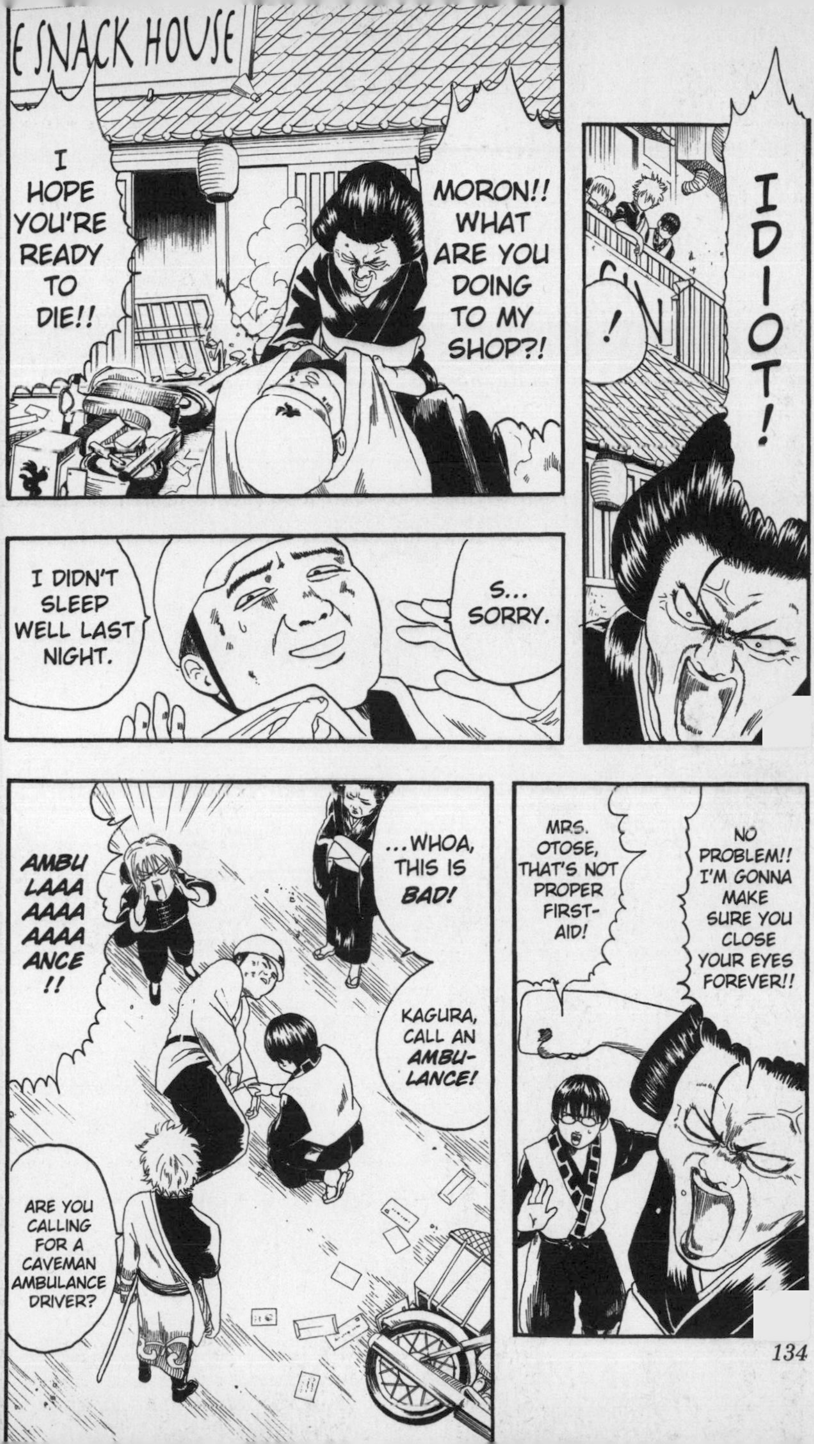
IDIOT!
!
E SNACK HOUSE
MORON!! WHAT ARE YOU DOING TO MY SHOP?!
I HOPE YOU'RE READY TO DIE!!
S... SORRY.
I DIDN'T SLEEP WELL LAST NIGHT.
NO PROBLEM!! I'M GONNA MAKE SURE YOU CLOSE YOUR EYES FOREVER!!
MRS. OTOSE, THAT'S NOT PROPER FIRST-AID!
...WHOA, THIS IS BAD!
KAGURA, CALL AN AMBULANCE!
AMBULAAAAAAAAAAAAANCE!!
ARE YOU CALLING FOR A CAVEMAN AMBULANCE DRIVER?

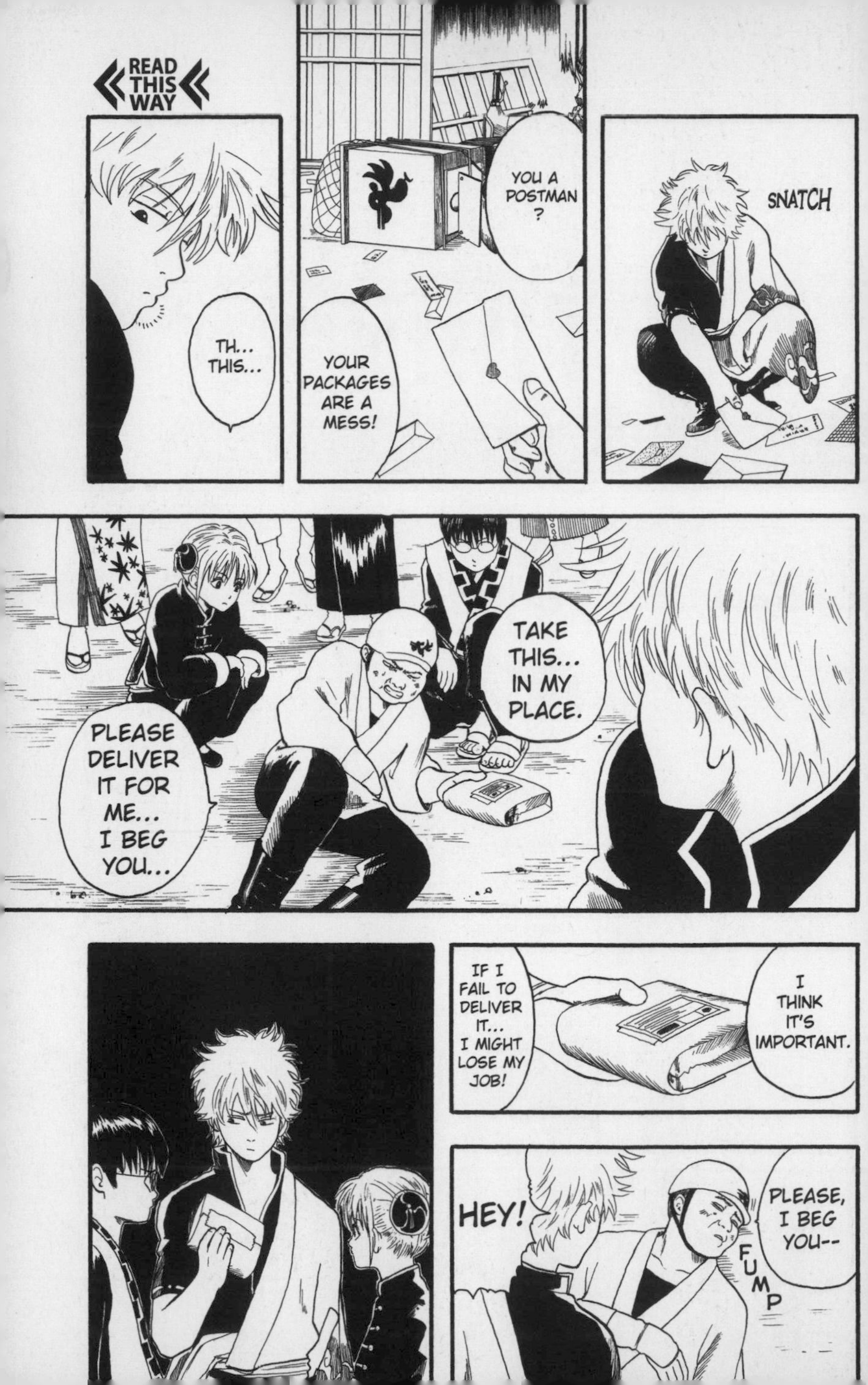
READ THIS WAY
SNATCH
YOU A POSTMAN?
YOUR PACKAGES ARE A MESS!
TH... THIS...
TAKE THIS... IN MY PLACE.
PLEASE DELIVER IT FOR ME... I BEG YOU...
I THINK IT'S IMPORTANT.
IF I FAIL TO DELIVER IT... I MIGHT LOSE MY JOB!
PLEASE, I BEG YOU--
FUMP
HEY!

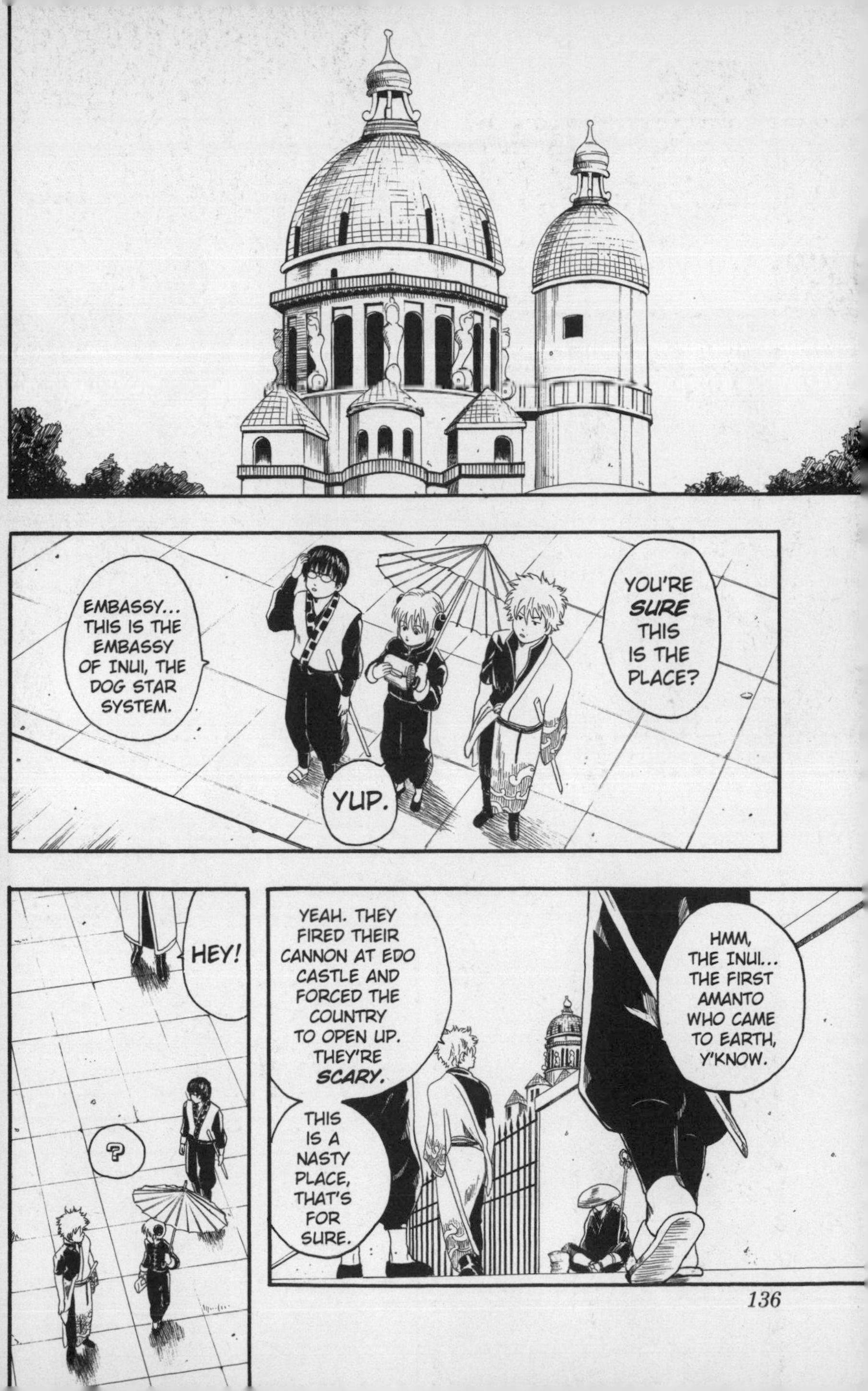
YOU'RE SURE THIS IS THE PLACE?
EMBASSY... THIS IS THE EMBASSY OF INUI, THE DOG STAR SYSTEM.
YUP.
HMM, THE INUI... THE FIRST AMANTO WHO CAME TO EARTH, Y'KNOW.
YEAH. THEY FIRED THEIR CANNON AT EDO CASTLE AND FORCED THE COUNTRY TO OPEN UP. THEY'RE SCARY.
THIS IS A NASTY PLACE, THAT'S FOR SURE.
HEY!
?

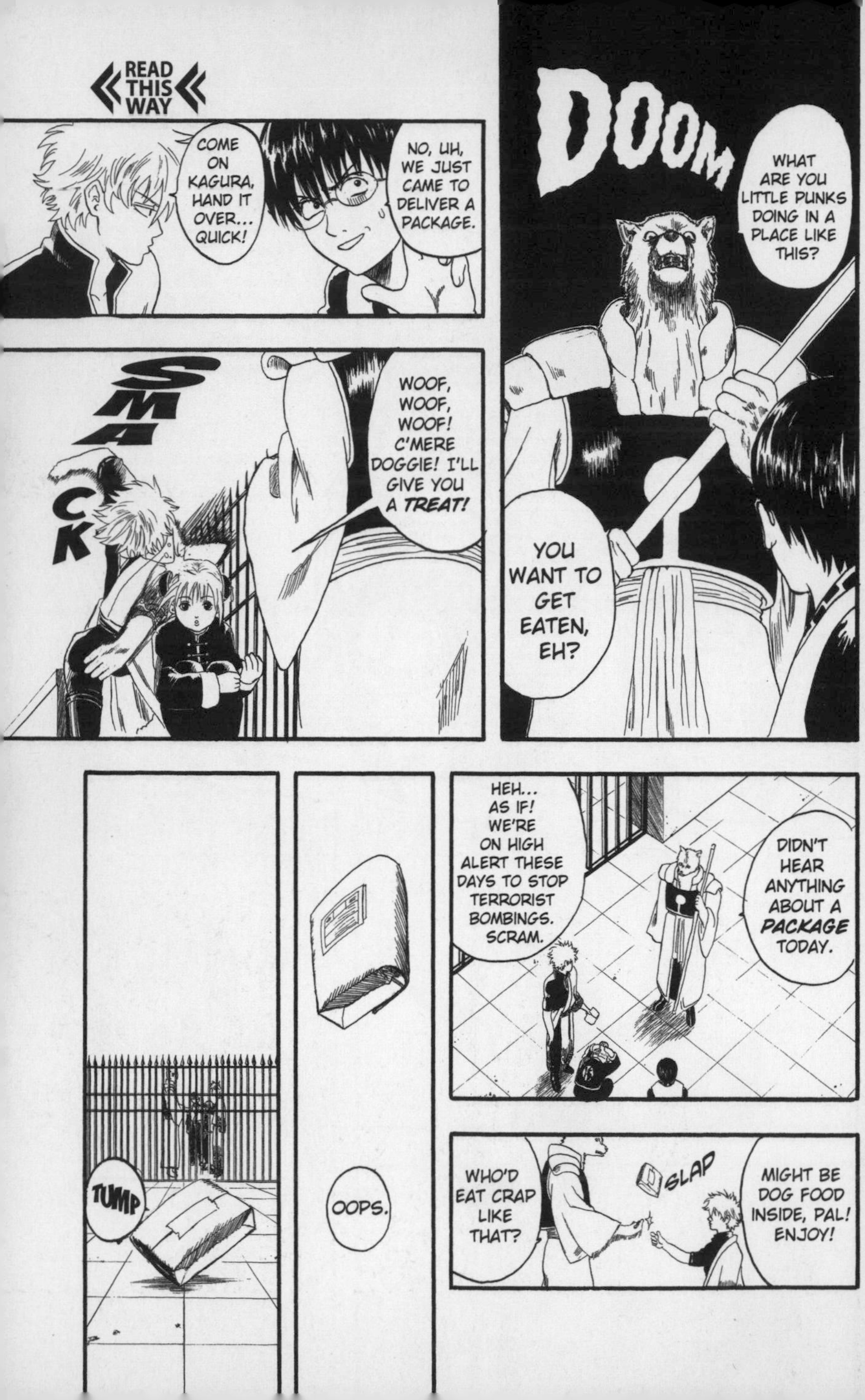
READ THIS WAY
DOOM
WHAT ARE YOU LITTLE PUNKS DOING IN A PLACE LIKE THIS?
YOU WANT TO GET EATEN, EH?
NO, UH, WE JUST CAME TO DELIVER A PACKAGE.
COME ON KAGURA, HAND IT OVER... QUICK!
WOOF, WOOF, WOOF! C'MERE DOGGIE! I'LL GIVE YOU A *TREAT!*
SMACK
DIDN'T HEAR ANYTHING ABOUT A *PACKAGE* TODAY.
HEH... AS IF! WE'RE ON HIGH ALERT THESE DAYS TO STOP TERRORIST BOMBINGS. SCRAM.
MIGHT BE DOG FOOD INSIDE, PAL! ENJOY!
SLAP
WHO'D EAT CRAP LIKE THAT?
OOPS.
TUMP

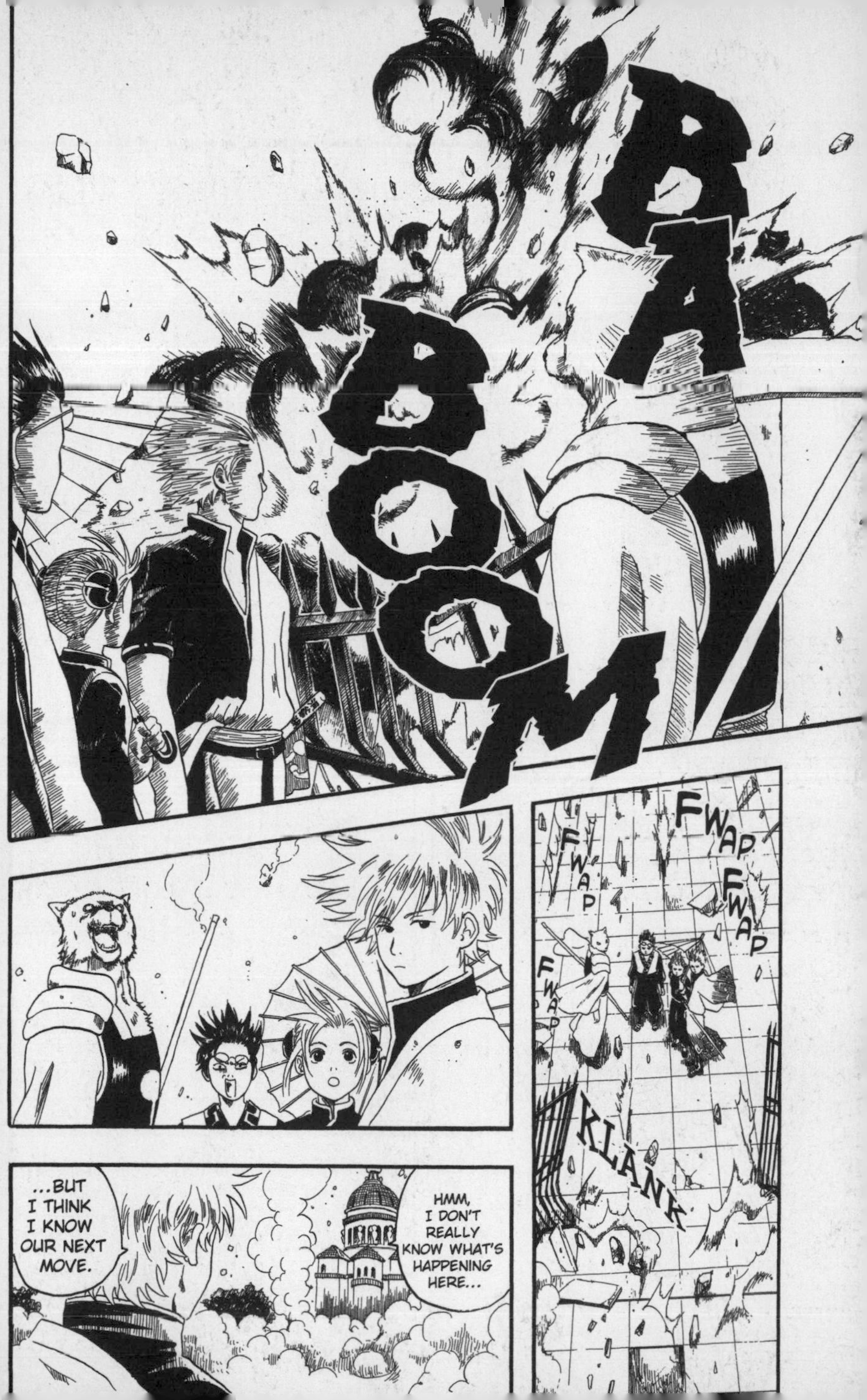
BA-BOOM
FWAP
FWAP
FWAP
FWAP
KLANK
HMM, I DON'T REALLY KNOW WHAT'S HAPPENING HERE...
...BUT I THINK I KNOW OUR NEXT MOVE.

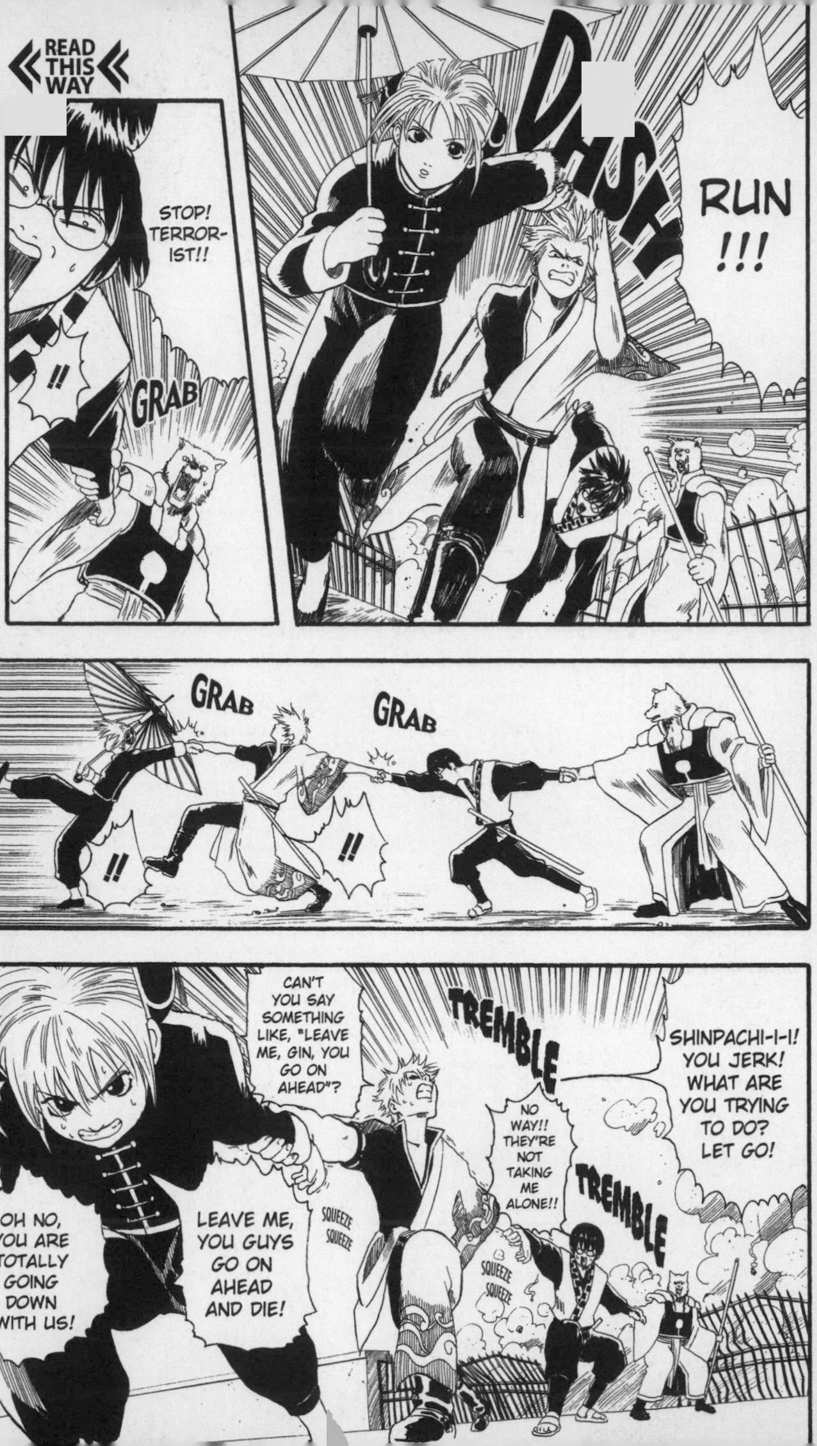
READ THIS WAY
DASH!
RUN !!!
STOP! TERROR-IST!!
!!
GRAB
GRAB
GRAB
!!
!!
SHINPACHI-I-I! YOU JERK! WHAT ARE YOU TRYING TO DO? LET GO!
TREMBLE
NO WAY!! THEY'RE NOT TAKING ME ALONE!!
TREMBLE
SQUEEZE SQUEEZE
CAN'T YOU SAY SOMETHING LIKE, "LEAVE ME, GIN, YOU GO ON AHEAD"?
SQUEEZE SQUEEZE
LEAVE ME, YOU GUYS GO ON AHEAD AND DIE!
OH NO, YOU ARE TOTALLY GOING DOWN WITH US!

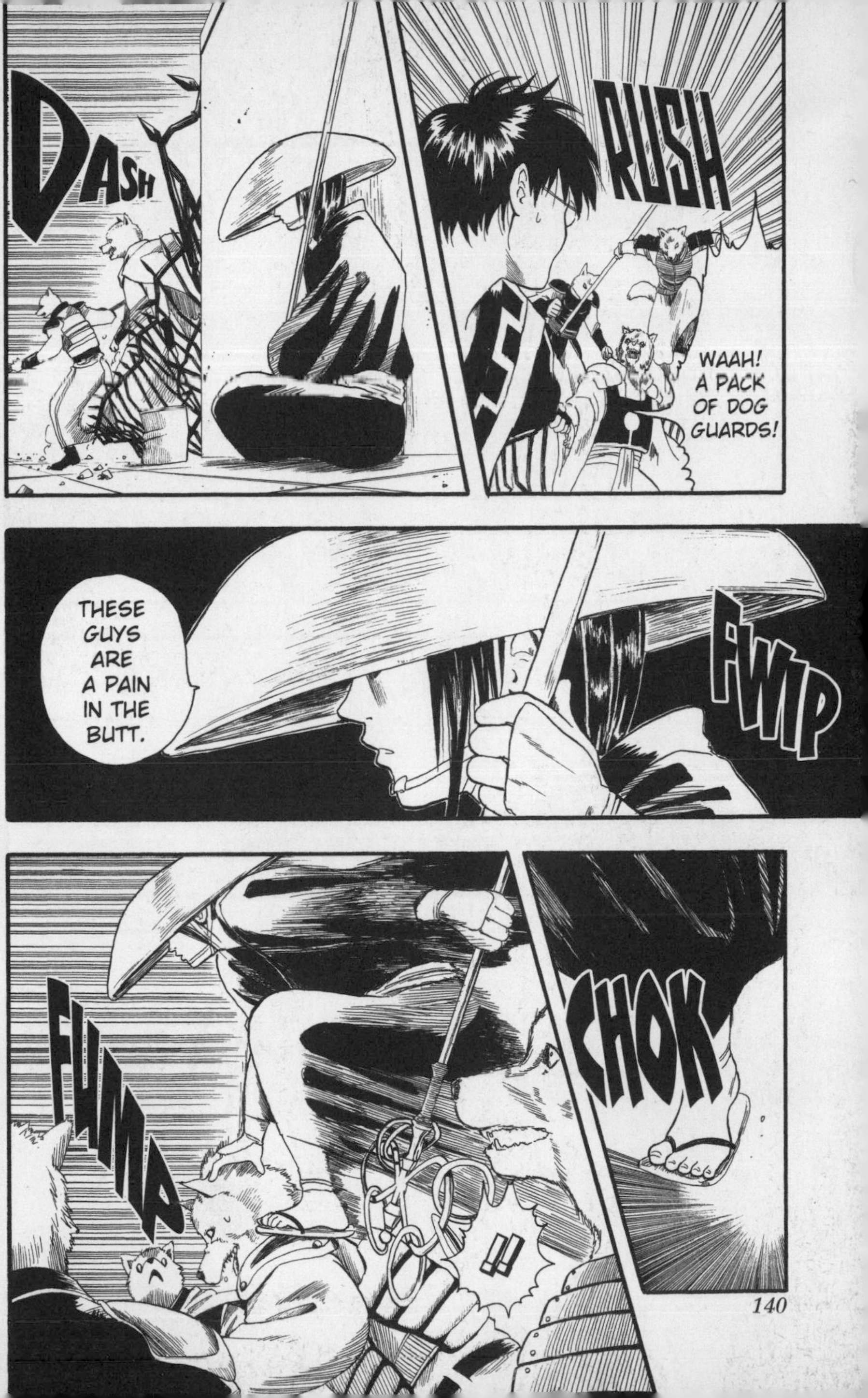

RUSH
WAAH! A PACK OF DOG GUARDS!
DASH
FWIP
THESE GUYS ARE A PAIN IN THE BUTT.
CHOK
!!
FUMP

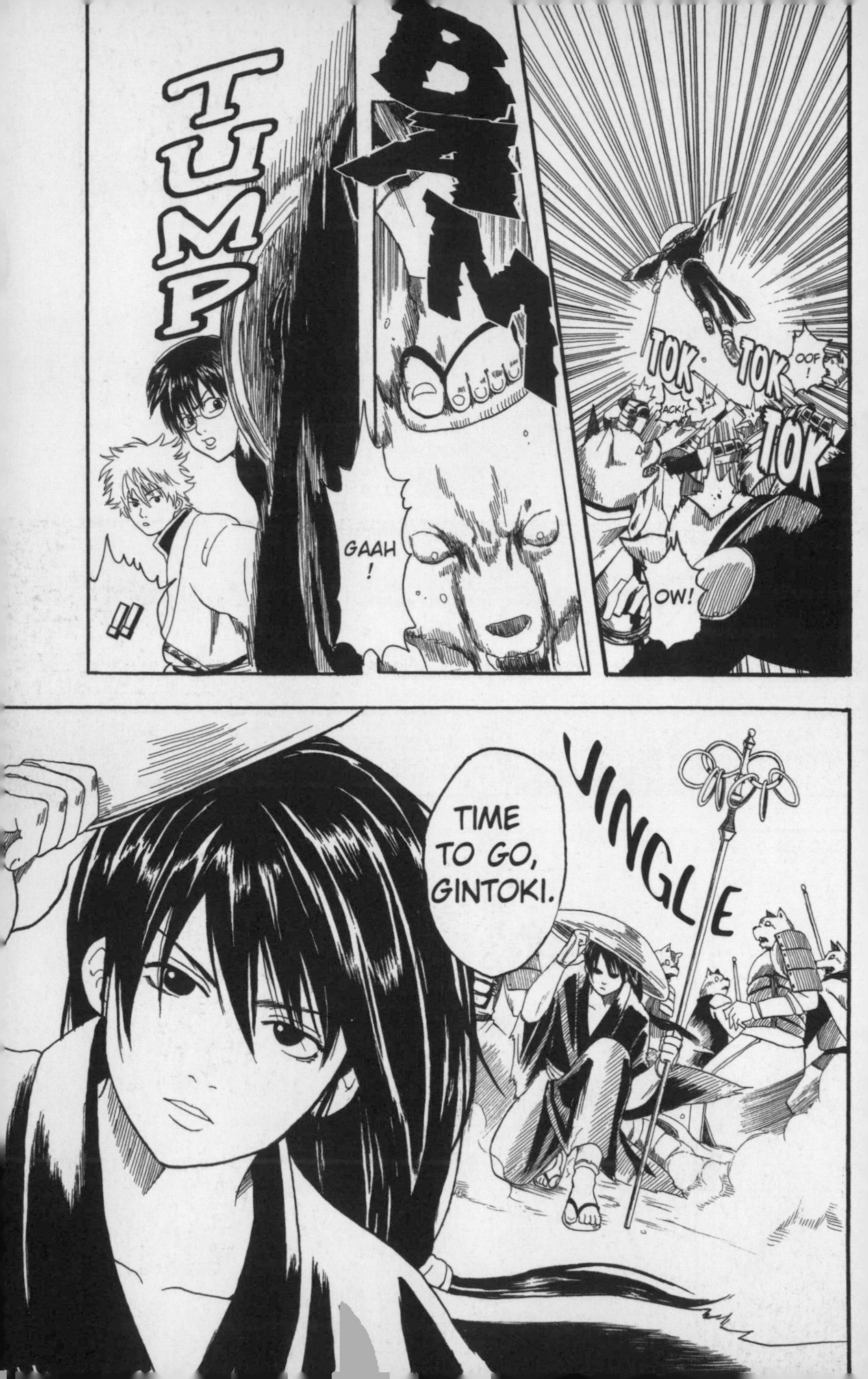
OOF!
TOK
TOK
ACK!
TOK
OW!
BAM
GAAH!
TUMP
!!
JINGLE
TIME TO GO, GINTOKI.

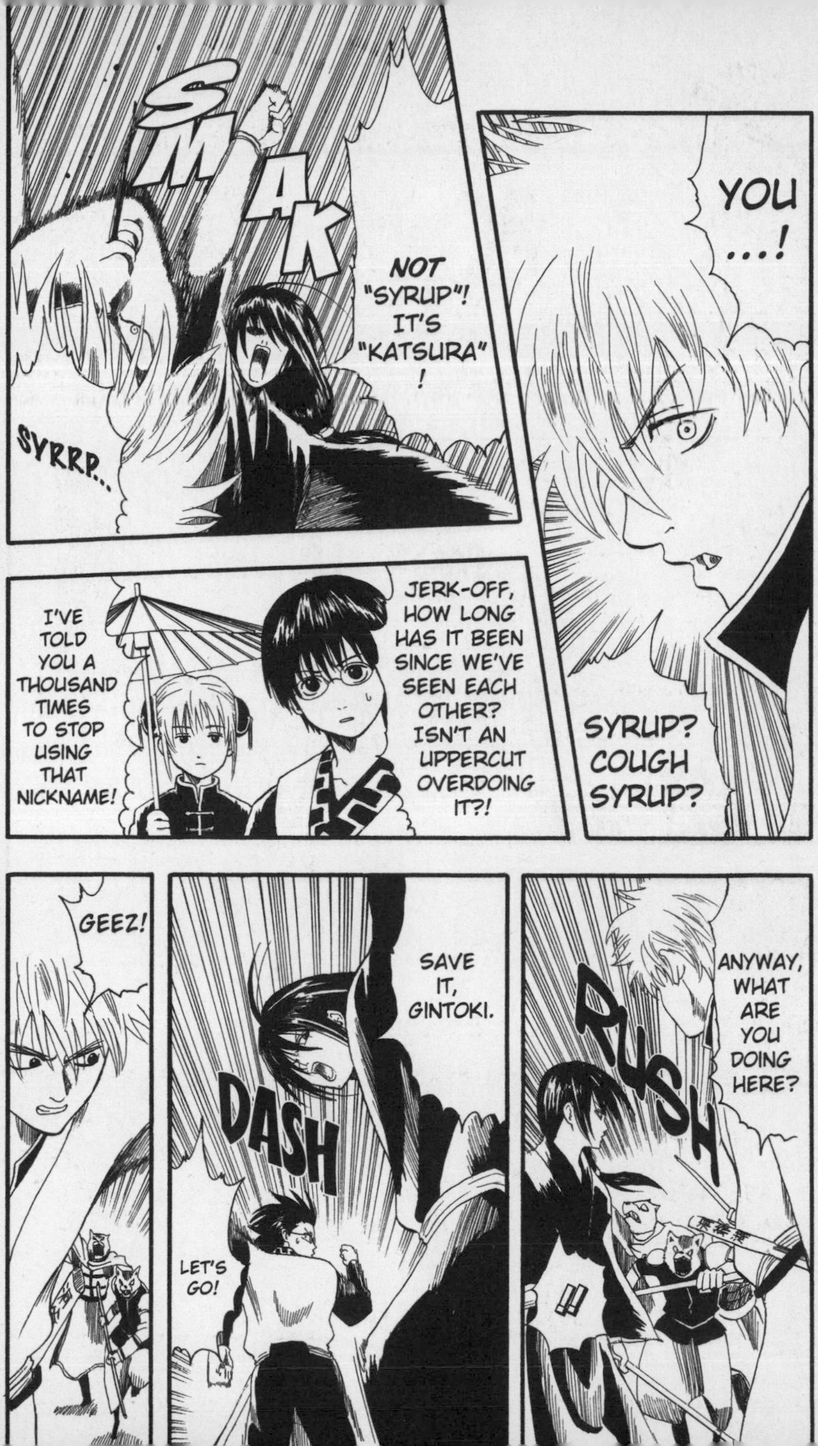
YOU ...!
SYRUP? COUGH SYRUP?
SMAK
NOT "SYRUP"! IT'S "KATSURA"!
SYRRP...
JERK-OFF, HOW LONG HAS IT BEEN SINCE WE'VE SEEN EACH OTHER? ISN'T AN UPPERCUT OVERDOING IT?!
I'VE TOLD YOU A THOUSAND TIMES TO STOP USING THAT NICKNAME!
ANYWAY, WHAT ARE YOU DOING HERE?
RUSH
!!
SAVE IT, GINTOKI.
DASH
LET'S GO!
GEEZ!

READ THIS WAY

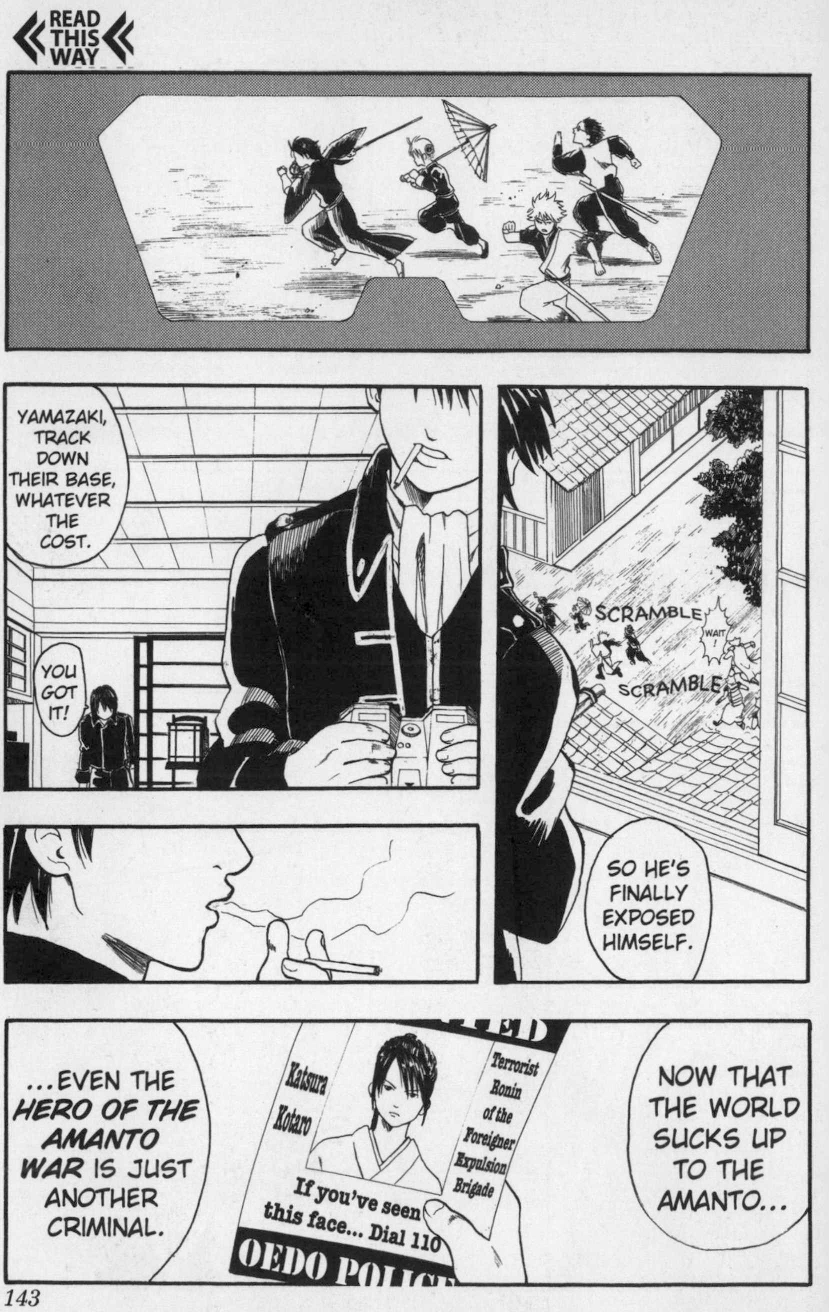

SCRAMBLE
WAIT!
SCRAMBLE
SO HE'S FINALLY EXPOSED HIMSELF.
YAMAZAKI, TRACK DOWN THEIR BASE, WHATEVER THE COST.
YOU GOT IT!
NOW THAT THE WORLD SUCKS UP TO THE AMANTO...
Terrorist Ronin of the Foreigner Expulsion Brigade
Katsura Kotaro
If you've seen this face... Dial 110
OEDO POLICE
...EVEN THE *HERO OF THE AMANTO WAR* IS JUST ANOTHER CRIMINAL.

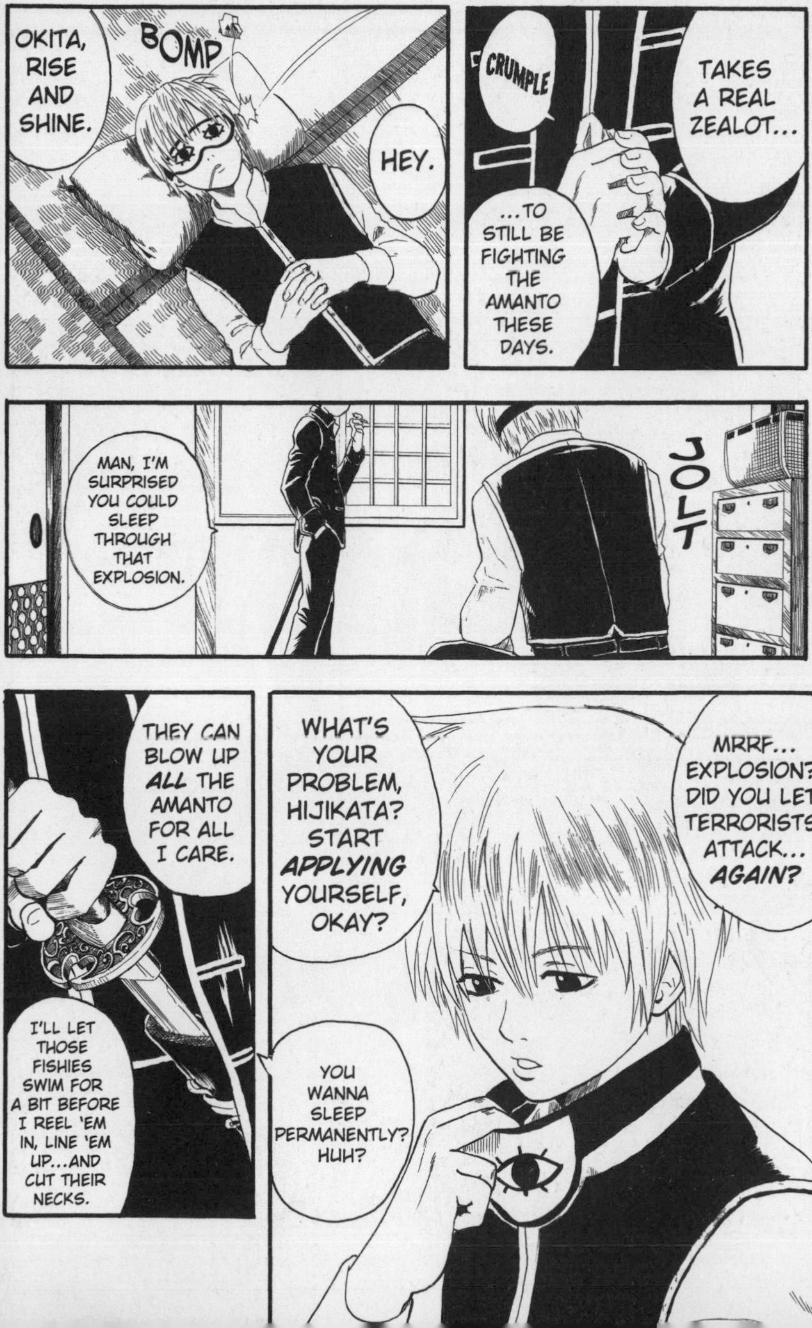

TAKES A REAL ZEALOT...
CRUMPLE
...TO STILL BE FIGHTING THE AMANTO THESE DAYS.
BOMP
OKITA, RISE AND SHINE.
HEY.
JOLT
MAN, I'M SURPRISED YOU COULD SLEEP THROUGH THAT EXPLOSION.
MRRF... EXPLOSION? DID YOU LET TERRORISTS ATTACK... AGAIN?
WHAT'S YOUR PROBLEM, HIJIKATA? START APPLYING YOURSELF, OKAY?
YOU WANNA SLEEP PERMANENTLY? HUH?
THEY CAN BLOW UP ALL THE AMANTO FOR ALL I CARE.
I'LL LET THOSE FISHIES SWIM FOR A BIT BEFORE I REEL 'EM IN, LINE 'EM UP...AND CUT THEIR NECKS.

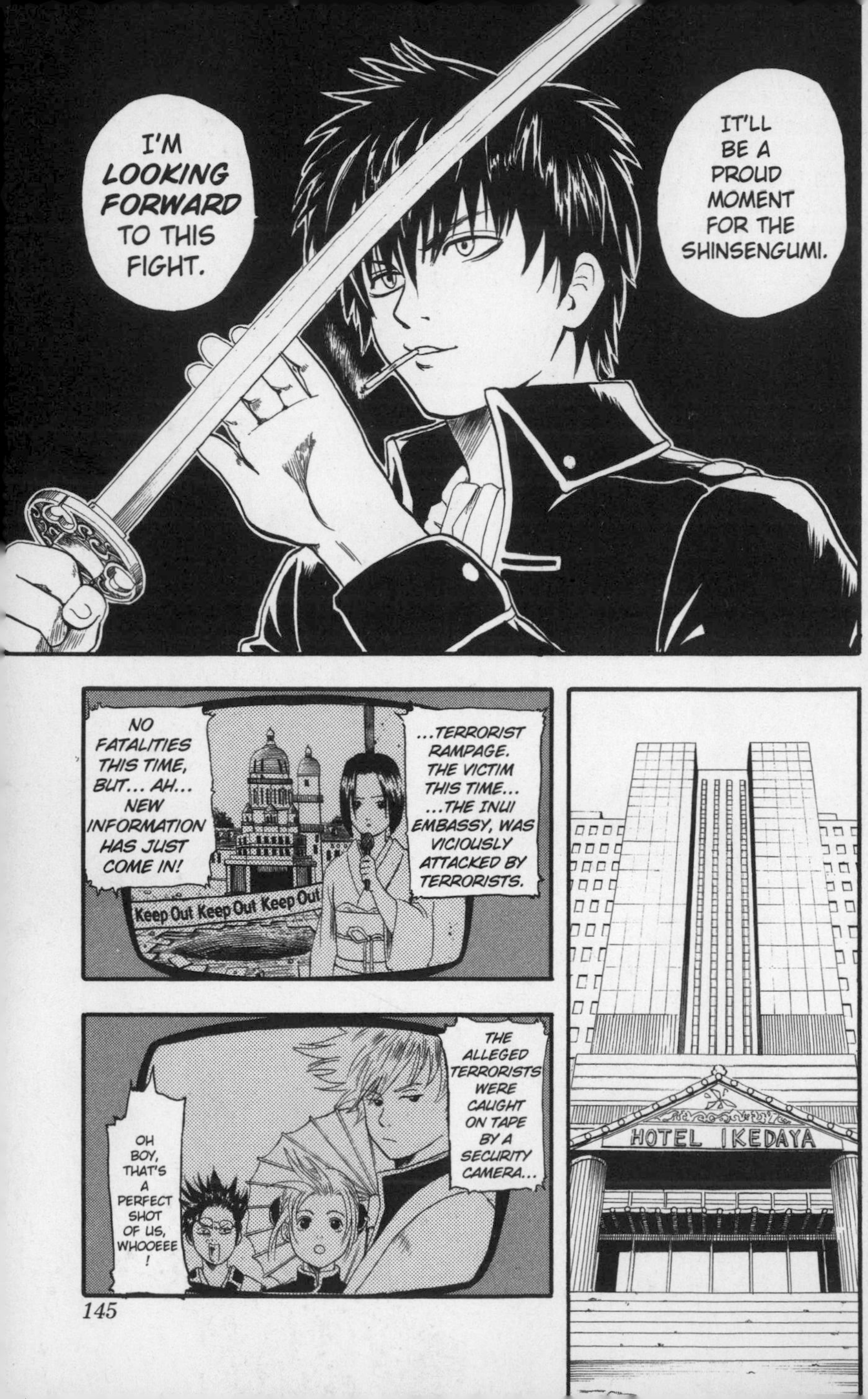
IT'LL BE A PROUD MOMENT FOR THE SHINSENGUMI.
I'M LOOKING FORWARD TO THIS FIGHT.
HOTEL IKEDAYA
...TERRORIST RAMPAGE. THE VICTIM THIS TIME... ...THE INUI EMBASSY, WAS VICIOUSLY ATTACKED BY TERRORISTS.
NO FATALITIES THIS TIME, BUT... AH... NEW INFORMATION HAS JUST COME IN!
Keep Out Keep Out Keep Out
THE ALLEGED TERRORISTS WERE CAUGHT ON TAPE BY A SECURITY CAMERA...
OH BOY, THAT'S A PERFECT SHOT OF US, WHOOEEE!

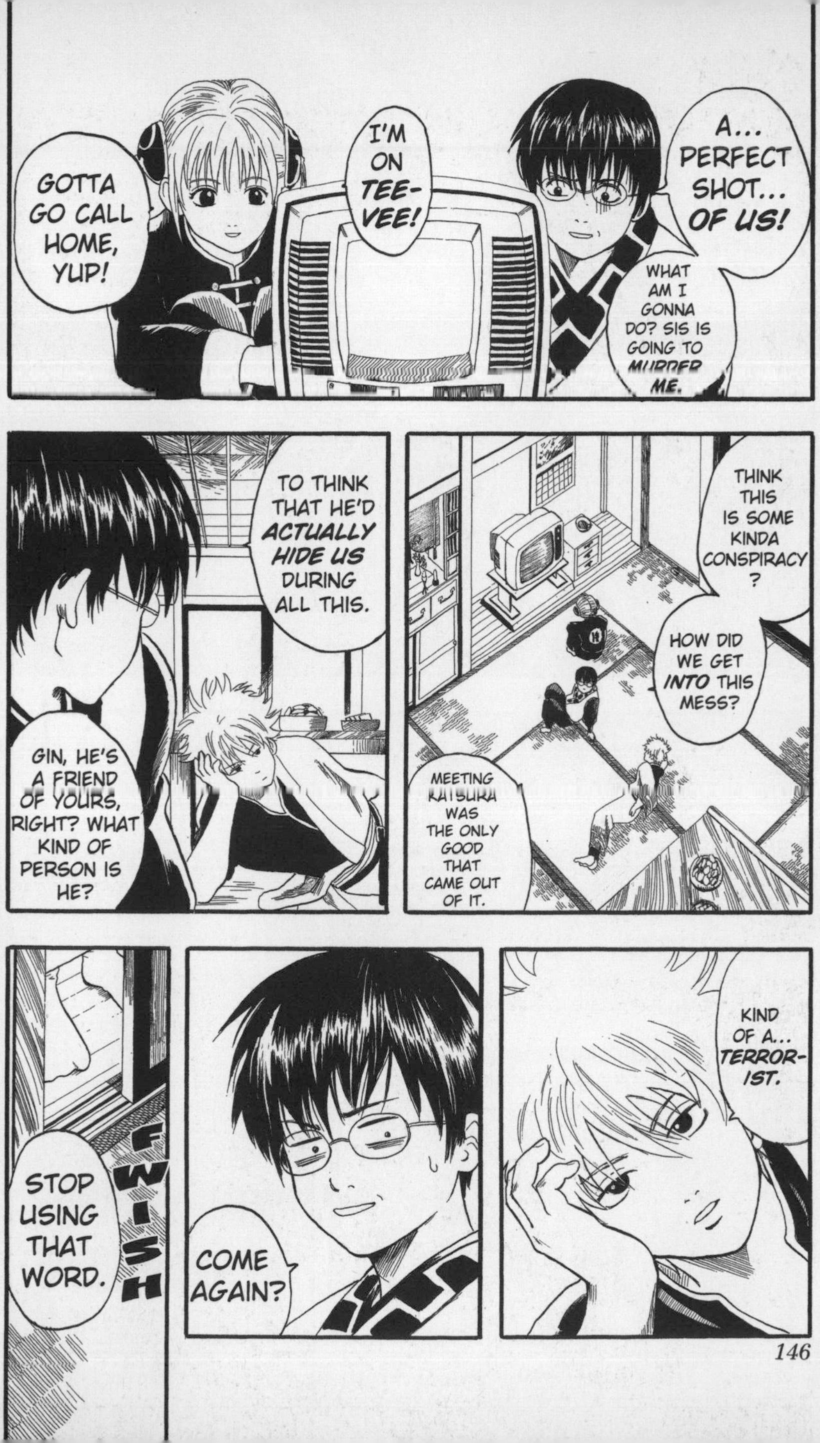
A... PERFECT SHOT... OF US!
WHAT AM I GONNA DO? SIS IS GOING TO MURDER ME.
I'M ON TEE-VEE!
GOTTA GO CALL HOME, YUP!
THINK THIS IS SOME KINDA CONSPIRACY?
HOW DID WE GET INTO THIS MESS?
MEETING KATSURA WAS THE ONLY GOOD THAT CAME OUT OF IT.
TO THINK THAT HE'D ACTUALLY HIDE US DURING ALL THIS.
GIN, HE'S A FRIEND OF YOURS, RIGHT? WHAT KIND OF PERSON IS HE?
KIND OF A... TERRORIST.
COME AGAIN?
FWISH
STOP USING THAT WORD.

READ THIS WAY

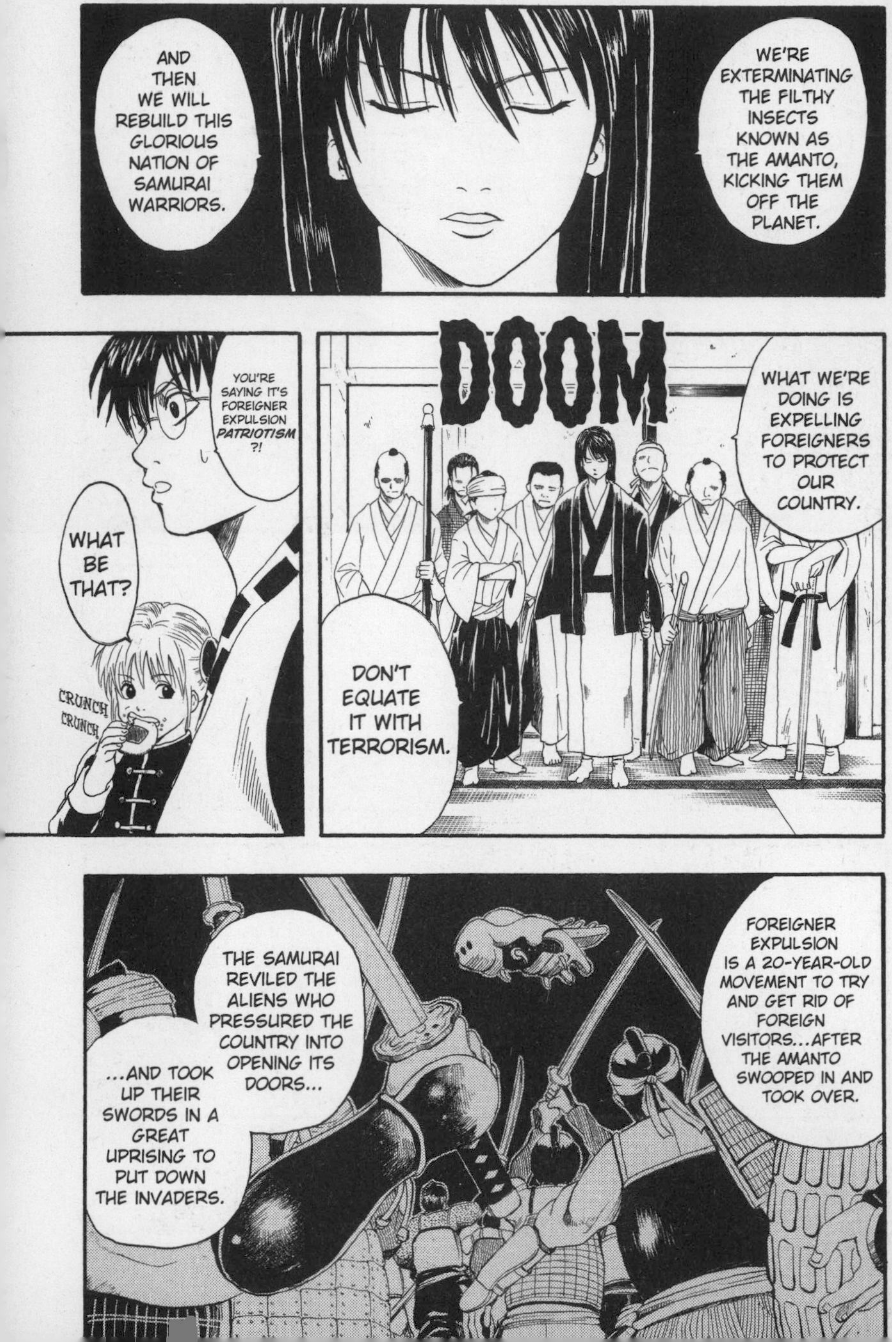

WE'RE EXTERMINATING THE FILTHY INSECTS KNOWN AS THE AMANTO, KICKING THEM OFF THE PLANET.
AND THEN WE WILL REBUILD THIS GLORIOUS NATION OF SAMURAI WARRIORS.
DOOM
WHAT WE'RE DOING IS EXPELLING FOREIGNERS TO PROTECT OUR COUNTRY.
DON'T EQUATE IT WITH TERRORISM.
YOU'RE SAYING IT'S FOREIGNER EXPULSION PATRIOTISM?!
WHAT BE THAT?
CRUNCH CRUNCH
FOREIGNER EXPULSION IS A 20-YEAR-OLD MOVEMENT TO TRY AND GET RID OF FOREIGN VISITORS...AFTER THE AMANTO SWOOPED IN AND TOOK OVER.
THE SAMURAI REVILED THE ALIENS WHO PRESSURED THE COUNTRY INTO OPENING ITS DOORS...
...AND TOOK UP THEIR SWORDS IN A GREAT UPRISING TO PUT DOWN THE INVADERS.

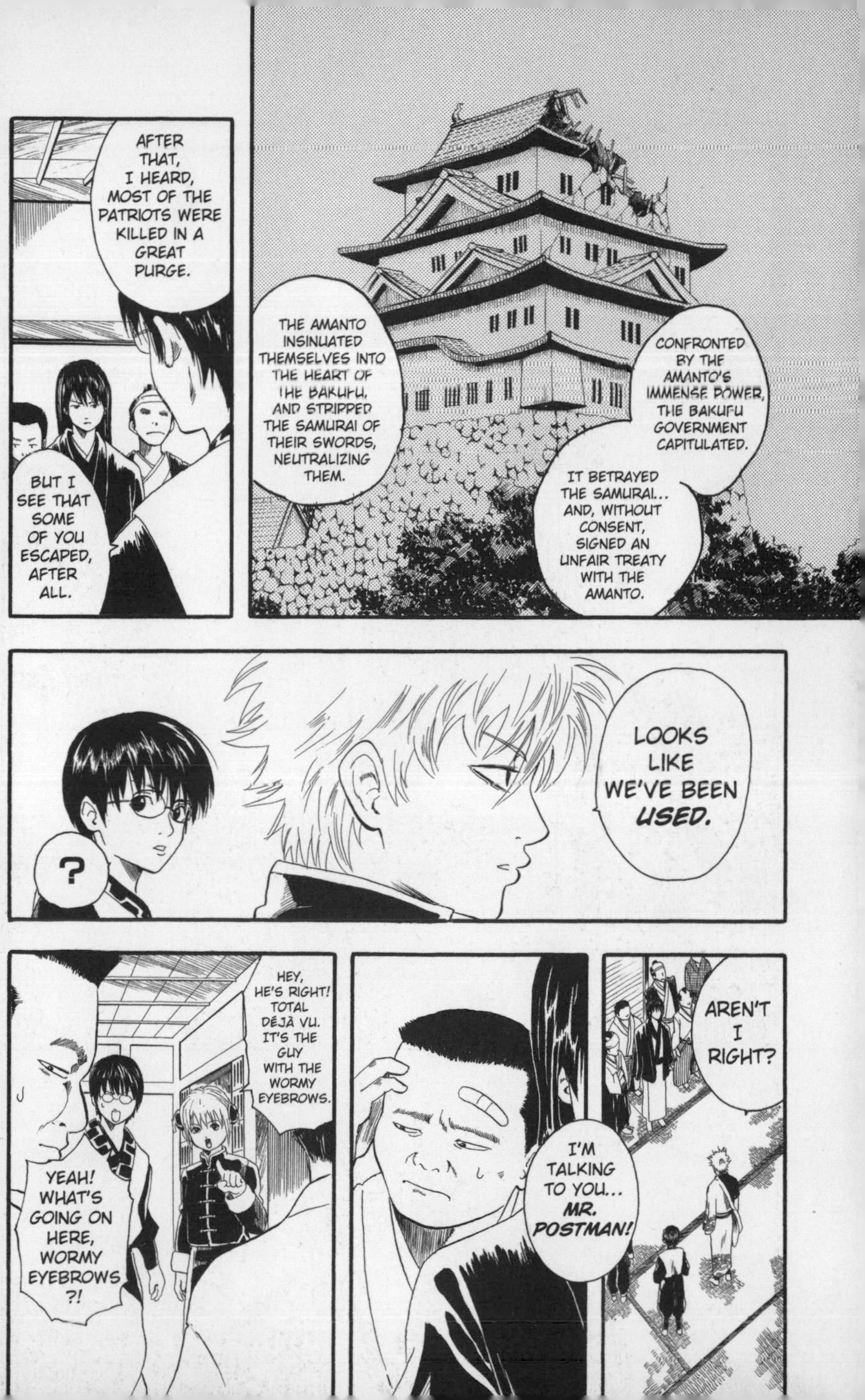
CONFRONTED BY THE AMANTO'S IMMENSE POWER, THE BAKUFU GOVERNMENT CAPITULATED.
IT BETRAYED THE SAMURAI... AND, WITHOUT CONSENT, SIGNED AN UNFAIR TREATY WITH THE AMANTO.
THE AMANTO INSINUATED THEMSELVES INTO THE HEART OF THE BAKUFU, AND STRIPPED THE SAMURAI OF THEIR SWORDS, NEUTRALIZING THEM.
AFTER THAT, I HEARD, MOST OF THE PATRIOTS WERE KILLED IN A GREAT PURGE.
BUT I SEE THAT SOME OF YOU ESCAPED, AFTER ALL.
LOOKS LIKE WE'VE BEEN ***USED.***
?
AREN'T I RIGHT?
I'M TALKING TO YOU... ***MR. POSTMAN!***
HEY, HE'S RIGHT! TOTAL DÉJÀ VU. IT'S THE GUY WITH THE WORMY EYEBROWS.
YEAH! WHAT'S GOING ON HERE, WORMY EYEBROWS ?!

READ THIS WAY

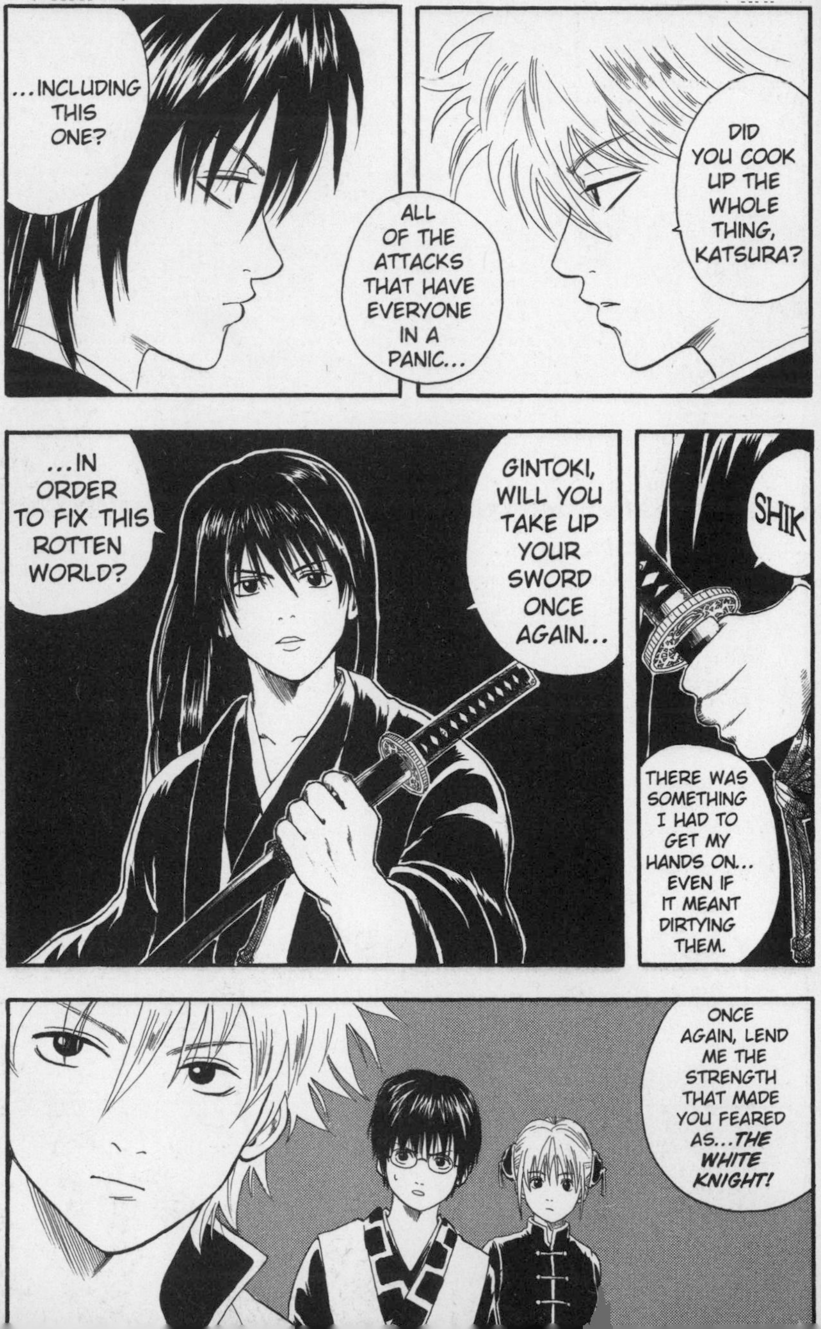
DID YOU COOK UP THE WHOLE THING, KATSURA?
ALL OF THE ATTACKS THAT HAVE EVERYONE IN A PANIC...
...INCLUDING THIS ONE?
SHIK
THERE WAS SOMETHING I HAD TO GET MY HANDS ON... EVEN IF IT MEANT DIRTYING THEM.
GINTOKI, WILL YOU TAKE UP YOUR SWORD ONCE AGAIN...
...IN ORDER TO FIX THIS ROTTEN WORLD?
ONCE AGAIN, LEND ME THE STRENGTH THAT MADE YOU FEARED AS...THE WHITE KNIGHT!

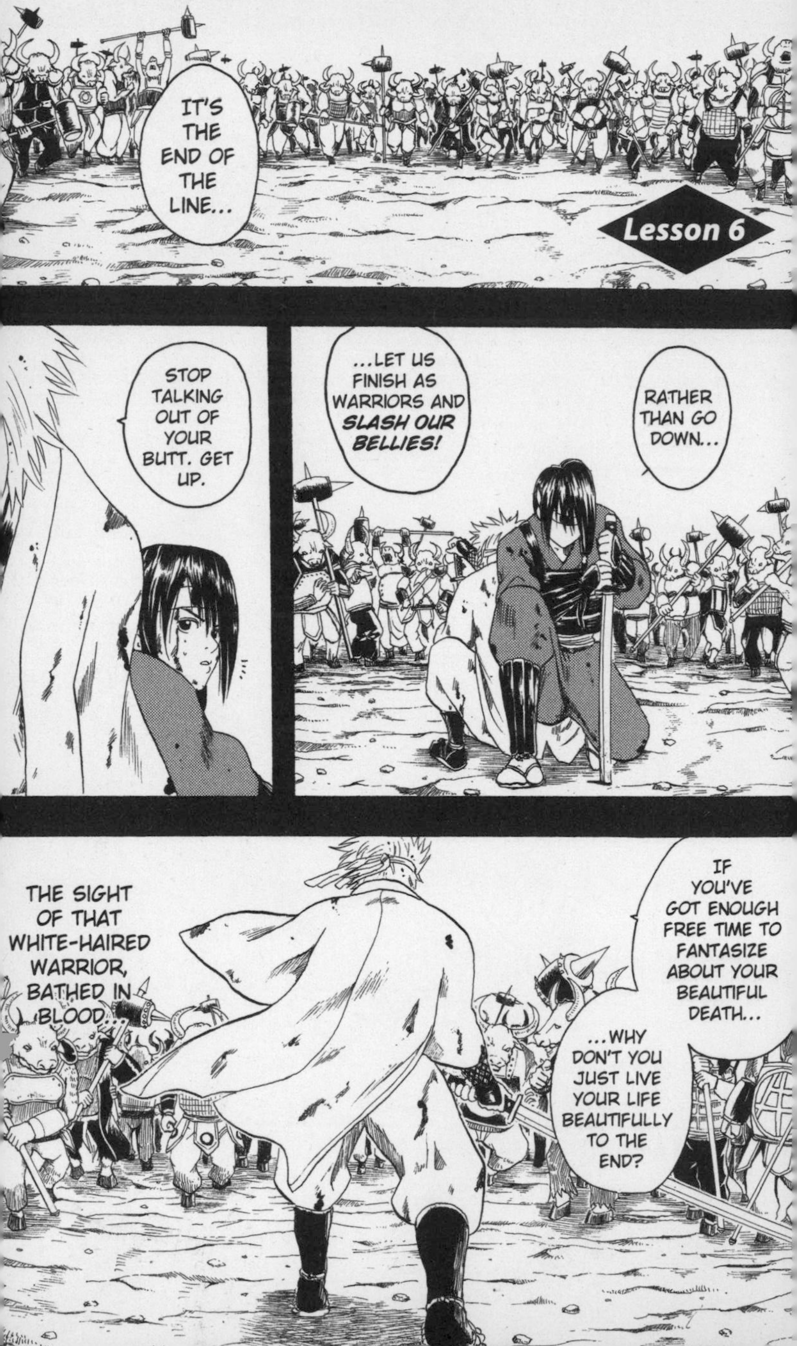
IT'S THE END OF THE LINE...
Lesson 6
RATHER THAN GO DOWN...
...LET US FINISH AS WARRIORS AND SLASH OUR BELLIES!
STOP TALKING OUT OF YOUR BUTT. GET UP.
IF YOU'VE GOT ENOUGH FREE TIME TO FANTASIZE ABOUT YOUR BEAUTIFUL DEATH...
...WHY DON'T YOU JUST LIVE YOUR LIFE BEAUTIFULLY TO THE END?
THE SIGHT OF THAT WHITE-HAIRED WARRIOR, BATHED IN BLOOD

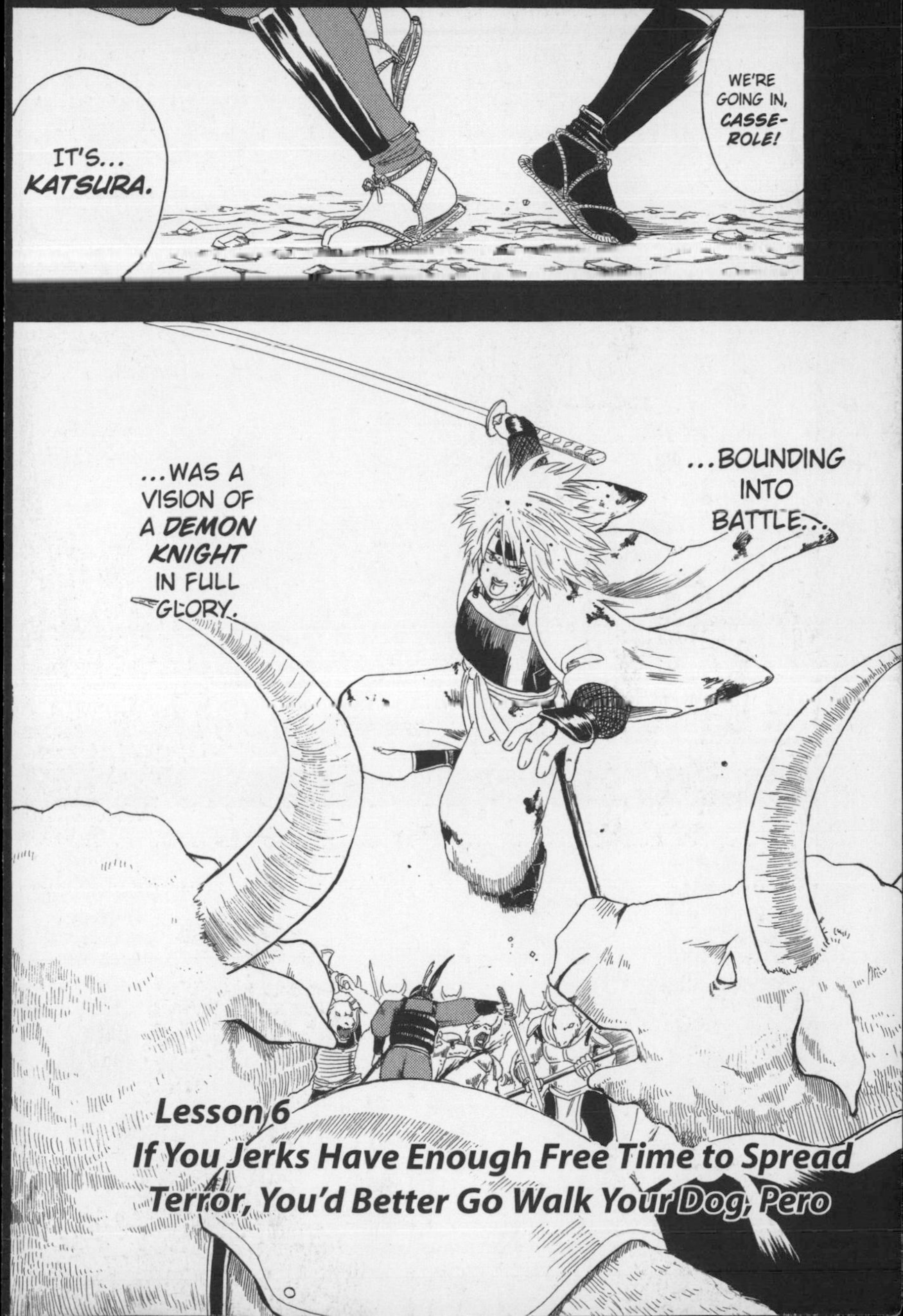
WE'RE GOING IN, CASSEROLE!
IT'S... KATSURA.
...BOUNDING INTO BATTLE...
...WAS A VISION OF A DEMON KNIGHT IN FULL GLORY.

Lesson 6
If You Jerks Have Enough Free Time to Spread Terror, You'd Better Go Walk Your Dog, Pero

READ THIS WAY

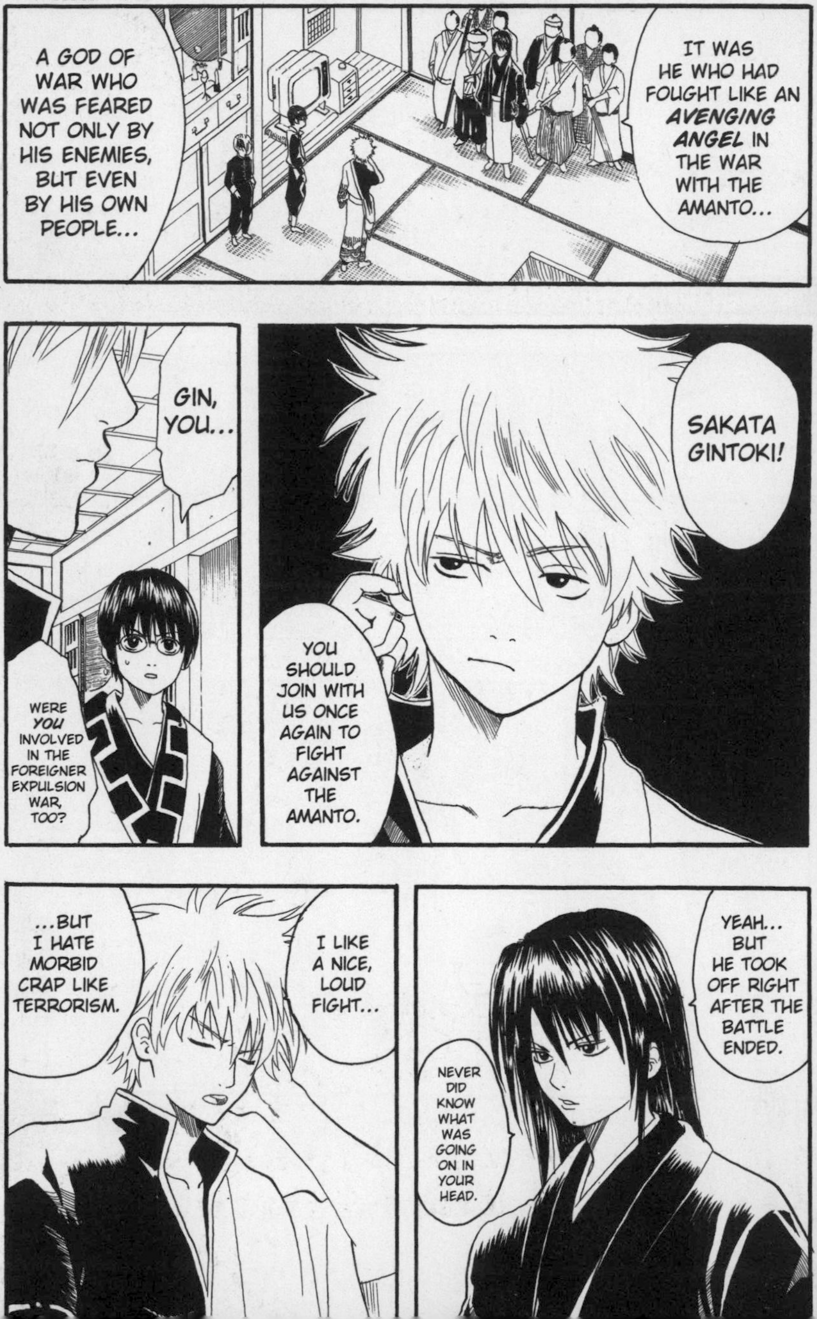
IT WAS HE WHO HAD FOUGHT LIKE AN *AVENGING ANGEL* IN THE WAR WITH THE AMANTO...
A GOD OF WAR WHO WAS FEARED NOT ONLY BY HIS ENEMIES, BUT EVEN BY HIS OWN PEOPLE...
SAKATA GINTOKI!
YOU SHOULD JOIN WITH US ONCE AGAIN TO FIGHT AGAINST THE AMANTO.
GIN, YOU...
WERE *YOU* INVOLVED IN THE FOREIGNER EXPULSION WAR, TOO?
YEAH... BUT HE TOOK OFF RIGHT AFTER THE BATTLE ENDED.
NEVER DID KNOW WHAT WAS GOING ON IN YOUR HEAD.
I LIKE A NICE, LOUD FIGHT...
...BUT I HATE MORBID CRAP LIKE TERRORISM.

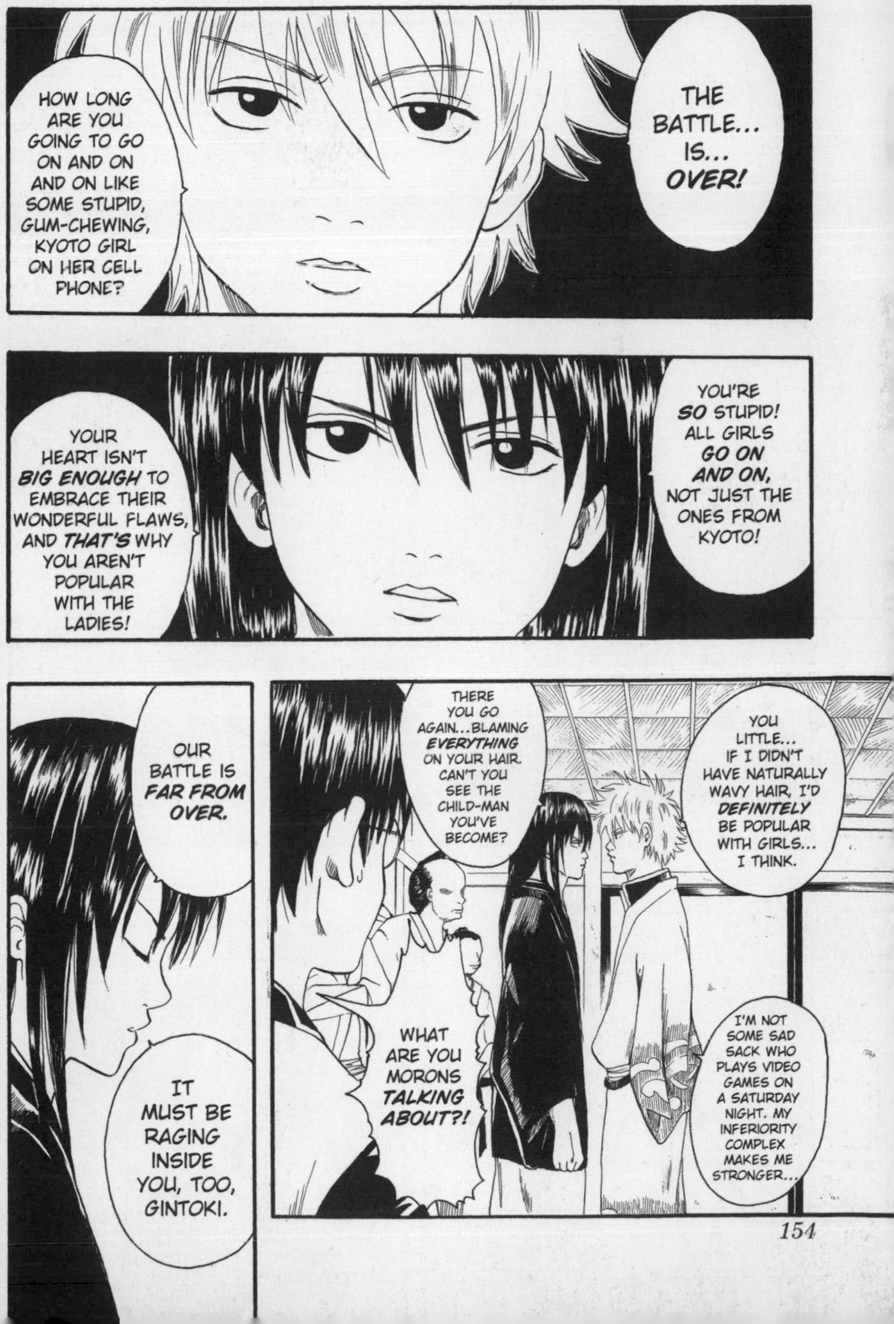
THE BATTLE... IS... OVER!
HOW LONG ARE YOU GOING TO GO ON AND ON AND ON LIKE SOME STUPID, GUM-CHEWING, KYOTO GIRL ON HER CELL PHONE?
YOU'RE SO STUPID! ALL GIRLS GO ON AND ON, NOT JUST THE ONES FROM KYOTO!
YOUR HEART ISN'T BIG ENOUGH TO EMBRACE THEIR WONDERFUL FLAWS, AND THAT'S WHY YOU AREN'T POPULAR WITH THE LADIES!
YOU LITTLE... IF I DIDN'T HAVE NATURALLY WAVY HAIR, I'D DEFINITELY BE POPULAR WITH GIRLS... I THINK.
THERE YOU GO AGAIN...BLAMING EVERYTHING ON YOUR HAIR. CAN'T YOU SEE THE CHILD-MAN YOU'VE BECOME?
I'M NOT SOME SAD SACK WHO PLAYS VIDEO GAMES ON A SATURDAY NIGHT. MY INFERIORITY COMPLEX MAKES ME STRONGER...
WHAT ARE YOU MORONS TALKING ABOUT?!
OUR BATTLE IS FAR FROM OVER.
IT MUST BE RAGING INSIDE YOU, TOO, GINTOKI.

READ THIS WAY

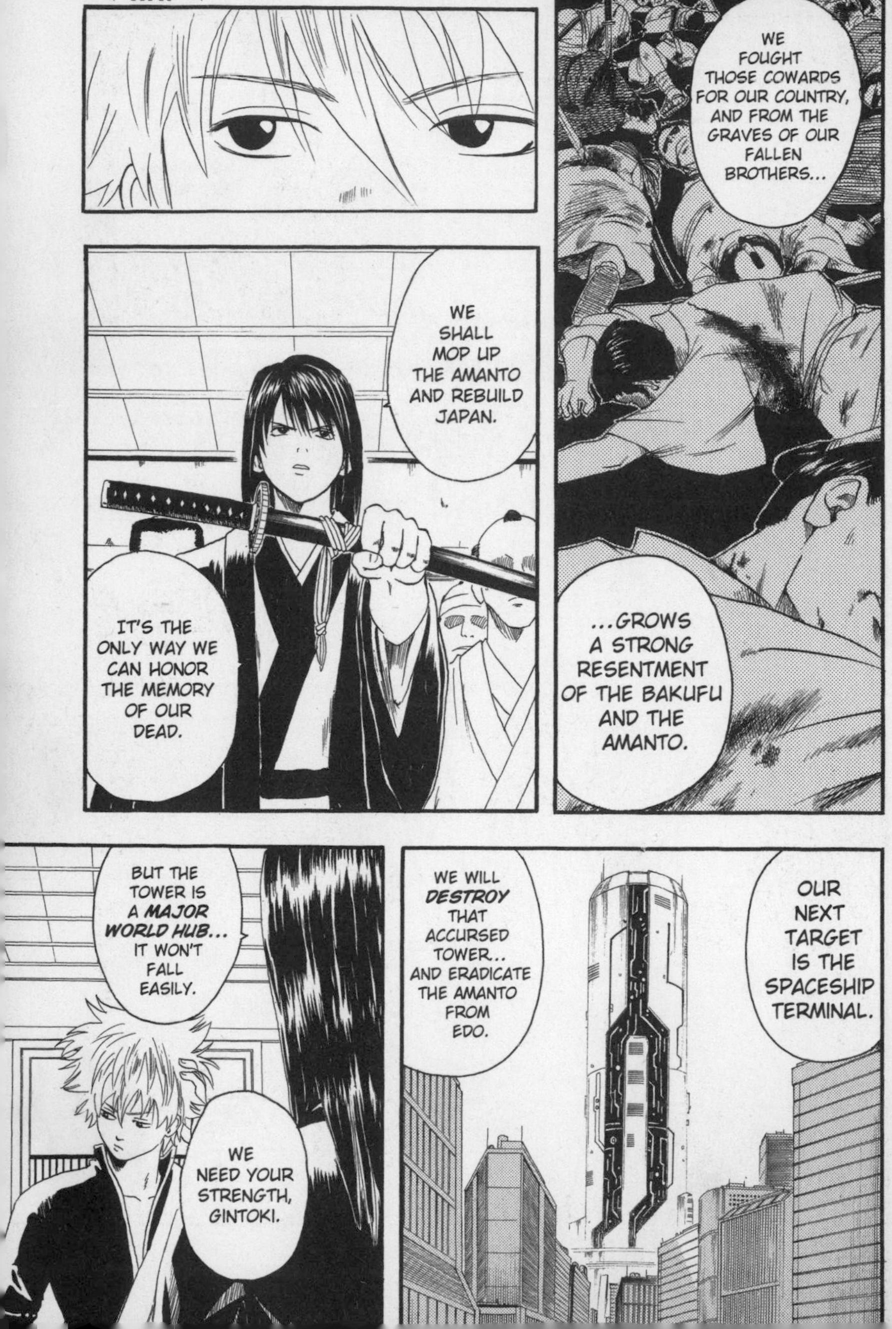
WE FOUGHT THOSE COWARDS FOR OUR COUNTRY, AND FROM THE GRAVES OF OUR FALLEN BROTHERS...
...GROWS A STRONG RESENTMENT OF THE BAKUFU AND THE AMANTO.
WE SHALL MOP UP THE AMANTO AND REBUILD JAPAN.
IT'S THE ONLY WAY WE CAN HONOR THE MEMORY OF OUR DEAD.
OUR NEXT TARGET IS THE SPACESHIP TERMINAL.
WE WILL *DESTROY* THAT ACCURSED TOWER... AND ERADICATE THE AMANTO FROM EDO.
BUT THE TOWER IS A ***MAJOR WORLD HUB...*** IT WON'T FALL EASILY.
WE NEED YOUR STRENGTH, GINTOKI.

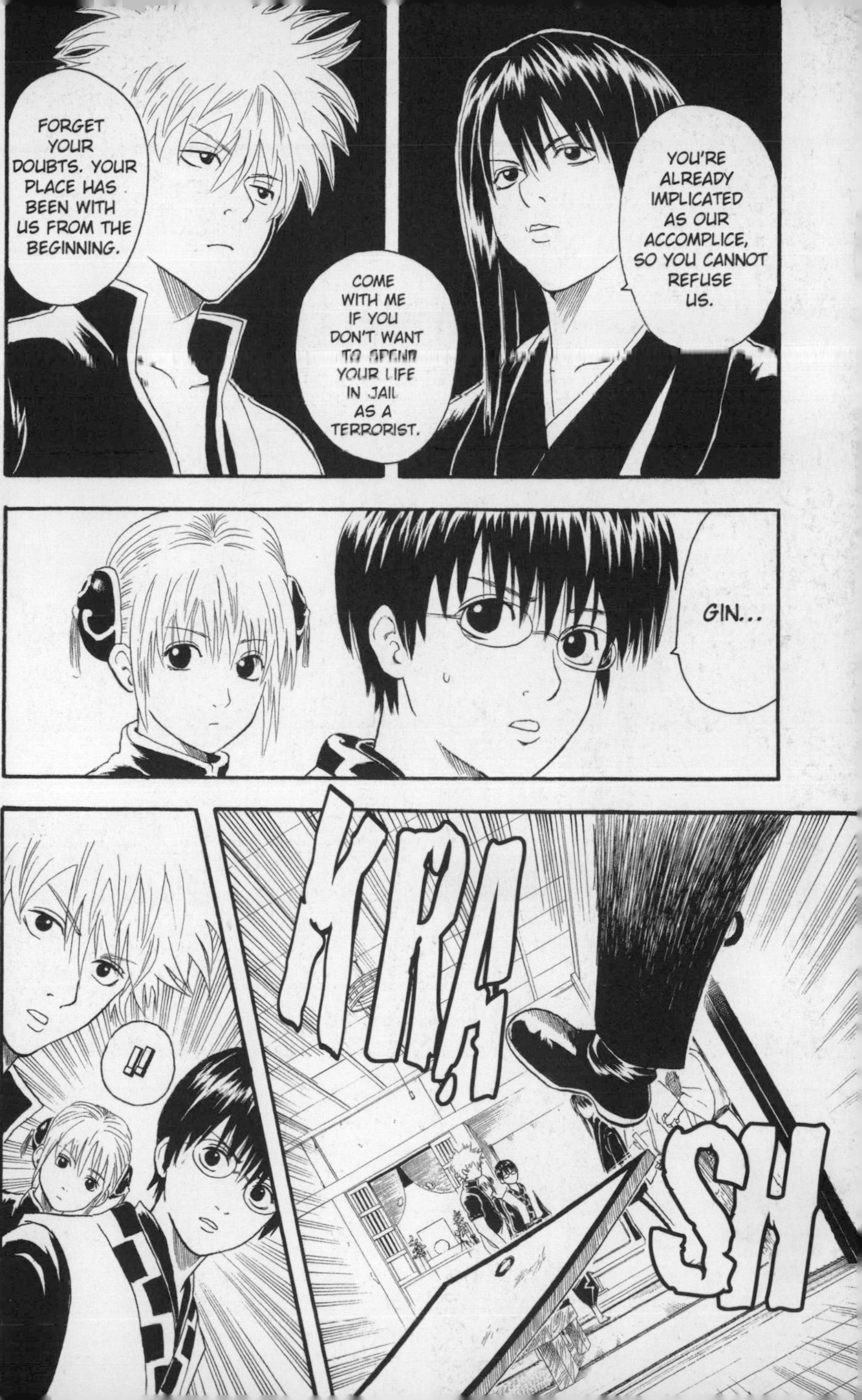
YOU'RE ALREADY IMPLICATED AS OUR ACCOMPLICE, SO YOU CANNOT REFUSE US.
COME WITH ME IF YOU DON'T WANT TO SPEND YOUR LIFE IN JAIL AS A TERRORIST.
FORGET YOUR DOUBTS. YOUR PLACE HAS BEEN WITH US FROM THE BEGINNING.
GIN...
KRA
SH
!!

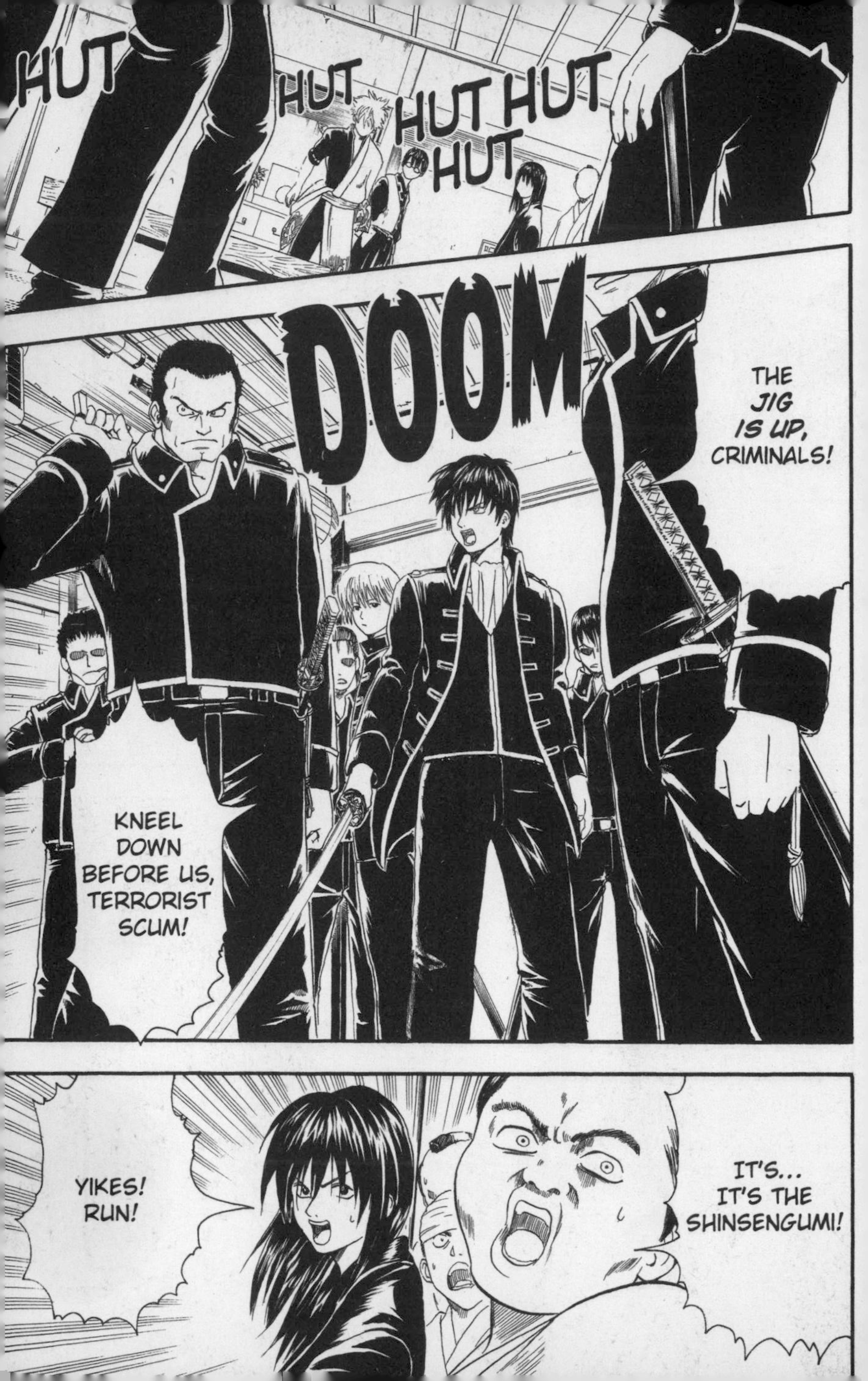
HUT HUT
HUT
HUT
HUT
DOOM
THE JIG IS UP, CRIMINALS!
KNEEL DOWN BEFORE US, TERRORIST SCUM!
IT'S... IT'S THE SHINSENGUMI!
YIKES! RUN!

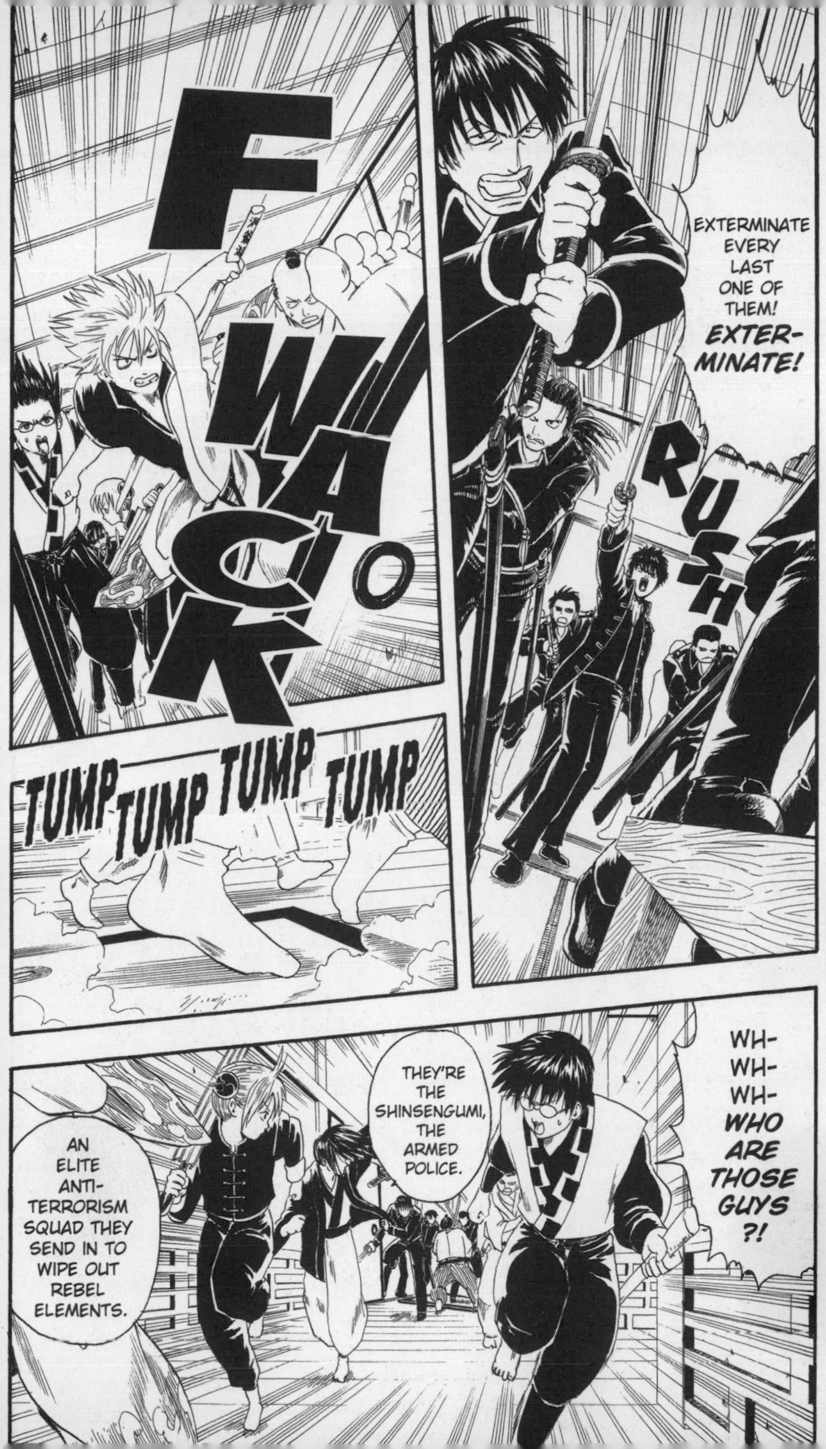
EXTERMINATE EVERY LAST ONE OF THEM! EXTERMINATE!
RUSH
FWACK
TUMP TUMP TUMP TUMP
WH-WH-WH-WHO ARE THOSE GUYS?!
THEY'RE THE SHINSENGUMI, THE ARMED POLICE.
AN ELITE ANTI-TERRORISM SQUAD THEY SEND IN TO WIPE OUT REBEL ELEMENTS.

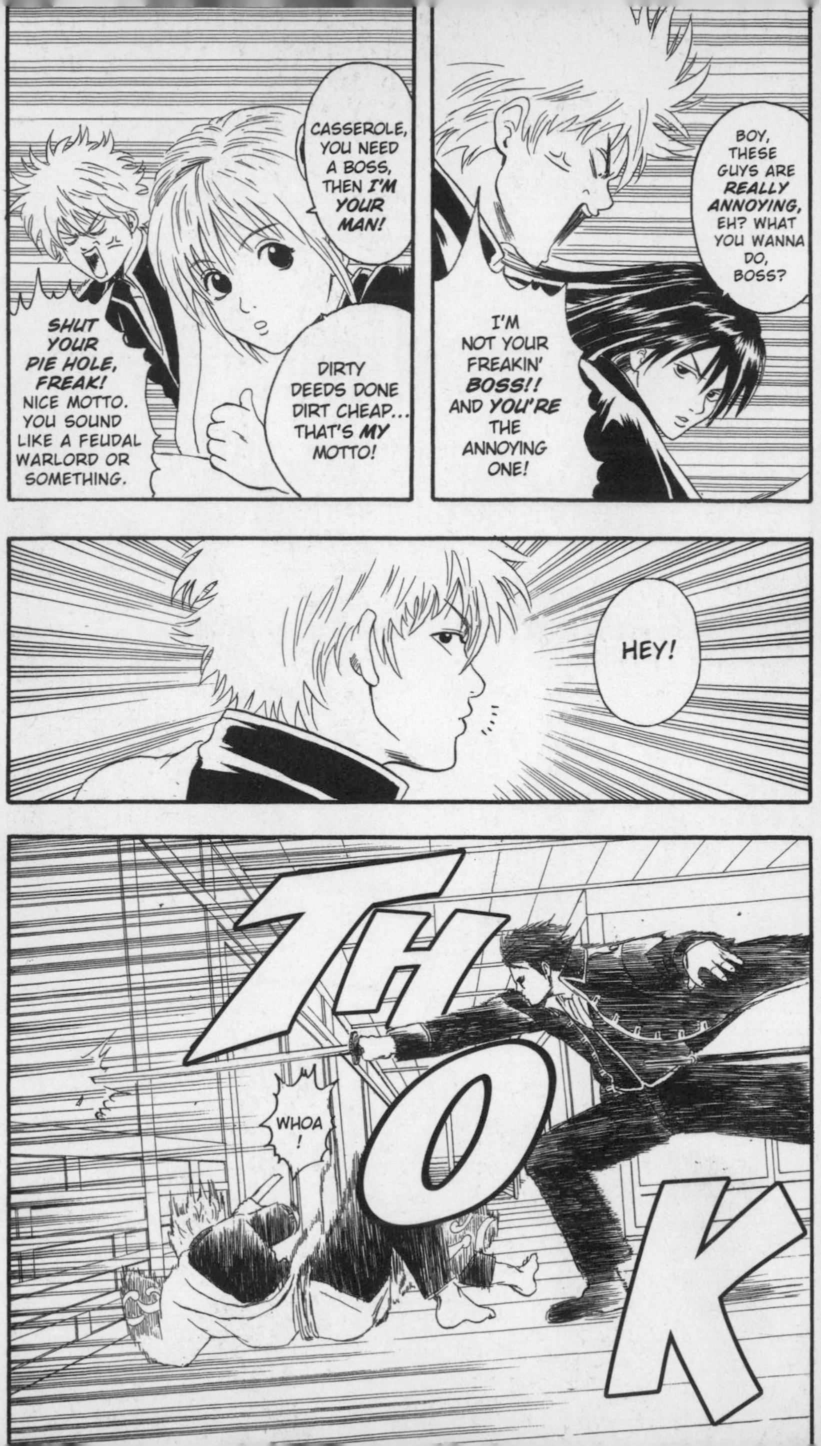

BOY, THESE GUYS ARE REALLY ANNOYING, EH? WHAT YOU WANNA DO, BOSS?
I'M NOT YOUR FREAKIN' BOSS!! AND YOU'RE THE ANNOYING ONE!
CASSEROLE, YOU NEED A BOSS, THEN I'M YOUR MAN!
DIRTY DEEDS DONE DIRT CHEAP... THAT'S MY MOTTO!
SHUT YOUR PIE HOLE, FREAK! NICE MOTTO. YOU SOUND LIKE A FEUDAL WARLORD OR SOMETHING.
HEY!
THOK
WHOA!

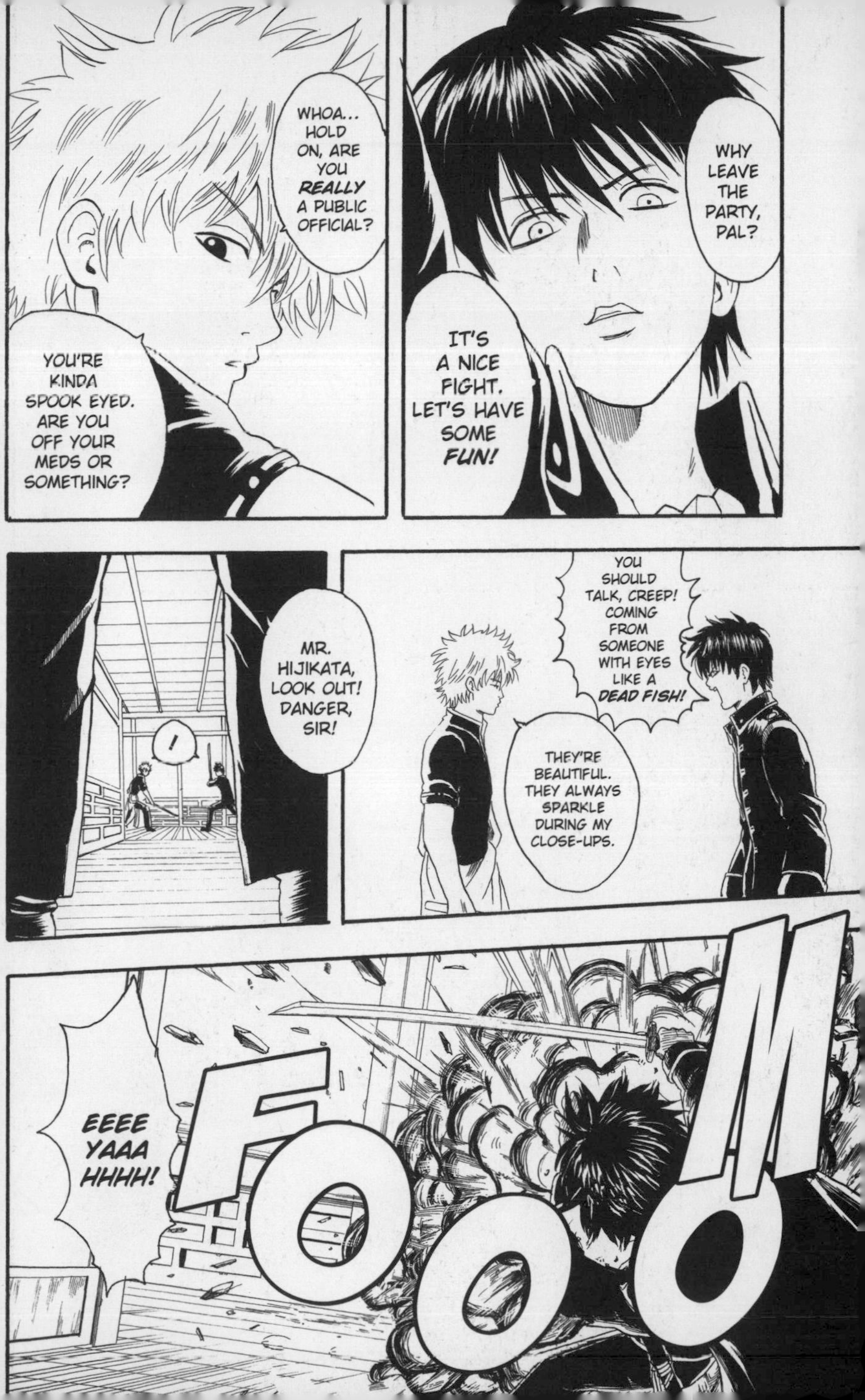
WHY LEAVE THE PARTY, PAL?
IT'S A NICE FIGHT. LET'S HAVE SOME *FUN!*
WHOA... HOLD ON, ARE YOU *REALLY* A PUBLIC OFFICIAL?
YOU'RE KINDA SPOOK EYED. ARE YOU OFF YOUR MEDS OR SOMETHING?
YOU SHOULD TALK, CREEP! COMING FROM SOMEONE WITH EYES LIKE A *DEAD FISH!*
THEY'RE BEAUTIFUL. THEY ALWAYS SPARKLE DURING MY CLOSE-UPS.
MR. HIJIKATA, LOOK OUT! DANGER, SIR!
!
FOOOM!!
EEEE YAAA HHHH!

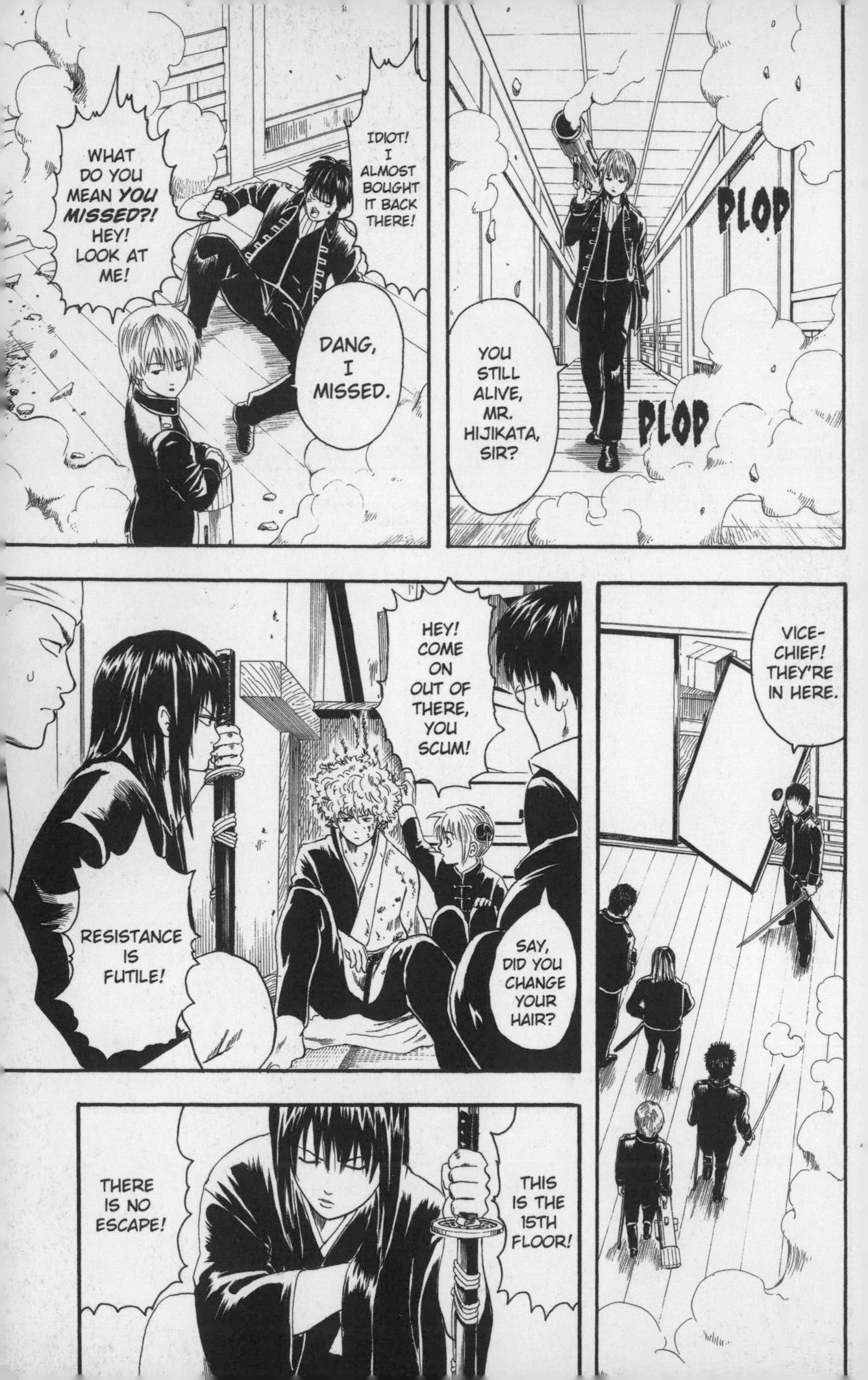
YOU STILL ALIVE, MR. HIJIKATA, SIR?
PLOP
PLOP
IDIOT! I ALMOST BOUGHT IT BACK THERE!
WHAT DO YOU MEAN *YOU MISSED?!* HEY! LOOK AT ME!
DANG, I MISSED.
VICE-CHIEF! THEY'RE IN HERE.
HEY! COME ON OUT OF THERE, YOU SCUM!
SAY, DID YOU CHANGE YOUR HAIR?
RESISTANCE IS FUTILE!
THIS IS THE 15TH FLOOR!
THERE IS NO ESCAPE!

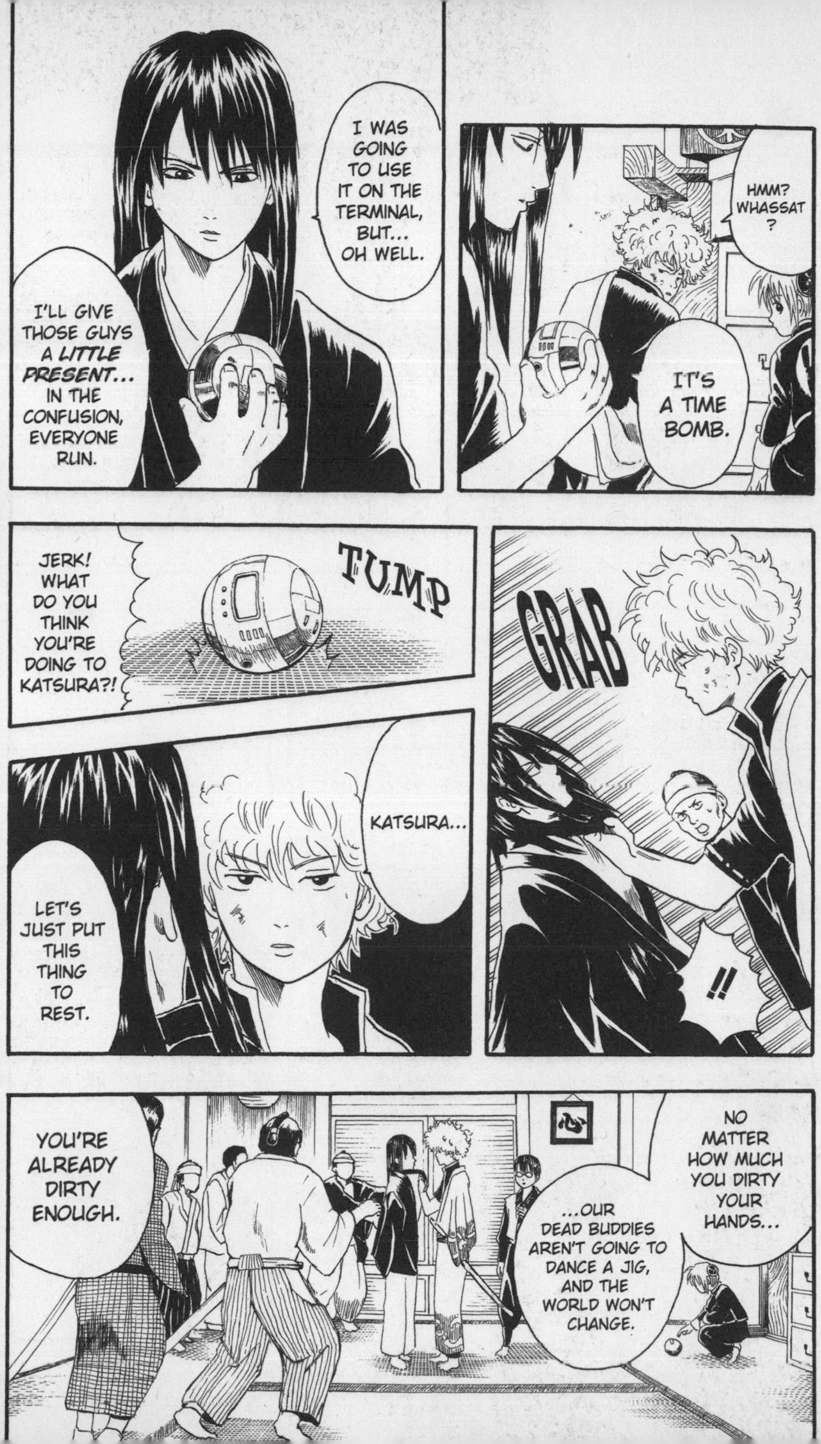
HMM? WHASSAT ?
IT'S A TIME BOMB.
I WAS GOING TO USE IT ON THE TERMINAL, BUT... OH WELL.
I'LL GIVE THOSE GUYS A *LITTLE PRESENT*... IN THE CONFUSION, EVERYONE RUN.
GRAB
!!
TUMP
JERK! WHAT DO YOU THINK YOU'RE DOING TO KATSURA?!
KATSURA...
LET'S JUST PUT THIS THING TO REST.
NO MATTER HOW MUCH YOU DIRTY YOUR HANDS...
...OUR DEAD BUDDIES AREN'T GOING TO DANCE A JIG, AND THE WORLD WON'T CHANGE.
YOU'RE ALREADY DIRTY ENOUGH.

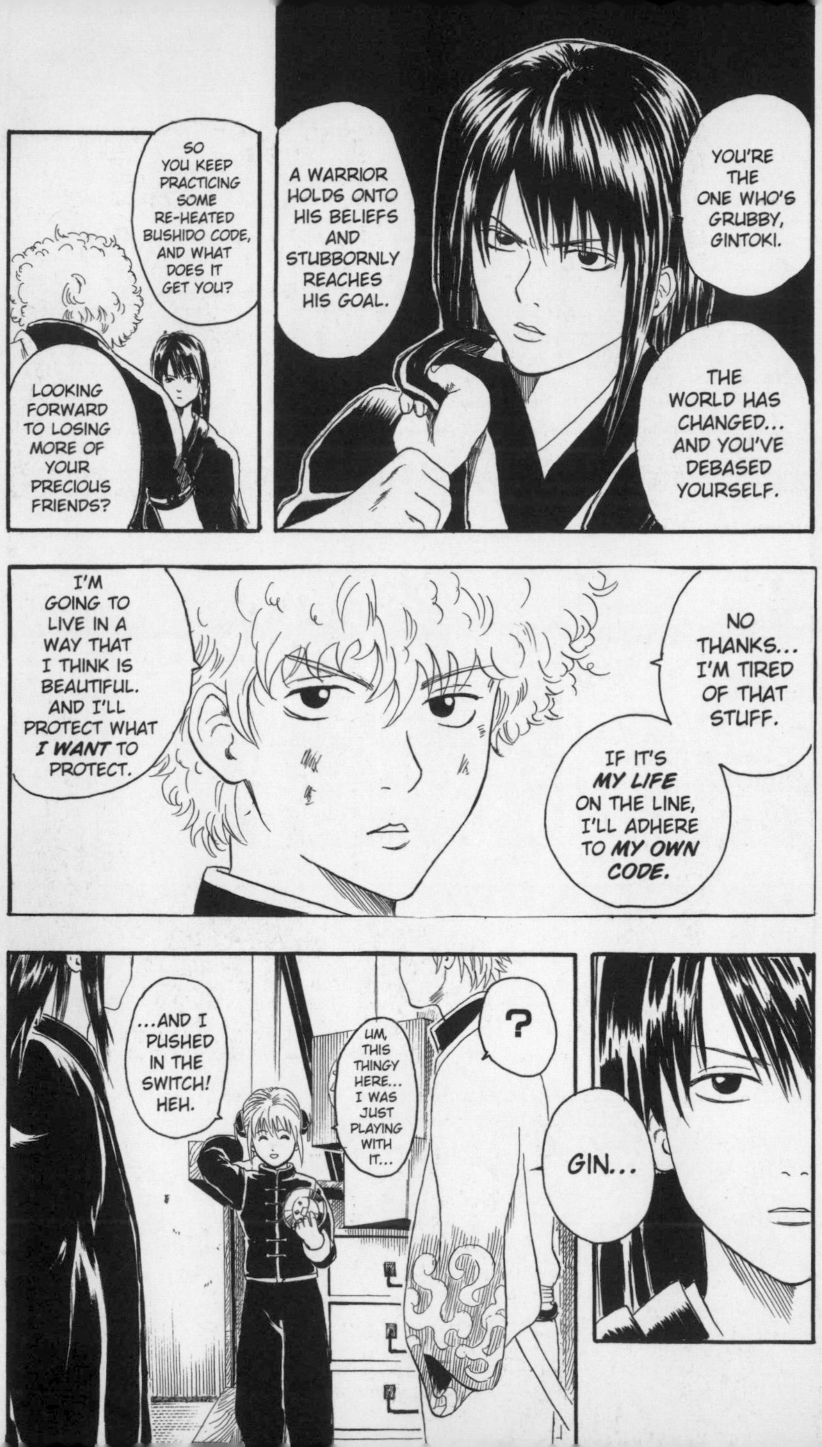
YOU'RE THE ONE WHO'S GRUBBY, GINTOKI.
THE WORLD HAS CHANGED... AND YOU'VE DEBASED YOURSELF.
A WARRIOR HOLDS ONTO HIS BELIEFS AND STUBBORNLY REACHES HIS GOAL.
SO YOU KEEP PRACTICING SOME RE-HEATED BUSHIDO CODE, AND WHAT DOES IT GET YOU?
LOOKING FORWARD TO LOSING MORE OF YOUR PRECIOUS FRIENDS?
NO THANKS... I'M TIRED OF THAT STUFF.
IF IT'S ***MY LIFE*** ON THE LINE, I'LL ADHERE TO ***MY OWN CODE.***
I'M GOING TO LIVE IN A WAY THAT I THINK IS BEAUTIFUL. AND I'LL PROTECT WHAT ***I WANT*** TO PROTECT.
GIN...
?
UM, THIS THINGY HERE... I WAS JUST PLAYING WITH IT...
...AND I PUSHED IN THE SWITCH! HEH.

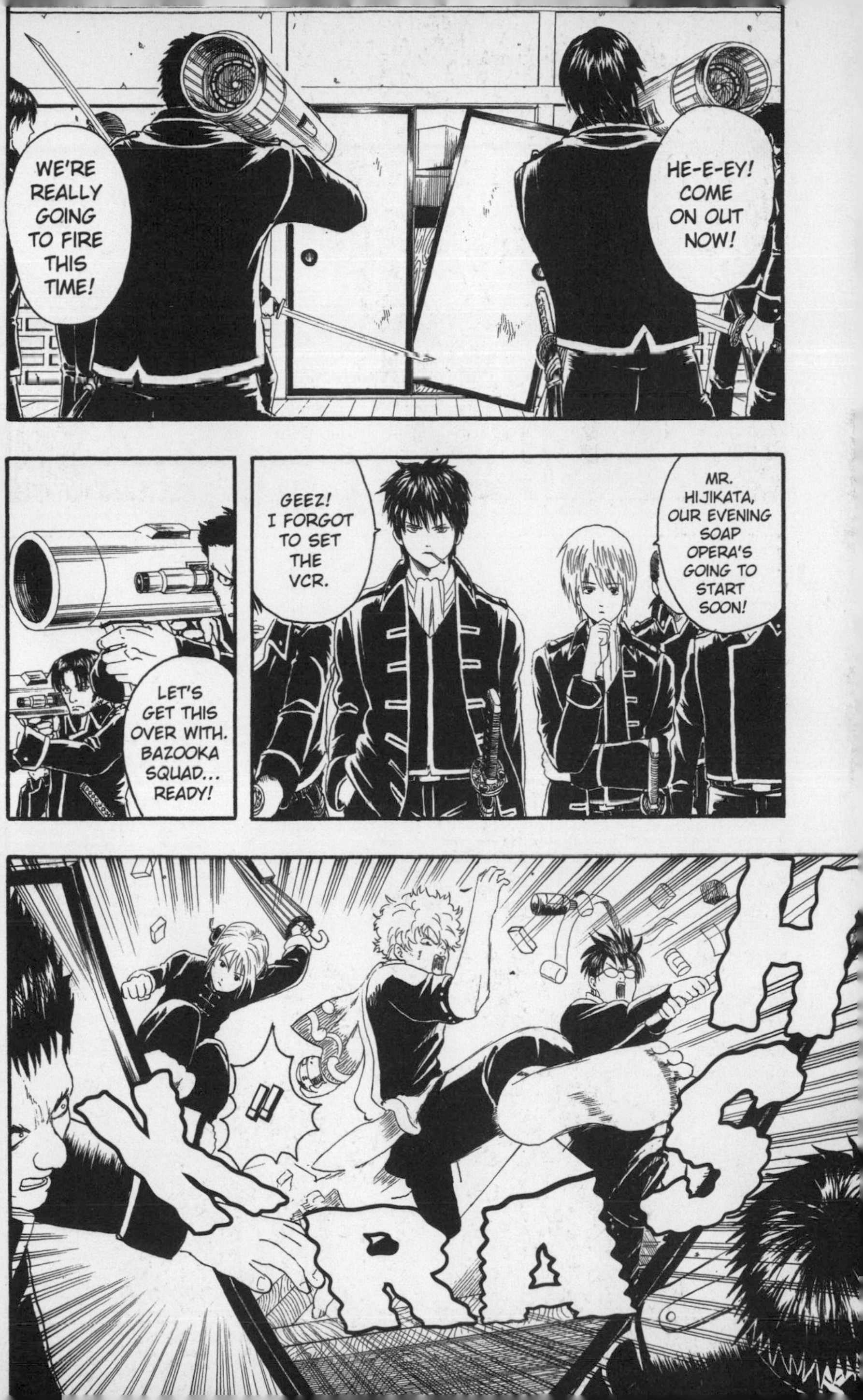
HE-E-EY! COME ON OUT NOW!
WE'RE REALLY GOING TO FIRE THIS TIME!
MR. HIJIKATA, OUR EVENING SOAP OPERA'S GOING TO START SOON!
GEEZ! I FORGOT TO SET THE VCR.
LET'S GET THIS OVER WITH. BAZOOKA SQUAD... READY!

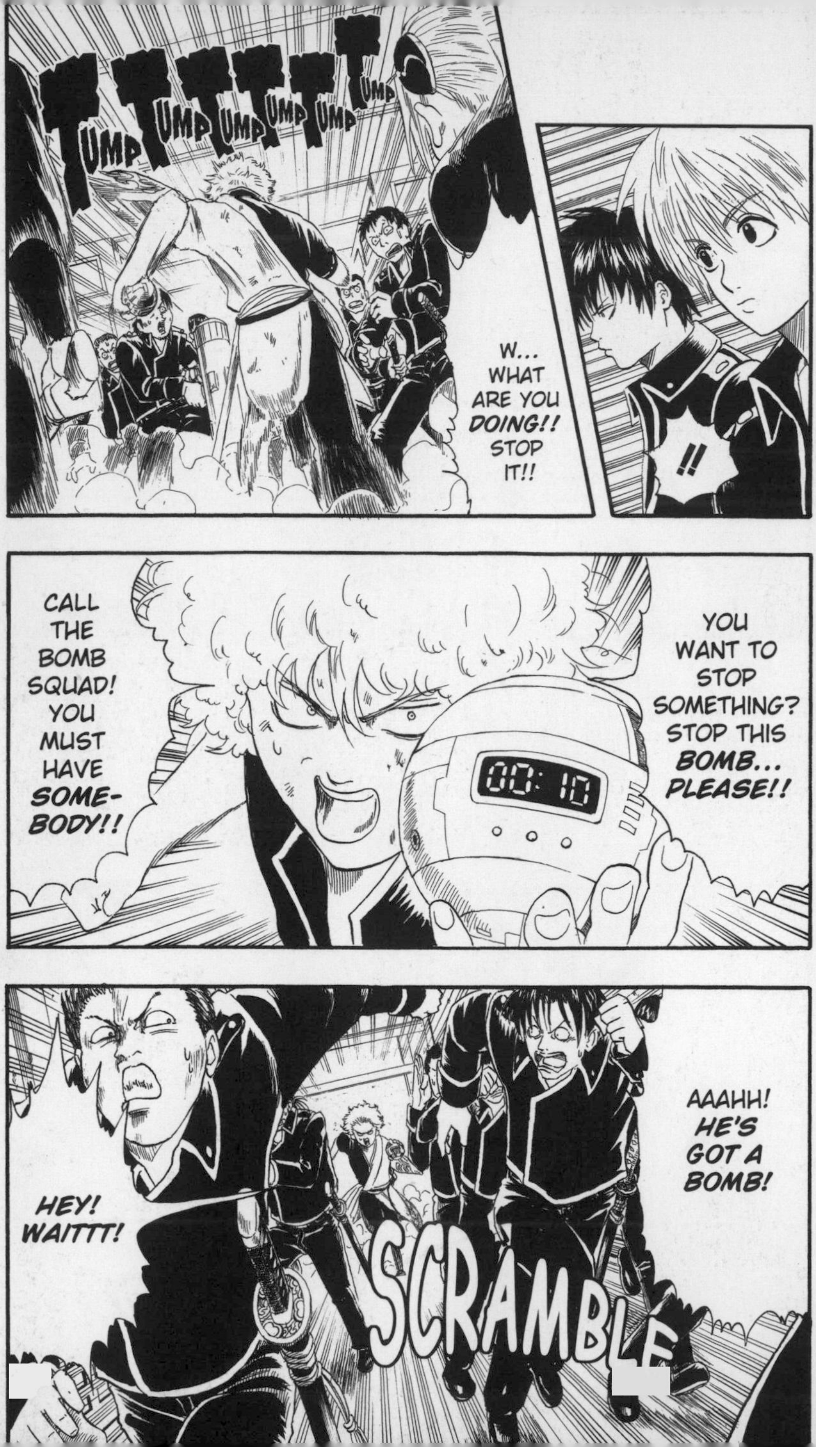
!!
TUMP TUMP TUMP TUMP TUMP TUMP
W... WHAT ARE YOU DOING!! STOP IT!!
YOU WANT TO STOP SOMETHING? STOP THIS BOMB... PLEASE!!
00:10
CALL THE BOMB SQUAD! YOU MUST HAVE SOME-BODY!!
AAAHH! HE'S GOT A BOMB!
SCRAMBLE
HEY! WAITTT!

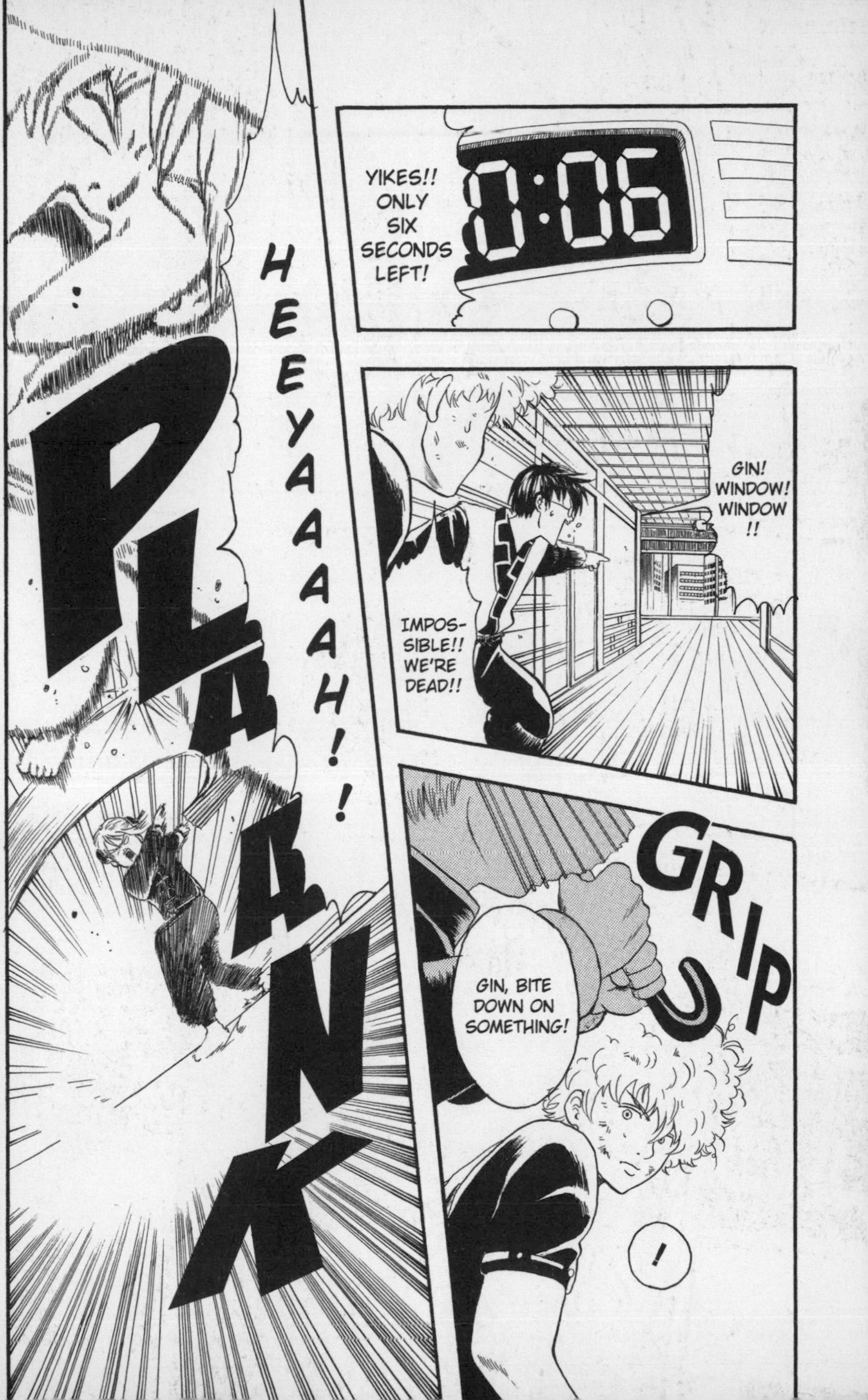
YIKES!! ONLY SIX SECONDS LEFT!
GIN! WINDOW! WINDOW!!
IMPOS-SIBLE!! WE'RE DEAD!!
GRIP
GIN, BITE DOWN ON SOMETHING!
!
HEEYAAAAH!!
PLANK

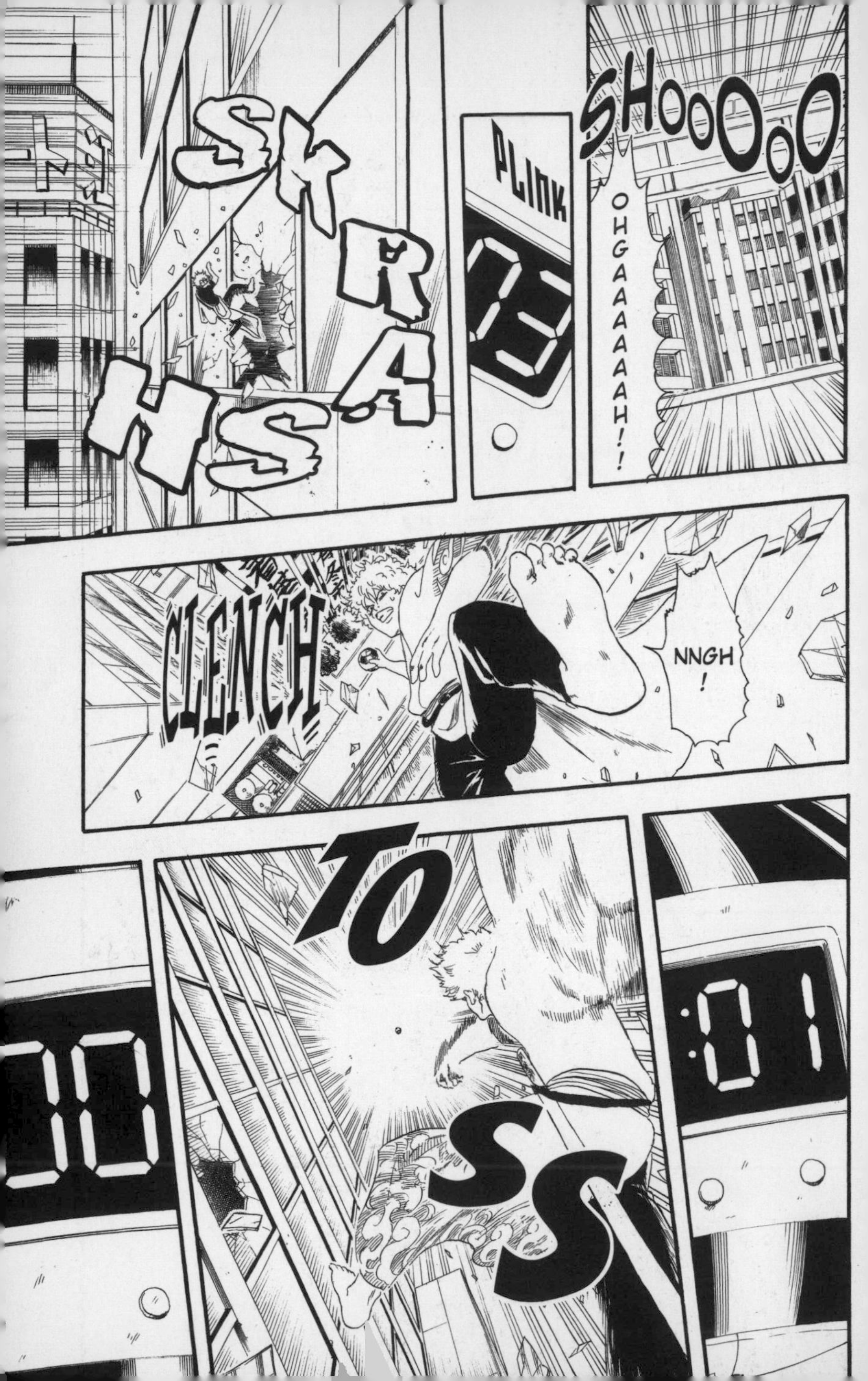
SHOOOOOO
OHGAAAAAAAH!!
PLINK
3
SHRASH
NNGH!
CLENCH
01
TOSS
00

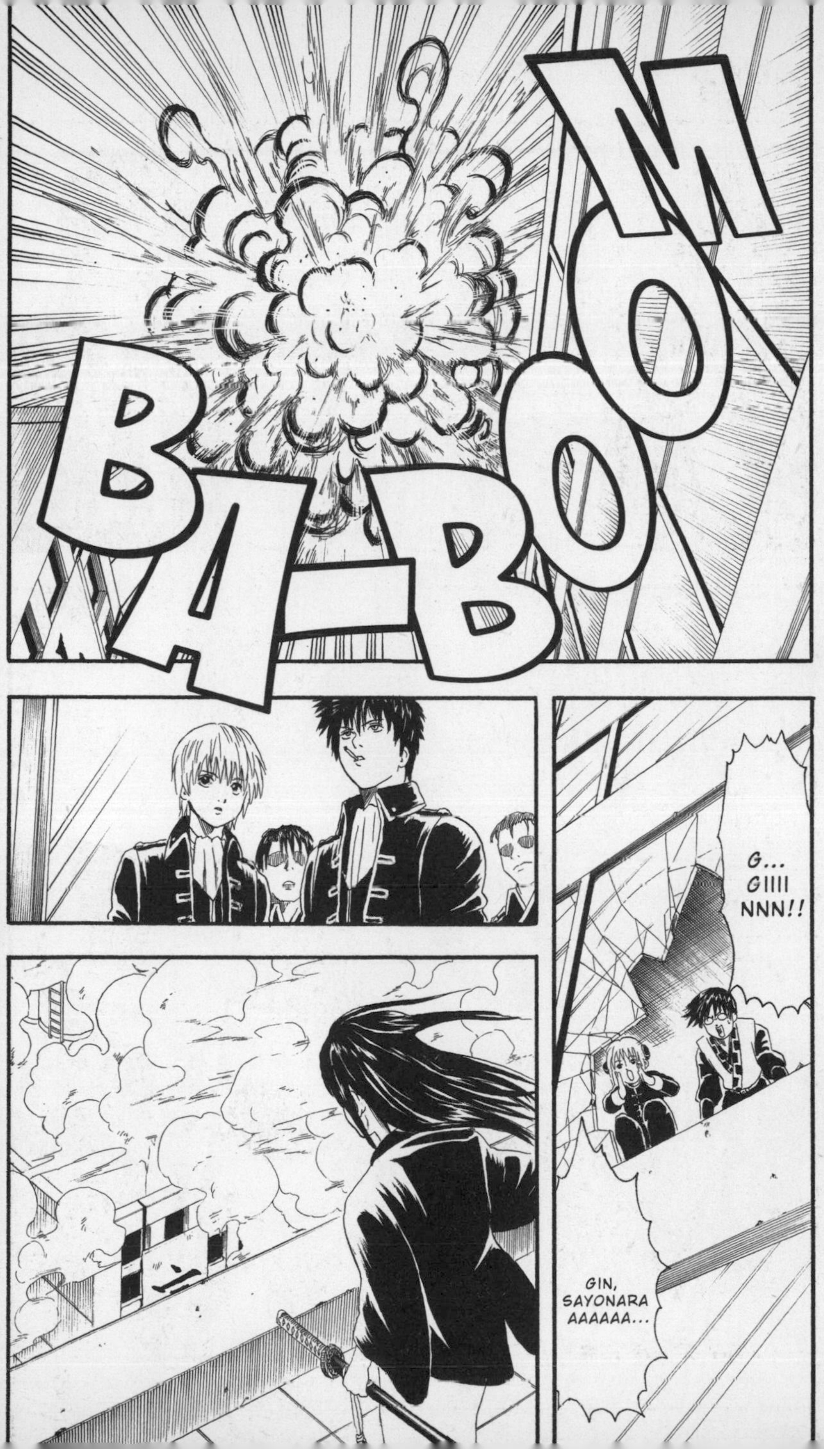
BA-BOOM
G... GIIII NNN!!
GIN, SAYONARA AAAAAA...

HMPH!

IF YOU'VE GOT ENOUGH FREE TIME TO FANTASIZE ABOUT YOUR BEAUTIFUL DEATH...

...WHY NOT JUST LIVE YOUR LIFE BEAUTIFULLY TO THE END?

WELL, I GUESS HAVING A FRIEND WHO NEVER CHANGES...

...ISN'T SUCH A BAD THING, AFTER ALL.

End of Volume 1

LIVE LIFE BEAUTIFULLY, HUH?

NOW ON SALE!

WINTER SALE!

FAIR

WHAT'S SO BEAUTIFUL ABOUT THAT?!

DANDELION

This was my very first story. It's just a stand-alone piece, but it was so popular that, even now, I sometimes receive letters about it. Some middle school students even perform plays based on it, for example. I've been privileged that this work has been enjoyed by a great many people. I like it myself, and would certainly like to redraw it if the opportunity arose.

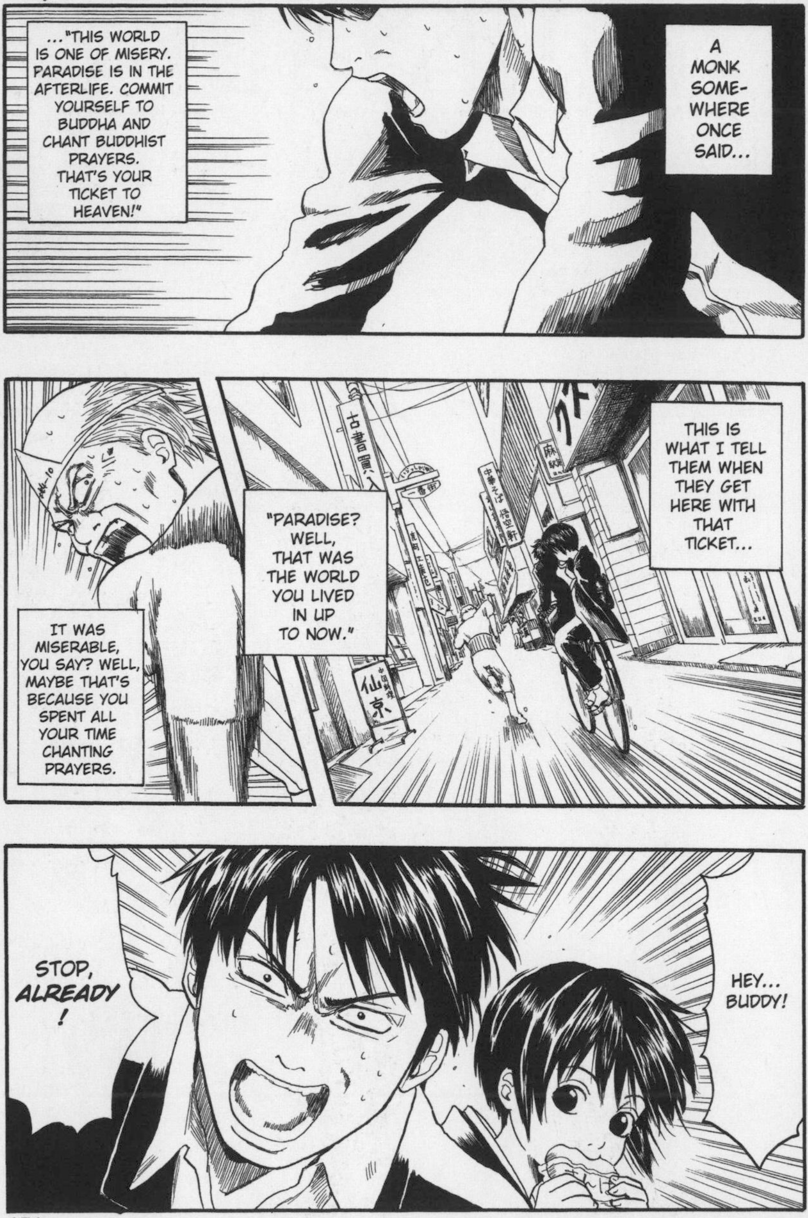
A MONK SOMEWHERE ONCE SAID...
..."THIS WORLD IS ONE OF MISERY. PARADISE IS IN THE AFTERLIFE. COMMIT YOURSELF TO BUDDHA AND CHANT BUDDHIST PRAYERS. THAT'S YOUR TICKET TO HEAVEN!"
THIS IS WHAT I TELL THEM WHEN THEY GET HERE WITH THAT TICKET...
"PARADISE? WELL, THAT WAS THE WORLD YOU LIVED IN UP TO NOW."
IT WAS MISERABLE, YOU SAY? WELL, MAYBE THAT'S BECAUSE YOU SPENT ALL YOUR TIME CHANTING PRAYERS.
HEY... BUDDY!
STOP, ALREADY!

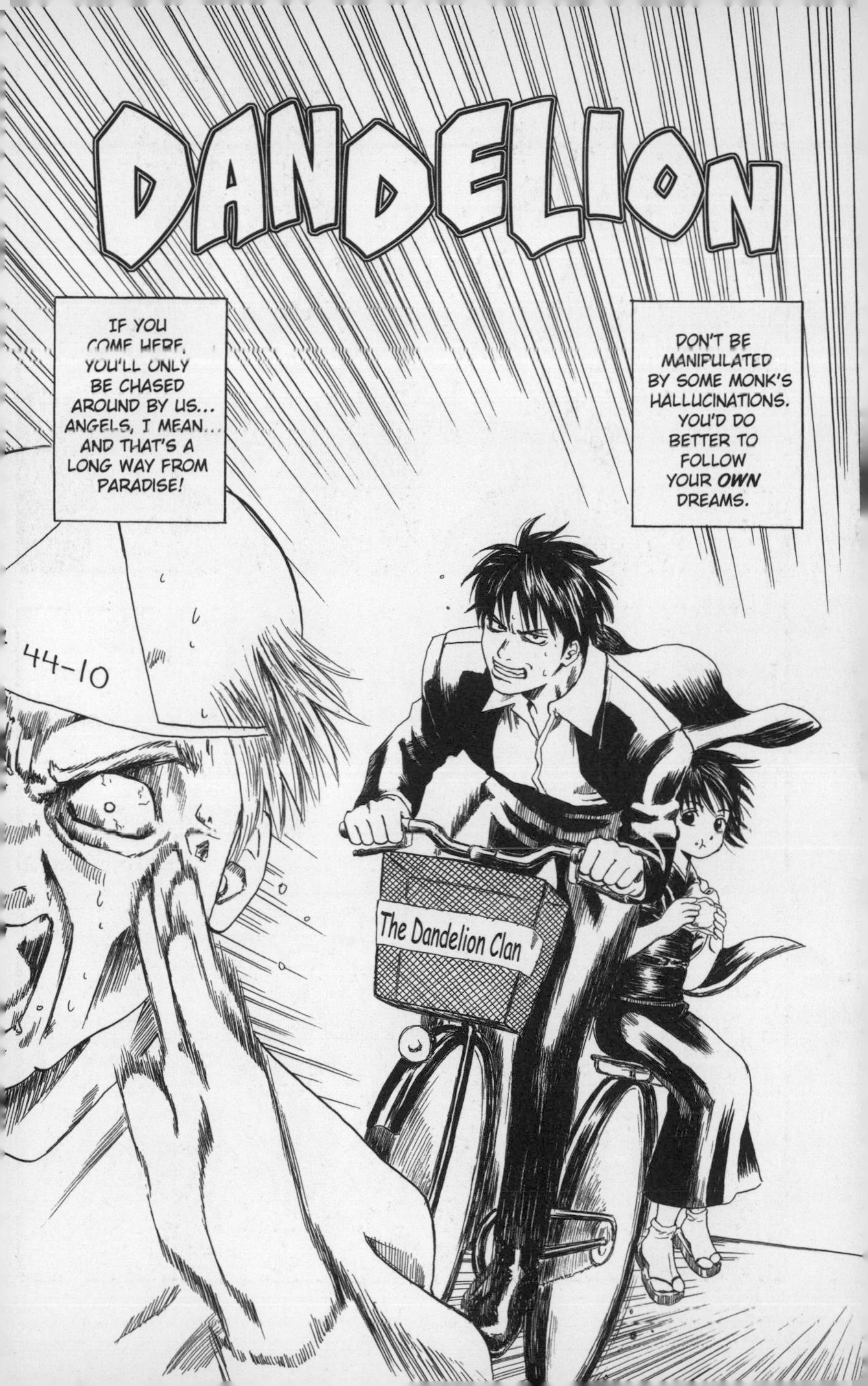
DANDELION
DON'T BE MANIPULATED BY SOME MONK'S HALLUCINATIONS. YOU'D DO BETTER TO FOLLOW YOUR *OWN* DREAMS.
IF YOU COME HERE, YOU'LL ONLY BE CHASED AROUND BY US... ANGELS, I MEAN... AND THAT'S A LONG WAY FROM PARADISE!
44-10
The Dandelion Clan

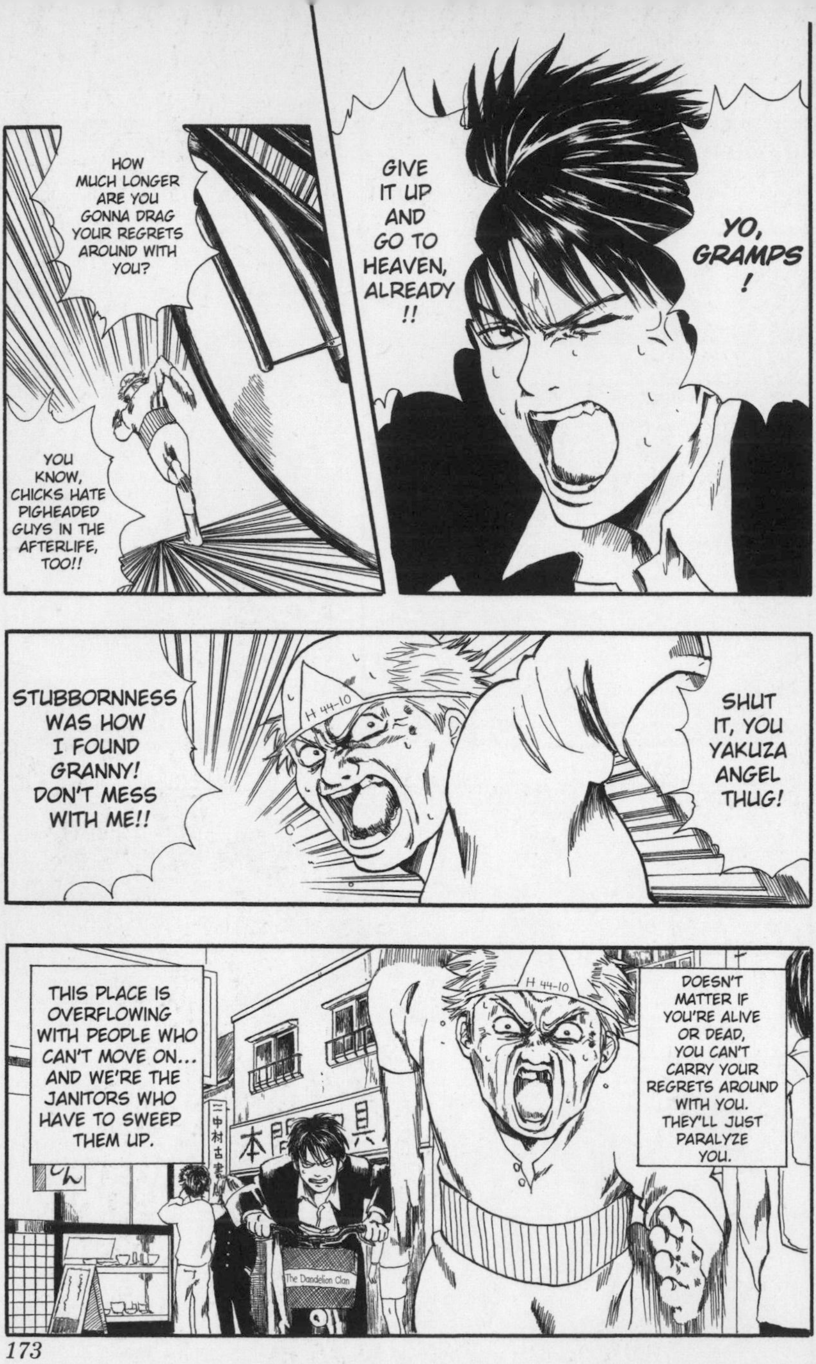
YO, GRAMPS!
GIVE IT UP AND GO TO HEAVEN, ALREADY!!
HOW MUCH LONGER ARE YOU GONNA DRAG YOUR REGRETS AROUND WITH YOU?
YOU KNOW, CHICKS HATE PIGHEADED GUYS IN THE AFTERLIFE, TOO!!
SHUT IT, YOU YAKUZA ANGEL THUG!
H 44-10
STUBBORNNESS WAS HOW I FOUND GRANNY! DON'T MESS WITH ME!!
H 44-10
DOESN'T MATTER IF YOU'RE ALIVE OR DEAD, YOU CAN'T CARRY YOUR REGRETS AROUND WITH YOU. THEY'LL JUST PARALYZE YOU.
THIS PLACE IS OVERFLOWING WITH PEOPLE WHO CAN'T MOVE ON... AND WE'RE THE JANITORS WHO HAVE TO SWEEP THEM UP.
The Dandelion Clan

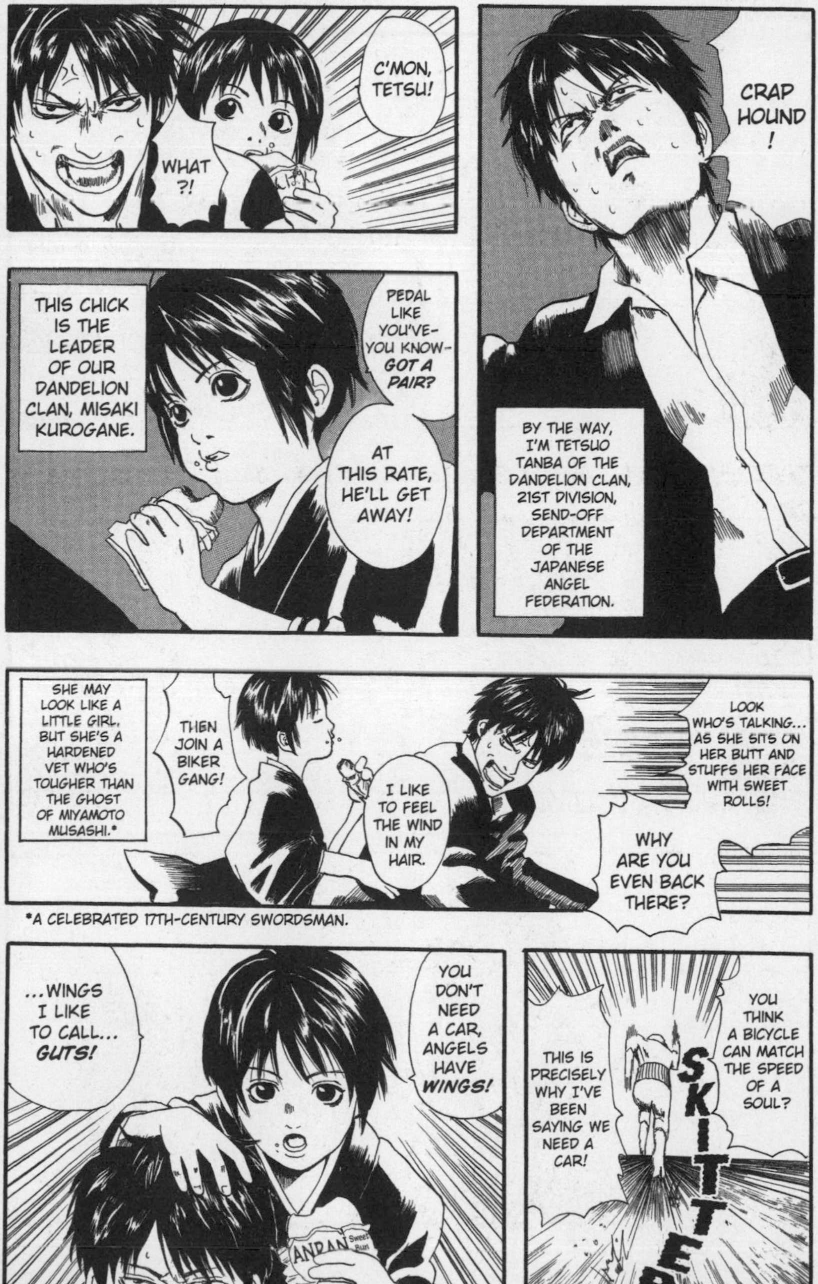
CRAP HOUND!
BY THE WAY, I'M TETSUO TANBA OF THE DANDELION CLAN, 21ST DIVISION, SEND-OFF DEPARTMENT OF THE JAPANESE ANGEL FEDERATION.
C'MON, TETSU!
WHAT?!
PEDAL LIKE YOU'VE- YOU KNOW- **GOT A PAIR?**
AT THIS RATE, HE'LL GET AWAY!
THIS CHICK IS THE LEADER OF OUR DANDELION CLAN, MISAKI KUROGANE.
LOOK WHO'S TALKING... AS SHE SITS ON HER BUTT AND STUFFS HER FACE WITH SWEET ROLLS!
WHY ARE YOU EVEN BACK THERE?
I LIKE TO FEEL THE WIND IN MY HAIR.
THEN JOIN A BIKER GANG!
SHE MAY LOOK LIKE A LITTLE GIRL, BUT SHE'S A HARDENED VET WHO'S TOUGHER THAN THE GHOST OF MIYAMOTO MUSASHI.*
YOU THINK A BICYCLE CAN MATCH THE SPEED OF A SOUL?
SKITTER
THIS IS PRECISELY WHY I'VE BEEN SAYING WE NEED A CAR!
YOU DON'T NEED A CAR, ANGELS HAVE **WINGS!**
...WINGS I LIKE TO CALL... **GUTS!**
ANPAN
Sweet Bun

*A CELEBRATED 17TH-CENTURY SWORDSMAN.

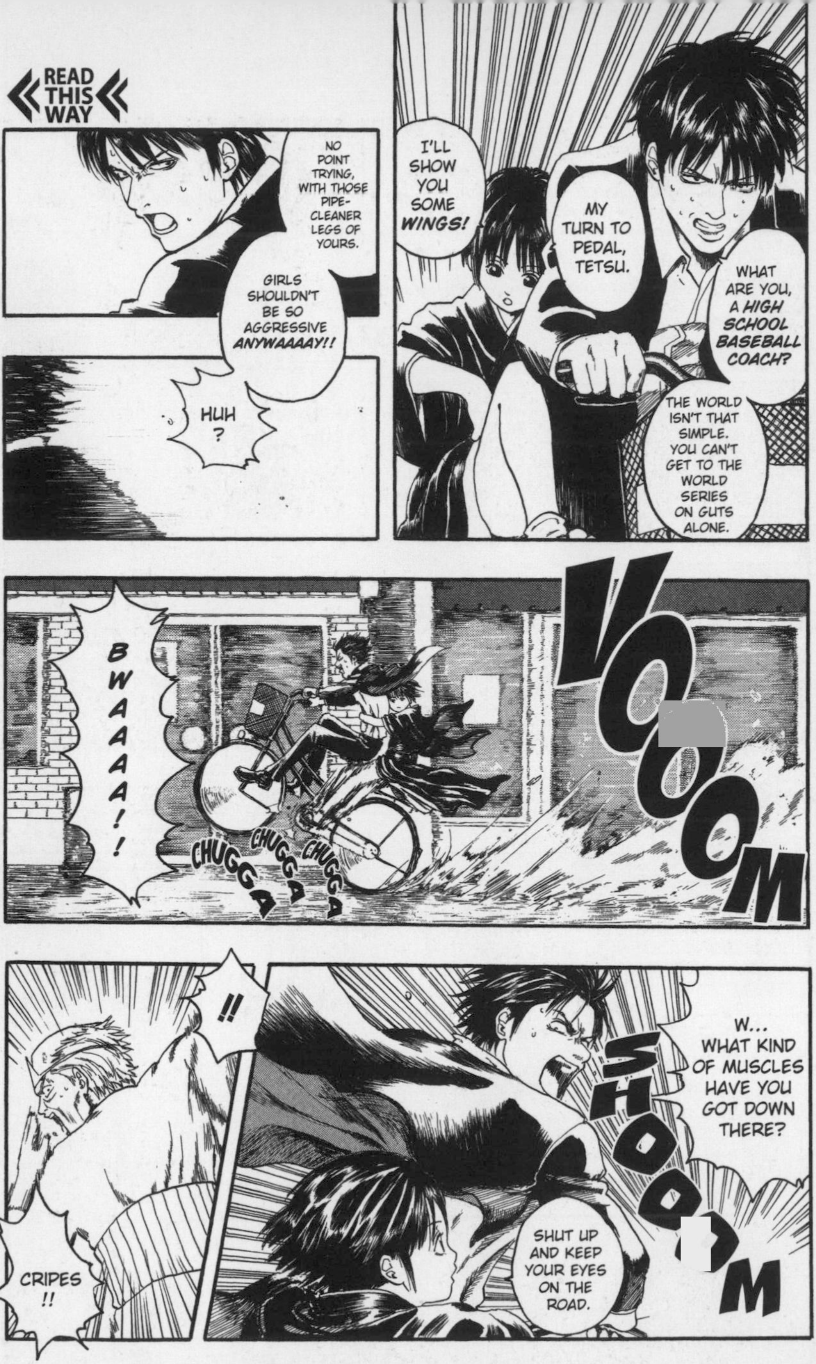
READ THIS WAY
I'LL SHOW YOU SOME WINGS!
MY TURN TO PEDAL, TETSU.
WHAT ARE YOU, A HIGH SCHOOL BASEBALL COACH?
THE WORLD ISN'T THAT SIMPLE. YOU CAN'T GET TO THE WORLD SERIES ON GUTS ALONE.
NO POINT TRYING, WITH THOSE PIPE-CLEANER LEGS OF YOURS.
GIRLS SHOULDN'T BE SO AGGRESSIVE ANYWAAAAY!!
HUH?
VOOOOM
BWAAAAA!!
CHUGGA
CHUGGA
CHUGGA
SHOOOOM
W... WHAT KIND OF MUSCLES HAVE YOU GOT DOWN THERE?
SHUT UP AND KEEP YOUR EYES ON THE ROAD.
!!
CRIPES!!

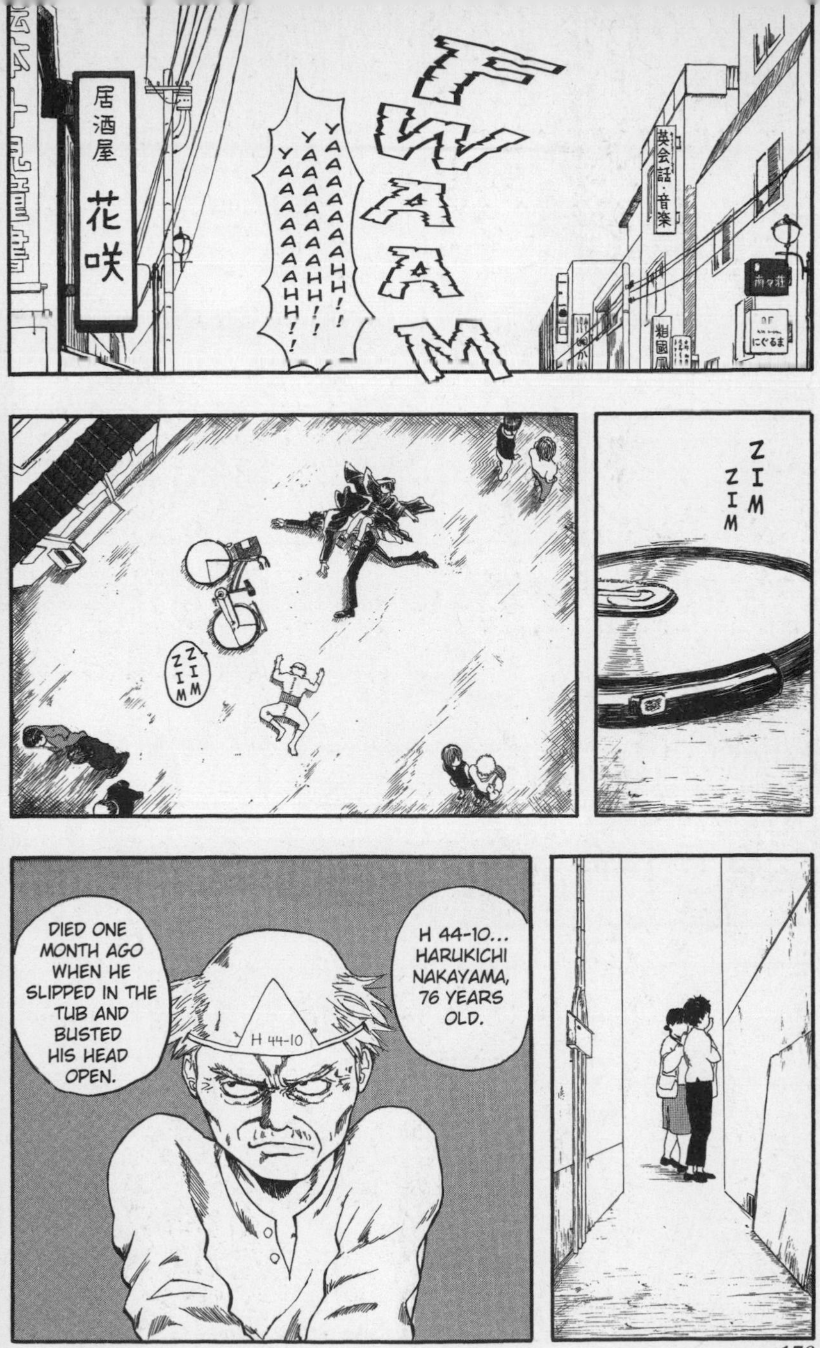

居酒屋 花咲
FWAM
YAAAAAAAAAHH!! YAAAAAAAAAAHH!! YAAAAAAAAAAHH!!
英会話・音楽
にぐるま
ZIM ZIM
ZIM ZIM
H 44-10... HARUKICHI NAKAYAMA, 76 YEARS OLD.
H 44-10
DIED ONE MONTH AGO WHEN HE SLIPPED IN THE TUB AND BUSTED HIS HEAD OPEN.

READ THIS WAY

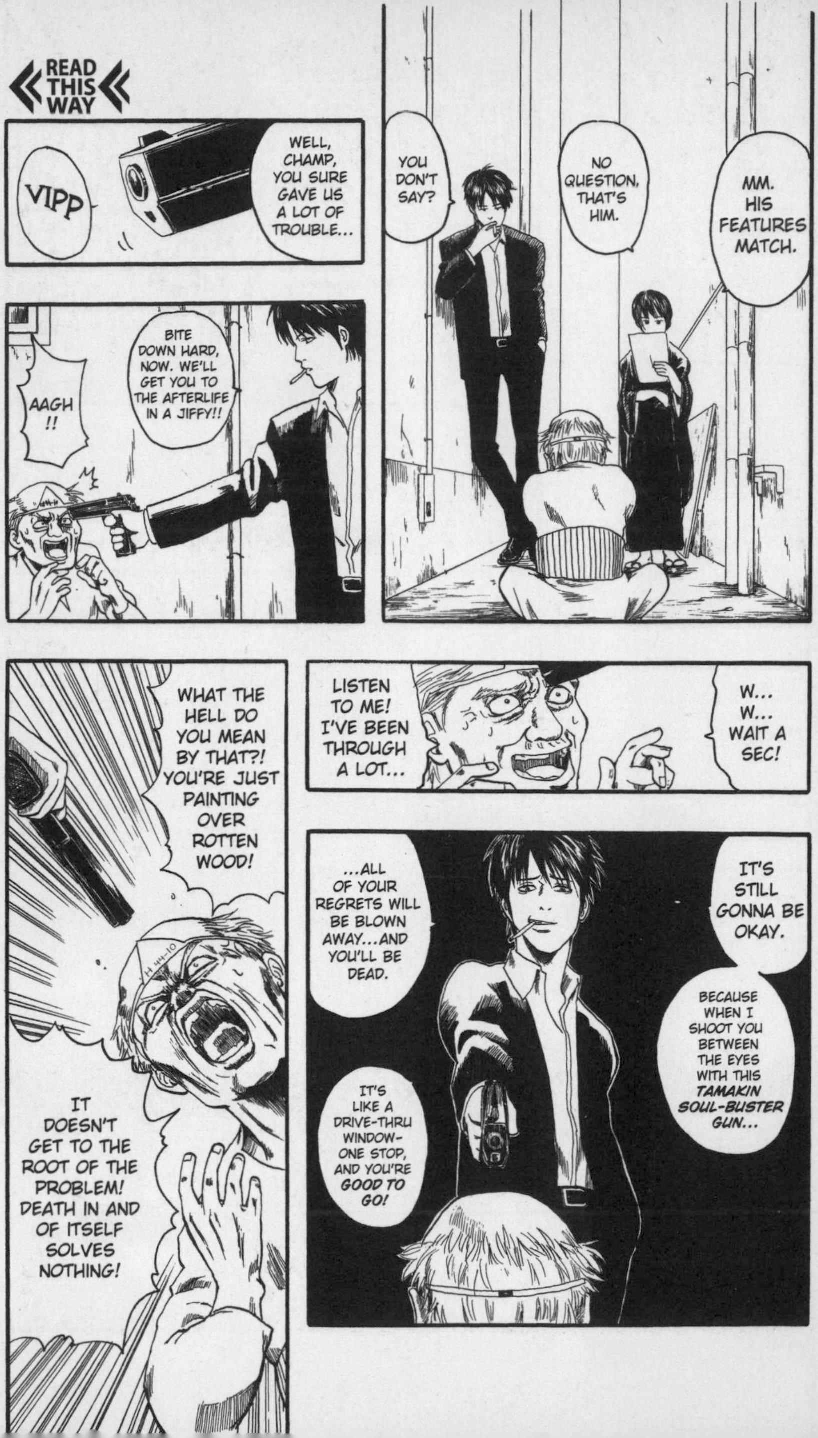
MM. HIS FEATURES MATCH.
NO QUESTION, THAT'S HIM.
YOU DON'T SAY?
WELL, CHAMP, YOU SURE GAVE US A LOT OF TROUBLE...
VIPP
BITE DOWN HARD, NOW. WE'LL GET YOU TO THE AFTERLIFE IN A JIFFY!!
AAGH !!
W... W... WAIT A SEC!
LISTEN TO ME! I'VE BEEN THROUGH A LOT...
IT'S STILL GONNA BE OKAY.
BECAUSE WHEN I SHOOT YOU BETWEEN THE EYES WITH THIS TAMAKIN SOUL-BUSTER GUN...
...ALL OF YOUR REGRETS WILL BE BLOWN AWAY...AND YOU'LL BE DEAD.
IT'S LIKE A DRIVE-THRU WINDOW-ONE STOP, AND YOU'RE GOOD TO GO!
WHAT THE HELL DO YOU MEAN BY THAT?! YOU'RE JUST PAINTING OVER ROTTEN WOOD!
IT DOESN'T GET TO THE ROOT OF THE PROBLEM! DEATH IN AND OF ITSELF SOLVES NOTHING!

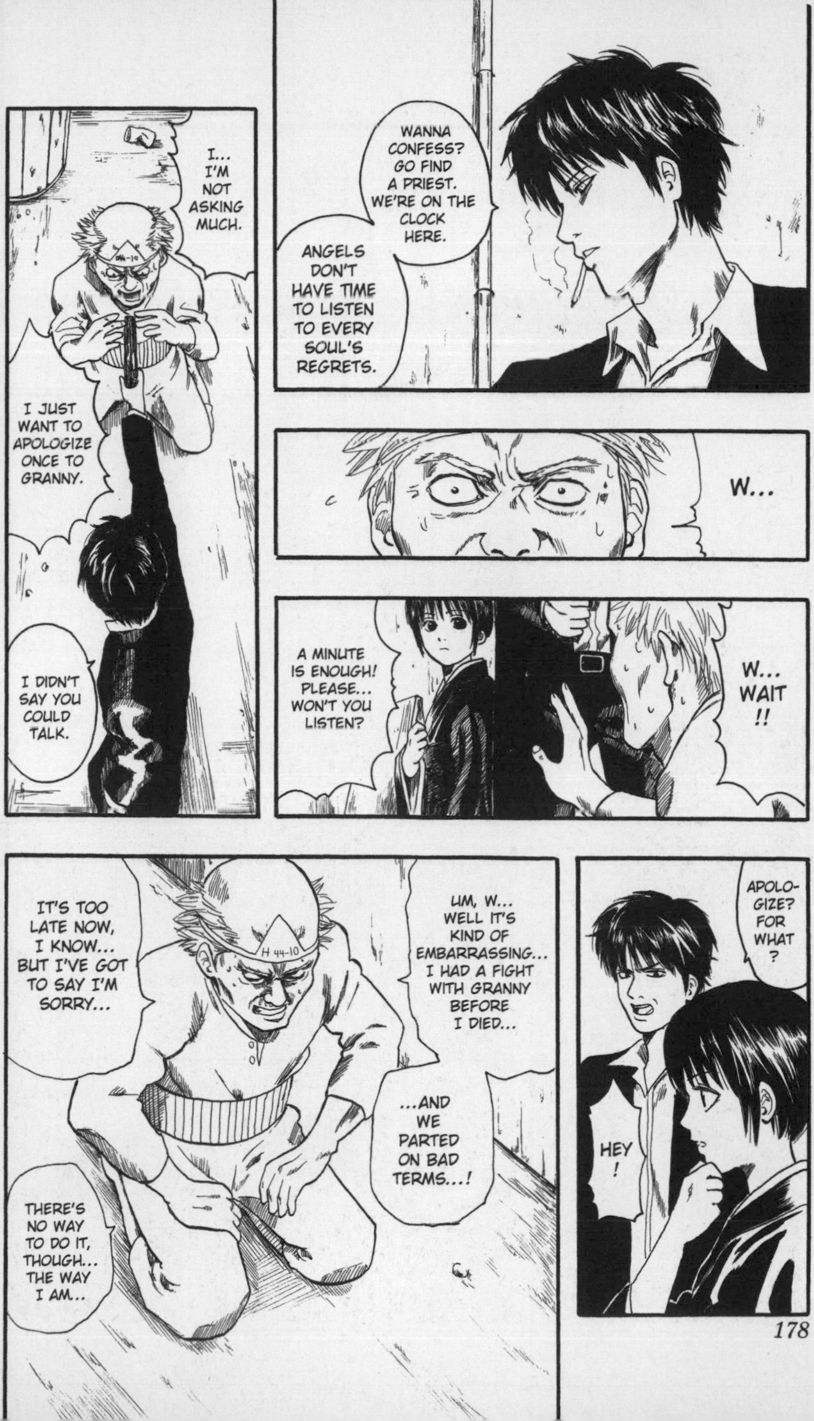
WANNA CONFESS? GO FIND A PRIEST. WE'RE ON THE CLOCK HERE.
ANGELS DON'T HAVE TIME TO LISTEN TO EVERY SOUL'S REGRETS.
W...
W... WAIT!!
A MINUTE IS ENOUGH! PLEASE... WON'T YOU LISTEN?
I... I'M NOT ASKING MUCH.
I JUST WANT TO APOLOGIZE ONCE TO GRANNY.
I DIDN'T SAY YOU COULD TALK.
APOLOGIZE? FOR WHAT?
HEY!
UM, W... WELL IT'S KIND OF EMBARRASSING... I HAD A FIGHT WITH GRANNY BEFORE I DIED...
...AND WE PARTED ON BAD TERMS...!
IT'S TOO LATE NOW, I KNOW... BUT I'VE GOT TO SAY I'M SORRY...
THERE'S NO WAY TO DO IT, THOUGH... THE WAY I AM...

READ THIS WAY

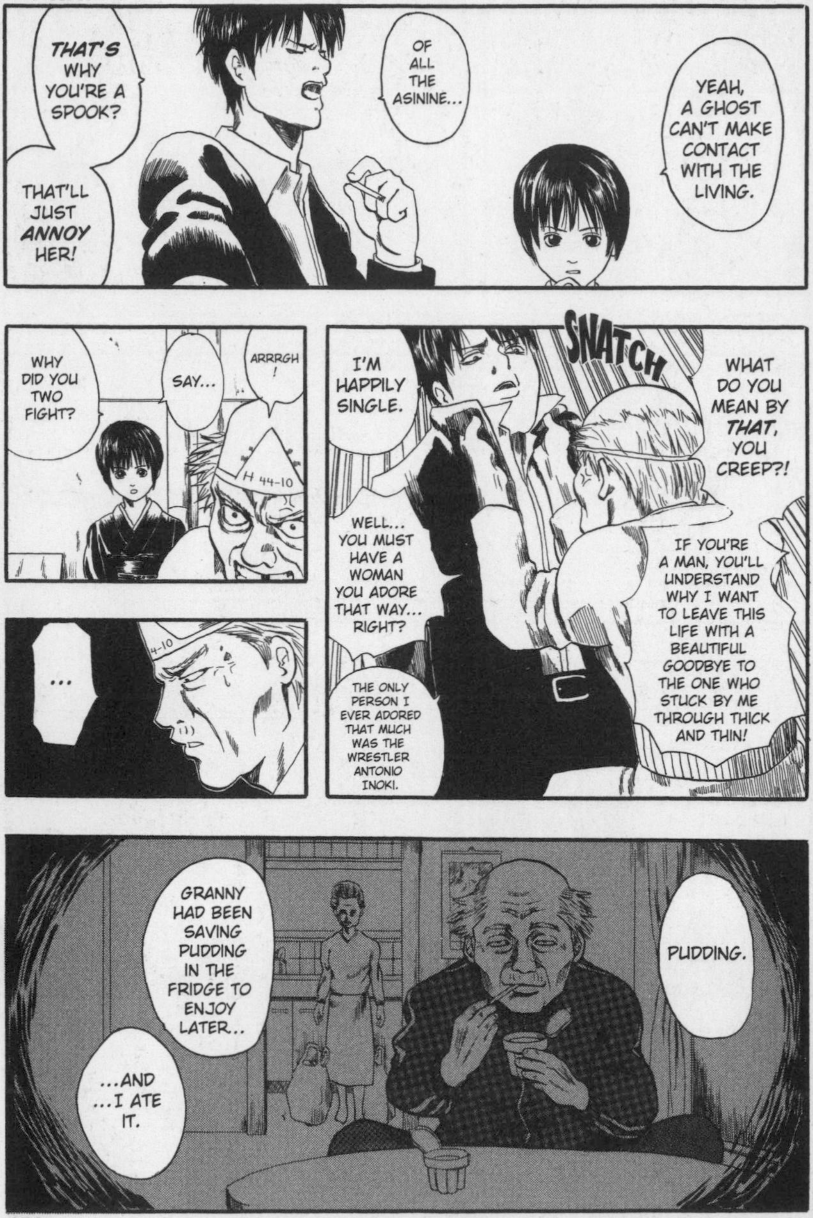
YEAH, A GHOST CAN'T MAKE CONTACT WITH THE LIVING.
OF ALL THE ASININE...
THAT'S WHY YOU'RE A SPOOK?
THAT'LL JUST *ANNOY* HER!
SNATCH
WHAT DO YOU MEAN BY *THAT,* YOU CREEP?!
I'M HAPPILY SINGLE.
IF YOU'RE A MAN, YOU'LL UNDERSTAND WHY I WANT TO LEAVE THIS LIFE WITH A BEAUTIFUL GOODBYE TO THE ONE WHO STUCK BY ME THROUGH THICK AND THIN!
WELL... YOU MUST HAVE A WOMAN YOU ADORE THAT WAY... RIGHT?
THE ONLY PERSON I EVER ADORED THAT MUCH WAS THE WRESTLER ANTONIO INOKI.
ARRRGH!
SAY...
WHY DID YOU TWO FIGHT?
H 44-10
4-10
...
PUDDING.
GRANNY HAD BEEN SAVING PUDDING IN THE FRIDGE TO ENJOY LATER...
...AND ...I ATE IT.

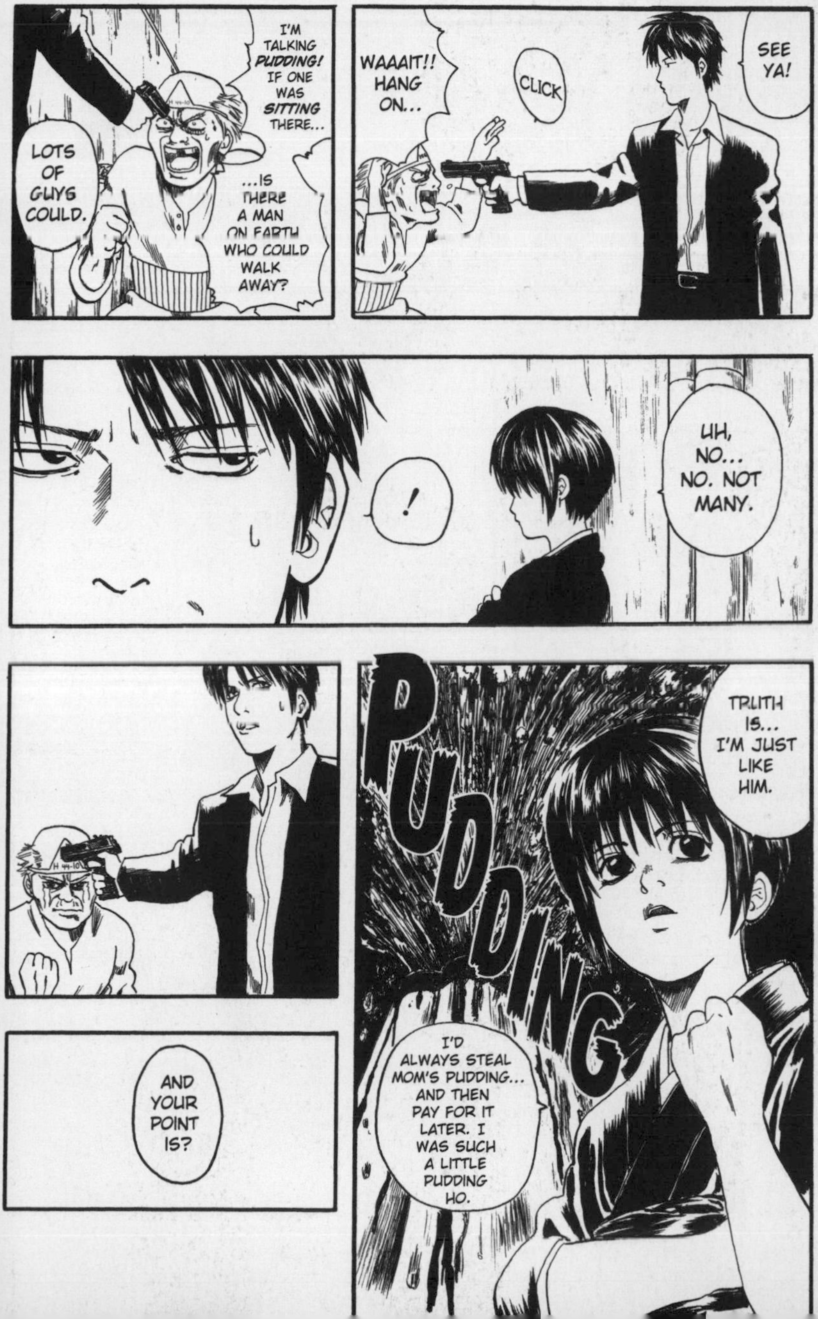
SEE YA!
CLICK
WAAAIT!! HANG ON...
I'M TALKING PUDDING! IF ONE WAS SITTING THERE...
...IS THERE A MAN ON EARTH WHO COULD WALK AWAY?
LOTS OF GUYS COULD.
UH, NO... NO. NOT MANY.
!
TRUTH IS... I'M JUST LIKE HIM.
PUDDING
I'D ALWAYS STEAL MOM'S PUDDING... AND THEN PAY FOR IT LATER. I WAS SUCH A LITTLE PUDDING HO.
AND YOUR POINT IS?

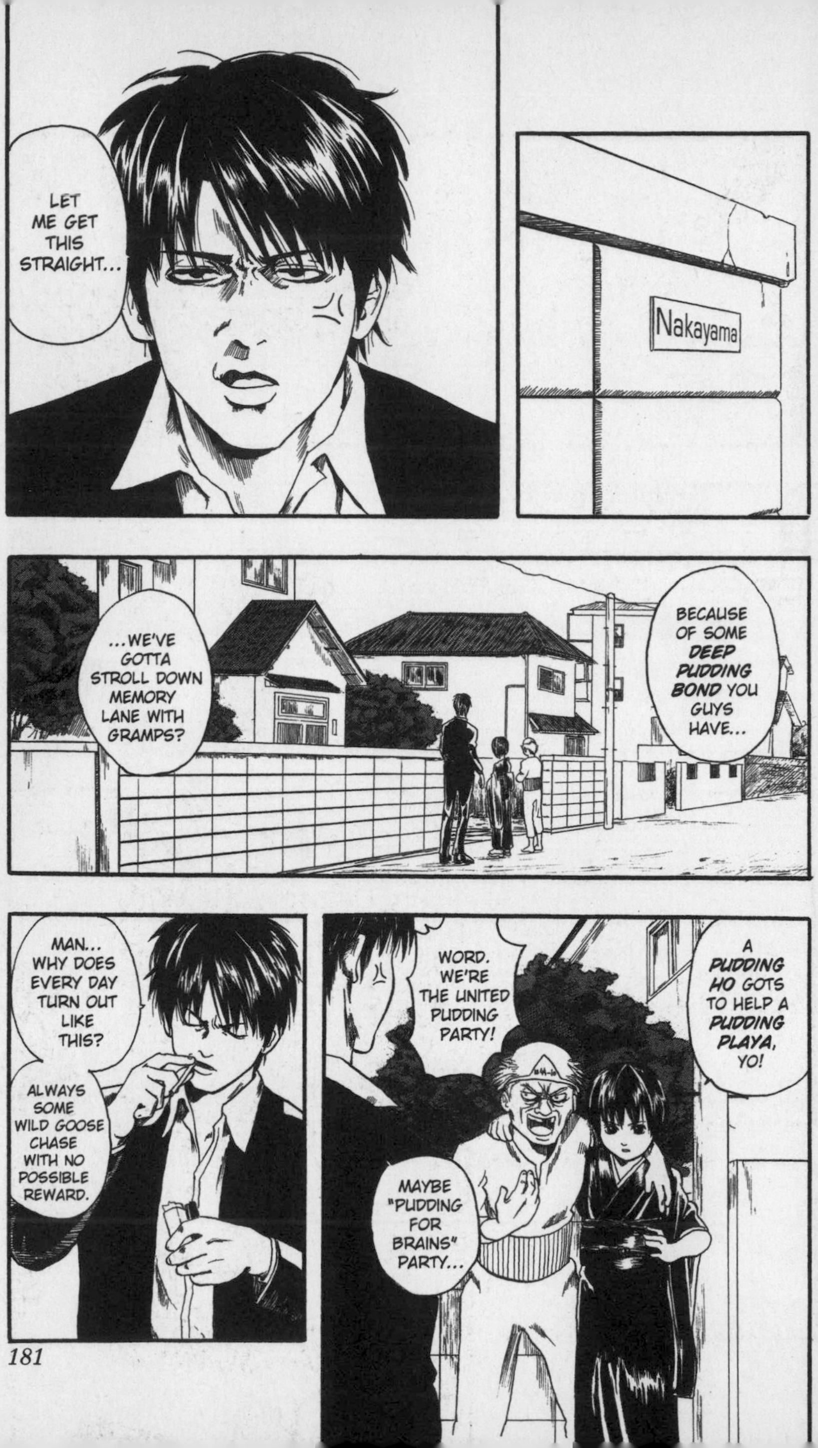
Nakayama
LET ME GET THIS STRAIGHT...
BECAUSE OF SOME DEEP PUDDING BOND YOU GUYS HAVE...
...WE'VE GOTTA STROLL DOWN MEMORY LANE WITH GRAMPS?
A PUDDING HO GOTS TO HELP A PUDDING PLAYA, YO!
WORD. WE'RE THE UNITED PUDDING PARTY!
MAYBE "PUDDING FOR BRAINS" PARTY...
MAN... WHY DOES EVERY DAY TURN OUT LIKE THIS?
ALWAYS SOME WILD GOOSE CHASE WITH NO POSSIBLE REWARD.

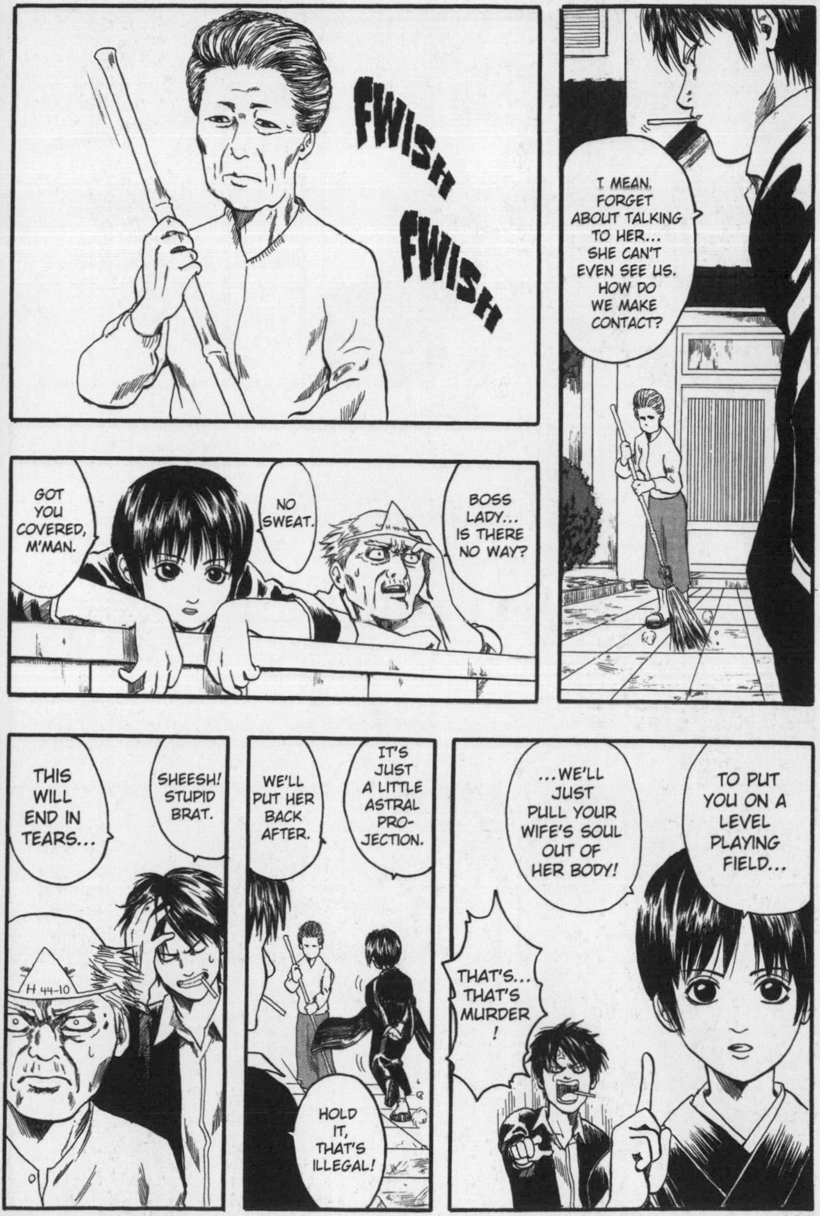
I MEAN. FORGET ABOUT TALKING TO HER... SHE CAN'T EVEN SEE US. HOW DO WE MAKE CONTACT?
FWISH
FWISH
BOSS LADY... IS THERE NO WAY?
NO SWEAT.
GOT YOU COVERED, M'MAN.
TO PUT YOU ON A LEVEL PLAYING FIELD...
...WE'LL JUST PULL YOUR WIFE'S SOUL OUT OF HER BODY!
THAT'S... THAT'S MURDER!
IT'S JUST A LITTLE ASTRAL PROJECTION.
WE'LL PUT HER BACK AFTER.
HOLD IT, THAT'S ILLEGAL!
SHEESH! STUPID BRAT.
THIS WILL END IN TEARS...
H 44-10

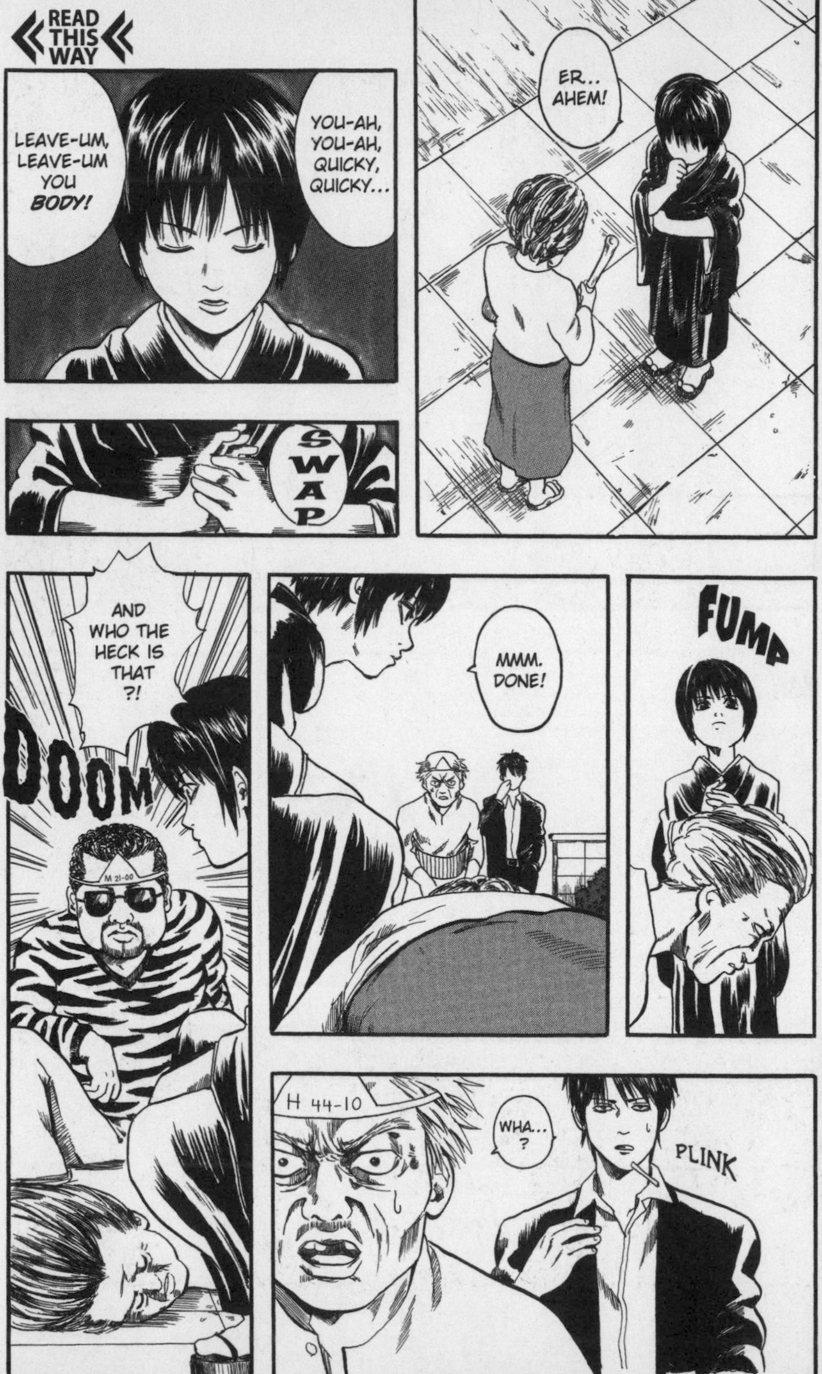
READ THIS WAY
ER.. AHEM!
YOU-AH, YOU-AH, QUICKY, QUICKY...
LEAVE-UM, LEAVE-UM YOU BODY!
SWAP
FUMP
MMM. DONE!
WHA... ?
PLINK
AND WHO THE HECK IS THAT ?!
DOOM
M 21-00
H 44-10

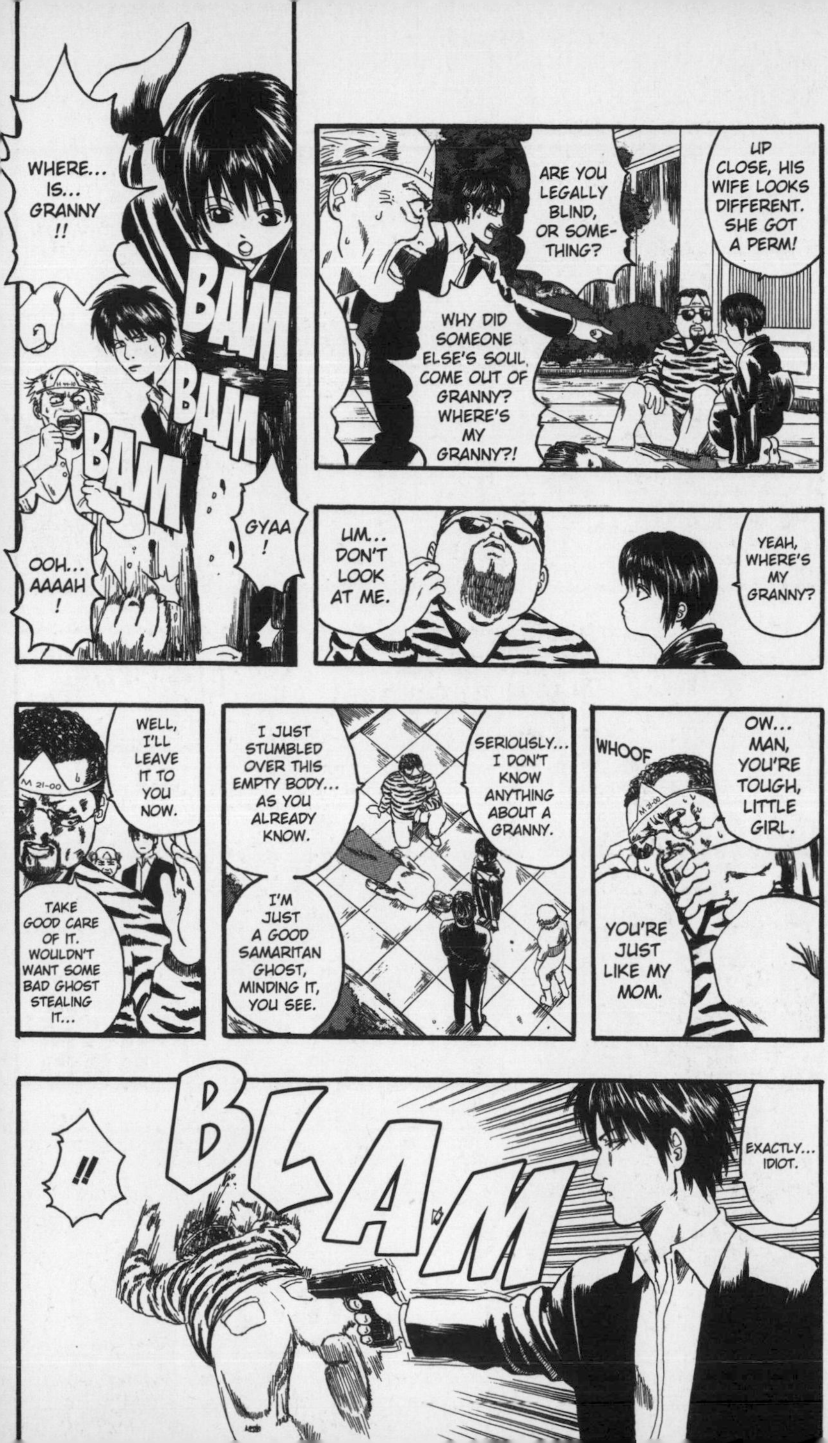
UP CLOSE, HIS WIFE LOOKS DIFFERENT. SHE GOT A PERM!
ARE YOU LEGALLY BLIND, OR SOME-THING?
WHY DID SOMEONE ELSE'S SOUL COME OUT OF GRANNY? WHERE'S MY GRANNY?!
YEAH, WHERE'S MY GRANNY?
UM... DON'T LOOK AT ME.
WHERE... IS... GRANNY !!
BAM
BAM
BAM
GYAA!
OOH... AAAAH!
WHOOF
OW... MAN, YOU'RE TOUGH, LITTLE GIRL.
YOU'RE JUST LIKE MY MOM.
SERIOUSLY... I DON'T KNOW ANYTHING ABOUT A GRANNY.
I JUST STUMBLED OVER THIS EMPTY BODY... AS YOU ALREADY KNOW.
I'M JUST A GOOD SAMARITAN GHOST, MINDING IT, YOU SEE.
WELL, I'LL LEAVE IT TO YOU NOW.
TAKE GOOD CARE OF IT. WOULDN'T WANT SOME BAD GHOST STEALING IT...
EXACTLY... IDIOT.
BLAM
!!

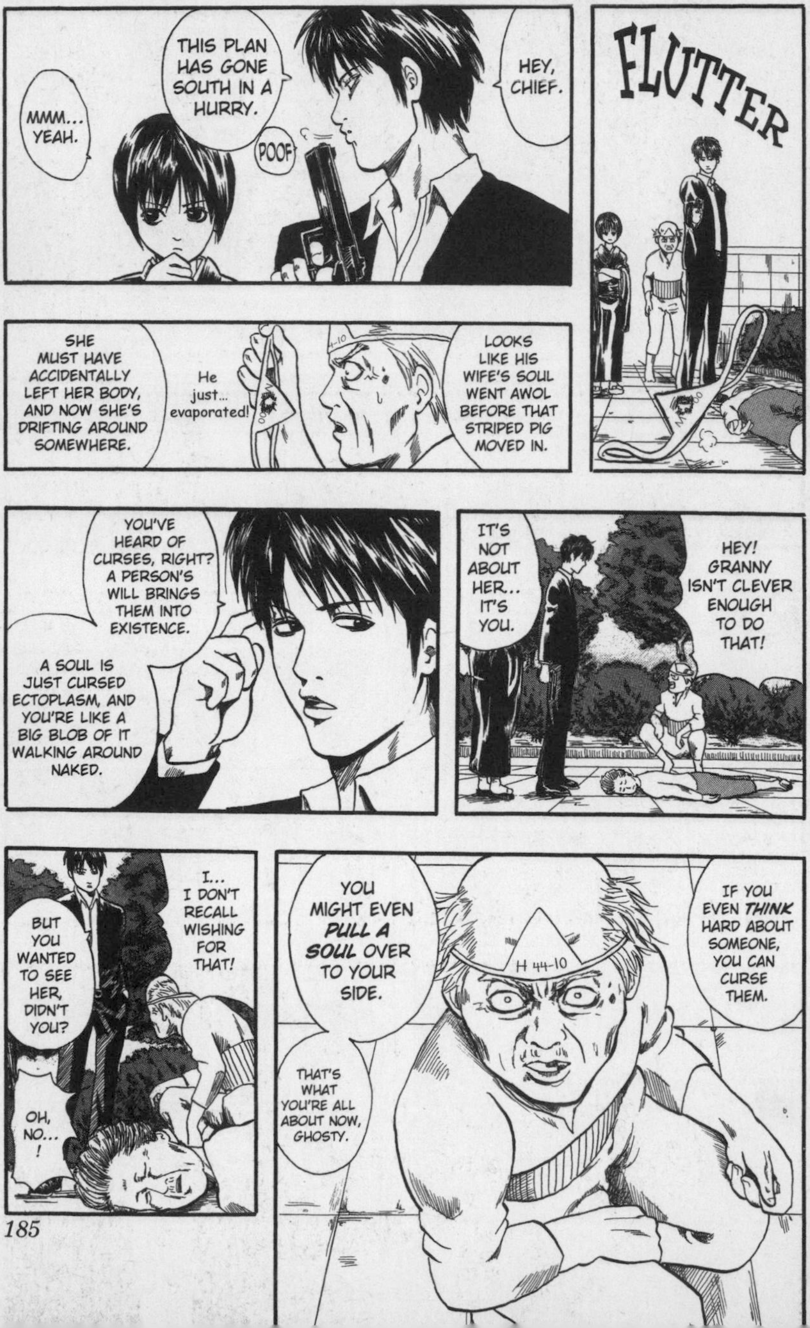
FLUTTER
HEY, CHIEF.
THIS PLAN HAS GONE SOUTH IN A HURRY.
POOF
MMM... YEAH.
LOOKS LIKE HIS WIFE'S SOUL WENT AWOL BEFORE THAT STRIPED PIG MOVED IN.
He just... evaporated!
SHE MUST HAVE ACCIDENTALLY LEFT HER BODY, AND NOW SHE'S DRIFTING AROUND SOMEWHERE.
HEY! GRANNY ISN'T CLEVER ENOUGH TO DO THAT!
IT'S NOT ABOUT HER... IT'S YOU.
YOU'VE HEARD OF CURSES, RIGHT? A PERSON'S WILL BRINGS THEM INTO EXISTENCE.
A SOUL IS JUST CURSED ECTOPLASM, AND YOU'RE LIKE A BIG BLOB OF IT WALKING AROUND NAKED.
IF YOU EVEN *THINK* HARD ABOUT SOMEONE, YOU CAN CURSE THEM.
YOU MIGHT EVEN **PULL A SOUL** OVER TO YOUR SIDE.
H 44-10
THAT'S WHAT YOU'RE ALL ABOUT NOW, GHOSTY.
I... I DON'T RECALL WISHING FOR THAT!
BUT YOU WANTED TO SEE HER, DIDN'T YOU?
OH, NO...!

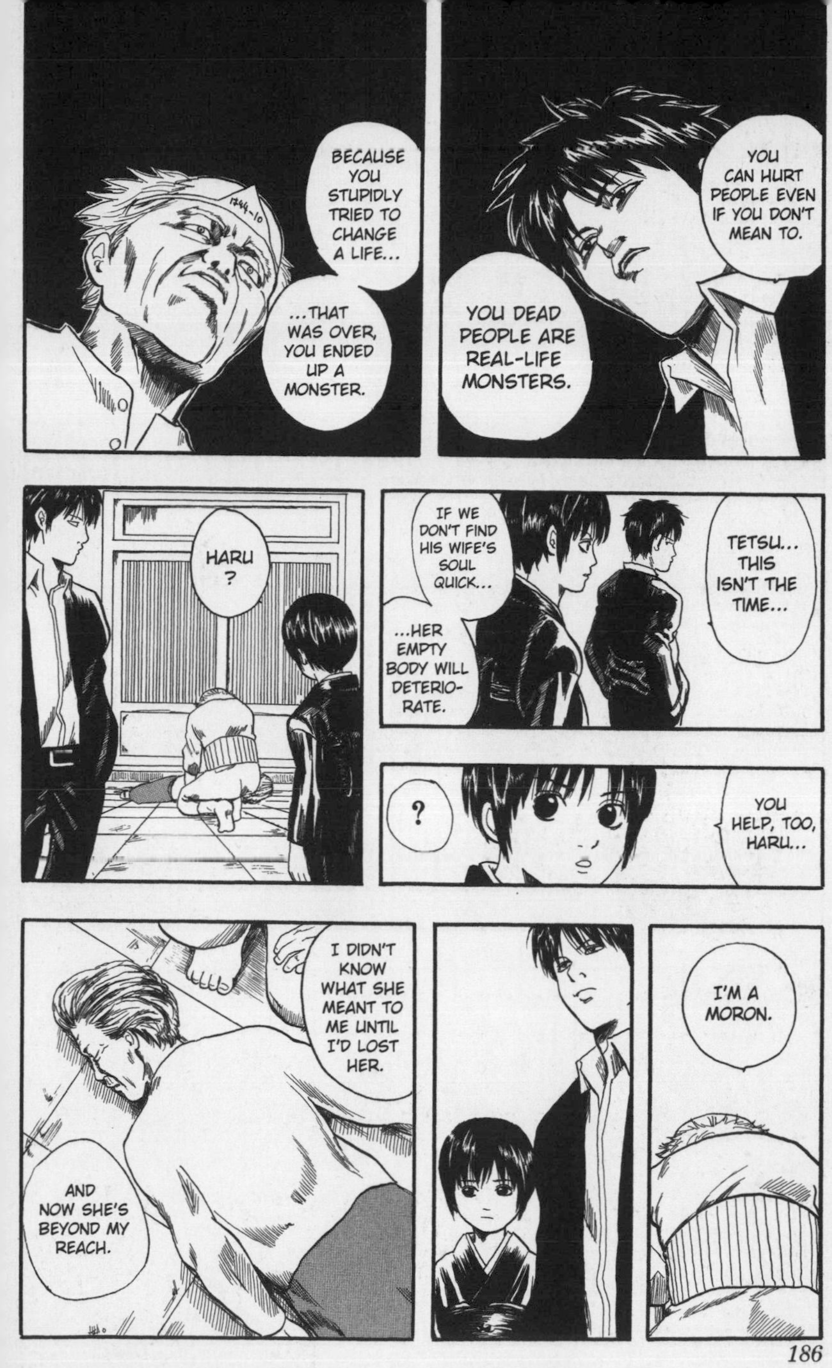
YOU CAN HURT PEOPLE EVEN IF YOU DON'T MEAN TO.
YOU DEAD PEOPLE ARE REAL-LIFE MONSTERS.
BECAUSE YOU STUPIDLY TRIED TO CHANGE A LIFE...
...THAT WAS OVER, YOU ENDED UP A MONSTER.
TETSU... THIS ISN'T THE TIME...
IF WE DON'T FIND HIS WIFE'S SOUL QUICK...
...HER EMPTY BODY WILL DETERIO-RATE.
YOU HELP, TOO, HARU...
?
HARU ?
I'M A MORON.
I DIDN'T KNOW WHAT SHE MEANT TO ME UNTIL I'D LOST HER.
AND NOW SHE'S BEYOND MY REACH.

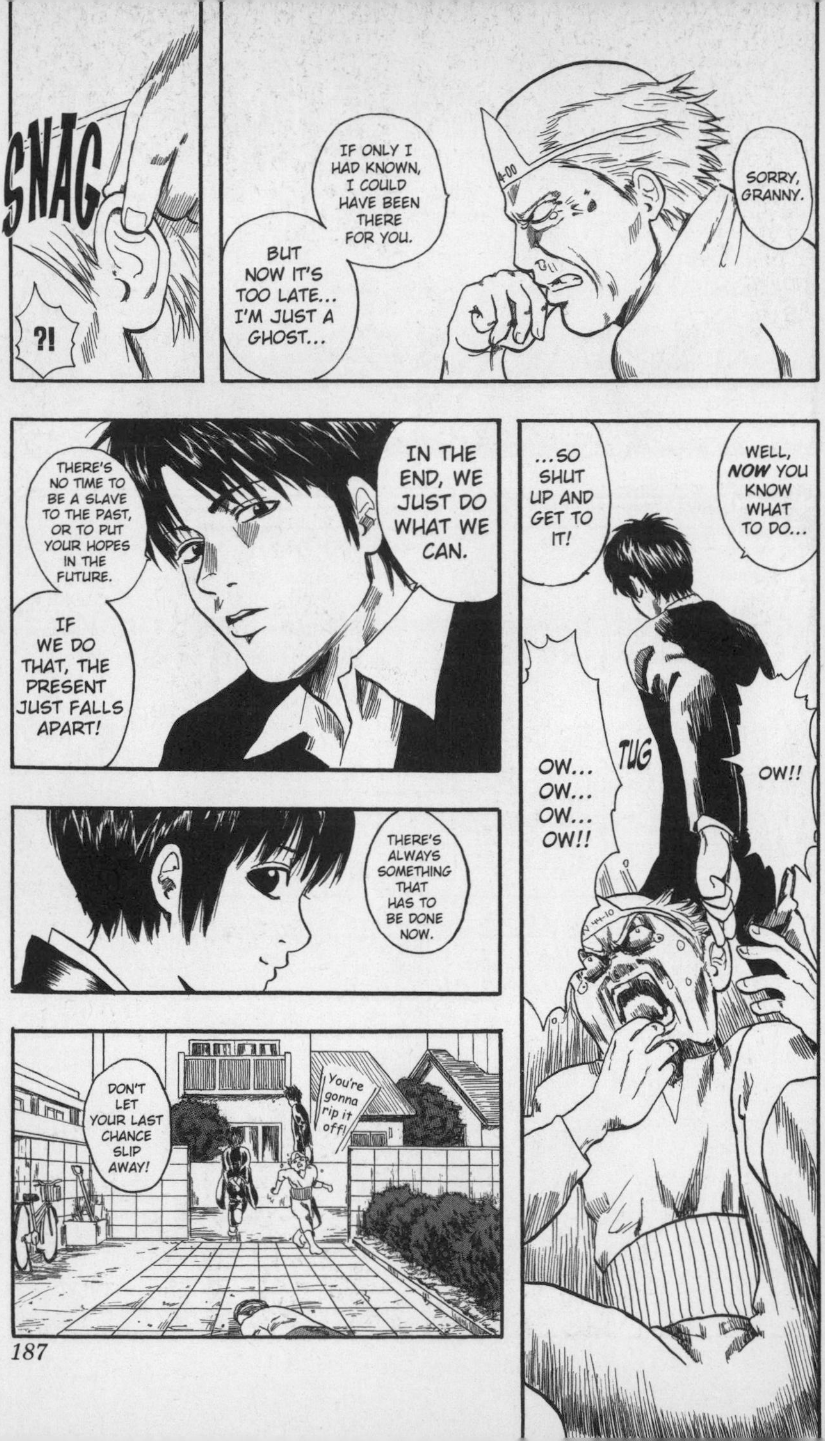
SORRY, GRANNY.
IF ONLY I HAD KNOWN, I COULD HAVE BEEN THERE FOR YOU.
BUT NOW IT'S TOO LATE... I'M JUST A GHOST...
SNAG
?!
WELL, NOW YOU KNOW WHAT TO DO...
...SO SHUT UP AND GET TO IT!
TUG
OW!!
OW... OW... OW... OW!!
IN THE END, WE JUST DO WHAT WE CAN.
THERE'S NO TIME TO BE A SLAVE TO THE PAST, OR TO PUT YOUR HOPES IN THE FUTURE.
IF WE DO THAT, THE PRESENT JUST FALLS APART!
THERE'S ALWAYS SOMETHING THAT HAS TO BE DONE NOW.
You're gonna rip it off!
DON'T LET YOUR LAST CHANCE SLIP AWAY!

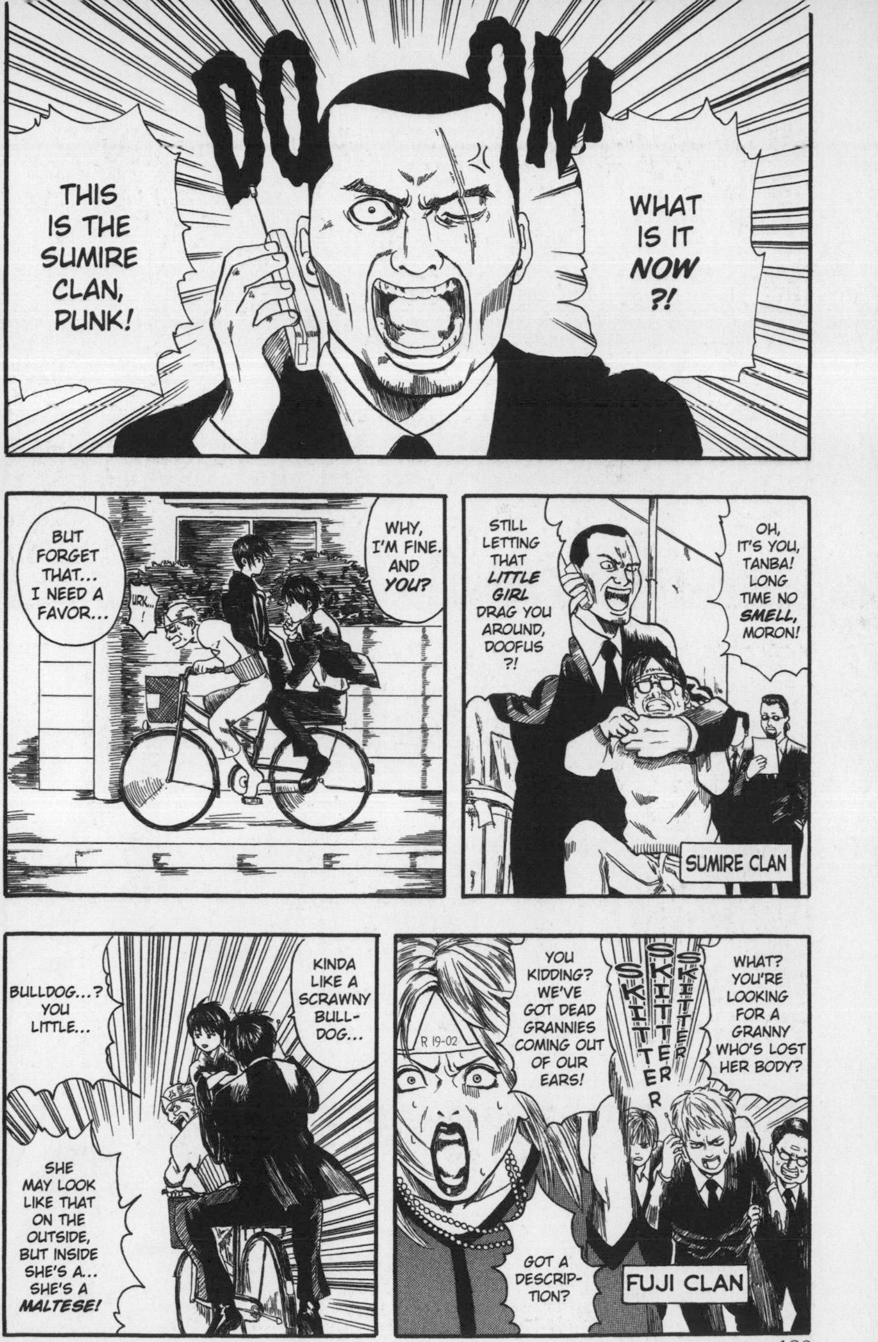
DOOM
WHAT IS IT NOW?!
THIS IS THE SUMIRE CLAN, PUNK!
OH, IT'S YOU, TANBA! LONG TIME NO SMELL, MORON!
STILL LETTING THAT LITTLE GIRL DRAG YOU AROUND, DOOFUS?!
SUMIRE CLAN
WHY, I'M FINE. AND YOU?
URK...!
BUT FORGET THAT... I NEED A FAVOR...
WHAT? YOU'RE LOOKING FOR A GRANNY WHO'S LOST HER BODY?
SKITTER
SKITTER
SKITTER
YOU KIDDING? WE'VE GOT DEAD GRANNIES COMING OUT OF OUR EARS!
R 19-02
GOT A DESCRIPTION?
FUJI CLAN
KINDA LIKE A SCRAWNY BULLDOG...
BULLDOG...? YOU LITTLE...
SHE MAY LOOK LIKE THAT ON THE OUTSIDE, BUT INSIDE SHE'S A... SHE'S A MALTESE!

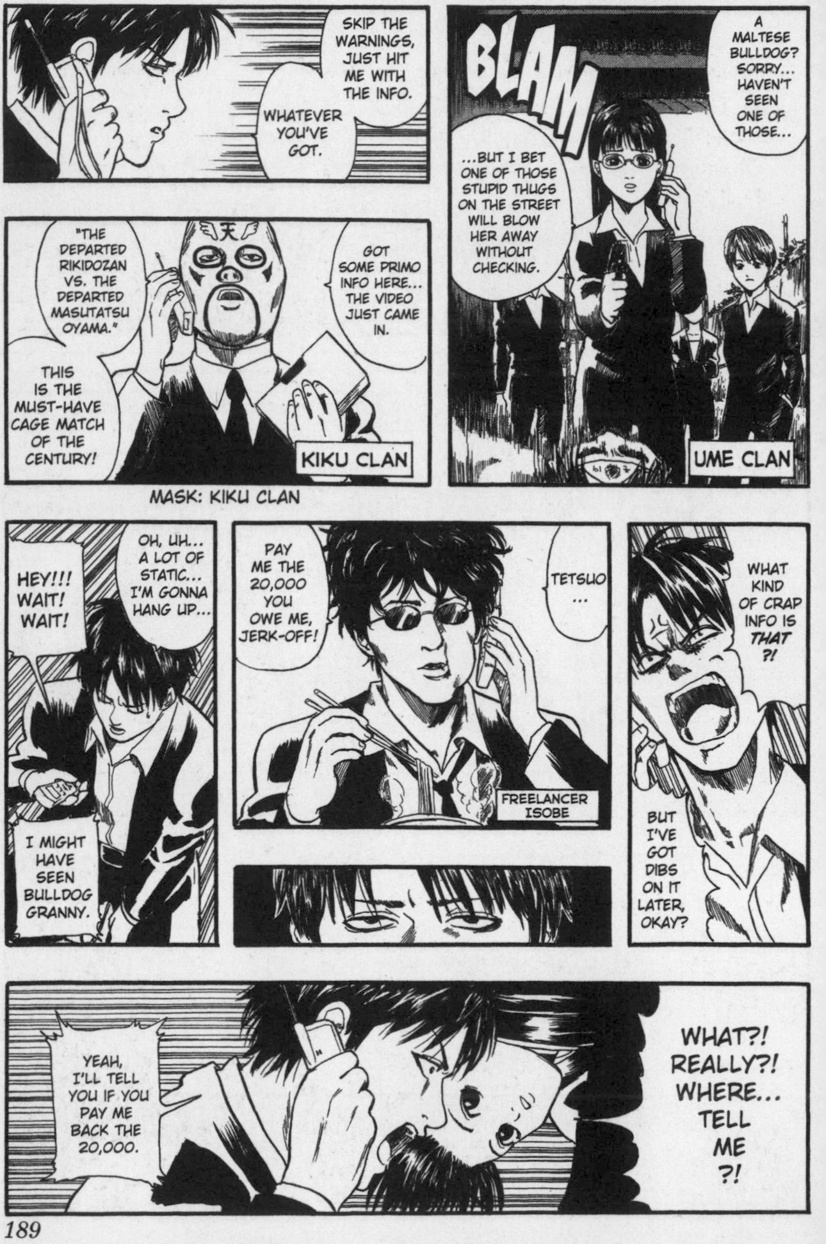
A MALTESE BULLDOG? SORRY... HAVEN'T SEEN ONE OF THOSE...
BLAM
...BUT I BET ONE OF THOSE STUPID THUGS ON THE STREET WILL BLOW HER AWAY WITHOUT CHECKING.
UME CLAN
SKIP THE WARNINGS, JUST HIT ME WITH THE INFO.
WHATEVER YOU'VE GOT.
GOT SOME PRIMO INFO HERE... THE VIDEO JUST CAME IN.
"THE DEPARTED RIKIDOZAN VS. THE DEPARTED MASUTATSU OYAMA."
THIS IS THE MUST-HAVE CAGE MATCH OF THE CENTURY!
KIKU CLAN
MASK: KIKU CLAN
WHAT KIND OF CRAP INFO IS *THAT* ?!
BUT I'VE GOT DIBS ON IT LATER, OKAY?
TETSUO ...
PAY ME THE 20,000 YOU OWE ME, JERK-OFF!
FREELANCER ISOBE
OH, UH... A LOT OF STATIC... I'M GONNA HANG UP...
HEY!!! WAIT! WAIT!
I MIGHT HAVE SEEN BULLDOG GRANNY.
WHAT?! REALLY?! WHERE... TELL ME ?!
YEAH, I'LL TELL YOU IF YOU PAY ME BACK THE 20,000.

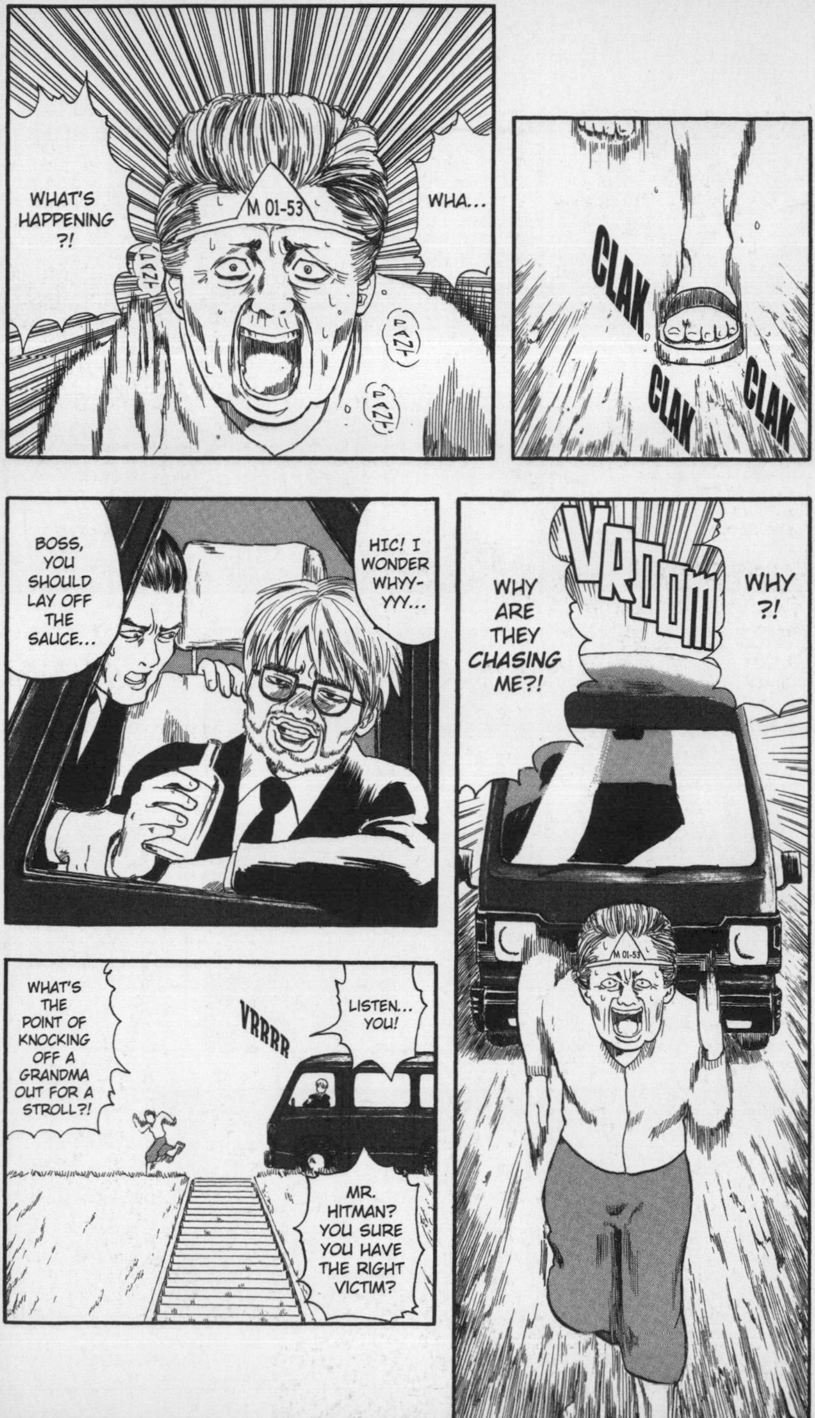
CLAK
CLAK
CLAK
WHA...
PANT
PANT
WHAT'S HAPPENING ?!
PANT
VROOM
WHY ?!
WHY ARE THEY CHASING ME?!
HIC! I WONDER WHYY-YYY...
BOSS, YOU SHOULD LAY OFF THE SAUCE...
LISTEN... YOU!
VRRRR
WHAT'S THE POINT OF KNOCKING OFF A GRANDMA OUT FOR A STROLL?!
MR. HITMAN? YOU SURE YOU HAVE THE RIGHT VICTIM?

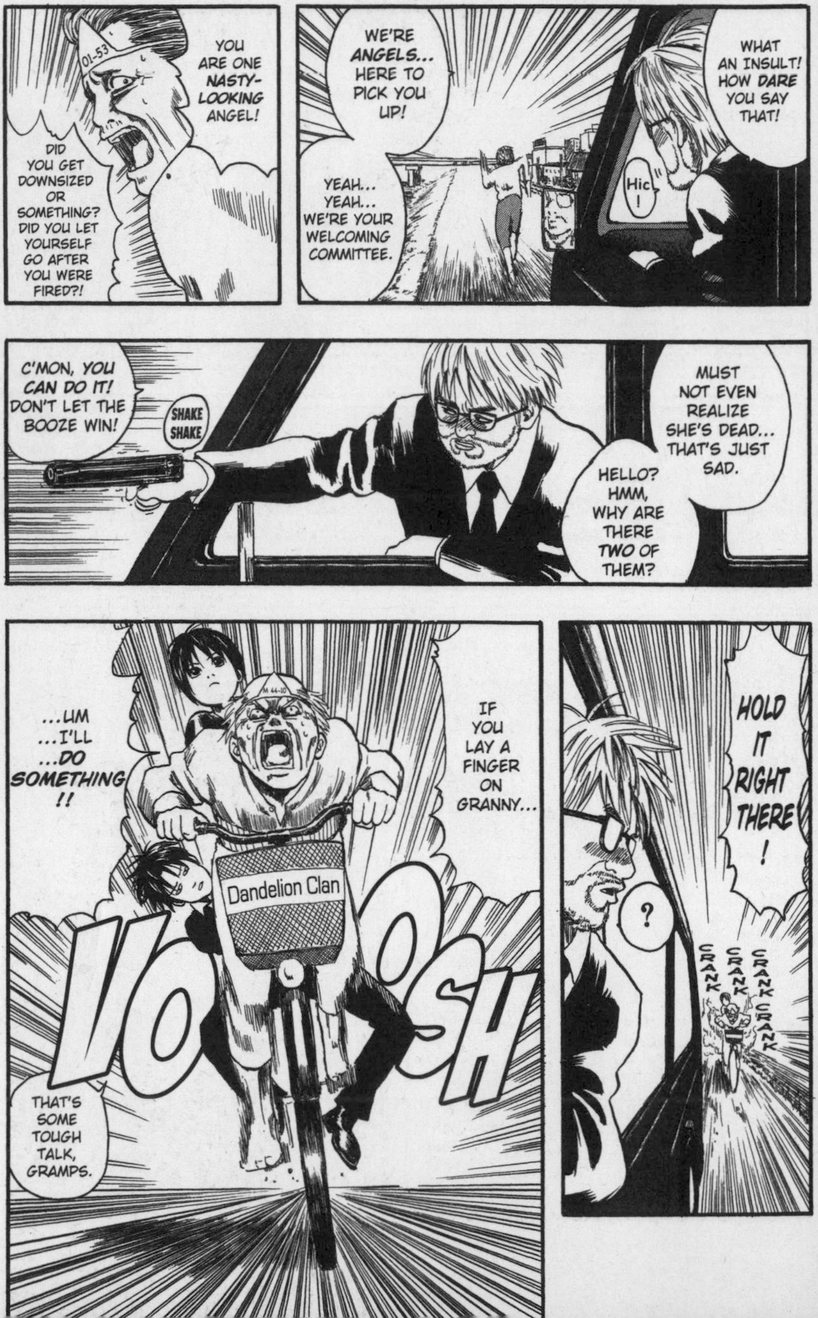
WHAT AN INSULT! HOW DARE YOU SAY THAT!
Hic!
WE'RE ANGELS... HERE TO PICK YOU UP!
YEAH... YEAH... WE'RE YOUR WELCOMING COMMITTEE.
01-53
YOU ARE ONE NASTY-LOOKING ANGEL!
DID YOU GET DOWNSIZED OR SOMETHING? DID YOU LET YOURSELF GO AFTER YOU WERE FIRED?!
MUST NOT EVEN REALIZE SHE'S DEAD... THAT'S JUST SAD.
HELLO? HMM, WHY ARE THERE TWO OF THEM?
SHAKE SHAKE
C'MON, YOU CAN DO IT! DON'T LET THE BOOZE WIN!
HOLD IT RIGHT THERE!
?
CRANK CRANK CRANK CRANK
IF YOU LAY A FINGER ON GRANNY...
M 44-10
...UM ...I'LL ...DO SOMETHING!!
Dandelion Clan
VOOSH
THAT'S SOME TOUGH TALK, GRAMPS.

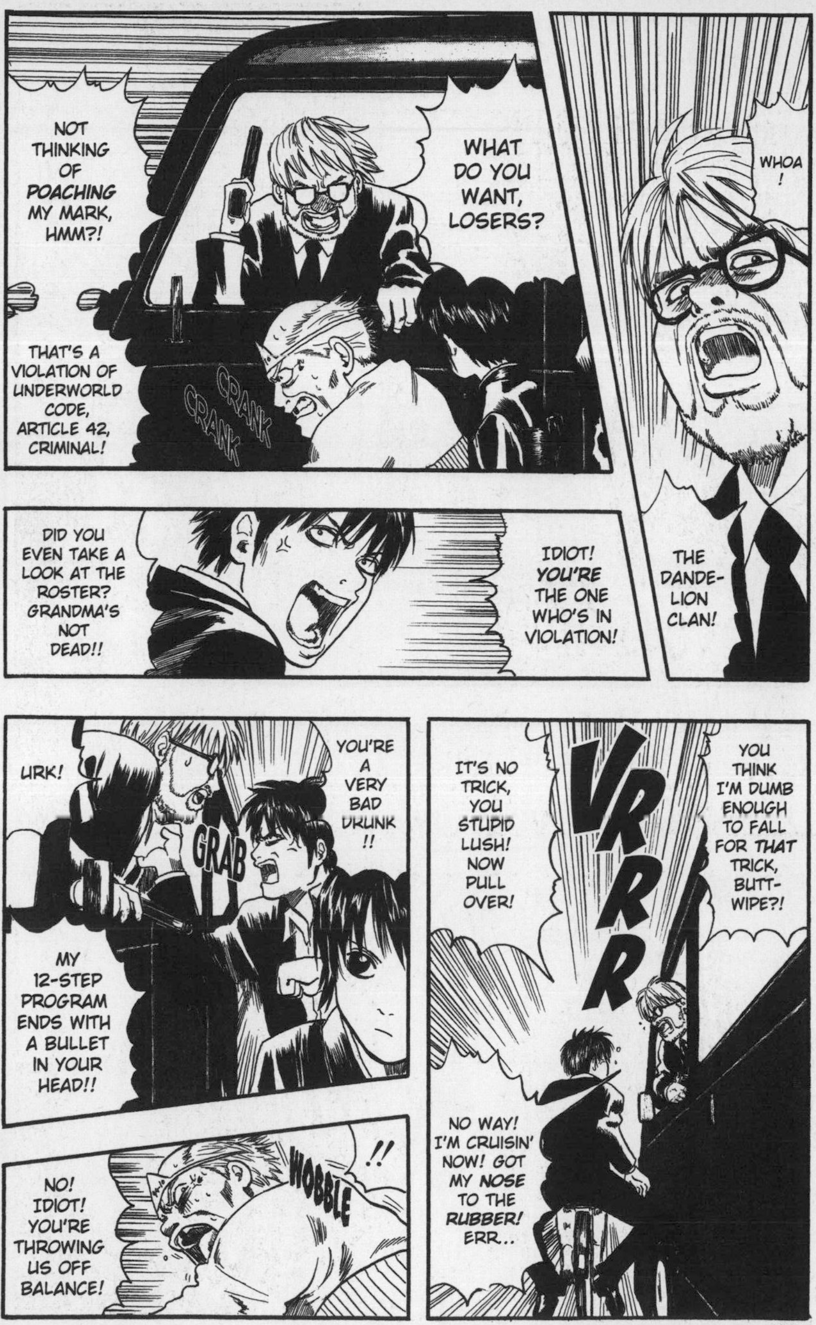
WHOA!
THE DANDELION CLAN!
WHAT DO YOU WANT, LOSERS?
NOT THINKING OF *POACHING* MY MARK, HMM?!
THAT'S A VIOLATION OF UNDERWORLD CODE, ARTICLE 42, CRIMINAL!
CRANK
CRANK
IDIOT! *YOU'RE* THE ONE WHO'S IN VIOLATION!
DID YOU EVEN TAKE A LOOK AT THE ROSTER? GRANDMA'S NOT DEAD!!
YOU THINK I'M DUMB ENOUGH TO FALL FOR *THAT* TRICK, BUTT-WIPE?!
VRRR
IT'S NO TRICK, YOU STUPID LUSH! NOW PULL OVER!
NO WAY! I'M CRUISIN' NOW! GOT MY *NOSE* TO THE *RUBBER!* ERR...
YOU'RE A VERY BAD DRUNK!!
URK!
GRAB
MY 12-STEP PROGRAM ENDS WITH A BULLET IN YOUR HEAD!!
!!
WOBBLE
NO! IDIOT! YOU'RE THROWING US OFF BALANCE!

READ THIS WAY

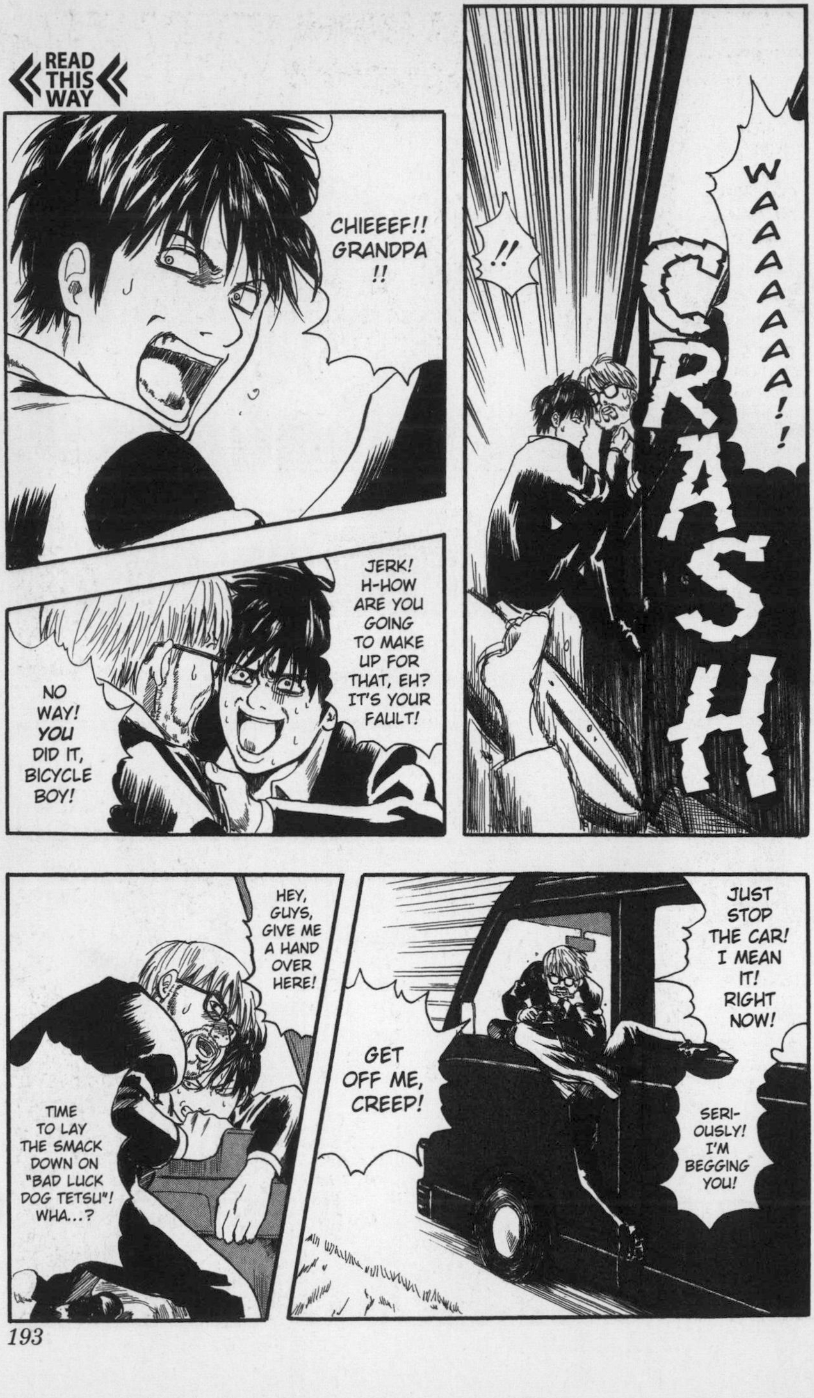
WAAAAAAAA!!
!!
CRASH
CHIEEEF!! GRANDPA !!
JERK! H-HOW ARE YOU GOING TO MAKE UP FOR THAT, EH? IT'S YOUR FAULT!
NO WAY! *YOU* DID IT, BICYCLE BOY!
JUST STOP THE CAR! I MEAN IT! RIGHT NOW!
SERI-OUSLY! I'M BEGGING YOU!
GET OFF ME, CREEP!
HEY, GUYS, GIVE ME A HAND OVER HERE!
TIME TO LAY THE SMACK DOWN ON "BAD LUCK DOG TETSU"! WHA...?

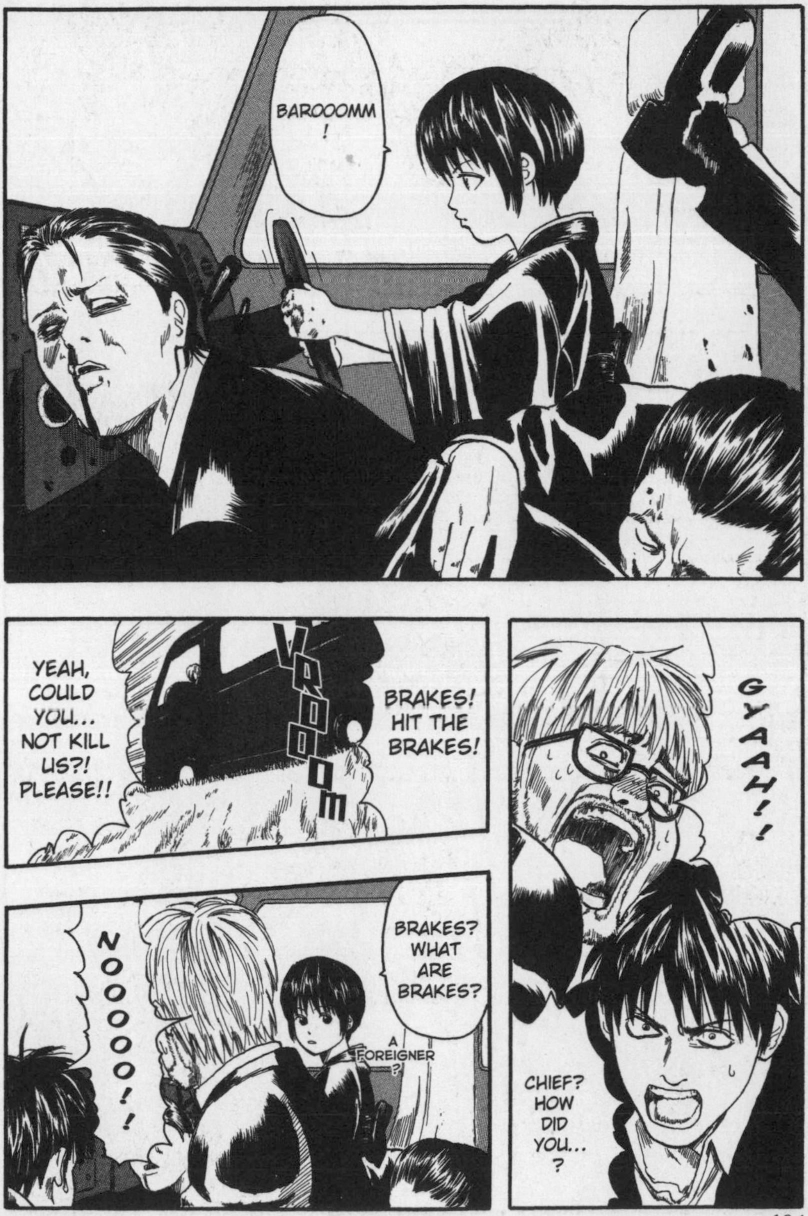
BAROOOMM!
GYAAH!!
CHIEF? HOW DID YOU...?
BRAKES! HIT THE BRAKES!
VROOOOM
YEAH, COULD YOU... NOT KILL US?! PLEASE!!
BRAKES? WHAT ARE BRAKES?
A FOREIGNER?
NOOOOOO!!

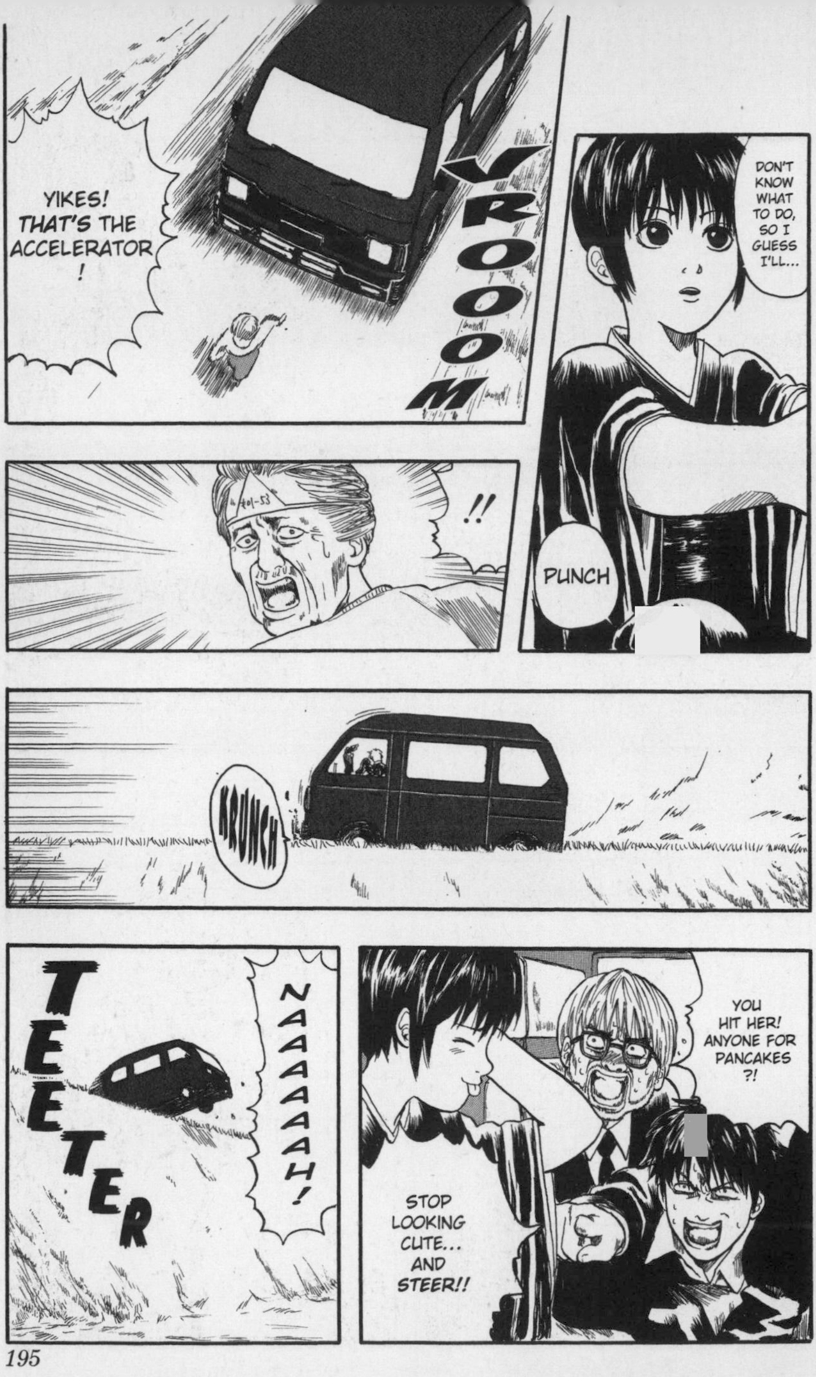
DON'T KNOW WHAT TO DO, SO I GUESS I'LL...
PUNCH
YIKES! THAT'S THE ACCELERATOR!
VROOOM
!!
KRUNCH
YOU HIT HER! ANYONE FOR PANCAKES?!
STOP LOOKING CUTE... AND STEER!!
NAAAAAAH!
TEETER

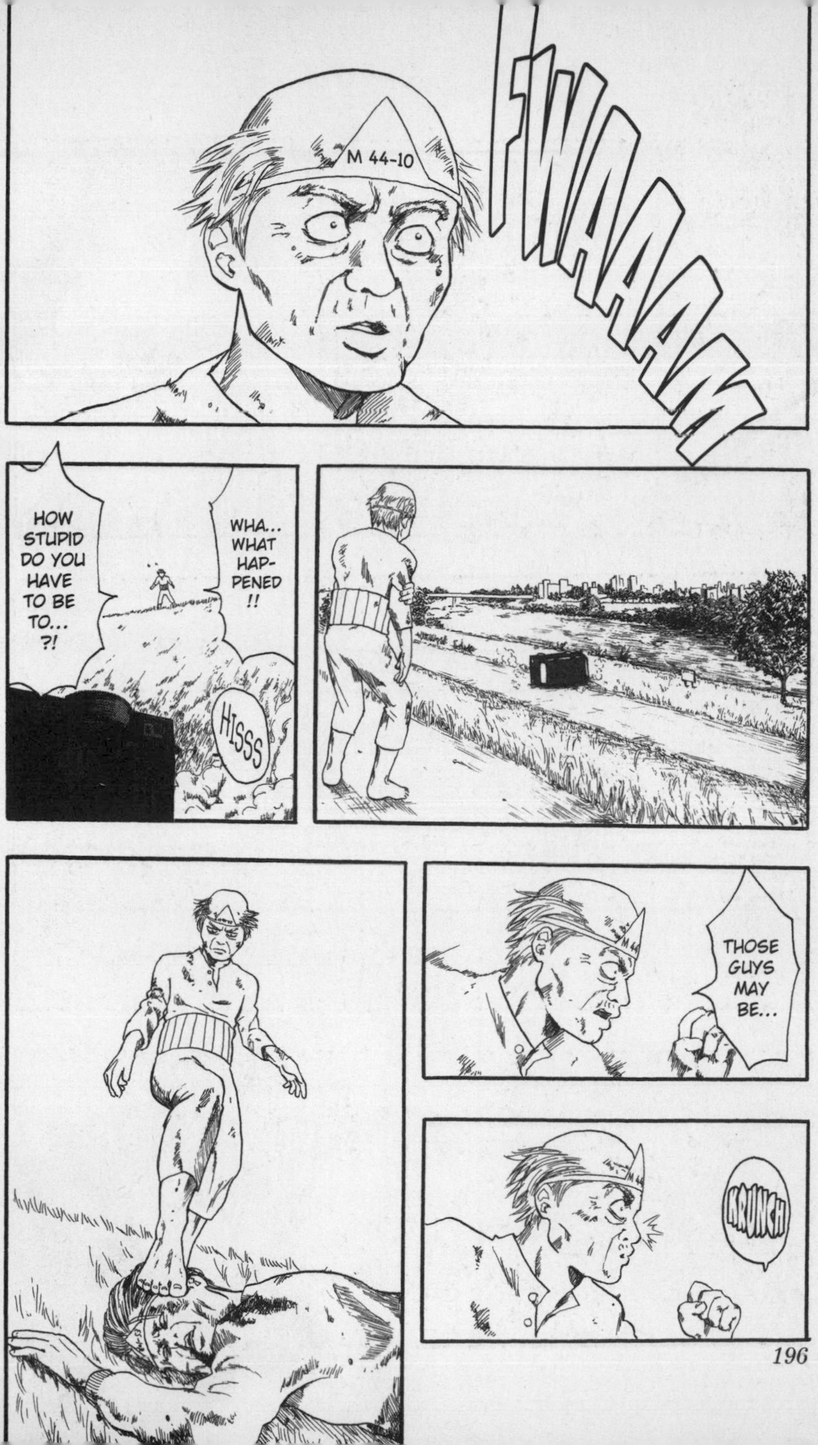
M 44-10
FWAAAM
WHA... WHAT HAP-PENED!!
HOW STUPID DO YOU HAVE TO BE TO...?!
HISSS
THOSE GUYS MAY BE...
KRUNCH

« READ THIS WAY «

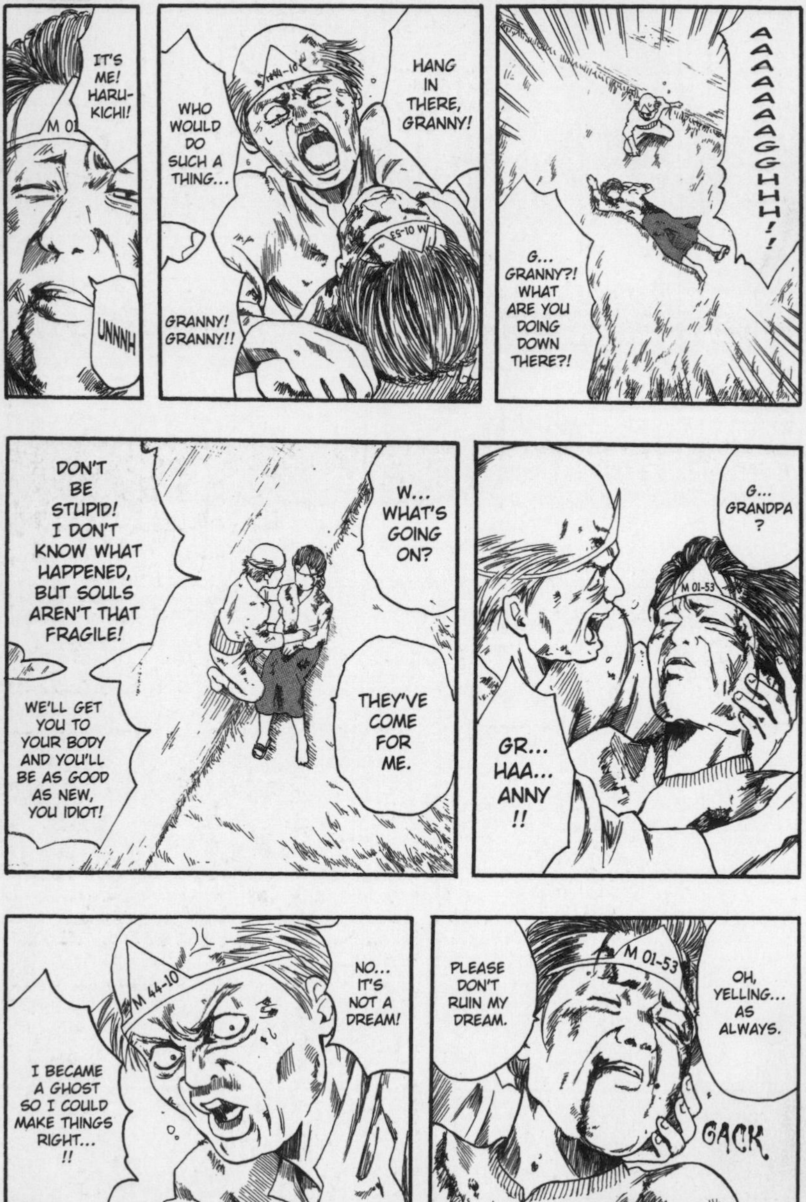
AAAAAAAAGHHH!!
G... GRANNY?! WHAT ARE YOU DOING DOWN THERE?!
HANG IN THERE, GRANNY!
WHO WOULD DO SUCH A THING...
M 01-53
GRANNY! GRANNY!!
IT'S ME! HARU-KICHI!
M 01
UNNNH
G... GRANDPA?
M 01-53
GR... HAA... ANNY!!
W... WHAT'S GOING ON?
THEY'VE COME FOR ME.
DON'T BE STUPID! I DON'T KNOW WHAT HAPPENED, BUT SOULS AREN'T THAT FRAGILE!
WE'LL GET YOU TO YOUR BODY AND YOU'LL BE AS GOOD AS NEW, YOU IDIOT!
OH, YELLING... AS ALWAYS.
M 01-53
PLEASE DON'T RUIN MY DREAM.
GACK
NO... IT'S NOT A DREAM!
M 44-10
I BECAME A GHOST SO I COULD MAKE THINGS RIGHT... !!

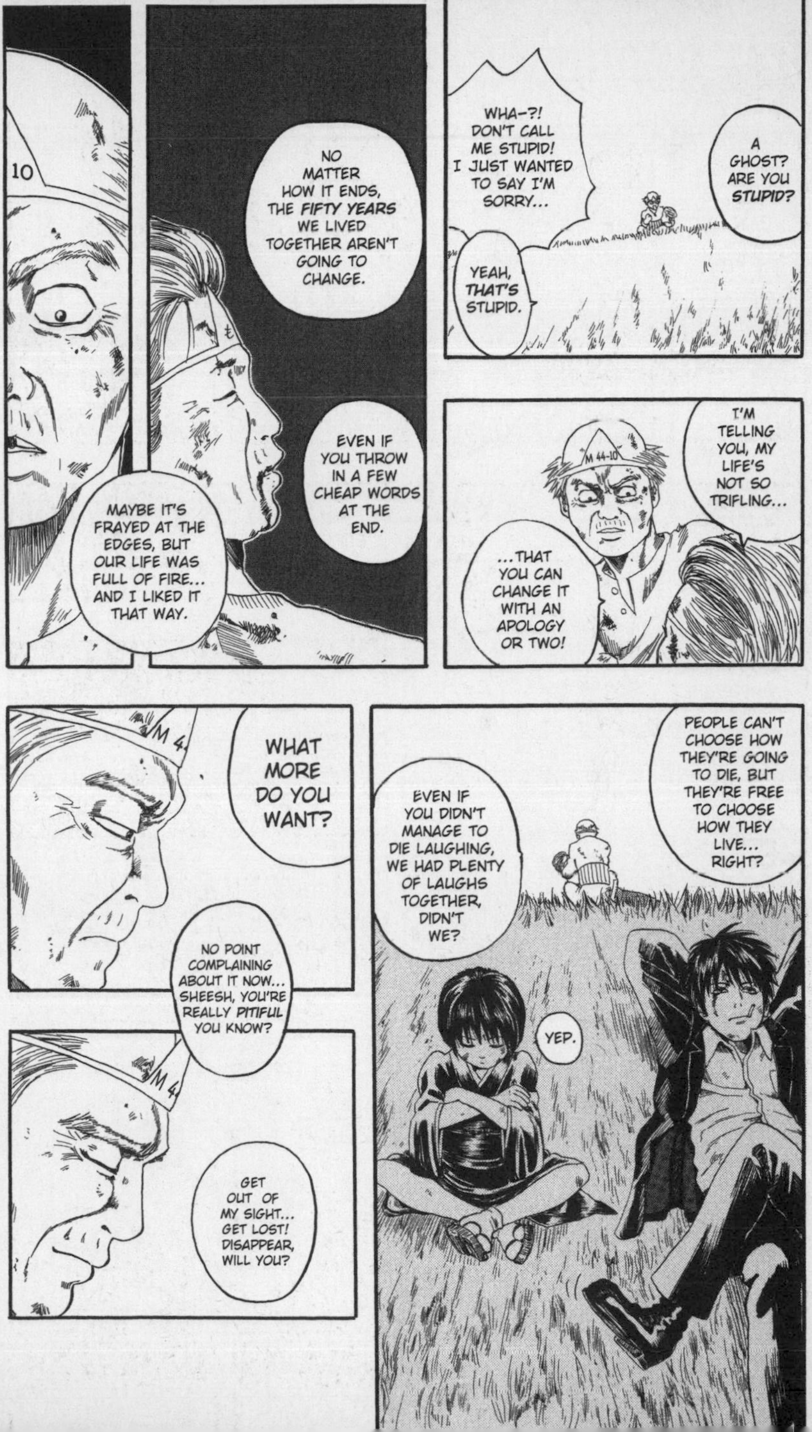
A GHOST? ARE YOU *STUPID?*
WHA-?! DON'T CALL ME STUPID! I JUST WANTED TO SAY I'M SORRY...
YEAH, *THAT'S* STUPID.
M 44-10
I'M TELLING YOU, MY LIFE'S NOT SO TRIFLING...
...THAT YOU CAN CHANGE IT WITH AN APOLOGY OR TWO!
NO MATTER HOW IT ENDS, THE *FIFTY YEARS* WE LIVED TOGETHER AREN'T GOING TO CHANGE.
EVEN IF YOU THROW IN A FEW CHEAP WORDS AT THE END.
MAYBE IT'S FRAYED AT THE EDGES, BUT OUR LIFE WAS FULL OF FIRE... AND I LIKED IT THAT WAY.
10
PEOPLE CAN'T CHOOSE HOW THEY'RE GOING TO DIE, BUT THEY'RE FREE TO CHOOSE HOW THEY LIVE... RIGHT?
EVEN IF YOU DIDN'T MANAGE TO DIE LAUGHING, WE HAD PLENTY OF LAUGHS TOGETHER, DIDN'T WE?
YEP.
WHAT MORE DO YOU WANT?
NO POINT COMPLAINING ABOUT IT NOW... SHEESH, YOU'RE REALLY *PITIFUL* YOU KNOW?
GET OUT OF MY SIGHT... GET LOST! DISAPPEAR, WILL YOU?

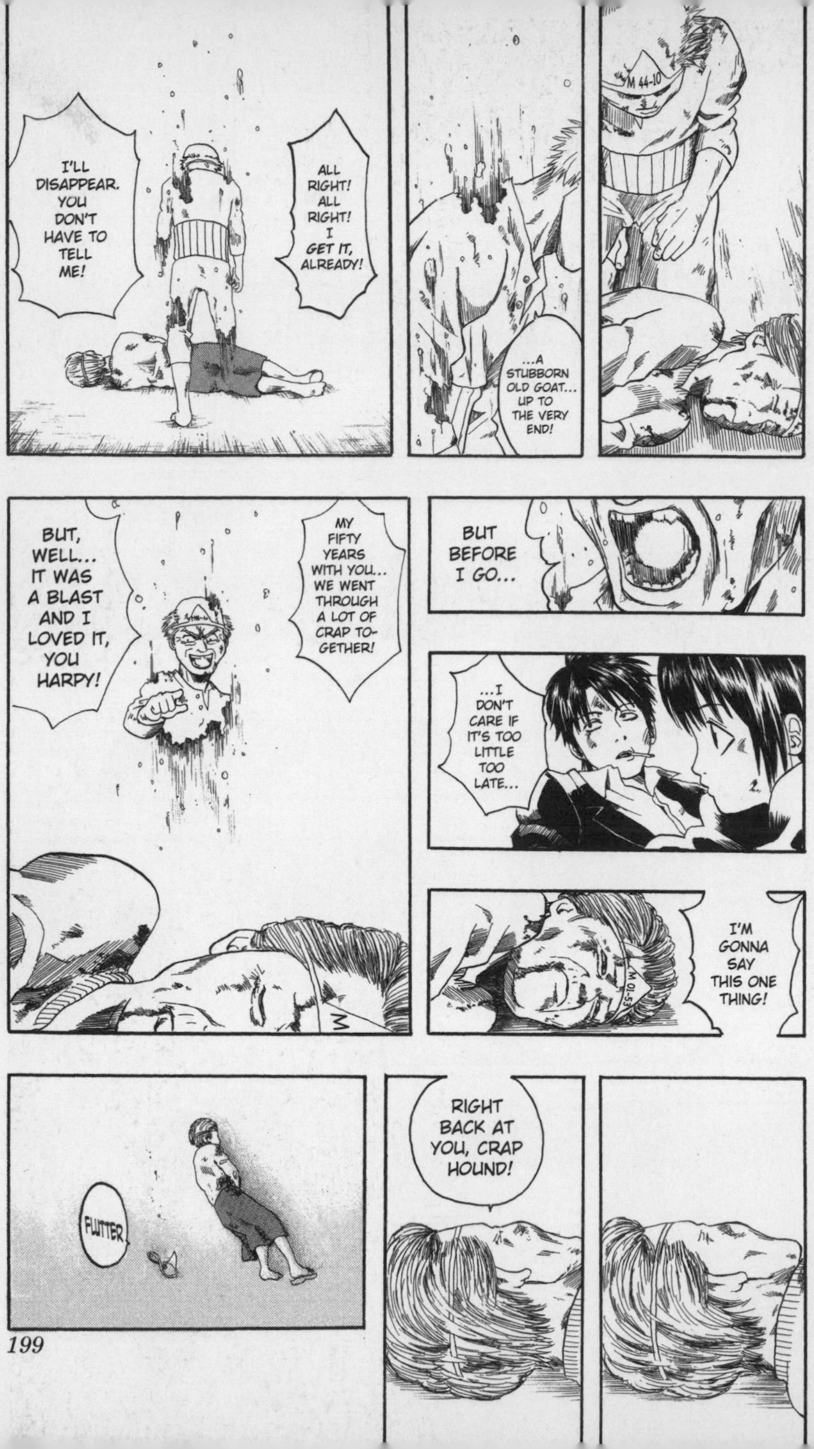
...A STUBBORN OLD GOAT... UP TO THE VERY END!
ALL RIGHT! ALL RIGHT! I GET IT, ALREADY!
I'LL DISAPPEAR. YOU DON'T HAVE TO TELL ME!
BUT BEFORE I GO...
...I DON'T CARE IF IT'S TOO LITTLE TOO LATE...
I'M GONNA SAY THIS ONE THING!
MY FIFTY YEARS WITH YOU... WE WENT THROUGH A LOT OF CRAP TO-GETHER!
BUT, WELL... IT WAS A BLAST AND I LOVED IT, YOU HARPY!
RIGHT BACK AT YOU, CRAP HOUND!
FLUTTER

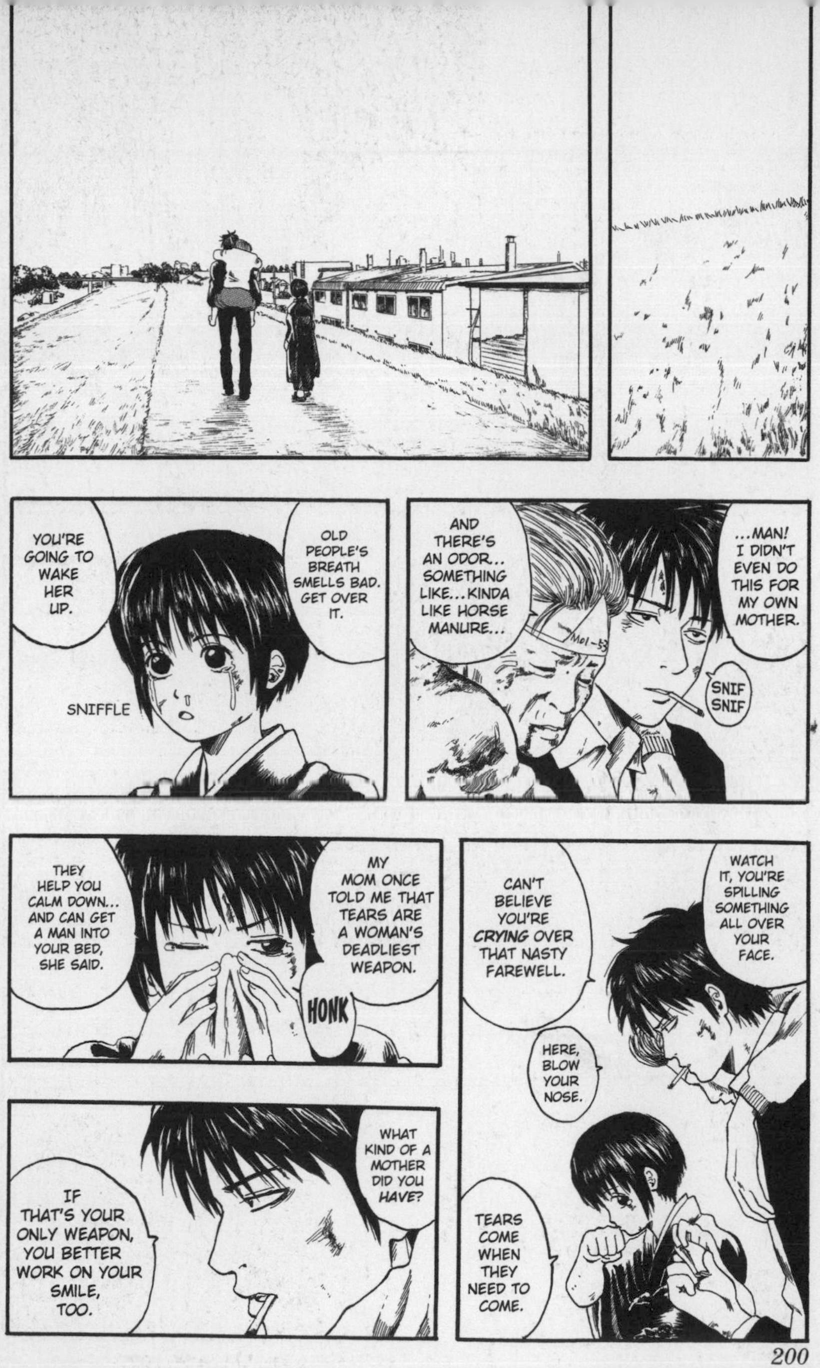
...MAN! I DIDN'T EVEN DO THIS FOR MY OWN MOTHER.
SNIF SNIF
AND THERE'S AN ODOR... SOMETHING LIKE...KINDA LIKE HORSE MANURE...
OLD PEOPLE'S BREATH SMELLS BAD. GET OVER IT.
YOU'RE GOING TO WAKE HER UP.
SNIFFLE
WATCH IT, YOU'RE SPILLING SOMETHING ALL OVER YOUR FACE.
CAN'T BELIEVE YOU'RE *CRYING* OVER THAT NASTY FAREWELL.
HERE, BLOW YOUR NOSE.
TEARS COME WHEN THEY NEED TO COME.
MY MOM ONCE TOLD ME THAT TEARS ARE A WOMAN'S DEADLIEST WEAPON.
HONK
THEY HELP YOU CALM DOWN... AND CAN GET A MAN INTO YOUR BED, SHE SAID.
WHAT KIND OF A MOTHER DID YOU *HAVE*?
IF THAT'S YOUR ONLY WEAPON, YOU BETTER WORK ON YOUR SMILE, TOO.

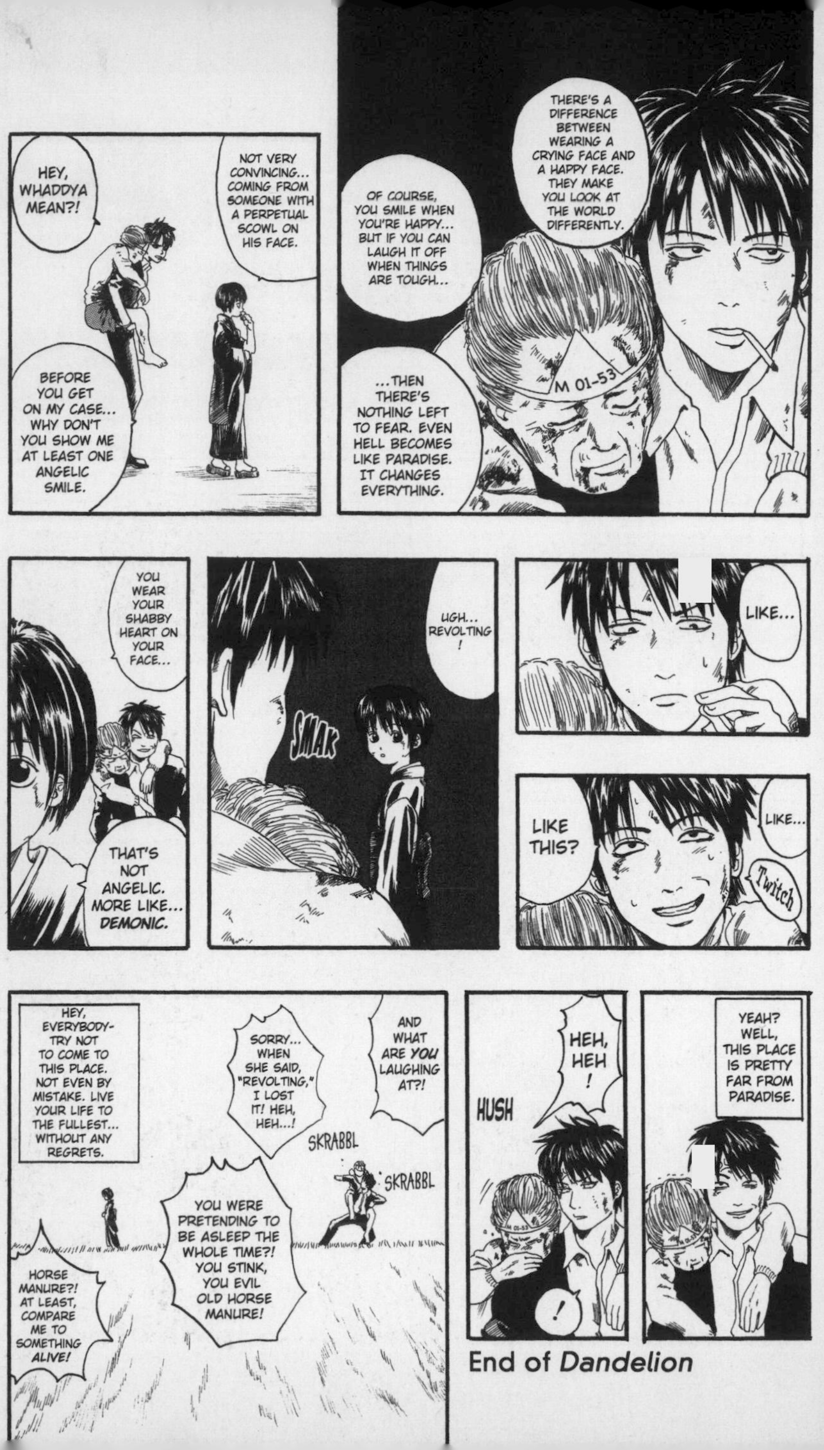
THERE'S A DIFFERENCE BETWEEN WEARING A CRYING FACE AND A HAPPY FACE. THEY MAKE YOU LOOK AT THE WORLD DIFFERENTLY.
OF COURSE, YOU SMILE WHEN YOU'RE HAPPY... BUT IF YOU CAN LAUGH IT OFF WHEN THINGS ARE TOUGH...
M 01-53
...THEN THERE'S NOTHING LEFT TO FEAR. EVEN HELL BECOMES LIKE PARADISE. IT CHANGES EVERYTHING.
NOT VERY CONVINCING... COMING FROM SOMEONE WITH A PERPETUAL SCOWL ON HIS FACE.
HEY, WHADDYA MEAN?!
BEFORE YOU GET ON MY CASE... WHY DON'T YOU SHOW ME AT LEAST ONE ANGELIC SMILE.
LIKE...
LIKE...
Twitch
LIKE THIS?
UGH... REVOLTING!
SMAK
YOU WEAR YOUR SHABBY HEART ON YOUR FACE...
THAT'S NOT ANGELIC. MORE LIKE... DEMONIC.
YEAH? WELL, THIS PLACE IS PRETTY FAR FROM PARADISE.
HEH, HEH!
HUSH
!
AND WHAT ARE YOU LAUGHING AT?!
SORRY... WHEN SHE SAID, "REVOLTING," I LOST IT! HEH, HEH...!
SKRABBL
SKRABBL
YOU WERE PRETENDING TO BE ASLEEP THE WHOLE TIME?! YOU STINK, YOU EVIL OLD HORSE MANURE!
HEY, EVERYBODY- TRY NOT TO COME TO THIS PLACE. NOT EVEN BY MISTAKE. LIVE YOUR LIFE TO THE FULLEST... WITHOUT ANY REGRETS.
HORSE MANURE?! AT LEAST, COMPARE ME TO SOMETHING ALIVE!

End of *Dandelion*

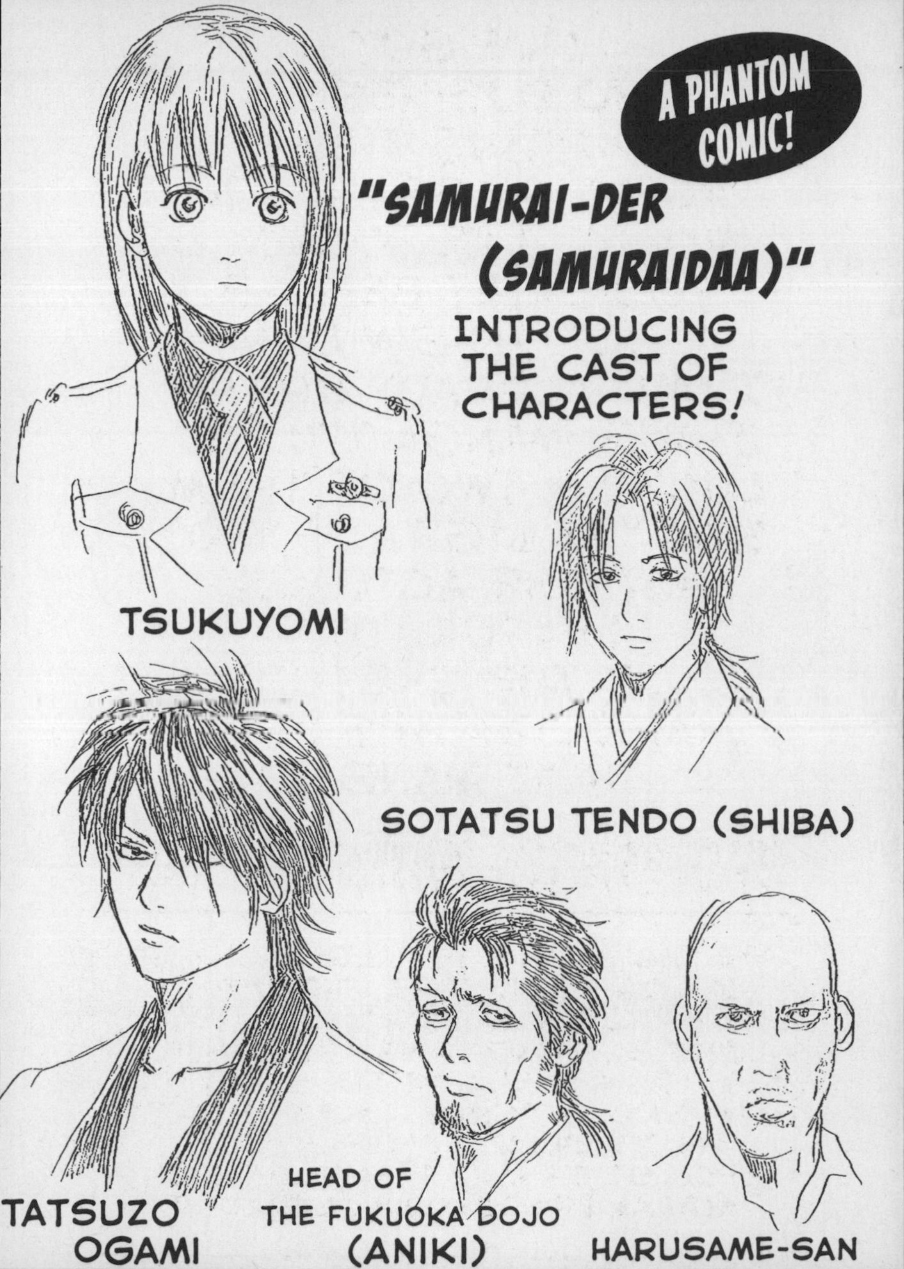
A PHANTOM COMIC!
"SAMURAI-DER (SAMURAIDAA)"
INTRODUCING THE CAST OF CHARACTERS!
TSUKUYOMI
SOTATSU TENDO (SHIBA)
TATSUZO OGAMI
HEAD OF THE FUKUOKA DOJO (ANIKI)
HARUSAME-SAN

I'VE GOT
NO BUSINESS
PUTTING THIS
KINDA STUFF INTO A
BOOK, BUT...OOPS...
TOO LATE! BEFORE
I GOT TO *GIN TAMA*,
I HAD ALREADY DRAWN
THREE MANGA TITLES.
LUCKILY, TWO OF THEM
SAW THE LIGHT OF DAY,
BUT ONE ACTUALLY
EVAPORATED
AT THE SKETCH
PHASE. THIS IS
THAT MANGA.

(TOUGH) WORDS FROM SUPERVISING EDITOR MR. 0

THE LEAD CHARACTER REQUIRES MORE
DEVELOPMENT. SURE, SHE TALKS A
LITTLE FUNNY, BUT BEYOND THAT, YOU'RE
JUST SLAPPING THINGS TOGETHER.
WHAT CAN THE STAR OF THE STORY DO?
WHAT KIND OF POWER DOES SHE HAVE?
WHAT HAPPENS TO THE SAMURAI
BECAUSE OF HER? PLEASE COME UP
WITH AN EPISODE AND DEVELOP IT.

TOTALLY NAKED GIN TAMA

ERM, SO WE HAD THESE TWO PAGES, SEE? I HAD NOTHING TO FILL THEM WITH, SO I FIGURED I'D JUST TAKE OFF MY CLOTHES AND GET NAKED, RIGHT? THAT'S ALL THERE IS TO DO. I'LL TAKE 'EM OFF NOW.

NOW, YOU YOUNG MEN OR LADIES OUT THERE ARE PROBABLY THINKING, "I DON'T WANT TO SEE YOUR FILTHY NAKED BOD'." WELL LET ME SET YOU STRAIGHT--YOU SHOULD REALIZE THAT WHAT'S FILTHY IS YOUR OWN HEART. SO, STARTING TOMORROW, GO LIVE YOUR LIFE BEARING THAT BURDEN ON YOUR BACK.

UH, YEAH. SO, I'D LIKE TO TALK NAKEDLY ABOUT HOW *GIN TAMA* WAS BORN. IT ALL STARTED WITH A SINGLE THING MY EDITOR MONCHICCHI ONISHI SAID TO ME. "YOU KNOW, NEXT YEAR, *TAIGA* (HISTORICAL) *DRAMA* IS GOING TO DO *SHINSENGUMI*, RIGHT? WELL, YOU COULD JUMP ON THE COATTAILS OF THAT."

I HAD BEEN THINKING UP A MANGA TO BE SERIALIZED...HAD IT IN MY HEAD TO SKIM BITS FROM *HARRY POTTER*, WHICH I HAD NEVER EVEN SEEN, WHIP IT UP JAPANESE-STYLE, AND MAKE A KILLING WITH A STORY ABOUT SOME KIND OF SCHOOL FOR DEMON DISPELLERS. OBVIOUSLY IT HAD NO CHANCE OF SUCCEEDING, AND SINCE I WAS PEEVED ABOUT ALREADY FAILING ONCE WITH A PERIOD DRAMA...

I TURNED AROUND TO MY EDITOR AND REPLIED, "I HATE PERIOD DRAMAS SINCE THEY ARE SO LIMITED IN THE STORYLINES THEY CAN USE. WHAT ARE YOU THINKING? THERE'S NO WAY I CAN JUST JUMP ON THE BANDWAGON. MONCHICCHI, YOU'RE AN IDIOT!!"

BUT HE SAID, "WHO ARE YOU CALLING MONCHICCHI, EH?! I'M SAYING THAT A SCHMUCK LIKE YOU MAKES MODERN-DAY DRAMA BORING! THE FACT IS, YOU'RE ALREADY TRYING TO JUMP ON THE *HARRY POTTER* BANDWAGON, AREN'T YOU?!"

OUR ARGUMENT REACHED A STALEMATE AND I SAID, "YEAH, BUT HARRY'S FINE! HE'S A FOREIGNER!" AND FINALLY MONCHICCHI BLASTED OUT, "WHO THE HECK CARES ABOUT WHAT PERIOD IT IS, ANYWAY? IT'S A FANTASY! A FANTASY PERIOD DRAMA!! IT'S SWORD FIGHTS WITH THE SHINSENGUMI AND MONSTERS!!" AND SO I GOT MYSELF ALL BOXED IN.

WELL, AFTER ALL THAT, I STARTED IN ON A SCRIPT, AND WHAT WITH MY ANNOYANCE OVER THE SETTING, MY IRRITATION WITH MY EDITOR, THE RAIN LEAKING INTO MY APARTMENT, THE INFLAMMATION IN MY MOUTH, MORE IRRITATION WITH MY EDITOR, AND OTHER STUFF-- SUCH AS IRRITATION WITH MY EDITOR--ALL PILING UP, MY PEN JUST STOPPED FLOWING.

"I TOLD YOU SO, MONCHICCHI! I'M NOT GOING TO LISTEN TO A SINGLE THING YOU SAY ANYMORE!!" AND WITH THAT, I TOTALLY CHANGED THE FLOW OF THE MANGA AROUND. IT BECAME *GIN TAMA*.

UM... WELL, THERE YOU GO... I'VE EVEN TAKEN OFF MY UNDERPANTS. HOW DO YOU LIKE THAT? I DON'T HAVE ANYTHING ELSE TO TAKE OFF, SO I'D LIKE TO PUT ON SOME CLOTHES AND SEE YOU AGAIN IN VOLUME 2. THANK YOU VERY MUCH FOR READING MY STUFF.

SORACHI

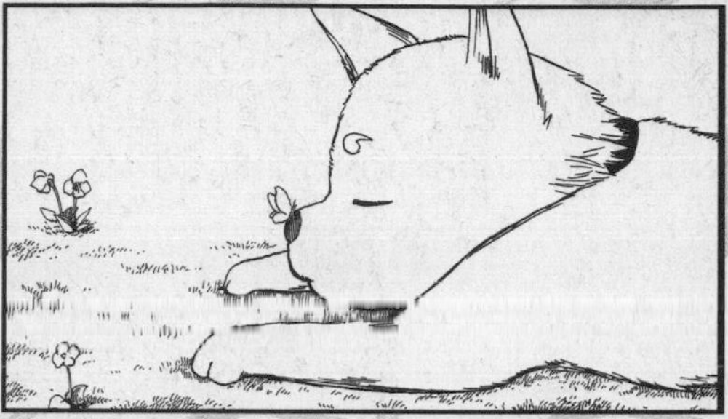

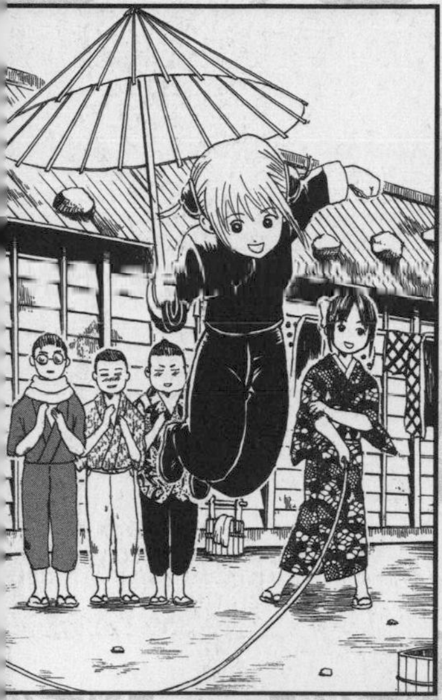

Next Volume Preview

Odd Jobs Gin, fellow *ronin* (independent samurai) Shinpachi, and alien combat girl Kagura aid and abet escaped convicts, long-lost lovers and homeless dogs! More importantly, is drinking milk the solution to all of Gin's problems…and maybe yours?

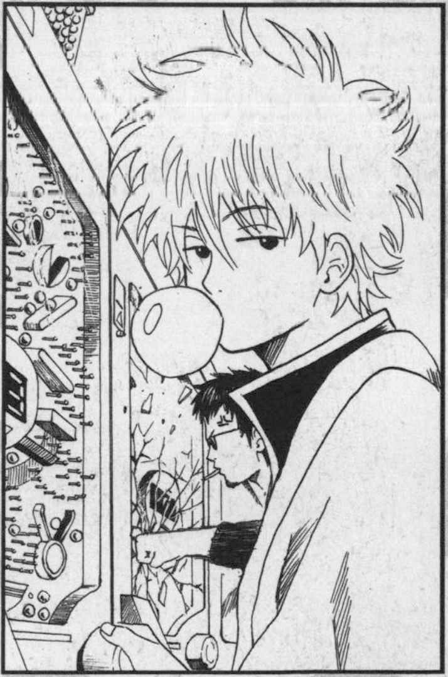

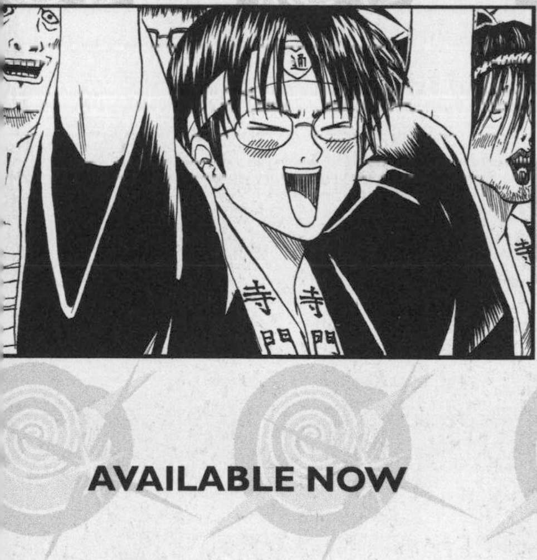

AVAILABLE NOW